On the Threshold of Freedom

On the Threshold of Freedom

Masters and Slaves in Civil War Georgia

CLARENCE L. MOHR

The University of Georgia Press   Athens and London

© 1986 by the University of Georgia Press
Athens, Georgia 30602
All rights reserved

Designed by Sandra Strother Hudson
Set in Linotron 202 eleven on fourteen Weiss
The paper in this book meets the guidelines for
permanence and durability of the Committee on
Production Guidelines for Book Longevity of the
Council on Library Resources

Printed in the United States of America

89 88 87 86   4 3 2 1

Library of Congress Cataloging in Publication Data

Mohr, Clarence L.
On the threshold of freedom.

Bibliography: p.
Includes index.
1. Slavery—Georgia—History.   2. Plantation life—
Georgia—History—19th century.   3. Georgia—Race
relations.   4. Georgia—History—Civil War, 1861–1865.
I. Title.
E445.G3M64   1985   975.8'041   85-5796
ISBN 0-8203-0793-9 (alk. paper)

FOR JANET AND THE POERS

CONTENTS

Contents

LIST OF TABLES

ix

List of Tables

ACKNOWLEDGMENTS

THIS STUDY first took shape at the University of Georgia, where I received the Ph.D. in history in 1975. A decade of subsequent research and writing has doubled the manuscript's length, altered its structure, and broadened its focus, but those who may wish to characterize the end product as a revised dissertation will hear no complaint from the author. On the contrary, I am delighted to affirm the direct link between this book and my graduate training, and to acknowledge, however inadequately, the profound debt I owe teachers and fellow students who helped me learn about the South during an epoch of regional change.

To embark upon the study of Southern history during the late 1960s was an exhilarating but intellectually treacherous experience. I was thus especially fortunate in securing the early guidance of Professor F. N. Boney, whose expert knowledge of the Old South and the historian's craft saved me from many serious blunders. In an era of academic turmoil Professor Boney presented aspiring historians with a model of tolerance and tact. After suggesting the topic of Confederate slavery to me in an early seminar, he waited patiently for over a year while I "discovered" an identical dissertation subject on my own. As a teacher, dissertation advisor, mentor, and friend, Nash Boney has contributed to my professional growth at every stage. Without his faith and encouragement I would not have become a historian.

A number of other Georgia faculty members, including William F. Holmes, Emory M. Thomas, Lester D. Stephens, Charles Crowe, Charles E. Wynes, and Kenneth Coleman, taught me a great deal about the South in its various incarnations. Will Holmes challenged a seminar of eager neophytes to grapple with the analytic complexities of post-Reconstruction social and political history. And, just as important, he persuaded many of us through the example of his own published work that narrative history was, at bottom, a literary art. Charles Crowe, during many stimulating conversations, compelled me to reexamine nearly all of my youthful assumptions concerning liberalism and American race relations. By the time I met Emory Thomas he was spearheading a major revitalization movement in Confederate historiography. I hope this book will contribute in some small way to that ongoing project. Lester Stephens introduced a generation of callow "TAs" to the bittersweet rewards of classroom teaching, and later braved America's first oil crisis to join me on a research trip to far-off Chapel Hill. Although I never had the opportunity to take classes under Professors Wynes and Coleman, each served on reading committees that critiqued my work and each offered helpful criticism. From all of these men, as well as from scholars like Numan V. Bartley, G. Melvin Herndon, and Willard B. Gatewood, I gained not only a wealth of factual knowledge but also the skills with which to move from research toward interpretative judgment.

Historical study in Athens possessed a special chemistry that I can only attribute to the presence of friends and classmates like Roger Martin, James P. Whittenburg, James M. Gifford, Tennant S. McWilliams, James C. Cobb, and Thomas G. Dyer. Their intelligence, camaraderie, and unfailing instinct for the historiographical jugular made graduate school as exciting as it was intellectually demanding. Exploring the South in such robust company represented a kind of secular equivalent to baptism by total emersion.

In the years since completing the dissertation my scholarly debts have multiplied so rapidly that I am reconciled to a lifelong imbalance of intellectual payments. Many obligations were incurred in the course of a four-year editorial stint with the Frederick Douglass Papers at Yale University during the late 1970s. Fellow Douglass Project staffers Carla Carr and Julie Saville dissected early drafts of what is now chapter 3 and subjected the remains to microscopic examination. Associate Editor C. Peter Ripley extended the right hand of fellowship to a weary pilgrim and shared with me his unrivaled knowledge of emancipation in the Department of the Gulf. Steven Hahn, from our first meeting in 1976, convinced me that I knew much less about Georgia history than I had previously supposed.

Acknowledgments

John W. Blassingame and Lawrence N. Powell took time from their own work to read my entire dissertation and offer an abundance of sage advice. Their suggestions, together with those of Eric Foner of Columbia University, who also read the unrevised manuscript, have been incorporated into the book whenever possible.

Many other scholars provided valuable assistance during and after my years in New Haven. The late Herbert Gutman of the City University of New York read a preliminary draft of chapter 3 and alerted me to important implications of my evidence. Larry E. Nelson of Francis Marion College invited me to adapt some of the same material for presentation at the 1977 meeting of the Southern Historical Association. John B. Boles read a slightly different version of the above paper prior to its publication in the *Journal of Southern History* and, in subsequent years, helped deepen my understanding of the antebellum religious context of Confederate racial liberalism. Paul D. Escott of the University of North Carolina at Charlotte offered useful comments concerning my treatment of black pamphleteer Harrison Berry in a 1983 article in the *Georgia Historical Quarterly.* With some modifications, material from that article has been incorporated into chapter 2 of the present study. John Cimprich of Southeast Missouri State University led me to important primary sources concerning the Forty-fourth Regiment, United States Colored Infantry, and other Tennessee units containing black recruits from Georgia. Jacqueline Jones of Wellesley College gave me the benefit of her expertise concerning postwar freedmen's education in Georgia. In an act of extraordinary generosity, Professor Charles B. Dew of Williams College provided me with copies of his laboriously compiled research notes concerning black labor in Georgia's wartime iron industry. Somewhat later, expressions of support and encouragement from Professor Dew and from Professor Harold M. Hyman of Rice University proved vital to the book's completion.

During a two-year sojourn at the University of Mississippi's Center for the Study of Southern Culture, I drafted several new chapters and revised or rewrote others. Research for chapters 5, 8, and 9 was supported by a 1978 grant from the Penrose Fund of the American Philosophical Society, and my initial writing year in Mississippi (1979–80) was made possible by a generous fellowship from the American Council of Learned Societies.

Acknowledgments

Both organizations have my sincere gratitude, as do William R. Ferris and Ann Abadie, whose friendship enriched my stay in Oxford.

My colleagues in the Department of History at Tulane University have been uniformly generous in their expressions of interest and confidence in my work. Among those who deserve special thanks for aid and counsel in particular matters are Bill C. Malone, Raymond A. Esthus, W. Burlie Brown, Sylvia R. Frey, F. Robert Hunter, and Patrick J. Maney. Writing itself is a solitary endeavor, but no one, I suspect, truly produces scholarship in isolation. For me, certainly, Tulane's stimulating and congenial environment has made a world of difference.

A variety of professional exigencies delayed completion of this book well beyond the time normally required for a monographic study. Progress would have been even slower without the diligent efforts of Miss Meriam Goldstein, who assisted me with important newspaper research while still a Yale undergraduate in 1978–79. Equally essential was the expert typing of Mrs. Ann Granger in Mississippi and Mrs. Elaine Siverio in New Orleans, who also rendered creative logistical aid during the final stages of the manuscript's preparation. My copy editor, Charles East, played a larger role in shaping the literary contours of the book than space permits me to describe. Working with him has been a real pleasure.

During periods of creative fallowness I sometimes feared that the book would require a lifetime to finish. For Thomas and Caroline Mohr it actually has, and in the circumstances their patience has been remarkable. It is difficult to know how to acknowledge the sixteen years of faithful support received from my wife Janet and her cousins the Poers of Decatur, Alabama. The book's dedication only hints at the magnitude of their contribution.

Clarence L. Mohr

Metairie, Louisiana
February 1985

INTRODUCTION

THIS is a book about the demise of chattel bondage in one of the states of the Confederate South. Like the slave regime itself, the story I have attempted to tell is biracial in character, embracing the perspectives of both blacks and whites as they struggled to comprehend the approach of black freedom within a framework of attitudes and assumptions shaped by decades of mutual exposure to Georgia's peculiar institution. Plantation society can be seen in retrospect as a vessel for the containment of powerful warring impulses, contradictory forces which were augmented and magnified under the pressure of a war environment. By exploring in detail the changing patterns of black-white interaction that preceded legal emancipation in 1865, the book seeks to define central tendencies within Georgia slavery and to suggest important links between antebellum life and the events of early Reconstruction. My approach to the subject matter rests upon a firm belief that historical insight admits of no color line and that neither slavery nor freedom can be understood without reference to developments which, by their very nature, defy the racial compartmentalization that Southern life and its chroniclers have frequently tried to impose.

II

FOR BOTH BLACKS AND WHITES in Georgia, the Civil War represented the closing act of a century-long drama. From the time slavery gained formal sanction in 1750 until the system was abolished by proclamation and military force in 1865, domestic race relations were in a state of constant flux. Far from being a static institution, chattel servitude constituted a dynamic nexus between superior and subordinate, a relationship that prescribed rigid boundaries within which change and adaptation could routinely occur. Indeed, over the course of eleven decades nearly every aspect of Georgia bondage underwent some modification. The demographic profile and cultural orientation of the state's black population changed profoundly during the nineteenth century, as did the political and economic environment surrounding nonfree labor. Between the 1780s and the 1850s the numerically typical Georgia slave ceased to be a young unassimilated male African engaged in rice production and became instead a third- or fourth-generation Afro-American man or woman laboring on an upland cotton plantation amid a complex web of kinship ties and indigenous cultural forms. With the end of the foreign slave trade after 1800, distinctly African customs and beliefs gave way to hybrid forms of music, dance, speech, religion, and group ethics. Culturally blacks and whites came to have more in common with each passing decade, although the social and psychological gulf separating the two groups remained immense. And as outward similarities between masters and slaves increased, a framework of caste etiquette evolved to ensure that personal interaction across racial lines could never imply equality.

In a variety of areas the line between black and white, slave and free, was drawn with greater precision and seeming permanence as the Civil War approached. As a legal system slavery hardened with age, although its physical rigors did not intensify correspondingly. On the whole, black Georgians probably lived longer, ate better food, and enjoyed greater access to primitive creature comforts in 1860 than at any previous time. The growth of industry and towns, together with widespread adoption of voluntary economic incentives for slave productivity, opened up limited avenues of opportunity for black workers. White artisans protested Negro involvement in skilled trades, but by the late antebellum era an enterprising urban bondsman could often arrange to live apart from his owner and reap the rewards of self-hire. Similarly, ambitious rice plantation hands or industrial slaves might also accumulate modest personal wealth through the system of "overwork" payments associated with task labor. A minority of black Georgians, in other words, could look forward to short-term personal rewards within slavery, but few could realistically anticipate that liberty would crown their efforts. Rising slave prices made the prospects for self-purchase remote, while a series of state laws and court decisions gradually closed off the last remaining avenues for domestic manumission.

With growing difficulty as the years passed Georgians of both races struggled to ignore the inconsistencies which lay at the heart of their evolving social system. At times the list of contradictions associated with Southern bondage seemed almost endless. Slavery in all of its settings was a relationship which simultaneously forced human beings together and drove them apart. Close white supervision was a central feature of the gang system of labor organization employed throughout the cotton belt, and even on coastal rice plantations blacks possessed only as much autonomy as masters or overseers found it in their interest to grant. Interracial contact was unavoidable, but for most whites a combination of ethnic chauvinism and paternalist ideology created the mental distance which made physical intimacy with slaves acceptable. Bondsmen, on the other hand, found exposure to whites hazardous and personally humiliating. The ritualized deference exacted by members of the ruling race impelled most blacks to a kind of self-segregation. Negroes routinely sought psychological refuge by withdrawing to rural slave quarters, urban fringe areas, and emerging "African" churches or less formal religious gatherings. In the process they fostered a type of racial separation as profound in some ways as any later imposed from above by white supremacist "Jim Crow" legislation.

By choice and through necessity black Georgians became a people apart during the years of slavery. Vulnerability quickened the pace of their strategic retreat from the white world and bequeathed a legacy of ambiguous ethnocentrism to the generation that would make the transition from slavery to freedom. By adopting a posture of outward subservience and defensive racial exclusiveness bondsmen minimized the inner damage of slavery, but they could not escape its pain. Instead of developing infantile personalities, Afro-Americans developed a fine sensitivity to human limits. Through a supple, expressive culture they were able to dispel anger and frustration, articulate forbidden aspirations, and sustain a rich fantasy life. Yet for all its vitality slave culture exhibited a deep ambivalence, an unstable dualism growing out of the tension between what blacks felt justified in desiring and the much different reality that slavery forced them to accept. The message conveyed through music, folktales, and other oral lore was complex but on some points remarkably consistent. The weak might confound the strong through cunning or artifice. The rabbit might win a skirmish with the fox, but the antagonists would retain their respective roles of prey and hunter. A degraded and scorned member of the animal kingdom could harbor secret longings and, at times, even aspire to greatness. But to stray too far from the conservative folk norm—to "get above" one's self—was to invite disaster. The portrait of life drawn in black folklore was, on the whole, quite uncompromising. Frequently its honesty was chilling. Happy endings were a luxury which those at the bottom could not afford.

III

FOR WHITE GEORGIANS slavery posed different but equally deep dilemmas and contradictions. First, last, and always there was the festering moral issue of human bondage in a free society. As David Brion Davis has noted, the American South was unique among slave regimes in the western hemisphere in being forced to resolve abolitionism's moral challenge by assimilating and transmuting it. Denied the option of becoming absentee landlords in the British Isles, Southern planters had no choice but to confront the emancipation issue at close quarters and to grapple with its concrete implications. Indigenous questioning of slavery during the era of the American Revolution posed ethical problems that conscientious whites found difficult to ignore and impossible to eliminate without repudiating black servitude and the social order that rested on it. A tiny handful of native white abolitionists were prepared to take precisely that step in the Upper South, but for the vast majority of slaveowners racial prejudice, economic self-interest, and fear of social chaos acted as powerful deterrents to antislavery measures. Increasingly during the early nineteenth century the humanitarian content of antislavery idealism was diverted into channels which followed the political and economic contours of plantation society. So formidable a reorientation was the work of decades rather than years, and its progress can be charted by the rise of systematic efforts to evangelize the slaves, or, less commonly, by planter endorsement of the American Colonization Society, which facilitated emancipation without challenging the right of slave ownership. A less tangible but more enduring change was the development of an elaborate religious and ethical rationale for slavery rooted in doctrines of paternalist reciprocity and Christian stewardship.

The collective moral reconciliation of Southern whites to racial bondage—that body of thought which came eventually to be known as the "proslavery argument"—represented a weaving together of three overlapping but ultimately irreconcilable strands of logic. Paternalism, when stripped of its embellishments, was simply the ideological medium through which a propertied ruling class justified the long-term exploitation of a dependent labor force. Themselves products of a patriarchal ethos, Southern planters seized upon the familial metaphor of parent-child reciprocity to explain their relationship to slaves. From the paternalist vantage point bondsmen assumed the role of perpetual children who toiled gratefully under the watchful guidance and control of fatherly masters. If few white Georgians truly believed this idealized version of plantation life, many nonetheless wished to do so, and their task was gradually made easier by Southern theologians who amassed biblical evidence that slavery was part and parcel of a rational and divinely sanctioned ordering of the universe. For slaveholders steeped in a culture of evangelical protestantism, the religious defense of black servitude was both reassuring and unsettling. By embracing proslavery theology masters could persuade themselves that ownership of human property was compatible with the dictates of Christian conscience, but the price for such ethical validation was an expanded definition of paternalism's self-imposed obligations. No longer could morally scrupulous whites content themselves with providing for the basic physical needs of "their people." In theory, at least, bondsmen joined the community of believers as "black brethren" whose souls and spiritual welfare required careful attention. With growing passion in the face of abolitionist assaults, Southern churchmen found themselves insisting that slavery was a "civilizing institution" providentially ordained to elevate blacks on the scale of morality and religious development.

Although the line of distinction between earthly and spiritual equality was sometimes difficult to maintain in proslavery theology, most white Christians in Georgia accepted bondage and black subordination as permanent conditions. Long-standing Anglo-European notions of Negro inferiority permeated Southern religion after 1800, shaping the context of slave evangelization and defining the limits of biracial humanitarianism. Eventually, however, problems arose when an explicitly biological conception of white supremacy began to emerge in the 1850s. Cloaked in pseudo-scientific garb, the new "hard racism" of late antebellum times became the third and increasingly dominant strand in proslavery thought. At both the local and national level, demagogues anxious to capitalize on popular prejudice found it expedient to argue that blacks were not culturally inferior fellow men but, on the contrary, a soulless subhuman species representing no more than an advanced order of brute creation. To liberate such creatures would be an act of madness, extremists argued, for only in slavery could whites restrain the Africans and curb their savage propensities.

Arguably the only constant elements in Georgia bondage were slavery's blighting influence on human potential and the system's ultimate foundation in violence. Masters might proclaim that slaves were contented peasants or fawning Sambos, but nagging doubts remained. Torn between allegiance to liberal, Christian, democratic values and the necessity of defending an institution that embodied the negation of those beliefs, white Southerners worried that blacks might react to oppression like other men and someday rise in rebellion. To most planters racial unrest was more than a theoretical concern. With disturbing regularity from the 1790s onward white Georgians were jolted by rumors of black insurrection. Most of the incidents were short-lived, but none were entirely forgotten. In what became an almost stylized pattern of response, local citizens inflicted summary punishment on persons implicated in alleged plots or conspiracies, while directing vigilante type repression against the state's black population in general. Frequently Georgia lawmakers responded with new statutes and municipal ordinances that rendered bondage more restrictive in theory and temporarily harsher in practice. After 1831, moreover, Georgia whites had before them the nightmarish example of Nat Turner and his exaggerated literary stereotype: the intractable black rebel who poisoned, butchered, raped, and exacted bloody retribution against white oppressors. Violent encounters between masters and slaves had long been a staple feature of Southern life, but from the 1830s onward rising sectional antagonism, hardening racial ideology, and the underlying reality of black discontent combined to make white Georgians acutely sensitive to even the rumor of Negro revolt.

IV

BY THE EVE OF SECESSION a variety of circumstances pointed toward an approaching crisis in Southern race relations. Escalating levels of political conflict over slavery made planters suspicious of Yankee intentions and increasingly prone to take a conspiratorial view of black behavior at home. Convinced that their way of life was under siege, white Georgians braced themselves for the assault that seemed certain to come. Abolitionist sentiments which a few decades earlier had produced only a vague sense of foreboding among slaveholders now met with militant rebuttal at the hands of fire-eating politicians who defended racial bondage as a positive good. It was almost as if a turbulent cloud of anxiety and belligerence descended on Southern life during the last half of the 1850s, an atmosphere unstable enough to be ignited by a single spark. Recklessness or spontaneous combustion might easily have touched off so volatile a mixture, but accident played little role in the conflagration that actually occurred. For it was neither insanity nor ineptitude but, on the contrary, deliberate revolutionary design which governed the conduct of free-state guerrilla fighter John Brown in 1859 as he prepared to strike flint and steel together in the mountains of northern Virginia.

From the "County Map of Georgia and Alabama, 1860." (Courtesy of the University of Georgia Libraries Special Collections.)

COUNTY MAP
OF
GEORGIA,
AND
ALABAMA.

SCALE OF MILES.

0   10   20   30   40   50   60

SOUTH CAROLINA

Eag...Grove
Anna...V.
Hollys...
ELBER
Elberton
Broad
...RPE
...ngton   Lincoln...
...WILKES   LINCOLN
Washington
...Fairplay   Applin...   AUGUSTA
TALIAFERRO   COLUMBIA
Crawf...   Thompson...Bel...   RICHMON
...fords V.   Camak Dearing   Berzelia
Warrenton   GLASCOCK   Gibson V.
...COCK   Sparta   St Clair   Waynesboro   Barnwell C.H.
...Devereaux   JEFFERSON   BURKE
...EDGEVILLE   Danisboro   Louisville   Sardis
Sanders V.   WASHINGTON   Jackson...boro
...ngton   Tennille   Holcomb
Oconee   Millen   SCREVE
...ngton V.   JOHNSON   Paris   Scarboro   Sylvania
...ns V.   Dublin   EMANUEL   Nevils   Halcyon dale
AURENS   Gt Ohoopee   Ohoopee   BULLOCK   Springfield
Anderson   Pendletons R.C.   Statesboro   Egypt
...le   Ohoopee C.C...   Cannochee   SAVANNAH
...Rockfish   MONTGOMERY   Mt   TATTNALL   Eden   ...CH.M...
...K Ocmulgee   Vernon   Reidsville   ...St...
...geland   Colquit   Taylors Cr.
...ELFAIR   LIBERTY   Ossabaws I.
Lumber City   Perrys...   Surrency   Hinesville   St Catherines...
...ackson V.   Ocmulgee   Holmesville   Jones...ville   ...Ri...   St Catherines S...
...le   Eg A Burrows   APPLING C.R.   Rushville   bor   ...S...
...md   middle   Pendarvis   Da...   ...Sa...
Coffee C.H.   ...Tuckers oville   St...
...lle   Strickland   Satilla R.   Waynes   R V.GLY...
...la   Bealetts V.   Waresboro   Blacka town   Bru...   St Simons S...
...Tomlinson   WARE   ...bur...   ...St Andrews S...
Magnolia   Cumberland I.
...CLINCH   Okefinokee   Traders H...   Cumberland S...
Swamp   Fernan...   Amelia I.
...Ft Gilmer   Nassau C.H.
Ellicott...   ATLANTIC
Lil. Suwan... R.   St Johns R.

PART ONE

*Rebellious Slaves
and the Slaveholders' Rebellion*

1. Harpers Ferry and the Limits of White Paternalism

D ESPITE the mounting tensions of the 1850s, Georgia was hardly a garrison state in mid-October 1859 when the telegraph clicked out the shocking news of a "Terrible Insurrection at Harpers Ferry."[1] The first reports, although garbled and inaccurate, still gave ample cause for alarm. From the very outset, newspaper accounts gave the raid racial overtones and accorded abolitionists a leading role.[2] Even before accurate reports were available an editor in Columbus, Georgia, described the event as an "outbreak and insurrection," stressing that the "insurgents" were composed "partly of negroes" undoubtedly "incited by abolitionists."[3] Two days later the same editor confirmed what he had previously surmised; not only had abolitionists incited the rebellion but the ringleaders were widely known as "blatant 'freedom shriekers.'"[4] To any white Georgian who read the papers or listened to street rumors during these tense few days, the signals were clear. The long familiar, almost stylized scenario was commencing. Inexorably and ominously, the cycle of terror had begun to build.

Within a week the facts concerning the Brown raid were available. John Brown himself was wounded and captured, and the majority of his followers were killed, wounded, or taken prisoner. Their plan for bringing immediate liberation to Virginia bondsmen had been thwarted.[5] In theory at least, the immediate cause of alarm was removed, but neither the swift suppression of the Harpers Ferry raid nor the subsequent trial and execution of its instigator brought calm to the troubled minds of white Georgians. On October 22, 1859, the Savannah *Morning News* in a lengthy

3

editorial sounded the theme which would be echoed by citizens from all walks of life during the months ahead. After attributing guilt for the Brown raid to Northern abolitionists and linking the outbreak directly to the doctrines of the major leaders of the Republican Party, the editor stressed the need for swift action to safeguard the slave regime's internal security. His argument had the ring of a call to arms: "What these insane abolitionists have accomplished . . . , the blood that they have caused to be shed, and the frightful scheme of insurrection, murder, and rapine which they have developed will, we trust, serve to convince the people of the South of the necessity of greater watchfulness, and of some concerted and effective means of protecting themselves from similar demonstrations of modern philanthropy."[6]

Although most slaveholders would probably have offered a fervent "amen" to the above sentiments, not all planters agreed that events in Virginia posed an immediate danger. From the beginning some white Georgians sought to preserve the important psychological crutch inherent in reaffirmation of black contentment under slavery. The Reverend Charles C. Jones of Liberty County found it easier to admit the existence of a monolithic sectional conspiracy against the South than to face the terrifying prospect of black unrest at home. Jones admitted that the Brown raid was more serious than he had originally thought—"not in reference to the Negro population, for that had nothing to do with it; but in reference to the hostility of . . . men of all classes in the free states." The young Savannah aristocrat George A. Mercer echoed these sentiments, while sprinkling the prose in his diary with disquieting images of violence: "The most remarkable feature of the [John Brown] affair is the refusal of the slaves to accept their freedom, and impale their masters upon the pikes furnished to them; not a single slave is implicated." In a similar vein, a woman from Charlton County sent newspaper accounts of the raid to her parents and stressed "how very anxious (I speak ironically) the slaves are to be liberated."[7]

Belief in the innate docility of local bondsmen died hard among Georgia planters, many of whom would continue to deny that slavery was in jeopardy even as the system crumbled around them during the Civil War. Yet optimists were probably always a minority in Georgia, and during the

tension-filled months after Harpers Ferry most whites were ready to believe the worst about any strange person or questionable situation. As
during previous insurrection panics, Yankee peddlers and traveling salesmen were especially vulnerable. Being both strangers and Northerners
they were doubly suspect, and an idle remark was often sufficient to link
them directly to the John Brown raid. In mid-November Columbus,
Georgia, was thrown into a state of "considerable excitement" by the
"arrest" of one Charles Scott, who represented a New York firm dealing in
embroideries and linens. Although "mild and inoffensive in appearance,"
Scott aroused suspicion by showing "more interest in the 'nigger question'
than in the . . . object of his visit" and reportedly expressed "great sympathy for 'Old Brown.'" After being ejected from a local merchant's shop
for undue "boldness," he tried to leave town but was "taken, brought back
and examined by a committee of citizens." They discovered nothing new,
but remained convinced that Scott "was an abolitionist 'dyed in the wool,'
and an unsafe man for any Southern community." Understandably, Scott
took the next train north.[8]

Even as Scott was leaving, the citizens of nearby Upson County were
in hot pursuit of several "suspicious looking individuals" thought to be "in
communication with negroes." This group, however, successfully eluded
pursuers and "left in the direction of Oglethorpe."[9] Barely two weeks later
Columbus residents were again aroused by the discovery of three book
salesmen thought to be "sympathizers with 'Old Brown,' and suspected of
tampering with slaves." As in the Scott case, no solid evidence existed to
substantiate such charges, but the salesmen were considered "suspicious
characters . . . engaged in a suspicious business" and soon returned to the
North by steamship from Savannah. In the wake of this incident a hastily
formed citizen's committee urged close scrutiny of the "many persons
from the free States now traveling through our neighborhood for the
ostensible purpose of selling books, maps, rat traps, etc."[10]

As whites grew more tense, the specter of John Brown seemed to lurk
everywhere. Unexplained events and local calamities immediately assumed a sinister character. The burning of numerous cotton gins throughout the state in the month of November produced wild rumors and some
actual violence. Accidental fires were common during the busy fall gin-

ning season and in normal years would scarcely have caused comment. But to panic-stricken editors the fires now became clear evidence of "Kansas Work in Georgia." When some seventeen Talbot County structures were destroyed within two weeks a Savannah newspaper observed pointedly that "incendiarism was one of the plans of 'Old Brown,' and that particular region was specifically designated on his map." During this same period a wildly exaggerated letter reached Milledgeville announcing that a "squad of Brown's emissaries" were hidden near Pine Mountain in Meriwether County, waiting to give battle to a force sent from the county seat to "secure that region."[11] In other parts of the state where no "emissaries" were reported, Brown's influence seemed to be at work among the slaves. Near Forsyth a slave reportedly burned twelve bales of his master's cotton, and in Jasper County a local planter shot and killed one of his own Negroes whom he discovered applying a lighted match to his gin house.[12] As far north as Elbert and Floyd counties, "incendiary" fires were also reported.[13]

Within a few weeks the apocalyptic vision of John Brown's army burning its way through Georgia and inciting black violence began to take a psychological toll. Heeding earlier calls for "concerted and effective" resistance, many white Georgians adopted the traditional expedient of extralegal vigilance committees. These grass-roots organizations bore a variety of names but shared common goals. Their primary concerns were to ferret out "abolition emissaries," enforce racial orthodoxy among whites, and suppress unrest among blacks.

The way in which local communities gave semiofficial sanction to lynch law is clearly illustrated by events in the southeast Georgia county of Effingham. On December 17, 1859, a crowd assembled at the county seat of Springfield to adopt measures for "common vigilance and security" against the "supposed presence" of Yankee abolitionists. The meeting authorized two principal committees of "citizen vigilants" to supervise the work of four subcommittees operating in separate militia districts.[14] Since this organization encompassed only a portion of the county, a second group met in January 1860 to form a "Committee of Safety." This group claimed authority in a precisely defined neighborhood bounded on the "North by Hudson's Ferry Road, East by the Savannah River, South by the district line, and West by the Middle Ground road." With equal precision, committee members spelled out their motivation and objectives. They were convinced by the Harpers Ferry raid that "Commotions of an incendiary character" were increasing throughout the North and that "thousands of emissaries" were overrunning the South "infusing" slaves with their "baneful opinions." Committee members resolved to exclude drummers, peddlers, or "other suspicious characters" from the area and to arm and equip themselves for instant response to any emergency. They were especially determined to rid the area of all free Negroes within a month's time and to "put down" all establishments where liquor could be obtained. [15]

The same racial anxiety which motivated Effingham County citizens stirred many other white Georgians to action. Throughout the state whites met to organize and take protective measures. In Rome a company of one hundred "minute men" armed with shotguns and revolvers stood ready to march to the aid of Virginia if "Northern fanatics" should attempt to rescue John Brown from the hangman. [16] The Savannah Vigilance Association threatened "condign punishment" for anyone attempting to excite insurrection or insubordination among local blacks. [17] White residents of Liberty County formed a "rifle corps and Vigilance Committee" to apprehend suspected abolitionists and "inflict such punishment as the nature of the case may require."[18] From Columbus, Augusta, Americus, Fort Valley, and elsewhere the summons was repeated again and again. [19] John Brown's body might be mouldering in the grave, but to Georgia whites his spirit seemed only too alive.

Although the Georgia response to Harpers Ferry followed familiar and well-established patterns, it far exceeded most previous insurrection scares in duration and intensity. As time passed and whites began to ponder the raid's broad implications, initial panic and hysteria solidified into cold fear. Instead of evaporating, the crisis mentality deepened and secured a firmer grip on the minds of many whites. "Never has the country been so excited before," wrote a Savannah resident in late December 1859. "[T]here was great feeling in 1820," he continued, "but not like the present. The South is deeply stirred." Similar reports came from Augusta, where pressure for racial solidarity among whites had thrown even the conservative American Colonization Society into disrepute. "Every day public affairs in this part of the country are getting more confused," reported a wealthy slaveholder seeking to manumit his bondsmen in Liberia. If his emancipation plans became public knowledge it would be "nearly impossible" to carry them out and the freedom promised to his slaves would be in "extremest jeopardy."[20]

II

PREVAILING SENTIMENT in Georgia left less and less room for even the most limited forms of Negro freedom in the winter of 1859–60. Fear of slave unrest during the Christmas holidays, together with a steady flow of insurrection rumors from neighboring states, kept local whites alert for signs of danger in their midst.[21] But itinerant rat-trap vendors and innocuous embroidery salesmen made unconvincing Yankee villains, and when genuine abolitionists failed to materialize, suspicion gradually settled over the state's entire black population. Prudence seemed to dictate that all possible precautions be taken against racial disturbances, particularly in those areas of black life that were sources of chronic concern to slaveholders. White moderates sounded a law-and-order theme calling for strict enforcement of state and local slave statutes. In Georgia's cities and villages the illegal sale of alcohol to bondsmen came under close public scrutiny. Larger towns like Macon placed the burden of surveillance on city police, while one Louisville resident urged that whites who sold slaves liquor be treated "as if they were followers of the 'sainted Brown'" and promptly chastised at the end of a "strong rope and a stout limb."[22]

White urban dwellers were also concerned over the unlawful assembly of large crowds of bondsmen at parades and other public events. In Savannah, where hundreds of blacks collected in "a perfect mob" on such occasions, the City Council adopted a tough new ordinance and followed up with mass arrests and subsequent floggings.[23] Rural residents renewed long-standing complaints about lax enforcement of patrol laws. In their January 1860 presentments, grand jurors of predominantly white Floyd County advocated a more aggressive approach to all aspects of slave discipline. After instructing district commissioners "to enforce the patrol laws rigidly," they demanded that slaves who acquired "bad habits" through hiring their own time or who became a "nuisance" by virtue of habitual intoxication should "be made an example of" as a warning to other blacks. [24]

Singling out troublesome bondsmen for harsh treatment was hardly a new idea in 1860, but the fears generated by John Brown threatened to transform slavery's sporadic brutality into a ground swell of anti-Negro violence. "Examples" took many forms in the wake of Harpers Ferry. Sometimes they involved black lawbreakers like the slave Leroy who was sentenced to receive sixty lashes for the theft of a string of sausage. [25] More often the philosophy of peace through intimidation was implemented outside the halls of justice by self-styled vigilantes or individual masters and overseers. Anxiety about patrol law infractions led whites near Ringgold to arrest a Walker County resident accused of forging slave passes. Although the prisoner claimed to be an Indian, he was "reported to actually be a Negro," and received one hundred lashes "upon a warrant from Judge Lynch."[26]

Farther south in Taliaferro County the slave Henderson, who ran away from an enraged overseer near Crawfordville, suffered an equally brutal fate when he was captured in Augusta. The overseer personally took Henderson out of the Augusta jail, "tied his hands behind his back and feet together and . . . dragged him in the roughest manner to Mr. Rappold's Bar Room where he knocked him down several times and dragged him by his hair over the whole house." Subsequently the overseer took Henderson, still bound hand and foot, into a vacant adjoining room and "hung him on a beam face or head downwards suspended in the air." The slave was finally rescued "in a fainting condition" by sympathetic bystanders who forced the overseer to leave the premises. [27] In Bibb County a white man named J. M. Brooks was actually arrested for killing one of the Negroes under his supervision. Within days, however, he was released on bond after witnesses swore that "the negro was killed while advancing upon Brooks with an axe raised to strike him." A similar incident took place in Columbia County, where a coroner's jury declared an overseer "fully justified" in killing a "crazy negro man" accused of murdering four other blacks and making a "desperate attempt" to kill the overseer himself.[28]

Throughout the early months of 1860 fear gradually secured a firmer grip on the minds of Southern slaveholders. Increasingly, it seemed, whites were transfixed by visions of black savagery, and united in their determination to forestall slave violence by any means necessary. How far local communities might go in enforcing Negro subordination became clear during April when Georgia newspapers reprinted graphic accounts of the capture and execution of a bondsman in Washington County, Mississippi. Apprehended after a lengthy chase, the black prisoner was taken to a nearby plantation "to consider what was best to be done in his case."

> Several highly respectable gentlemen were present at the council, who concluded the severest punishment possible should be inflicted upon the black desperado . . . as it might be the means of repressing at once any similar ebullition of passion on the part of other desperate negroes in the neighborhood. They decided to burn him at the stake, which was done in the presence of all the negroes on that and several of the adjoining plantations, all of whom seemed terrified out of their wits on viewing so awful a scene. The spirit of the doomed negro was never subdued. He died cursing his judges—his last words being that he would "take vengeance on them when they met each other in h——l."

The editor of the Vicksburg *Sun* expressed confidence that the "awful fate" of this "bloodthirsty, desperate fellow" would go far toward ensuring the "peace and safety of the community."[29]

Whether or not most Georgians drew any specific lessons from such stories, there can be little doubt that life grew increasingly hazardous for local blacks. During the last week of April, for example, a veteran overseer in Oglethorpe County lost his composure and shot a valuable slave who had fled to escape punishment for damaging a farm wagon.[30] A few weeks later residents of the same county were involved in a far more serious incident that bore a striking resemblance to the Mississippi tragedy. The trouble began while William Smith, a local planter, was threshing wheat one Saturday afternoon. Hoping to finish the job early, Smith ordered one of his slaves standing nearby to "take hold and help." Perhaps

10

the work infringed upon what Smith's bondsman regarded as customary free time. In any event, an argument ensued. Soon the dispute became more heated and Smith attempted to chastise his bondsman for replying in an "impudent manner." At this point a fight broke out and the black man drew a knife, with which he rapidly inflicted sixteen fatal stab wounds upon his master. The Negro fled from the scene but was captured the next day and held until the following morning, when "a number of citizens from Lexington and the surrounding country" assembled and after "due investigation of the facts" summarily burned their prisoner at the stake.[31]

III

ORIGINATING in a commonplace work dispute between master and slave, the Oglethorpe episode offers a telling illustration of how Georgia's deepening climate of fear and tension could foster racial conflict. Although few, if any, black Georgians were plotting insurrection during the post–John Brown era, reports of increased bellicosity among slaves were not necessarily inaccurate. When frightened whites threatened normally acquiescent bondsmen with death or severe physical punishment, violence sometimes became a self-fulfilling prophecy. All else being equal, desperate resistance was not an illogical alternative for the intended victim of an angry lynch mob. Usually, however, blacks managed to avoid physical harm by minimizing direct contact with whites and shying away from suspicious individuals or dangerous situations. Circumspection was the quality most evident to disinterested observers of black behavior in 1860.

The apprehensive mood and cautious demeanor of Georgia Negroes made a particularly strong impression on William McLain, an American Colonization Society representative who visited Savannah to arrange for the departure of a vessel carrying black immigrants to Liberia. Hostile public sentiment forced the veteran colonizationist to conceal his true mission and operate in a clandestine fashion. Local blacks who had once been friendly now treated McLain as if he were a carrier of plague. Writ-

11

ing to a colleague in Washington, D.C., he graphically summed up the attitude of wary Savannah Negroes: "I have seen but two or three of my friends—they said nothing & I did the same. It grieves me to find my Colored friends afraid to be seen speaking to me."[32]

Physical security was perhaps the uppermost concern of black Georgians in the wake of John Brown's raid. Having acquired the skills necessary for survival in a hostile environment, bondsmen drew upon the entire range of their personal and collective experience in order to insulate themselves from the destructive impulses unleashed by Harpers Ferry. Slave folkways were usually resilient enough to withstand the pressures that white society brought to bear, but in the repressive atmosphere of the times even the supportive psychological environment of the black community sometimes failed to sustain individual hope and resolve. In such cases the violence spawned by fear and desperation was directed inward. After clinging tenaciously to life through decades of adversity, a number of black Georgians made the sudden, and highly unusual, decision to die by their own hands. In March 1860, for example, a slave woman in Penfield became "tired of life" and attempted to commit suicide by jumping down a 65-foot well, after first throwing in her three young children. She was subsequently pulled out by her enraged owner and placed in jail to stand trial for murder. When questioned as to her motives she would say only that "she wished to die and didn't want to leave any of her children behind."[33]

An even more revealing incident occurred the following month in Jones County, where a slave named John was on trial for "striking and stabbing a white man." Apparently hoping to avoid extreme punishment, John pled guilty and "put himself upon the mercy of the court." To his dismay he was sentenced to be branded and then imprisoned. The judge justified this "light" punishment on the basis of John's age and "the injuries he received at the time of the difficulty." The slave was locked up in the county jail at Clinton to await his branding, but the following afternoon he hanged himself. Circumstances left little doubt that the strangulation was self-inflicted: "He fastened a strip of cloth around his neck and over a hinge on the jail door inside and deliberately choked himself to death, for his knees were on the floor of the jail and he had to hold up his feet in order to suspend himself at all."[34]

In June 1860 eyewitnesses reported the suicide of London, a slave who came in conflict with the black driver on a Chatham County rice plantation. Apparently terrified by the prospect of a flogging, London waded into the Savannah River and vowed to drown himself rather than surrender. Promises to delay punishment until the return of a white overseer were of no avail, and, in full view of the driver and other slaves, London sank beneath the water and perished. His death posed an implicit challenge to plantation discipline which could not be ignored. Hoping to discourage future sacrifices of costly human property, the overseer directed that the drowned bondsman's corpse be left floating in the river until carried out by the tide. "[T]his I have done," he explained, "to let the negroes see when a negro takes his own life they will be treated in this manner."[35]

Several weeks later a tragedy unfolded near Hawkinsville which bore a marked resemblance to the Chatham County episode. In this case the trouble began when a black foreman "who generally superintended matters when his master was not at home" attempted to break up an argument between the slaves Joe and Henry. A general fight ensued during which Joe killed the black supervisor and then, realizing the inevitable consequences, fled in terror. He was later discovered "at no great distance from the house, hanging by the neck from the limb of a tree, . . . his life extinct. He had procured a pair of reins, and deliberately hung himself, thinking that he was but anticipating the gallows in so doing."[36]

Unique circumstances surround any act of human self-destruction, and certainly no historian can presume to know why particular persons seek death at a given moment. It seems apparent, however, that the events just described bore more than an incidental relationship to the social context in which they occurred. At least three of the four cases cited above involved fear of impending punishment during a period when whites were bent on "making examples" of black offenders. This fact, together with the apparently low incidence of slave suicide in previous years, suggests that the oppressive reality of black life on the eve of disunion forced bondsmen toward, and sometimes beyond, the outer limits of their emotional endurance.[37]

IV

FREE BLACKS as well as slaves exhibited signs of a crisis mentality as the Civil War approached, and not without good reason. The situation of nonslave Negroes in Georgia had never been an enviable one. Economically marginal and few in number, they were less a legitimate "third caste" than a grudgingly tolerated minority, dependent on the uncertain patronage of white guardians in a society that equated dark skin with servitude. Throughout the Lower South the position of free Negroes deteriorated in direct proportion to the rise of "positive good" justifications for slavery during late antebellum times. Periodic efforts to harass or intimidate black freemen achieved little, however, until Harpers Ferry gave white extremists the upper hand in public affairs. Then, in the aftermath of John Brown's raid, Georgia's "free people of color" found their basic right to liberty under sudden and serious attack.[38]

A wave of hostile legislation from state and local authorities became the focus of initial concern among free blacks. What developed after Harpers Ferry was a concerted attempt to shore up the structure of chattel bondage by eliminating nonslave Negroes whenever possible and subjecting all remaining free blacks to tighter controls. In December 1859 the state legislature addressed the problem in a comprehensive manner. New legislation closed loopholes in earlier laws prohibiting slave manumission, thus making doubly certain that morally troubled slaveowners would not augment the state's free black population through deathbed acts of conscience.[39] Another law prohibited nonresident free blacks from entering the state and required that violators be sold into slavery.[40] A third especially important act "to define and punish Vagrancy in free persons of color" formed the core of the state's legal assault on free blacks. The always dangerously nebulous concept of vagrancy received a definition in the 1859 statute which made a mockery of the legal process. The law defined as a vagrant any free black found "wandering or strolling about, or leading an idle, immoral or profligate course of life" and provided that all such offenders should be sold into chattel slavery. The bondage would be limited to two years for a first offense but would become perpetual upon a second conviction. [41]

These general statutes were supplemented by a host of local laws which posed immediate threats to free blacks in many parts of the state. At least nine towns and cities received special police power or taxation authority over free blacks. [42] Grants of local police power sometimes took the form of blanket permission to "pass all by-laws and ordinances, for the control and government of slaves and free persons of color," or in other cases consisted of precisely worded statutes aimed at specific offenses. Still, the result was much the same and enslavement was often the primary objective. In Crawfordville and Warrenton, for example, free blacks were forbidden to reside on lots separate from their white guardians, to keep an "eating house" or "public table," or to "in any manner traffic in chickens, butter, eggs, ducks, turkeys, etc." Free blacks who were convicted of these trivial offenses faced stiff fines of from one hundred to two hundred dollars, and if unable to pay they could be sold into slavery for an unspecified period of time. [43]

In the realm of taxation a similar pattern emerged. Frequently new tax laws subjected free Negroes to financial coercion and harassment. This is clearly revealed by the tax structure of small towns such as Bainbridge, where free blacks bore a triple economic burden in the form of a poll tax, a personal property tax, and a special street tax of five dollars per person. [44] Other municipalities employed a more direct form of economic pressure. In Louisville the town commissioners could impose an annual tax of one hundred dollars upon all free blacks living or working within the corporate limits, regardless of age or sex. Anyone who failed to pay this tax would be "levied on" and sold into slavery "for such time as will be required to pay said tax."[45]

There is abundant evidence that these laws were not simply hollow legislative pronouncements destined to become dead letters. The growing white hostility toward free Negroes which moved the legislature to action in the first place ensured that the laws would be implemented when passed. [46] The legal and extralegal intimidation of free blacks was well

15

under way at the grass-roots level by January 1860. During that month a Savannah justice's court sentenced John Taylor, a free Negro seaman, to receive 128 lashes for cutting a shipmate. The court expressed regret that the law did not permit a harsher sentence. In Effingham County a local vigilance committee avowed that "there shall be *no* free negro location in our neighborhood, and that all free negroes in our limits shall immediately be informed that within thirty days from this date they must either choose a master or . . . be dealt with as the committee see fit."[47] On January 17 the inferior court in Waynesboro convicted two free blacks of violating an obscure 1835 statute and sentenced them to pay fines and court costs. When they were unable to do so, one of them was sold for a period of twenty-two months and the other was "bound to a gentleman for twelve years." Armed with new authority by the recent act of the state legislature, local officials announced that "such offenders for the future will be sold into slavery."[48]

Although Georgia's free blacks faced growing hostility throughout the state, conditions were probably worse in and around the city of Augusta than in any other single locality. In the wake of the John Brown raid the city's 386 free blacks became the focal point of white fear and suspicion. The City Council began rigorously enforcing local ordinances controlling the activities of free Negroes, and in order to prevent potentially dangerous contacts with the city's large slave population, officials even advocated forcibly removing free blacks from the state or enslaving them. On December 20, 1859, the latter alternative became frighteningly feasible when the legislature authorized the city recorder of Augusta to order the enslavement "either for life or a term of years" of any "free person of color or nominal slave" convicted of violating any city ordinance.[49] In practical terms this act had essentially the same object as the state's general vagrancy law, and was even easier to enforce.

As the new year began, the range of options open to Augusta's free blacks had narrowed considerably. With little hope of legal protection or just treatment by local authorities, they could either leave the city or else remain and hope for a favorable shift in white sentiment. The second course of action was hazardous, to be sure, but it must certainly have appealed to many black people who were loath to sever personal ties or to incur the unavoidable economic loss of a hasty exodus. In any event, Augusta's free blacks were not entirely devoid of allies in the white community. One of their most vocal supporters was the wealthy Augusta resident Robert Campbell, long active in the American Colonization Society. On at least two occasions Campbell spoke out forcefully against the "inhuman, unprincipled and therefore disgraceful law" permitting enslavement of free blacks. He asserted that the law was flagrantly unconstitutional and quoted statements by former Governor George M. Troup in support of this view.[50]

Although Campbell's unpopular public stand required considerable courage, it apparently had little or no effect on the city's climate of racial hostility. Surviving evidence indicates that for a number of Augusta's more prosperous and socially well-established free blacks, conditions finally became intolerable. Several longtime residents made the hard decision necessary for survival, arranged their affairs, and prepared to leave the city. In January 1860 the movement began when Robert Harper, a "civil and orderly" free Negro piano tuner with five children and real estate valued at two thousand dollars offered his pianos and picture frames for sale prior to departing.[51] Others would soon follow him, but even as they bowed to public pressure some of the city's free blacks received covert assistance from sympathetic local whites. The aid came generally from supporters of African colonization, who took advantage of the prevailing crisis to gain black converts. By holding out emigration to Liberia as an alternative to the increasing persecution facing free blacks at home, white colonizationists neatly fused principle with expediency, and thus perpetuated the moral ambivalence which had always surrounded their movement. However, the situation was not entirely an exploitive one. Most of Augusta's free blacks were far from naive about white motives. Although some may have been frightened into hasty action, others saw Liberian emigration as the most rational course of action available in the face of burgeoning domestic repression. There were also a few black Georgians for whom the goal of reaching Africa had long been a cherished objective. Some of these people seized upon the growing antipathy toward free blacks as a vehicle to transform their dreams into reality.[52]

Persecution, despair, hope, and humanitarianism combined in varying proportions to create a small African exodus among free black Augustans during the spring of 1860. A select group of sympathetic whites, who were aware that a Liberia-bound vessel would touch briefly at a Georgia port in May, conveyed this knowledge to prospective black emigrants and helped arrange for their departure. In February Alfred Cuthbert (who would soon send his own slaves to Liberia) informed American Colonization Society officials that a free black woman of "excellent character" and with an estate of at least forty thousand dollars would soon leave the city. She had "determined to emigrate to Liberia, in consequence of a law lately passed in Augusta that all free colored persons found in Augusta, after a certain date must leave instantly or be sold into slavery." Cuthbert promised that if she was able to sell her property, he would "inform her in time" to take the May ship. [53]

While this woman quite clearly acted in response to direct legal pressure and harassment, the motives of other free Negroes were more complex. For Silas Pope the events of early 1860 offered a unique opportunity to fulfill a lifelong ambition. Indeed, the outline of Pope's career constitutes a tribute to the struggles of many other historically anonymous Georgia blacks who overcame seemingly insurmountable obstacles in their quest for freedom and human dignity. Described as "a negro man of dark complexion," Pope had spent much of his life on a plantation in Greene County, where he became "used to heavy agricultural labor." In March 1860 he was forty-seven years old but still "active, vigorous and healthy." If his actions are any indication, he was even stronger psychologically than physically. Sometime prior to 1860 he had purchased his own freedom for $1,072, and in March 1860 he had just finished paying $667 for his forty-five-year-old wife Louisa and their eight-year-old daughter. He and his family could at last obtain the necessary legal documents enabling them to emigrate to Liberia. No doubt urged on by Augusta's rapidly worsening racial climate, Pope wished to leave as soon as possible "lest something should occur to throw difficulties in his way." As in the case of most prospective emigrants, his main problem was money. Working through a white friend he sought aid from the American Colonization Society, which agreed to grant the Pope family free passage to Liberia on the ship leaving in May. If Pope felt any apprehensions or misgivings about leaving his home of nearly half a century to face the

18

rigors of life in Africa with a wife and young child, he concealed his feelings well. His white allies in Augusta reported that upon learning of the society's decision he was "delighted at the prospect of being enabled to obtain a permanent home, to secure which he and his wife have been struggling for many years."[54]

Whatever regrets the Popes may have felt over leaving their home and friends could be at least partially offset by the comforting knowledge that their family would remain intact. Other black emigrants were not so fortunate. Mary, a former Augusta slave emancipated in the will of her late mistress, Martha Moderwell, faced a heartrending choice between equally unacceptable alternatives. Her mistress had fully intended that Mary be accompanied to Liberia by her husband Alfred and their four children. However, Mrs. Moderwell failed to purchase Alfred before her death and thus the emancipation clause of her will applied only to Mary and the children. The situation was further complicated when some "friends of the heirs" of the Moderwell estate strongly advised Mary to "make her option to remain in slavery." Understandably Mary "determined to reject" this gratuitous and obviously self-serving advice. Yet once she had steeled herself to ignore white pressure and demand her freedom, she still faced a painful dilemma which may itself have been an indirect form of coercion. Although friends assured her they were making "strenuous efforts" to purchase her husband, they held out little hope of success. Thus, as the time for departure approached Mary lived with the sobering realization that "the choice she has made will probably result in separation, at least for a time, from her husband, to whom she is devotedly attached." We have no record of her private emotions in the final days and weeks before departure. Perhaps this is just as well. It is enough to know that her resolve held firm and that when the *Mary Caroline Stevens* sailed from Georgia its passenger list included Mary and her children but not their father. Certainly Mary perceived the tragic irony of her situation, whether or not she allowed herself to dwell upon it. In escaping slavery she had incurred the fate most dreaded by those in bondage— forced separation from family and loved ones. Her choice, however, was freedom or slavery and she chose freedom. Thousands of Georgia's black people would make similar choices in the years ahead.[55]

2. Politics, Secession, and the Continuing Reign of Terror

T HE SUMMER of 1860 emerges in retrospect as a critical juncture in Southern race relations. Given time enough, the hysteria generated by a single event, even one as traumatic as Harpers Ferry, would inevitably have run its course. While early claims that the John Brown panic had "died a natural death" were clearly premature, the logic undergirding them was basically sound.[1] Had all other factors remained constant, there can be little question that the second half of 1860 would have witnessed a significant reduction of racial fear and tension. This trend failed to develop for several reasons, all of which were linked directly or indirectly to the 1860 presidential contest. Within Georgia itself the key factor was perhaps the minority position of Southern extremist candidate John C. Breckinridge. Despite support from most Georgia newspapers, all of the state's Democratic congressmen, and such influential figures as Senator Alfred Iverson, Senator Robert Toombs, and Governor Joseph E. Brown, radical Breckinridge supporters were waging an uphill fight in the months of July and August.[2] Even had their position been stronger, Georgia radicals, like fire-eaters elsewhere in the South, would undoubtedly have exploited to the fullest the racial fears generated by Harpers Ferry. Racial demagoguery was nothing new to Southern politics, and in 1860 Georgia secessionists were often as susceptible to racist appeals as the electorate they hoped to manipulate.[3] It was scarcely surprising, therefore, that Breckinridge agitators in Georgia seized upon a rash of mysterious fires in the distant state of Texas to rekindle the flames of racial fear and hostility at home.

20

The "Texas Troubles," as the fires and their aftermath came to be known, originated on the afternoon of July 8 when the neighboring towns of Dallas, Denton, and Pilot Point were almost simultaneously swept by flames. The cause of the fires remains unclear, but many tense and frightened local whites immediately assumed the worst. On the basis of dubious confessions extorted from terrified blacks by threats of violence, reports soon spread that the fires represented the opening phase of a vast abolitionist-inspired campaign of arson, murder, and insurrection. The plot theory was effectively promoted in a series of letters from Charles R. Pryor, editor of the pro-Breckinridge Dallas *Herald*. As the startling stories from north Texas became known, the conspiracy thesis gained numerous white adherents. By August, Texas was in the throes of the most serious and widespread slave insurrection panic in its history. Terrorism reigned, and by the most conservative estimates at least fifty black and white victims were murdered by lawless mobs and vigilante groups.[4]

Historians continue to differ over both the origin of the Texas fires and the degree of actual slave unrest in the Lone Star State. Neither of these questions, however, is of central importance when assessing the effect of the Texas Troubles on black life in Georgia. Whether true or false the insurrection rumors had a profound impact on the racial climate of Georgia as well as other Southern states. The Georgia experience fully and tragically confirms the judgment of a noted historian that following the Texas fires the South experienced "one of the greatest witch hunts in American history."[5]

II

GEORGIA WAS RIPE for an insurrection panic in the summer of 1860, with or without outside stimulation. The increasingly shrill tone of radical Breckinridge supporters, in conjunction with an already tense atmosphere of mutual distrust and hostility between blacks and whites, produced a situation that was dangerously volatile. Almost any questionable event or happening might have touched off a new spasm of racial hysteria, but

21

because of their incendiary origin the Texas Troubles reverberated through Georgia like a veritable fire bell in the night.

Developments during the spring of 1860 had made white Georgians especially sensitive to rumors of arson by slaves or free blacks. Arson was always one of the most effective weapons of reprisal available to bondsmen, and it became a subject of renewed concern for Georgia slaveholders in the wake of Harpers Ferry. Although the tendency in late 1859 was to blame followers of John Brown for the rash of mysterious fires in cotton gin houses, local slaves were never fully exonerated.[6] When a second wave of unexplained fires swept the state beginning in April 1860, suspicion centered almost exclusively on Georgia's black population. The spring fires played a major role in shifting white attention away from external threats to seemingly more immediate internal dangers.[7] With each new clang of the fire bell John Brown became less a harbinger of abolitionist invasion and more a white Nat Turner, capable of generating black unrest through his clear example of naked, raw courage. Most important, however, the spring fires paved the way for the Texas Troubles in the minds of white Georgians, and gave the wild rumors of insurrection and conspiracy a credibility they might otherwise have lacked.

Concern over suspected slave arson appeared first and was most intense in and around the city of Macon. Beginning in late March 1860 Macon experienced a series of individual blazes occurring in rapid succession over a two-week period.[8] The very frequency of these occurrences—at one point townsmen extinguished three separate fires in the space of ten hours—seemed to rule out accidental causes. Almost immediately the mayor offered a $500 reward for capture of the unknown arsonist, but by mid-April no arrests had yet been made. It was at this point that white suspicion first began to focus on local blacks. Although no hard evidence existed implicating any single individual, city policemen were urged to investigate various "suspicious looking" Negroes seen "lurking around the alleys and in the dark streets of the suburbs . . . after the lawful hour." Police should be "doubly vigilant," wrote one local resident, since "another burning dwelling might be the consequence of their neglect."[9]

In spite of such warnings the fires continued during the second half of April, and by the end of the month vague suspicion against blacks had hardened into specific accusations.[10] The first charges against a particular individual came on April 26, after the home of a Macon minister was badly damaged by a fire which appeared to have been deliberately set. According to one account, the blaze was started by a black woman "on the lot" who "had taken offense at something." Fearing the consequences of intense public excitement and hostility, the woman's owners almost immediately "sent her off into the country." This action enraged the editor of the Macon *Telegraph*, who demanded that city authorities "take the matter in hand, and if . . . the evidence appears conclusive, let her be severely punished—with death if the law demands it. . . . Some example must be made as a warning to others."[11]

Throughout most of May the town was relatively free from fires and it appeared, for a time at least, that the arsonist had been either "sent off" or intimidated. By the month's end, however, the fires began anew and the press resumed its strident calls for vigilance and retribution. During the two-week period ending just prior to mid-June there were a dozen separate fires or attempts at arson. The *Telegraph* editor alluded grimly to the "settled determination" of "incendiaries" to burn the city and asserted that, if captured, the arsonists would "meet with but little mercy." Suspicion continued to focus on blacks, and the fires began attracting notice even in the neighboring state of Alabama, where the Montgomery *Mail* urged Macon whites "to get up a hanging party."[12] The situation reached another crisis point on the evening of June 30 when three different buildings in the city were set on fire. An intensive investigation culminated on July 6 with the arrest of a slave named Bob, who was examined by local magistrates and confined in jail to await trial at the next term of Bibb County Superior Court.[13]

Bob's arrest marked the beginning of another month-long period of calm for Macon-area whites, but elsewhere in the state quite the opposite was true. Like some malignant tumor the plague of arson had seemingly spread outward to neighboring communities. In nearly every unexplained fire, whites now assumed almost automatically that slaves were involved. Three mysterious fires in the same section of Columbus during mid-July caused a local white resident to deplore the fact that "negro incendiaries . . . are and have been protected from the law by their owners."

Unless black arsonists were severely punished, he asserted, neither life nor property would be safe from the "ruthless savage incendiary." The "horrid state of affairs" existing in Columbus and elsewhere resulted largely, he felt, from a breakdown of slave discipline during the late antebellum period: "Of late years entirely too much latitude is given negroes—their feelings and wishes are too much consulted, and to such an extent has lax discipline been practiced, until a lady really fears, . . . to speak short to a negro for fear of insulting her or him. Such occurrences happen daily, and if owners of negroes uphold them in their rebellion, we may not be surprised to awake any night with the flames over our heads."[14] In other parts of the state there was equal concern over slave arson, but increasingly secessionist agitators sought to link such occurrences directly to the influence of Northern abolitionists—especially followers of John Brown. One of the most forceful statements of this viewpoint came from Joseph Addison Turner of Putnam County. A lawyer and planter as well as a marginally successful author, publisher, and literary critic, Turner devoted his professional career largely to promoting Southern nationalism in the realm of both literature and politics.[15] Writing in the July 1860 issue of *De Bow's Review,* he referred to recent conflagrations that had erupted almost simultaneously in the towns of Atlanta, Griffin, Warrenton, and Newnan, Georgia, and asked rhetorically, "Whence come all the fires of which we read? Is it at all probable that so many in so short a time are the result of accident?"

Turner's "answer" to these questions was in reality an elaborate conspiracy thesis, intended to channel white racial fears in support of Southern economic and political independence. "In view of the Harpers Ferry affair and the developments which have followed it," Turner argued, white Southerners should speedily adopt strong defensive measures. Letters from John Brown's followers, avowing that "Southern people are easily gulled," were damning enough, but when added to the sinister maps in Brown's possession pointing out high concentrations of black population in Georgia as well as other states, they were proof positive of Northern intentions. According to Turner, the South faced "actual invasions" by hordes of Yankee emissaries disguised as teachers, clergymen, merchants, and peddlers. Northerners engaged in these occupations were frequently "base, bitter, malignant abolitionists" seeking only to "instil the poison of their opinions" into the minds of Southern slaves. Such charges, of course, were not new to white Southerners in 1860, but when linked directly to local events like the Georgia fires they took on a new air of urgency. Thus, Turner concluded in a carefully chosen metaphor that throughout Georgia and the South abolitionists were "working silently, slowly, insidiously, but constantly, . . . to kindle a fire of servile insurrection, which shall wrap in flames and involve in ruin the whole broad expanse of our . . . Southern country. . . . The danger is in our very midst and we must meet it now."[16]

III

IT WAS AGAINST THIS BACKGROUND of suspected arson among local slaves and conspiratorial rhetoric among local whites that news of the Texas Troubles first reached Georgia in late July of 1860. In this crucial election year any rumor of an abolitionist-inspired slave revolt would certainly have produced profound emotional shock waves. It is, however, only within a sequential context—as part of a *perceived* chain of sinister events—that the impact of the Texas Troubles upon white Georgians can be properly understood. The numerous fires attributed to Georgia blacks during the spring and early summer made the Texas burnings seem doubly terrifying. The conspiratorial arguments of Turner and other Southern extremists made the reports of an extensive abolitionist plot in Texas seem entirely plausible. To many white Georgians in July 1860, John Brown's raid seemed to mark the beginning of a clear and ominous progression of events that threatened seriously to disrupt the established racial order. In part this conclusion may have been, like secession itself, the product of "logical reasoning within a framework of irrational perception."[17] If so, the perceptions of white society were most irrational, and the consequences of such irrationality were most tragic, where they directly involved Georgia's black community.

In most important respects, the response of white Georgians to the Texas Troubles closely paralleled their reaction to the John Brown raid eight months earlier. At first many people expressed open skepticism and disbelief at the seemingly incredible rumors from the Lone Star State. Upon receiving the first garbled telegraphic reports from Texas on July 27, the editor of a Macon newspaper casually dismissed the entire matter. He was confident that once the facts were available this "very vague account of a servile insurrection" would "be found to amount to nothing." Within less than a week, however, his complacency had vanished. "The trouble in Texas seems to be more serious than we supposed," he confessed, while expressing hope that none of the "white conspirators" had been hanged before "all the facts of the plot" were discovered. [18]

The Savannah *Republican* was also cautious in its initial judgments and "abstained from comment" for several days to await further details. As late as July 30 reports were still "too indefinite . . . to warrant a fixed opinion," but the editor had already begun to draw the inevitable parallels. In his view, the Texas Troubles presented "many features" of a virtual "re-enactment of the John Brown affair." Should early accounts of a "widespread conspiracy" be substantiated, there would, he grimly prophesied, be "no little excitement among the Southern states of the Union."[19]

In the following weeks the rumors of conspiracy and insurrection in Texas, while seldom factually confirmed, received increasing public attention. Georgia newspapers were literally deluged with letters from Charles R. Pryor and other Texas residents, giving "firsthand" accounts of a "most diabolical plot" by white abolitionists to bring on a "general insurrection and civil war at the August election." Stories reprinted from newspapers in every section of Texas appeared to lend credence to such individual reports. On the surface at least, the sheer volume of evidence seemed overwhelming. [20]

Not all white Georgians were immediately persuaded, of course, but as reports of black unrest began trickling in from other parts of the South the Texas Troubles became more and more difficult to ignore. [21] Within a matter of days it became apparent that racial paranoia was again increasing. The crisis mentality which had shown signs of abating in June gained new life in July and was again at full strength by the middle of August. In tragically ironic fashion the Savannah *Republican's* earlier analogy was proving all too accurate. A "re-enactment of the John Brown affair" was indeed taking place—not in north Texas, but in the minds and actions of white Georgians.

IV

WHILE SOME of the Texas rumors may have been politically motivated, there is little question that the Georgia response was spontaneous and genuine. The very rapidity with which many whites succumbed to this new wave of racial hysteria all but precludes the possibility of a preconceived secessionist conspiracy. Long before old vigilance committees could be revived, or new ones created, and weeks in advance of any formal declarations from local public meetings, the state was rife with rumors of black rebellion. Newspaper accounts of these insurrection panics, while offering little direct evidence of actual black attitudes, still reveal much about the harsh realities of life daily confronted by many Georgia bondsmen.

At first glance, published reports of alleged plots or conspiracies during this period seem to possess a surprising, even suspicious, degree of internal uniformity. In the sequence of events described, the characterization of individuals involved, and the literary imagery used, most accounts of suspected slave revolts present strikingly similar features. Yet, in the last analysis, the very frequency with which these immutable themes are repeated ultimately strips them of any artificial or contrived appearance. No group of secessionist editors, however cynical, determined, or skillful, could possibly have fabricated so many separate accounts of insurrection panics, all differing in factual details but exhibiting almost universal thematic consistency. In a very real sense, these press reports were the literary equivalent of a public dissection of the Southern psyche, laying bare the deepest racial fears of white society.

For many white Georgians the slave insurrection panics of the summer and early fall took the classic form of self-fulfilling prophecies. The wave of racial paranoia set off by the Texas Troubles led inevitably to "discoveries" which were soon magnified into large-scale conspiracies. In every instance the procedure followed was essentially the same. Some initial incident, often trivial in nature, aroused white suspicions against an individual slave. This person was then arrested and whipped or beaten until a "confession" was obtained, usually implicating other blacks who were similarly coerced until they confirmed the "truth" of the original confession, and perhaps implicated still more bondsmen. Through this process the outlines of an elaborate conspiracy could be established, at least to the satisfaction of local whites, within a relatively short time.

Another common element in most accounts of insurrection panics was the existence of a hostile and recalcitrant black villain. This figure, conforming generally to the familiar "Nat" stereotype, appeared consistently as either the main instigator of an insurrection plot or, if white "abolitionists" were allegedly involved, as a second-echelon "ringleader." Far from allaying white fears, however, this "demotion" of "Nat" to a secondary role actually made the specter of black violence even more terrifying. The same white-supremacist frame of reference which initially produced the "demotion" (itself a racist judgment) also made "Nat" seem doubly threatening when aided by a white accomplice. This new union of "brains and brawn," intellect and savagery, deprived white Georgians of even the minor psychological crutch inherent in affirmations of black racial inferiority. If the security of white society rested upon black inferiority or incompetence, then such security vanished as soon as white abolitionists entered the picture. With increasing desperation as the weeks went by, white Georgians began to flail blindly at these dual enemies who seemed to grow simultaneously more menacing and elusive. Every strange white man became a potential "abolition emissary," out to convert the many "Nats" who lurked secretly behind the impassive ebony countenances of outwardly servile bondsmen.

The earliest reports of an actual insurrection plot came from Floyd County in northwest Georgia during the first week of August. The trouble began when three slaves from different plantations were allegedly "overheard concerting a plan to rise and destroy the whites." From this initial discovery, the drama unfolded with almost mathematical precision. After being "whipped by his master" one of the slaves "confessed the truth," and his statements were soon "corroborated" by the other blacks when publicly questioned before a meeting of the local "neighbors." On this occasion the slave Green, "a notoriously bad character," admitted to being the "ringleader" and "divulged the whole plot." The three black conspirators "had determined to instigate an insurrection" sometime between August and December, and had discussed the plan with several other slaves, some of whom agreed to join. The "first point of attack" was to be an upcoming revival meeting at a local Baptist church.

These disclosures so enraged the assembled whites that they "were on the eve of hanging . . . Green," but the crowd ultimately relented and agreed to set him free upon assurances that he would immediately be sent out of the state. In true "Nat" fashion, Green "persisted to the last in saying that he still intended to carry out his diabolical design." Subsequent attempts by local authorities to bring Green back for legal prosecution proved fruitless.[22]

For Georgia's black community the Floyd County incident was a somber warning of things to come. Growing out of the tense racial atmosphere following the Texas Troubles, it served as an emotional catalyst triggering new and more violent reactions. Response came quickly from white Georgians who felt that their worst conspiratorial fears were now confirmed. Almost immediately the event itself was obscured by a complex array of speculative embellishment. As early as August 9 a number of white accomplices were written into the script by the editor of the Rome (Floyd County) *Courier*. There was, he acknowledged, "no evidence" that white men were implicated but such was "doubtless the case" since several "suspicious individuals" were "prowling about in the county."[23] Within less than a week these suspicious whites became Yankee abolitionists. The transformation was effected through the discovery of a letter ostensibly written by a Boston abolitionist to an "emissary" in Rome. The document, possessing "some marks of genuineness," summarized reports from other abolitionist "agents" in Augusta, Savannah, Columbus, Macon, and Atlanta, and outlined "the measures which have been adopted in Georgia to accomplish a general insurrection."[24] This theme struck a responsive chord with the Augusta *Dispatch*, which editorialized grimly about the prevailing "insurrectionary tendency of things." The Floyd County developments, in conjunction with newly discovered plots in Mobile and Pine Level, Alabama, made it "perfectly apparent" that "emissaries of Republicanism" were operating secretly in Georgia through "gentlemen niggers" and itinerant Northern preachers.[25]

While it is unlikely that most white Georgians took such extreme assertions completely at face value, neither did they reject them out of hand. In the wake of the Floyd County insurrection panic, skepticism over the reports from Texas all but vanished. "The plan for a negro conspiracy in Texas appears . . . well organized & extensive," a previously cautious Savannah resident confided to his diary on August 22. With even greater conviction a writer concluded in the Columbus *Sun* that the existence of a "deeply laid scheme" to incite a slave revolt in Texas was now "reduced to a certainty." He was especially concerned that guilty parties not escape punishment, and he left little doubt that recent events in Floyd County weighed heavily on his mind. In "more than one instance," he wrote indignantly, "ringleaders" of insurrection plots had been captured and subsequently ordered to leave the "neighborhood and State." Describing this practice as "dangerous and suicidal," he urged that in the future "no individual, white or black, who is detected in such work . . . be allowed to escape hanging to the most convenient limb."[26]

Subsequent events in Floyd County as well as other parts of the state rendered sadly inappropriate such warnings about undue leniency. As Georgia whites implemented increasingly repressive policies in anticipation of further black unrest, violent racial clashes occurred with predictable regularity. The existence of machinery for systematic law enforcement and the proximity of local newspapers make this "repression-violence" syndrome most apparent in towns and cities, although it was clearly operative in rural areas as well. Less than three weeks after the initial panic in Floyd County, a night watchman in the county seat of Rome leveled a shotgun blast at two local bondsmen whose only offense consisted of engaging in "close conversation." One of the blacks was seriously injured, "about eighteen buck shot having taken effect upon his person."[27]

In Macon, whites had never fully recovered from the waves of alleged arson by slaves during the spring and early summer. A series of nighttime robberies attributed to local bondsmen, coupled with the severe beating of a city policeman by unknown black assailants, kept the community on edge during June and July.[28] When the home of a prominent Macon physician was destroyed by fire in the early morning darkness of August 27, white reaction was instantaneous. Suspicion focused at once upon a thirteen-year-old black "servant girl" named Becky or Rebecca who "had been refractory for a day or two past." Becky's arrest and confinement followed as a matter of course, but local whites were eager for decisive action. "The house was set afire there is no mistake about that," wrote a man who had helped extinguish the blaze. "The Girl is in the Guard house but refuses to tell anything about the origin of the fire."[29] Some two weeks later, when Becky finally received the legally required hearing before three county justices, public feeling was obviously running high. The justices returned her to custody to await trial at the next term of Superior Court, virtually ignoring the fact that no adequate evidence existed upon which to base prosecution.[30]

For two more months Becky languished in the Bibb County jail, while her owner refused even to employ legal counsel. Ultimately, however, the latter circumstance actually worked in her favor, for the presiding judge in her mid-November trial appointed the competent young lawyer Lamar Cobb (son of the prominent Georgia politico Howell Cobb) to defend her. Eager to make a good impression in his debut before the Macon bar, Cobb diligently prepared a legal brief demonstrating that "there was no proof against [her] except her own confession—made under threats of punishment." The judge declared such evidence inadmissible and pronounced a verdict of "not guilty." Legally, at least, Becky was now exonerated. Her subsequent fate at the hands of her master is not recorded.[31]

In view of the tense racial atmosphere in Macon, Becky's acquittal on the basis of what many whites undoubtedly considered a legal technicality seems especially fortunate. Certainly not all blacks fared so well during this period. The slave Joe, accused of murdering a white storekeeper in rural Talbot County, is an excellent case in point. Joe was arrested in mid-July, barely one month after a black man in Oglethorpe County had been burned to death for a similar offense. From the very outset white hostility was intense. The crime itself seemed especially savage, the storekeeper's head having been "frightfully macerated by repeated blows from some heavy iron instrument." On the basis of information supplied by another slave, Joe was summarily charged with the murder, but initial attempts to convince local whites that the law would exact full retribution proved fruitless.[32] Only a day or two after entering the county jail at Talbotton, Joe was confronted by the frightening spectacle of "an excited crowd of about two hundred people from the neighborhood of the murder, armed with axes and sledges, and avowing the intention to take possession of the negro and *hang* him."[33] After much argument from a local judge and "other respectable gentlemen," the crowd finally agreed to disperse, but not before exacting at least a ritualistic form of psychological gratification. In response to the crowd's demands, Joe was brought out of the jail in custody of the sheriff and several deputies and, "being examined, confessed to all the facts of the murder and how it was performed."[34] Having thus reaffirmed both "Nat's" reality and their own ability to neutralize his racial threat, local whites were content to let the law take its course. What followed was largely a formality—or from Joe's viewpoint, perhaps, a hollow mockery. Late in September Joe was tried for murder in Talbot County Superior Court. "The case was fully made out by the State, and went to the Jury without arguments." Joe's hanging, now thoroughly legalized, was ordered to take place on the nineteenth of October.[35]

This execution was touted by many contemporaries as evidence of the state's basic commitment to law and order. Yet in retrospect the episode seems most significant as a barometer of white paranoia following the Texas and early Georgia insurrection panics. The growing pervasiveness of racial fear was reflected not only in the actions of the Talbot County mob, but also in the response to the Talbotton incident among whites in other parts of the state. Surviving evidence suggests that the initial rumors of a lynching in Talbotton were magnified into reports of another burning similar to that in Oglethorpe County two months earlier. This, at least, was the explanation offered by several editors for a mid-August story in the Augusta *Dispatch* of a "Murder and Lynching" in southwest Georgia. According to this account, "a negro boy who had killed a white man" was "burnt at the stake" by a mob at station number 11 on the Southwestern Railroad. Twelve people reportedly took the black man from the sheriff's custody, giving bond for his return, and in apparent mockery of the legal process tried, sentenced, and executed the murderer, and "returned his ashes to the officer."[36] The substance of this report was confirmed by at least one other contemporary source, although the location of the burning was shifted to a separate branch of the railroad.[37] With grim but unconscious irony, a number of newspaper editors who rushed to the defense of "law abiding and law enforcing" Georgia whites cited the trial and hanging of Joe as conclusive proof that no such burning had occurred.[38]

The very existence of such a "hanging vs. burning" debate, conducted in tones of high moral indignation, aptly symbolized the growing preoccupation with racial violence among white Georgians. The reaction triggered by the early insurrection panics had now begun to expand and assume new dimensions. From August through October white racial paranoia quite literally fed upon itself as violence, rumors, and new insurrection panics continuously interacted to produce a deepening crisis mentality. During late August and early September reports of impending slave revolts poured in from Cobb, Floyd, Cass, Gordon, and Whitfield counties in northwestern Georgia. The most serious of these panics began on the night of August 25 near Dalton, when thirty-six blacks were arrested and charged with plotting to burn the town and lead a large-scale rebellion. Initial reports alleged that after setting fire to Dalton the blacks planned to fan out over the surrounding countryside and "accomplish all they could in the work of destruction." On the following day they would "go in a body to the Railroad and after taking possession of the train, . . . proceed down the road stopping as long as they saw fit at each station, intending to reach Marietta in the night, where it was designed to pursue the work of killing and burning, and thence as far on the road as they were successful."[39] These rumors immediately touched off a wave of panic among whites in the entire region south of Dalton along the line of the Western and Atlantic Railroad. From Dalton to a point several miles north of Marietta "the people were under arms and adopted measures to protect the women and children."[40] When the southbound train from Chattanooga reached Marietta, a similar reaction occurred. A cadet at the Georgia Military Institute there gave a graphic firsthand account of white response to the shocking reports from Dalton: "There was a good deal of excitement here last night when it was rumored that the negroes were rising, that they had hung an abolitionist and had thirty negroes in jail in Dalton, and tonight was the time appointed to burn Marietta. The citizens in town had patrols out last night, and we [posted] a double guard part of the night [;] no one could move scarcely without being challenged by sentinels."[41]

Like previous insurrection panics, the Dalton affair reveals much about the steady drift toward irrationality and racial violence among white Georgians, but sheds little direct light on black attitudes or behavior. If anything, the testimony of bondsmen who were swept suddenly into the grasp of panicked white mobs constitutes the least reliable and most potentially misleading historical evidence available. Immediate survival frequently required blacks to make incriminating statements which would inevitably leave the surrounding black community under a pall of suspicion long after surface calm was restored. Yet in most cases the blacks immediately involved had no realistic alternative except to gratify even the wildest fantasies of their white captors. In the Dalton panic, for example, whites were clearly determined to extract the "right" answers as they whipped a group of slaves "for the purpose of drawing from them a confession." The slaves wisely chose to comply, knowing that only a profession of guilt could bring an end to their torment. "Some confessed one thing and some another," but no one seemed bothered by the inconsistencies. Frightened Dalton whites accepted the confessions as proof that a revolt was "in contemplation."[42]

As racial tension rose to new heights in the month of September, occasional pleas for moderation appeared in the Georgia press. The ever cautious Savannah *Republican* could "see no good in publishing the rumored attempts at insurrections" which appeared regularly in other newspapers. Not only did such reports cause undue public excitement, but they also led to the "consideration of a subject which otherwise might . . . never . . . enter the brain of those whom we should see engaged in such a movement." In a similar vein the Macon *Telegraph* cautioned its readers about uncritical acceptance of recent insurrection rumors from Talladega, Alabama, describing a supposed plan by rebel blacks to burn the town and kill adult white males and "old and ugly" females while keeping all the "young and lovely" white women as mistresses. Expressing grave concern over the growing mob psychosis in Georgia and elsewhere, the *Telegraph* editor urged his readers to ascertain "how the testimony of the negroes was taken," since "there might be something in the *manner* of obtaining this testimony . . . which would establish its credibility."[43]

Such appeals to reason, however, were too belated and too infrequent to have any appreciable effect on Georgia's rapidly deteriorating racial climate. In northwest Georgia, the Dalton and Floyd County incidents continued to reverberate, triggering minor insurrection panics near Adairsville and Cartersville. In central Georgia, Macon authorities were urged to investigate the reported sighting of three strange black men "each armed with a new double-barrelled gun." From Screven County, located south of Augusta on the Savannah River, came even more alarming reports which reveal quite clearly the continuing psychological impact of John Brown's raid. A patrol party visiting the plantation of one Peyton L. Wade had allegedly unearthed "a box of dirks, a lot of Sharp rifles, several swords and a good many likenesses of old John Brown." Local newspapers pointedly reminded their readers that this particular section of Screven County was among the many areas of high slave population especially "marked out" on the maps found in John Brown's possession.[44]

V

IN ADDITION to pointing out the continuing impact of Harpers Ferry, the Screven County rumors also revealed the beginning of an important shift in the overall pattern of white response to threats (real or imagined) against the established racial order. By late September or early October the type of disorganized panic which followed the first insurrection rumors in August had largely given way to the more structured and formalized activities of local vigilance committees. This change involved more than the determination of community residents to close ranks. In terms of the basic attitudes of Georgia whites, the vigilante approach implied a major change, if not an outright reversal, in psychological posture. Initially the Texas insurrection rumors had triggered a simple and

35

spontaneous defensive reflex, as white Georgians recoiled in terror and dismay while bracing themselves for similar disturbances at home. The reappearance of local vigilante groups beginning in late September reflected the emergence of a more defiant and aggressive attitude on the part of many whites. Having recovered from their initial shock, whites throughout the state began to mount a grass-roots offensive.

Also implicit in this new arrangement was an increased tendency to link racial unrest with the political agitation of the 1860 presidential campaign, then actively under way in Georgia. The growing preoccupation of Georgia whites with national politics led many of them to ponder the impact of heated partisan debates upon local blacks. Were white Southerners inadvertently giving Republicans and Yankee abolitionists a dangerous amount of free publicity? Those who answered this question affirmatively became increasingly vocal as the campaign progressed. Some urged that blacks be rigorously excluded from all political rallies and public debates. This, of course, was not a new idea. As early as February 1860 a newspaper in Rome, Georgia, cautioned against the "loose and unguarded discussion before negroes, of the political excitement of which they are the cause." Describing the practice as "general, if not universal," the paper urged its readers to "reflect upon this thing and be more careful and circumspect."[45] By September many people were demanding positive action instead of mere reflection. To be sure, such demands often possessed a decidedly shrill tone and contained substantial amounts of exaggeration. Yet they cannot be entirely dismissed as valid historical evidence. They undoubtedly indicated a certain degree of genuine black political awareness, especially in urban areas, and also revealed some of the pragmatic strategies which blacks employed to gain political news and information without attracting undue attention.

From Columbus came complaints that the city's "colored population" was "manifesting an unusual interest in politics, and the result of the Presidential election." The frequent presence of blacks at political speeches caused the mayor to order city police to exclude all Negroes from "the meetings and discussions of the different political parties."[46] A similar situation existed at political gatherings in Macon, but blacks in that city were able to evade local regulations through a number of effective and sophisticated techniques. The key was to exploit the system's weaknesses, while always stopping short of any open or direct challenge. Writing in early September 1860, a white resident of Macon asserted that through-out the presidential campaign "every political speech . . . delivered in Macon had attracted a number of negroes, who, without entering the Hall, have managed to linger around and hear what the orators say until the bell rings, when they leave. They do not congregate in sufficient numbers to make an unlawful assembly, but scatter themselves around— some at the Hall door and some in the streets where it is very easy to hear what is said within, when the windows and doors are open."[47]

Whites in Macon and elsewhere were also concerned over slave literacy as a possible avenue by which blacks could gain political information. As early as March of that year a Macon newspaper demanded that the com-mon practice of illegally selling books to slaves be investigated, and in September a Penfield woman accused a local white man of taking blacks into "the old fields and woods on Sundays and . . . teaching them to write and cipher."[48] White concern in this regard was not entirely ground-less, for although literate blacks were few in number, the information they acquired could be easily disseminated by word of mouth throughout the black community.[49]

Yet on the whole there is little evidence that most whites considered abstract political theory a major or immediate source of racial conflict. Although moderate Unionists sometimes accused secessionist newspapers of creating "dangerous" and "disastrous" hopes in the minds of Georgia bondsmen by depicting all presidential candidates except Breckinridge as hostile to slavery, such arguments apparently had little impact.[50] The link which white Georgians perceived between black unrest and national pol-itics was less direct but far more tangible in nature. With increasing fury and intensity as election day approached, white society lashed out at that familiar straw man, the seemingly ubiquitous abolition emissary.

This shift in emphasis reflected a number of political and psychological pressures, the most obvious of which was the impending loss of Southern control of the presidency. By October Lincoln's election was nearly a foregone conclusion, and although united in defense of white supremacy, voters in Georgia and throughout the South seemed powerless to prevent

37

the racial threat implicit in a Republican victory.[51] Thus, in several important respects, Georgia's preelection abolitionist witch hunt was directly
related to the South's gloomy political fortunes. Not only could radical
Breckinridge editors gain support for their candidate through promoting
rumors of abolitionist plots in Georgia but, perhaps more important,
white Georgians could vent their political frustrations against the North
by focusing upon helpless Northerners close at hand.

It was, therefore, with a special sense of mission—or even face-saving
vindication—that many local vigilante groups set out to purge their communities of whites whose racial views were in any way suspect. Early in
September of 1860 the citizens of McIntosh County clearly announced
their intentions in this regard after arresting a strange white man for the
vague offense of "talking to a number of negroes . . . under very suspicious circumstances." In a subsequent public meeting county residents
resolved to "take some action upon the too prevalent practice of allowing
strangers to interfere with our institutions." Later the same month white
Georgians learned of the arrest in Memphis, Tennessee, of an alleged
"underground railroad agent" attempting to reach Cincinnati with two
runaway slaves from Georgia. Amid reports that he had promised to take
the slaves to a place "where negroes were as good as white men," the
supposed "agent," identified only as Mr. Amason, was forcibly returned to
Albany, Georgia, to confront the owner of one of the black runaways.
Amason's arrival created a "high state of excitement" among Albany's
white residents, a majority of whom "were in favor of making an example
of this man, by hanging him." Mob violence was successfully headed off
on this occasion, but white hostility remained intense. A Macon newspaper editor who personally witnessed the Albany incident no doubt
spoke for many white Georgians when he asserted that "those who advocated lynch law in this instance had reason on their side."[52]

The rising tide of anti-Northern feeling was even more evident in the
up-country town of Athens, home of the University of Georgia. In early
October a white man "suspected of inciting the negroes to insurrection"
was "taken up and tried" by a local vigilance committee, which granted
him one week in which to "fix his things up & leave." Some Athenians,
however, were convinced that still further action was necessary. A young

38

man from one of the town's most wealthy and influential families voiced an antipathy toward Northerners which was apparently quite widespread:

> There is another man[,] a Yankee[,] living just above here who is suspected & there are men watching him now . . . [,] if anything certain can be proved . . . I think that he will be dealt with according to the most approved style of "Lynch Law."
>
> The people here are very much excited on the subject . . . ; they are outraged at the idea of these miserable Yankees living among us a[s] friends & making fortunes by swindling & at the same time inciting our negroes to cut our throats.[53]

Additional testimony illustrating the Southern white viewpoint could readily be obtained, but some of the most useful insights into conditions faced by Northerners in Georgia during the fall of 1860 come from the diary of Jennie Akehurst Lines, a New York woman who moved to Georgia in the 1850s. Mrs. Lines's descriptions of life as a boarder with a Southern family in Atlanta just prior to the November presidential election is especially revealing. Perhaps because she was herself strongly opposed to the abolition movement, Jennie Lines was slow to comprehend the relationship between Lincoln's impending victory and her landlady's growing sensitivity over Mrs. Lines's treatment of black house servants. On November 3, three days before the national election, Jennie Lines innocently advised the hired slave Caroline to "bathe her feet and take some hot tea" as treatment for a "hard cold." Mrs. Gardner, the Southern landlady, responded instantly, ordering her Northern boarder to "express no sympathy at all for the negro." The following day Mrs. Lines furnished Caroline with a vile of camphor for her illness, and was dismayed when the gift drew an "excited" rebuke from Caroline's mistress. By November 5 the landlady and her son had become "very silent and reserved" in Mrs. Lines's presence. Unable to understand the dynamics of fear, racism, and sectionalism which was transforming the attitudes of white Georgians around her, Mrs. Lines was more perplexed than angered by her landlady's hostility. "When I have [previously] boarded with those who owned servants," she mused, "I could not please them better than to notice their servants kindly, but it is not so in this house. I have been sorry that we ever came here."[54]

VI

ON NOVEMBER 6 Georgians cast their votes for president, and although John C. Breckinridge led the field of candidates, his popular vote total fell slightly short of a clear majority. Two days later, as if by way of contrast, newly assembled state legislators received news of Abraham Lincoln's landslide victory. At last, the final turbulent act in the drama begun at Harpers Ferry a year earlier was at hand. The news of Lincoln's election evoked responses among white Georgians ranging from bewilderment and disbelief to angry defiance. The scene in Savannah's Monument Square on the night of November 8 was described by one observer as an unprecedented "uprising of the people *of all* parties. With the vast multitude, the excited harangues & equally excited responses, the fireworks etc. etc., it was emphatically a demonstration of popular feeling upon the recent election. There was no stemming the emeute."[55]

In other parts of the state, public demonstrations were smaller and individual reactions slightly more subdued, but in varying degrees nearly all public and private utterances echoed a common theme: Lincoln's election was a threat to slavery.[56] And for a majority of Georgia's white population, the protection of slavery was inextricably bound up with the maintenance of white supremacy. From the very outset, secessionist leaders (whose political views were themselves partially molded by racial anxieties) sought to capitalize on the floodtide of racial fear loosed by Lincoln's victory and channel it in support of disunion. In some areas, most notably the predominantly white counties of northwest Georgia, this strategy failed when nonslaveholders were apparently more influenced by economic and class antipathy toward wealthy planters than by appeals to racial unity. The central fact remains, however, that within the space of two months a Breckinridge plurality became a secessionist majority, with the bulk of prosecession votes concentrated in plantation counties with large black populations. Not all whites were transfixed by insurrectionary fears, of course, but there is abundant evidence that secessionist attempts to foster racial panic for political purposes led to a further exacerbation of the crisis confronting Georgia blacks.[57]

With the "Black Republican" Party about to assume control of the executive branch of the Federal government, warnings about abolitionist activity in Georgia took on new urgency. In his opening message to the legislature Governor Joseph E. Brown painted a grim picture of Georgia's future under a national Republican administration. As soon as Lincoln assumed the presidency, Brown warned, a "hungry swarm of abolition emissaries" would come south as Federal officeholders to "eat out our substance, insult us with their arrogance, corrupt our slaves, and engender discontent among them; while they flood the country with inflammatory abolition documents, and do all in their power, to create . . . a war of extermination between the white and the black races."[58] Even as the legislature debated during its first week whether or not to authorize a special state secession convention, rumors of black rebellion swept over the capital. Stories circulated in Milledgeville that throughout central Georgia blacks had been told "they were to be free on the day of Lincoln's election," and that "several" slaves had made "impudent speeches" to that effect. On November 12 reports reached the capital that only seven miles away a gang of slaves had openly rebelled, "declaring themselves free."[59]

It was also on November 12 that Thomas R. R. Cobb, scholar, jurist, and ardent secessionist brother of Howell Cobb, rose to address a night session of the General Assembly. With a keen sense of drama and a sure instinct for the psychological jugular vein of the tense legislators, he delivered the type of racial soliloquy which would become the stock-in-trade of a later generation of Southern politicians. Fully aware of the day's insurrection rumors, he began with an invitation:

Recur with me to the parting moment when you left your firesides, to attend upon your public duties at the Capitol. Remember the trembling hand of a loved wife, as she whispered her fears from the incendiary and the assassin. Recall the look of indefinable dread with which the little daughter inquired when your returning footsteps should be heard. And if there be manhood in you, tell me if this is the domestic tranquility which this "glorious Union"

41

has achieved. Notice the anxious look when the traveling peddler lingers too long in conversation at the door with the servant who turns the bolt— the watchful gaze when the slave tarries long with the wandering artist, who professes merely to furnish him with a picture—the suspicion aroused by a Northern man conversing in private with the most faithful of your negroes, and tell me if peace and tranquility are the heritage which this Union has brought to your firesides. Take up your daily papers and see the reports of insurrections in every direction. Hear the telegram read which announces another John Brown raid. Travel on your railroads and hear, as I did this day, that within seven miles of this Capitol, a gang of slaves have revolted from their labor, declaring themselves free by virtue of Lincoln's election. . . . Our slaves are the most happy and contented . . . laboring population in the world. . . . But a discontented few, here and there, will become the incendiary or the poisoner, . . . and . . . your home or your family may be the first to greet your returning footsteps in ashes or in death.[60]

While Cobb's principal object was to promote the cause of secession, his oratory typified the sort of extremist political tactics which contributed most directly to the deterioration of Georgia's racial climate. In reality Cobb had done little more than digest the substance of the courthouse politician's diatribe and the rural stump speaker's frenzied harangue, and present their arguments with the literary polish necessary to render them palatable to the assembled state legislators.

In at least one sense, however, Cobb's rhetoric was not exaggerated. Reports of slave insurrections were quite literally coming from "every direction," and would continue to do so well into 1861. Inevitably, of course, greater racial paranoia among Georgia whites meant increased violence and repression for the state's blacks. During November and December instances of racially inspired mob violence became almost commonplace. Even when the victims were white, as was the case in Athens, Americus, Savannah, and elsewhere, the message for blacks was clear enough.[61]

As often as not, black people themselves were the initial targets and primary recipients of actual violence or torture. Even as Cobb skillfully played upon the racial fantasies of the legislators in Milledgeville, a slave insurrection panic of major proportions was occurring only forty miles away in rural Crawford County. Events there followed a familiar pattern, but violence against blacks was unusually widespread. Beginning with "confessions" obtained "under the whip" from some fifteen to twenty bondsmen on the plantation of one W. C. Cleveland, violence spread rapidly throughout the county as other blacks were "implicated." For several days the "examination among the negroes continued and a good many were found to know a good deal about the [planned] insurrection." The reign of terror finally ended when a special twelve-man "Investigating Committee" singled out a white native Pennsylvanian living in the area as "the chief cause of all the difficulty."[62]

Later in November a similar drama was acted out in Habersham County, where several slaves and one free black man (allegedly "their leader") were "arrested and severely whipped" for conspiring to murder a local white woman and throw her into a well. At almost the same moment a free black man named Joseph W. Ribero was receiving equally harsh punishment at the hands of a mob near Savannah. Accused of inciting local slaves to rebel on the day of Lincoln's inauguration, Ribero was taken to a "sparsely settled section" near the city where a self-appointed jury of "twelve quiet gentlemen [and] property holders" gave him twenty-eight lashes and shaved one side of his head. He was then held prisoner on Skidaway Island until nightfall, when he was put on board a steamship bound for Boston.[63]

Throughout December Savannah remained "under the . . . strictest police . . . that it ever had," with rival vigilante groups vying for preeminence.[64] To a considerable extent the city during this period provides an accurate mirror of developments in the state as a whole. The racial violence spawned by insurrection panics in Savannah and elsewhere was, in reality, only the most extreme manifestation of a broader campaign of repression directed at black Georgians in the fall of 1860. At the grassroots level, blacks could usually avoid encounters with lynch mobs, but they could seldom entirely escape the impact of steadily tightening legal and institutional restraints. In the Thermidorian atmosphere of the secession crisis, few areas of black life were left untouched.

In virtually all of Georgia's major towns and cities blacks faced increasing restrictions on their daily activities, as local authorities began rigidly enforcing long-neglected city ordinances. Just as after the John Brown raid, the illegal sale of liquor to blacks was a subject of great concern to many whites. Early in September Augusta officials took steps to reduce the illicit liquor traffic, and within a matter of days white residents of Columbus were demanding similar action. A local newspaper editor, who reported having personally seen as many as fifty blacks enter a local liquor shop on a single Sunday afternoon, urged citizens to follow Augusta's example and "break up the dens which infest every ward of our city." Since black testimony was generally inadmissible in court, the goal could, in his view, best be achieved through a "calm, determined and peaceful vigilance organization." Other white residents felt, however, that the problem was linked to the "nefarious practice" of allowing Columbus blacks to engage in a variety of illegal commercial pursuits. "While negroes keep drinking and gambling saloons," wrote one man indignantly, "you may expect them to drink and gamble; and decoy or encourage others to do so."[65]

Another subject of major concern to white urban dwellers was the practice of allowing blacks to live separately from their owners and to hire themselves out to whomever would pay the highest wages. Columbus citizens complained, with considerable hyperbole, that blacks who hired their own time were "in a state of virtual freedom." Other Columbus whites found such bondsmen utterly "unfit for domestic duties" and "insufferably insolent" to both owners and employers.[66] Between October 1860 and February 1861 the towns of Athens, Augusta, Macon, Milledgeville, Columbus, and Savannah all took special steps to prevent blacks from "living out" or independently hiring themselves. Macon revised city ordinances on the subject; Athens imposed a tax of from five to twenty-five dollars per person to discourage the practice; and Milledgeville authorities even wrote letters to slaveowners in other parts of the state, reminding them of an 1831 state law which required that bondsmen be placed "under the control and oversight of some responsible white person" or else removed from the city.[67]

In their zeal to guard against possible black unrest, whites in some Georgia towns went to truly extraordinary lengths. A week after Lincoln's election a mass meeting in Athens organized a force of citizen volunteers to patrol every ward in the city. Fear of a slave rebellion was especially strong during the Christmas holidays, when slaves traditionally enjoyed considerable freedom of movement. Planters in the Columbus area were asked to discourage their bondsmen from coming into the city in large numbers, and Augusta authorities actually went so far as to organize a force of secret police.[68] Perhaps the mayor of Savannah best captured the increasingly reactionary temper of white urbanites when he complained in late October that "great laxity has obtained in reference to the conduct of the Negro population. The consequence is that they have forgotten their places—are guilty of gambling, smoking in the streets, drinking, and disorderly conduct generally. To remedy this I intend to devote, and am devoting, my every energy."[69]

In rural Georgia, blacks also faced a growing amount of legal and institutional repression. It was impossible, of course, to surround rural bondsmen with the same complex web of legal restrictions applied to urban blacks, and in normal times the law seldom impinged upon the basic autonomy of the white planter in matters of slave discipline. Yet the rural enforcement machinery of the patrol system, while frequently inefficient, was always available in periods of crisis. At the local level, calls for stricter enforcement of patrol laws became insistent enough by the fall of 1860 to produce meaningful action from the Georgia legislature.[70] In December the patrol systems in a number of Georgia counties were modified in order to improve their effectiveness. Generally speaking, the old system requiring that Inferior Court justices appoint patrol commissioners, who in turn organized patrol companies and appointed company captains, was abandoned in favor of various types of simpler organization, where responsibility was easier to fix. If the previous deterioration of patrol machinery reflected a sense of relative security among rural whites, no doubt many state legislators agreed with the November pronouncement of the Bibb County Grand Jury "that [such] security no longer exists."[71]

Nowhere was the racial anxiety of Georgia lawmakers more evident than in legislation directed at illicit commerce between blacks and whites. It was clearly against the "Nats"—the "discontented few" whom T. R. R.

Cobb had characterized as potential murderers, poisoners, and arsonists—that these laws were directed. Since colonial times slaves had been forbidden to carry firearms except in special circumstances, but in December 1860 this ban was reenforced. New legislation provided a prison sentence and possible $500 fine for white men furnishing slaves or free blacks with "any gun, pistol, bowie knife, slung shot, sword cane, or other weapon used for the purpose of offense or defense." The employment of slaves by apothecaries to prepare or sell drugs had also been prohibited for many years, as had selling poison to slaves or free blacks. Now, however, the legislature passed a more stringent law requiring doctors and druggists to record the names and addresses of all persons buying poison, and authorizing prison terms of up to twenty years for selling poisonous drugs to blacks. In cases where a black actually administered poison, the person furnishing it could face the death penalty.[72]

As indicated in several of the above statutes, free blacks were also prime targets of both legislative and judicial harassment during this period. But for free blacks, even more than for slaves, the crisis of late 1860 and early 1861 was an ongoing phenomenon. Nearly all of the repressive legislation precipitated by the John Brown raid still remained on the books, and was refined late in 1860 by further enactments designed to close loopholes in earlier laws.[73] Perhaps of greater significance, however, was the fact that deep-seated white hostility toward free blacks remained relatively constant throughout the entire fifteen-month period following the raid on Harpers Ferry. Although in January 1860 the Augusta City Council modified its ordinance concerning the sale of convicted free blacks into slavery, and accepted appeals from decisions of the city recorder in such cases, there is little evidence that this action reflected any basic change in white attitudes. Certainly those free black Augustans who, some four months after the modification of the enslavement ordinance, followed through on their plans to emigrate to Liberia were unconvinced that Augusta's whites had experienced a change of heart. Subsequent developments throughout the state reveal that the skepticism of these black people was well founded.[74]

In actual fact, the campaign to reduce all black Georgians to chattel slavery gained considerable momentum during 1860 and was not finally abandoned until late in 1863. That this campaign arose and largely culminated amid the tumult of the secession crisis was neither surprising nor entirely accidental. Georgia's attempt to enslave free blacks was a logical, almost inevitable, result of the convergence of two historical forces, one ideological, the other political. Throughout the 1850s Southern defenders of slavery as a "positive good"—even those who frequently espoused a reactionary class ideology—came increasingly to rest their arguments on doctrines of black racial inferiority. Their reasons for doing so were at least partly expedient. As white America stood poised to embark upon an age of "scientific" racism, Georgia's strongly democratic white middle class apparently found little that was appealing or persuasive in the quasi-feudalistic world view of such isolated and alienated proslavery intellectuals as George Fitzhugh. In terms of political viability, race rather than class was the wave of the future. Recognizing this fact, many proslavery theorists shifted their ground accordingly.[75]

Between October 1859 and January 1861 a new component was added to this strongly flowing tide of racism which channeled it away from the realm of ideology and into the area of direct action. Simply stated, this new component was the momentary ascendancy of the radical fire-eaters and secessionists. These were the men who, in the main, had labored diligently throughout the 1850s to establish devotion to slavery as the only valid test of "Southernism."[76] On the eve of secession some even pressed this doctrine to its extreme limits, abandoning ancient taboos and demanding the reopening of the African slave trade.[77] The implications, then, were clear. If slavery was the *sine qua non* of Southern society and if black racial inferiority was slavery's ultimate justification, the elimination of nonslave Negroes became desirable and even mandatory. Not all white Georgians accepted these doctrines, of course, and many who did also voiced more immediate and "practical" reasons for enslaving free blacks. But there can be little question that the temporary juncture of racism and political extremism between 1859 and 1861 added measurably to the pressures upon Georgia's free black community.

Probably few of Georgia's free black people spent time reflecting upon the origins of the crisis confronting them in 1860. What concerned them most was its immediate and frightening reality. The Augusta City Council's January decision to modify its enslavement ordinance was more than offset by negative developments elsewhere in the state. Georgia newspapers carried ominous accounts from Petersburg, Virginia, of free blacks sold into slavery for failure to pay city taxes, and in August the Columbus *Sun* launched its own scathing editorial attack on Georgia's free blacks. Describing them as a "dangerous element" in the population of "any community," the *Sun* editor urged the next legislature to abandon "false philanthropy" and admit "that the true and safe policy of the Southern states and of Georgia, is to rid the country of this element in the negro population." Two months later, in October, the Jones County Grand Jury condemned free blacks as a "nuisance to society" and urged state lawmakers "to pass a law in our next legislature to remove them from our State or sell them into slavery." During the same month the clerk of Muscogee County's Inferior Court took advantage of laws already on the books and imposed a fine of $110 upon Willis Smothers, a free Negro who had failed to re-register his name in the clerk's office as required. When Smothers was unable to pay so large a sum, the sheriff was ordered to "sell him for the shortest time to any purchaser for the amount of the fine." On October 2 Smothers was "'knocked down' to Col. R. J. Moses" for a period of five years.[78]

Early in November the Georgia General Assembly convened, and almost immediately the previous year's assault upon the basic legal status of free blacks was renewed. On November 14 the state House of Representatives began considering a bill "to allow free persons of color to go into voluntary slavery, or to compel them to move from the state." Finally, on December 8, after several unsuccessful attempts at amendment, the bill was adopted by a vote of 83 to 48, but apparently failed to reach the Senate soon enough to be acted on before the session ended.[79] Thus, for the second time in twelve months the threat of immediate mass enslavement was averted, but pressure on individual black people continued. While the bill for general enslavement was still being considered, the Georgia House adopted special legislation authorizing several free blacks to enter slavery on a supposedly "volunteer" basis. One, a woman named Emiline Cole, would also "carry with her her two children."[80]

Even when due allowance is made for the unique circumstances of each individual case, there can be little question that such enslavement "petitions" from free blacks were in large measure the product of intense white hostility and prolonged public pressure. It is not inconceivable that, in the face of seemingly insurmountable social and economic barriers, some Georgia free blacks may actually have chosen "voluntary slavery" as the best available alternative in 1860—especially if the other choice was being sold on the auction block like Willis Smothers. Perhaps it was to avert such a fate, and thus to avoid or at least postpone the possibility of family separation, that Emiline Cole acted. Yet, by any standards, entering chattel bondage was a drastic step, and it surprised even some white Georgians who favored free black enslavement. One white Savannah resident jubilantly described the petitions as "a nut for the Abolitionists to crack," and the Milledgeville correspondent of the Savannah *Republican* could hardly conceal his amazement in reporting the fate of the petitions in the Georgia House. "This is a sensible move on the part of these negroes," he wrote. "They actually petition the Legislature to allow them to become slaves!"[81]

Georgia's free black people may have breathed slightly easier in early 1861, when it became apparent that their legal claim to freedom had survived another legislative session. Yet most of them probably realized that the battle was far from over. They could not know that the war years would witness three more legislative attempts at mass enslavement as well as a continuing series of individual "petitions." They could, however, perceive that the racial crisis which had swirled around the black community since Harpers Ferry showed little sign of abating during the first nine months of 1861. Whether free or slave, black Georgians could hardly fail to conclude that the emotional frenzy which accompanied creation of the Southern Confederacy reflected more than simply politics or patriotism. Any doubt on this score was removed in mid-January, only one day after the Georgia Convention first endorsed secession, when a major state newspaper proudly heralded the event as the establishment of "a white man's Republic."[82] Two months later Alexander H. Stephens, vice-president of the new republic, developed this point at greater length before an emotional audience in the city of Savannah. In a classic affirmation of the concept of "*Herrenvolk* democracy," Stephens stressed the natural right of all whites to complete legal equality, but: "Not so with the negro. Subordination is his place. He, by nature, or by the curse against Canaan, is fitted for that condition which he occupied in our system. . . . Our new government is founded upon . . . its corner-stone rests upon the great truth that the negro is not equal to the white man, that slavery—subordination to the superior race—is his natural or normal condition."[83] Clearly, for Georgia's black people the time for rejoicing was not yet at hand.

VII

THROUGHOUT most of 1861 black Georgians lived in an atmosphere of hostility and suspicion which differed little from that of the preceding year. As Georgia rapidly mobilized for war, some temporary strengthening of the slave system's repressive mechanism was all but inevitable. The thousands of white Georgians who rushed to enlist in state or Confederate military service constituted a potential police force of unprecedented dimensions. Ultimately conscription of adult white males into the Confederate Army helped undermine both the rural patrol system and the disciplinary structure of individual plantations, but in 1861 the impact of volunteering on Georgia's total supply of white manpower was negligible, and many troops destined for Confederate service remained in the state for lengthy periods to be trained, armed, or organized. The military presence in Georgia was further augmented by Governor Brown's dogged struggle to retain a separate force of state troops under his own control and by his frequent attempts to increase the number of Confederate troops allotted for coastal defense.[84]

The simple knowledge that thousands of armed soldiers were on hand in 1861 undoubtedly served as a major inhibiting factor for many black Georgians. From the very outset, whites throughout the state recognized the army's potential value in controlling recalcitrant bondsmen, and in May 1861 a Savannah woman even suggested the type of military tactics which should be employed. If slaves became "refractory," a "company of soldiers" should "march them off at the point of the bayonet, while companies of cavalry scour the whole woods about the neighborhood, with the understanding that every negro out will be shot down." Less than six months later squads of Confederate soldiers were actively assisting individual planters whose slaves had grown "insubordinate." Beginning in 1862 the army was, to all intents and purposes, converted into a gigantic slave patrol on the Georgia coast, charged both with regulating black passage in and out of Savannah and, more important, with preventing black escapes to the Union-held sea islands.[85]

In spite of the army's vast potential as a coercive instrument, most bondsmen in 1861 had less to fear from Confederate soldiers than from local white authorities or vigilante groups. White fears ran especially high in the isolated plantation country of southwestern Georgia, where rumors of black rebellion persisted from April through July. One of the most serious of these panics began in mid-June when a group of patrollers in Decatur County captured a slave named Israel away from his home plantation and questioned him "very clost." Israel's statements helped convince the patrollers that a widespread insurrection plot existed among local blacks, involving slaves on Israel's own plantation and many others as well. Almost immediately basic white anxieties began to surface, and reports soon spread that blacks near the county seat of Bainbridge had secretly collected guns and pistols with which to "kill all of the men and old women and children and take the younger ones for their wives." Two alleged leaders of the plot were soon arrested, amid grim assertions that "if they ever turn them out we are going to kill them."[86] In reality, however, slave insurrection panics account for only a small portion of the violence actually inflicted upon black people during this period. Most violent encounters can be traced directly or indirectly to attempts by Georgia slaveowners at stricter regulation and control of local bondsmen.

Widespread uncertainty among whites over the way slaves would respond to a war with the "abolitionist" North gave many public utterances on the subject an almost schizophrenic quality. In the columns of local newspapers ringing affirmations of the loyalty and devotion of Georgia slaves went hand in hand with proposals to prevent insurrections and crush black unrest. Privately some whites acknowledged the hollowness and lack of conviction beneath much of the "loyal slave" rhetoric. Writing to Howell Cobb in early May, a Macon resident spoke prophetically of the effect upon black behavior which a Federal invasion would produce. "We ought . . . to remember," he cautioned, "that the fidelity of our colored population depends upon our success in effectively defending our soil. Let us falter or fail and our present security will be at an end. . . . Is anybody so blind as to feel sure that a vast majority of the slaves would not with avidity escape from bondage if they felt there was a power to secure them that boon?"[87]

Denying slaves the opportunity for escape or rebellion was a central goal of local paramilitary organizations formed throughout the state during the spring and summer. Known variously as "Home Guards" or "Committees of Safety" these reconstituted vigilante groups shared common visions of a Northern-inspired racial bloodbath. At countless public meetings and village assemblies vigilantes demanded rigid enforcement of Georgia's newly revised patrol laws. Frequently they resolved to ignore the existing legal structure and conduct their own patrols, believing the "ordinary process of law . . . too slow to insure safety."[88] Coastal residents went beyond normal surveillance procedures and launched a determined campaign to eliminate by whatever means necessary the colonies of fugitive slaves who inhabited swamps along the Savannah and Ogeechee rivers. Even trusted plantation "drivers" saw their autonomy reduced when masters collected old muskets previously given black foremen for hunting purposes, and donated the weapons to the state for military use. The trend toward closer regulation of black activity also extended into the purely social realm, and many privileged bondsmen found access to railroad travel significantly restricted, as both civil authorities and previously indulgent masters complied with public demands to curtail "the social privileges between slaves in distant localities." For similar reasons some rural white churches temporarily suspended separate worship services for blacks, when the assemblies conflicted with state law.[89]

Attempts to isolate blacks from each other by banning religious assemblies, restricting travel, and expanding slave patrols represented a tacit recognition by whites that individual or collective acts of slave resistance would generally receive sanction and support from other bondsmen. In this regard the numerous incidents of antiblack violence in 1861 are especially revealing. When individual slaves were threatened with immediate punishment or serious bodily harm, they frequently turned to fellow bondsmen for aid and protection. Such behavior often appeared to result less from a reasoned choice than from an almost automatic survival reflex. Long experience under slavery had taught blacks that in moments of crisis whites were far more likely to become enemies than allies. Thus, when the slave George, accused of sexually assaulting a white woman in rural Harris County, became the object of a search with bloodhounds, he fled first not to his master or employer but to a "neighboring house where . . . [he] had a wife." Shortly afterward he was captured and placed in the county jail to await trial. George's lack of confidence in white protection proved fully warranted. The "boldness" of his alleged crime "incensed" local whites who "could not content themselves with the law's delay." A large mob soon assembled at the county seat, broke into the jail, and took George some two miles into the country, "where they fastened him to a stake and burned him." George's master briefly considered legal action, but soon abandoned the idea and announced that he had "withdrawn all suits instituted against persons engaged in the burning."[90]

The actions of other blacks in and around the city of Savannah revealed a basic mistrust of white society. During the spring and summer of 1861 white Savannahians waged a prolonged battle against a number of black runaways known to be in the area. Although numerous blacks were killed, wounded, or captured in a well-organized campaign, certain incidents shed especially valuable light upon the fundamental attitudes and priorities of the blacks involved. One of the most thoroughly documented fugitive slave captures took place in early March and involved Paul, the slave of wealthy planter and former Savannah mayor Edward C. Anderson. Paul's trouble began when a white man named Patrick Brady attempted to arrest him on suspicion of being a runaway. Brady enticed the black man into his house with an offer of food and then "took hold" of him without warning. In the ensuing struggle Brady was killed and Paul soon became the object of a manhunt by veteran Constable A. E. Jones with his pack of highly trained "Negro dogs."

No longer simply a runaway but now a fugitive accused of murdering a white man, Paul might reasonably have concluded that his best chance for survival lay in returning to his wealthy and powerful master. He chose instead to seek aid from fellow blacks, and for three desperate days remained hidden from pursuers in a house on Indian Street in Savannah occupied by the slave couple Palmer and Dolly. Ultimately, however, a Captain Skinner of the "Louisville road patrol" learned of his whereabouts, surrounded the residence with a large detachment of men, and cut off all avenues of escape. Palmer and Dolly had apparently extended their aid to Paul with full awareness of the risks involved, for they met the patrollers with determined resistance despite the inevitable consequences. In the space of a few minutes the door was battered down, the house searched, and the slave discovered hiding in a brick oven. Although patrol captain Skinner ordered that no shots be fired, Paul was seriously wounded in the leg and taken away to jail barely in time to avoid being lynched by a crowd of whites who had gathered at the scene. Palmer and Dolly were also arrested, given thirty-nine lashes each, and placed in jail "until further orders." Shortly after entering the Chatham County jail, the three blacks faced still another enraged mob composed of "friends and countrymen" of the murdered white man. Only the prompt appearance of a military force summoned by Savannah Mayor Charles C. Jones, Jr., prevented a lynching. For Paul, however, Mayor Jones's defense of law and order came too late. The following morning the slave was officially pronounced dead from gunshot wounds in his leg and foot, inflicted by some "person or persons unknown."[91]

Such episodes are particularly revealing because all black people involved were presented with clear alternatives and options. Their actions resulted from a conscious choice and thus reflected personal priorities and values. Since Paul eluded his pursuers for several days, he might have chosen to seek help from his master, who, at the very least, had an economic interest in saving his bondsman from the gallows. The slaves Palmer and Dolly, on the other hand, might have refused to conceal Paul because of the great personal risk which such complicity entailed. They might even have reported his presence to local authorities in order to protect themselves, or out of a sense of loyalty and duty to white masters. Their actions at the time of Paul's arrest, in the face of impending harsh reprisals, clearly demonstrate the rejection of all these alternatives.

For Georgia slaveholders evidence of group solidarity among bonds-men, while hardly a new discovery, was probably more unsettling in 1861 than at any previous time. Confronted with the prospect of a bloody war, few white Georgians cared to be reminded of the glaring discrepancies between the infantile Sambo of proslavery polemics and the autonomous personalities of flesh-and-blood bondsmen. In fact, it is only within the context of paternalist stereotypes that the concerted drive to eliminate slave rebels and runaways can be properly understood. Small bands of black fugitives who emerged from swamps or forests to commit occasional "depredations" posed little real danger to white society. They did, how-ever, intrude upon the idealized version of master-slave relations which many whites were anxious to accept as reality. The actions—indeed the very existence—of these defiant fugitives effectively undermined the cherished image of the universal slave-child who lived for no higher pur-pose than to reciprocate the affection of a patriarchal master.

Some of the clearest testimony on the latter point is to be found in the response of white Savannahians to the capture in mid-July 1861 of the famous black runaway chieftain Toney. The accolades which local resi-dents heaped upon A. E. Jones, the ubiquitous slave-hunting constable, require no explanation beyond the characterization of Toney presented in newspaper accounts of his capture. Widely known as a "desperate runaway and the head of a gang of runaways who . . . had their camp in Shaw's swamp," Toney successfully eluded captors until July 16 when, as one Savannah newspaper reported, "Mr. Jones' dogs got upon the trail of *Toney* in Mr. McAllen's woods and pursued it to the Augusta road near Dundee bridge where they came up with him. Refusing to surrender, he fought the dogs with great desperation, killing two and wounding several of them with his Bowie knife; he also made a cut at Mr. White, when one of the party in pursuit fired on him with a double barrelled gun, the shot taking effect in his shoulder and back, after which he was captured."[92]

Many antebellum whites undoubtedly dismissed such rebellious blacks as atypical, the occasional exceptions to an otherwise universal pattern of slave docility. In one sense this view was correct, since at any given pe-riod of Southern history the number of blacks who rejected slavery with dramatic gestures of self-affirmation through violence was understandably small. But in ways that stopped short of open rebellion, succeeding generations of bondsmen resisted the personal debasement which complete internalization of the white world's roles and stereotypes would have entailed. And if some blacks accepted the ethic of planter paternalism, many others harbored lifelong resentment against white exploitation even as they accommodated themselves to the realities of power in a planter-dominated society.

One of the key elements in black resistance and solidarity, both during and after slavery, was the general adherence of Georgia Negroes to an intensely personal form of fundamentalist Christianity which offered them crucial links to a broader moral universe. Religious faith played a central role in enabling many blacks to survive the collective psychological traumas of bondage, as well as individual personal tragedies. By affirming their faith in God, blacks were in reality affirming their own moral worth as human beings. And if black preaching was seldom openly millenial in character, it frequently tapped the universal Christian theme of collective deliverance through faith. Some of the most eloquent testimony on this point comes from the Reverend Joseph Williams, a black Presbyterian preacher who had ministered to bondsmen in various parts of Georgia since the 1840s. In 1860 he was attached to the white Presbyterian church in Athens, where in the course of six months he had gathered a rapidly growing black congregation. We do not know precisely what Williams said when he preached to blacks in the basement of the church on Sunday evenings, or if his sermons there differed from those he delivered in the separate black church three miles from town. But in a time of personal crisis several years earlier Williams expounded a spiritual theme which would have been equally appropriate in the repressive atmosphere of late 1860. One may speculate that his sermons to Athens blacks echoed his earlier affirmation that "the darkest hour . . . . is the best time to serve and trust the Lord. Man's extremity has always been God's opportunity. This has been true in all the ages of the world. Therefore I must do as primitive Christians when they were in darkness [—] wait on the Lord until the light came."[93] In spite of its implicit reference to the early Christian martyrs, this message is basically one of hope, strength, and fortitude rather than one of despair or Paulistic acquisescence. Williams's faith possessed a quality of enduring steadfastness which strengthened but did not immobilize. Such a faith gave black people the courage to act and the calmness not to act foolishly.[94]

There can be little question that religion was a major source of strength to many Georgia bondsmen in the crisis of 1860. Even at this early stage the black church, whether it took the form of a clandestine prayer meeting or an officially sanctioned worship service, was a major source of social and cultural cohesion in the slave community. Some whites realized this fact and viewed the church as a potential source of unrest or even rebellion. The entire slave experience had, of course, taught black people the need for caution and circumspection in religious gatherings. Amid the white paranoia of the secession crisis, however, normal precautions sometimes proved insufficient. Susie King Taylor, a Savannah slave woman who escaped to Federal lines early in the war, recounted one such incident involving her grandmother, Dolly Reed. In late 1860 or early 1861 Mrs. Reed had the misfortune to attend a prayer meeting in a Savannah suburb where the black worshipers temporarily let down their guard. As they fervently sang the dangerously ambivalent hymn verse "Yes, we shall all be free/Yes, we shall all be free/Yes, we shall all be free/When the Lord shall appear," local police rushed in and arrested the entire congregation on the charge of "planning freedom." The lesson was not lost on any of the black people involved, including Mrs. Reed. Susie King Taylor later recalled, "Grandmother never forgot that night, although she did not stay in the guard-house, as . . . her guardian . . . came at once for her; . . . this was the last meeting she ever attended out of the city proper."[95]

Much of our knowledge concerning the attitudes of Georgia slaves must be deduced from their collective behavior or from the potentially misleading comments of white masters. Yet a limited amount of direct testimony from slaves and free blacks is also available. In weighing the significance of such evidence, form as well as content becomes important. Firsthand testimony from black Georgians in 1860–61 consists almost exclusively of published letters and pamphlets directed primarily at a white audience. Obviously the documents cannot be taken entirely at face value. They do, however, shed considerable light on the techniques employed by literate, sophisticated blacks to manipulate white sentiment. By early 1861 a number of Georgia Negroes were engaged in what amounted to a shrewd public-relations campaign aimed at staving off further repressive measures and neutralizing white hostility. Certainly this educated, urbane minority did not, in any direct sense, speak for all segments of Georgia's black population. Perhaps they spoke only for themselves. Or perhaps their education enabled them to express attitudes and emotions which illiterate field hands shared but were incapable of articulating. In either case, their opinions deserve a fair hearing.

One of the most significant and intriguing documents produced by a black writer during this period was a forty-one page pamphlet entitled *Slavery and Abolitionism as Viewed by a Georgia Slave*.[96] Its author was Harrison Berry, a slave owned by S. W. Price of Covington, but employed in Atlanta as a shoemaker in 1861. At first glance this pamphlet appears to be simply a violent anti-abolitionist polemic, representing either Berry's cynical attempt to curry favor with whites or his complete acceptance of the slave system's values. Viewed from this superficial perspective, it has apparently proved no less embarrassing to twentieth-century liberals than to nineteenth-century abolitionists, and one modern writer has even questioned its authenticity.[97] Yet a careful reading of *Slavery and Abolitionism* reveals that Berry was saying considerably more than most white Georgians realized in 1861. When placed within the context of Berry's earlier career and later writings, the pamphlet all but loses its apparent moral ambiguity.

At one level *Slavery and Abolitionism* was a direct mirror of its time, reflecting both the precarious racial situation of the 1850s and, more immediately, the wave of anti-Negro violence touched off by John Brown's raid. Although not published until the spring of 1861, the pamphlet was written and revised during late 1859 and 1860. Berry's thinking was obviously influenced by the rising tide of terrorism during this period, and his essay may be regarded in part as an attempt to calm white racial fears, or at least to channel them away from blacks and toward elusive Northern "emissaries." Through a careful recitation of the major tenets of the proslavery argument, Berry skillfully established his credibility with Georgia whites. Dutifully he affirmed slavery's biblical sanction, stressed the paternalistic

58

nature of the master-slave relationship, attacked Northern economic exploitation of free laborers, and drew favorable comparisons between the material condition of Southern slaves and the lower classes of other nations. Again and again he assured Southern masters that their bondsmen were overwhelmingly loyal, citing the failure of John Brown to gain black converts as conclusive proof.

Much of Berry's essay was ostensibly addressed to Northern abolitionists, whom he castigated for disrupting supposedly harmonious relationships between masters and slaves. In reality, however, such passages can probably be best understood as descriptions of Georgia's prevailing climate of racial violence, viewed from the perspective of a potential victim. The likelihood seems equally strong that Berry's remarks were aimed primarily at a local audience. Consider, for example, the following extraordinary descriptions of white violence and repression which, if lifted out of their anti-abolitionist context, can hardly be viewed as unqualified endorsements of the Georgia slave system. Predicting that a Republican presidential victory would "put manacles on every Slave South of Mason & Dixon's line," Berry asserted bluntly that:

Even now the oppression has commenced, but where it will end God only knows. . . . Yes, indeed, you [abolitionists] are absolutely the worst enemy the Slave has ever had. . . . Now, as the master waits all night for the return of his Slave that has run away from him, seeing, in the morning, he is yet absent, he goes over to his neighbor's house, and asks him to look out for him. Says, he, "I went to town yesterday after my paper, and when I had gotten it, I saw a statement of the organization of an Abolition Convention, resolving that Slavery was a sin, and a reproach to any free people, and that they would never desist . . . until they had eradicated the last string that bound it to the country. I, of course, became somewhat grum when I saw it; and, on going to the field after getting home . . . I, perhaps, might have been too much vexed to have judged correctly the amount of work that should have been done. I, at any rate, thought they had not done enough, and scolded Tom for not having done more; he commenced muttering, which only added fuel to the fire already kindled within me; so I was in a bad fix to take his insolence, and made at him, when he run away. . . ."

Now let us hear the consolation of his neighbor. He says: "Yes; and let me tell you what happened at my house last Sunday. As I was going to the lot, I saw my Bob have a newspaper, reading very attentively; and on going to him, and asking him to let me see it, I found that he was reading the paper that had the very same proceedings of that Convention of the Abolitionists you were speaking of. So I lurked about my negroes' houses that night, to see if I could hear Bob say anything about the Convention to the other Negroes; and, sure enough I did, for I heard him tell them that they would not be slaves much longer, for the Abolition party intended to set them all free. . . . He was going on at a terrible rate; and, on peeping through a crack, I saw two of Mr. Jones' boys there too. So I slipped back to the house, and thought I would watch their maneuvers the next morning; and when morning came I found them to be dull, careless, and very slothful. So I took them up, and whipped every one of them, and gave Bob two hundred lashes, then I got on my horse and rode over to Mr. Jones' and told him what I had heard Bob say in the presence of his two boys, and what I had done to mine. He called up his two boys and whipped them too. So you see how this thing is shaping. We must have our property protected against this diabolical set of Abolitionists, and our Legislatures must give us more power over our Slaves. Any man that will not agree to make the laws more binding on Slaves can't get my vote. . . ."

Thus they extort from their candidates a promise to legislate on the laws regulating the privileges of Slaves. . . . Now, it is not at all astonishing to me to see this law so vigorously enforced, when aided by such an allied army of fiends as you Abolitionists are. . . . But when we view the treason of John Brown at Harpers Ferry we must beg leave to pause, for a moment at least. . . . The horror lying at the bottom of that attempt is more than I could describe. . . . My nerves would not suffer me to write it down, even were I calculated to do so. Therefore, I can give you nothing but my imagination. I can imagine that I see gibbets all over the Slave-holding States, with negroes stretched upon them like slaughtered hogs, and pens of lightwood on fire! Methinks I hear their screams—I can see them upon their knees, begging, for God's sake, to have mercy! I can see them chained together . . . and shot down like wild beasts. These are but shadows to what would have been done, had John Brown succeeded.[98]

What is one to make of such chilling vignettes from the pen of a Georgia black man? At the very least they suggest that Berry considered planter paternalism a fragile shield against persecution in times of crisis. Writing in an atmosphere of unparalleled racial tension, Berry anticipated the methods employed by later generations of Southern black writers when he relied upon ambiguous syntax and multiple levels of meaning in order to express a dissenting viewpoint which white society would tolerate. Implicitly *Slavery and Abolitionism* acknowledges force and violence as the ultimate foundation of Southern race relations, and offers a somber assessment of the consequences of black vulnerability. Within this framework the author's assertion that "slaves are much worse treated when the slavery question is agitated" can hardly be construed as a contented bondsman's repudiation of freedom. [99]

All of this is not to say, however, that Berry's skepticism over the antislavery movement was merely a cynical ploy to disarm Southern whites. His doubts were quite real but they were not confined to abolitionists alone. Throughout the pamphlet Berry's arguments deal less with the stated issues of "slavery" and "abolitionism" than with the more fundamental problem of white supremacy. That Berry perceived the essential similarity of Northern and Southern racial attitudes more clearly than other black Georgians was undoubtedly due in part to his decade-long association with the American Colonization Society, which sought to encourage black emigration to Africa by stressing the permanent nature of white race prejudice. [100] The influence of Colonization Society propaganda is evident throughout Berry's pamphlet in both overt and subtle ways. His repeated attacks on Northern prejudice represent an individual application of the Colonization Society's general strategy of skillfully manipulating Southern sectional and racial phobias. Thus, we find Berry's white employer, A. M. Eddleman, naively applauding his bondsman's affirmation of the universality of white racism: "He has often remarked in my hearing, that there was no such thing as a free negro in this country (meaning the whole country)." By setting his remarks in an anti-Northern context, Berry was able to assert bluntly in his pamphlet: "The colored man is a colored man anywhere. He is but the tool North and the servant South." [101]

In some portions of *Slavery and Abolitionism* Berry ventured beyond this

essentially negative strategy of veiled or implicit criticism of white prejudice. To stereotype Harrison Berry as an embryonic black nationalist
would be a gross overstatement, ignoring both the complexity and the
ambivalence of his evolving attitudes toward white America. Yet much in
his writing does reflect a groping quest for a sense of historical identity,
informed and directed by an underlying sense of black pride. Here again,
the American Colonization Society's influence cannot be disregarded. As
George M. Fredrickson has noted, major Colonization Society officials,
in spite of their expedient manipulation of white Negrophobia, espoused
a philosophical position which was essentially nonracist. They consistently rejected claims that blacks were innately or permanently inferior
to whites, and within this quasi-egalitarian context they frequently
stressed the dignity and achievements of the African past. [102]

There can be little question that Berry was influenced by these appealing, if often self-serving, themes in colonizationist literature. Twice in his
essay he stops just short of openly endorsing emigration to Africa. But in
each reference to this subject Berry casts the issue in religious terms,
invoking a biblical analogy with potentially revolutionary implications.
His remarks, to be sure, appear within an outwardly proslavery context,
but one may logically argue that Berry's entire literary approach was predicated upon the ability of literate blacks to look beyond external form to
inner substance. When one considers the central role of religion in antebellum black life, it is difficult to imagine that the juxtaposition of the
following passages on the same page was accidental:

I contend that the overthrow of Jerusalem, by the wicked and idolatrous
Nebuchadnezzar and the carrying away of the children of Israel to Babylon,
affording them an opportunity of embracing the true Religion, was a manifestation of the Higher Law.

I contend that the circumstance of the Africans being sold to the Euro-
peans, and from them to the Americans, . . . thereby bringing them into a
land flowering, as it were, with the milk and honey of the Gospel, . . .
and . . . fitting them for useful missionaries to their benighted brethren in
Africa . . . is a manifestation of the Higher Law. [103]

Even without further elaboration, the implication of this historical parallel could hardly have been lost upon black Georgians, whose faith placed major stress upon the theme of collective deliverance. Southern slaves were latter-day children of Israel, and who were the Israelites if not "God's Chosen People"? The point emerges still more clearly in a section of Berry's pamphlet which he requested masters to read aloud to their illiterate slaves: "Now, my kind brethren in bondage, if it be so that the children of Israel were enslaved for the express purpose of saving much people now alive, how much more might it be possible that the Slaves of America are enslaved to save many Africans alive?"[104] Depending upon one's individual perspective, such passages may be viewed as biblical justifications of slavery, pleas for African colonization, or assertions that life held some higher destiny for Georgia blacks than perpetual bondage. When *Slavery and Abolitionism* is placed alongside Berry's postwar writings proclaiming black racial equality and demanding protection of black constitutional rights, the latter interpretation becomes especially persuasive.[105]

One can only speculate as to how many bondsmen actually read or listened to the contents of *Slavery and Abolitionism*, but it is clear that Berry was not alone in his attempt to manipulate white prejudice and insecurity for strategic purposes. During this same period a slave preacher in southwest Georgia dutifully delivered to his black congregation a sermon "on the subject of slavery, presenting the Bible argument in support of it." At the end of the service, with white observers apparently present, "he took a vote to see how many of his congregation agreed in believing that slavery was right according to the Bible." Taking their cue smoothly, "the whole congregation without a single exception arose to their feet." A literate slave in the city of Macon "took some pains" to read to his "fellow servants" a proslavery sermon by the Reverend J. Henry Van Dyke of New York, observing blandly as he did so that "it was the ablest vindication of Bible truth, upon that subject, he had ever seen." There is ample evidence that these bondsmen correctly judged the temper of the times, recognizing what was required of them as de facto "spokesmen" for a slave community rendered especially vulnerable by external events.[106]

Harrison Berry's pamphlet was particularly well suited to the emotional needs of numerous white Georgians who faced growing frustration in

their attempts to reconcile the idealized view of slavery as benign paternalism and reciprocal affection with the harsh reality of racial fear and
anti-Negro violence. Some white Southerners may, indeed, have experienced neither guilt feelings nor psychological tensions over the system of
racial bondage, but if so, E. W. Warren, pastor of the First Baptist Church
of Macon, was not among them. Upon learning the contents of *Slavery
and Abolitionism* he could scarcely conceal his sense of relief and elation.
Warren was delighted at the "moral spectacle of a negro slave teaching
ethics, religion, history, and slavery" to the "misguided fanatics" who
sought to liberate Southern bondsmen. In his view *Slavery and Abolitionism*
was quite literally a godsend, offering clear proof that "Providence" was
"raising up faithful and gifted men" among Southern blacks "to defend the
institution which enslaves them." With a characteristic antebellum flourish, Warren threw down the gauntlet to global opinion. "I challenge the
world", he boasted, "to produce another instance in which the enslaved of
any land have believed it morally and religiously right to be held in bondage; and have . . . come to the defence of those who held them in bondage." For Warren, and no doubt other white Georgians as well, *Slavery and
Abolitionism* had clearly touched a responsive chord. It is reasonable to
suppose that this was precisely the reaction Harrison Berry hoped his
pamphlet would evoke. [107]

If *Slavery and Abolitionism* may, in some measure, be regarded as a piece
of defensive propaganda intended to diminish or deflect white hostility,
the highly publicized activities of Georgia's free blacks fall even more
clearly within this vein. For bondsmen the key to survival was outward
submissiveness and passivity. For free blacks the opposite tended to be
true. The two legislative sessions since John Brown's raid had amply demonstrated to free blacks that their future legal status was, at best, uncertain. In a nation which affirmed slavery as its "cornerstone," free Negroes
soon came to realize that more was required of them than neutral acquiescence if they were to strengthen their increasingly precarious hold on
freedom. Only through overt, positive actions could they hope to convince white society of their trustworthiness and loyalty, and thereby stave
off further repressive measures.

Historians have offered a variety of explanations for the apparent enthusiasm with which some free blacks embraced the Confederate cause early in the war. The factors most often cited include local loyalty and patriotism, the prevailing climate of military fervor, economic interests such as ownership of real estate or slaves, a desire to improve civil and political status by supporting the government in power, and threats of harassment or bodily harm from local whites. [108] No doubt all of these forces helped shape the pro-Confederate posture of certain free black Georgians in early 1861. Available evidence suggests, however, that those free Negroes who offered to take up arms for the state or to perform military labor acted less out of a sense of duty or patriotism than out of simple fear and apprehension.

In the most numerically significant case of such "voluntary" service, a fairly direct cause and effect relationship can be established between white pressure and free Negro response. The origin of this somewhat less than spontaneous display of Southern nationalism was a June 1861 newspaper article attacking Savannah's large and vulnerable free black community. Stressing the crucial need for labor on nearby fortifications, the article described Savannah's free Negroes as "drones in the hive" who should be rescued from lives of "indolence and vice" in local grogshops and "made useful" in Georgia's war effort. Rebuttals to these charges appeared almost immediately in city newspapers. The correspondent "Justice" pointed out that Savannah's free blacks had rendered "signal service" as pioneers in the War of 1812 and that as early as April 1861 over sixty of them had made a "written tender" to Governor Brown of "their services in any capacity in which he would employ them." The offer had, however, been rejected. A number of free Negro women, "actuated by the same public spirit," had agreed to make one hundred suits of clothes for local volunteer companies, and were "willing to work so long as a Southern soldier shall need a garment." Such actions were cited as proof that the "Loyalty of this class of our population has never been questioned. No people were ever more attached to the government which protects them."[109]

During the next two months Savannah's free black community (aided occasionally by sympathetic whites) worked diligently to create a favorable public image. In mid-June, for example, a group of fifty-five free

Negro men published the following carefully worded letter in the Savannah *Morning News:*

> *To Brigadier General Lawton*
> *Commanding Military District*
>
> The undersigned free men of color, residing in the city of Savannah and county of Chatham, fully impressed with the feeling of duty we owe to the State of Georgia as inhabitants thereof, which has for so long a period extended to ourselves and families its protection, and has been to us the source of many benefits—beg leave, respectfully, in this the hour of danger, to tender to yourself our services, to be employed in the defense of the state, at any place or point, at any time, or any length of time, and in any service for which you may consider us best fitted, and in which we can contribute to the public good. [110]

This offer was followed several weeks later by an article listing the names of twenty-four "Free Colored Volunteers" who had been "honorably discharged" by the commander of Fort Pulaski in Savannah harbor, after "having faithfully served the time for which they volunteered." The article promised that a second detachment of twenty-four free blacks would leave for the fort promptly. Within less than a month still another notice appeared, giving the names of a large group of free black women who, for "some months past," had been "diligently sewing for the soldiers."[111]

In other parts of the state such public displays by free blacks were infrequent. When they occurred they involved only isolated individuals whose motives cannot be explicitly determined. The possibility does, of course, exist that some free blacks were influenced by genuine feelings of community loyalty. Yet probably few were totally unmindful of the personal benefits to be derived from cultivating a "good press" with local whites. In January 1861, for example, Joe Clark, a free Negro barber in Columbus, wrote Governor Brown offering to raise a military company for state service. Georgia newspapers described the offer as "patriotic" and pointed out that Clark had served in the Seminole War of 1836 and "still limps occasionally from a wound received in that campaign." In Milledgeville the well-known free Negro Wilkes Flagg was praised for "Commendable Liberality" when he contributed twenty-six dollars to a local military company. "Well done for Wilkes," exclaimed a Milledgeville newspaper editor, obviously pleased by support from an unexpected quarter.[112]

In the final analysis Georgia's nonslave Negroes stood at the periphery of the Confederate revolution, tied to the Southern cause by their weakness and need for white protection from extremist elements within the secession movement itself. The position was ambiguous in the best of circumstances and productive of little that could be called genuine patriotism. Indeed, for most black Georgians, whether free or slave, loyalty to the Confederacy as a political entity was all but impossible in 1861. The moral gulf between blacks and whites under slavery fostered racially distinct value systems for oppressor and oppressed—modes of perception and thought that were outwardly compatible but inwardly at odds. White Georgians spoke of the sectional struggle in terms of abstract principles and moral absolutes. Blacks necessarily took a different view as they weighed alternatives on a scale of relative advantage. Slave "loyalty" and self-interest overlapped in most circumstances prior to emancipation, and it was largely this ethical fusion which guided the conduct of bondsmen during the secession crisis. Once the Civil War was actively under way, black Georgians would demonstrate beyond all question their willingness to form independent moral judgments, and to act upon those judgments decisively.

3. Black Georgians and the Union War Effort, 1861–1865

FROM a white standpoint the continued tightening of controls over black life in 1861 did not seem abnormal. On the contrary, repressive racial policies acquired new legitimacy as logical and necessary steps in the larger task of securing the Confederate revolution. For many months the entire process of nation-building seemed to transfix Southerners, causing them to suspend critical judgment and ignore the somber implications of the hostilities initiated at Fort Sumter. Shielded from attack by geography and early success on distant Virginia battlefields, white Georgians found the idea of Yankee conquest all but inconceivable during the springtime of their independence. Few allowed themselves to doubt that the struggle for Southern nationhood would prove short and successful, and that it would preserve the racial status quo. Few, that is, except coastal rice and cotton planters whose vulnerability to amphibious assault was made vividly apparent by the Union capture of Port Royal, South Carolina, in November 1861. With the arrival of Federal warships off the South Atlantic coast the realities of war flooded in abruptly on a peacetime culture. In Savannah local whites were thrown into a state of confusion and panic by news of the Union victory. With booming Federal cannon clearly audible in the distance, crowds milled excitedly in the streets and outbound trains were crammed with fleeing residents. For several days the city remained in "great commotion" as the chaotic exodus of civilians continued. Savannah soon acquired a deserted look reminiscent of the city's appearance in "yellow fever time."[1]

68

Apprehension over the possibility of a Federal invasion was not the only cause of concern among white Georgians in the wake of Port Royal. Even if Savannah remained impregnable, many coastal residents wondered how the proximity of a large Union army would affect local bondsmen, and in this regard reports from the invaded region of South Carolina were anything but reassuring. On Port Royal Island whites had barely abandoned their elegant Beaufort town houses and fled to the mainland before angry black field hands from the surrounding plantations began to vent years of pent-up frustration through the destruction and pillaging of their late masters' property. "Beaufort is reported completely gutted by the negroes," wrote one white Savannahian. Black women had appropriated their mistresses' best apparel, while black men were "rioting over their masters' wine." Equally disturbing were the reports reaching Savannah that most slaves had refused to evacuate the sea islands at the time of the Federal attack, and that a number of black runaways had already found shelter behind Union lines. One Georgia woman lamented the fate of a friend from Beaufort whose slaves had "left her in a body" as soon as they realized the Federal attack would succeed. Savannah aristocrat George A. Mercer undoubtedly reflected the fears of many local whites when he described the Port Royal expedition as "a great John Brown Abolition raid" aimed at enticing "ignorant and susceptable" Southern bondsmen away from their masters. "[W]e well know what this means," he wrote ominously.[2]

For blacks along the Georgia seaboard the white reaction to Port Royal may have ushered in the beginnings of a new consciousness of the war's potential implications. The sight of supposedly omnipotent and secure masters fleeing in terror at the first approach of Northern soldiers undoubtedly produced a significant psychological effect on many Savannah-area blacks. White actions spoke considerably louder than the barrage of fabricated atrocity stories and anti-Yankee propaganda which Georgia slaveowners directed at their bondsmen. Even prior to the Port Royal expedition probably few, if any, Georgia slaves accepted uncritically rumors that Union soldiers would sell blacks to Cuba or use them as draft animals. "[D]on't mind what the white people say," an elderly black woman advised her teenage granddaughter who asked whether the

Yankees were as evil as reported. No doubt many black children received comparable advice from parents or other adults as Union forces consolidated their South Carolina foothold and prepared to begin operations along the Southern coast.[3]

Georgia planters began leaving the sea islands shortly after the fall of Port Royal. Union forces landed on Tybee and Wassaw islands during the closing weeks of 1861, and by early 1862 only Confederate garrisons remained at most offshore locations. Their stay, however, was destined to be brief. Bowing to tactical necessity General Robert E. Lee ordered the military evacuation of St. Simons Island in February 1862, and by late March all of Georgia's coast was under Federal control except Fort Pulaski in Savannah Harbor, which surrendered on April 11 after a two-day bombardment.[4]

The Northern conquest of Georgia's "golden isles" had been bloodless and for the most part undramatic, but its significance was not lost upon nearby slaves. Almost immediately local bondsmen began making their way to the scattered offshore outposts that Union authorities optimistically designated the "Department of the South." Although unprompted by official declarations, the black exodus could hardly be called "spontaneous" in the sense of an unreasoning or impulsive act. On the contrary, both the timing and the method of slave escape efforts were matters of careful choice, reflecting a clear sense of the value of liberty and a highly concrete definition of what freedom should entail. After decades of circumspection, low-country bondsmen were poised to assert their latent values and aspirations behind the protection of Yankee gunboats.

II

PRECISELY how many slaves escaped bondage along the Georgia seaboard is a subject for speculation. Union naval officers in the South Atlantic Blockading Squadron afforded protection and assistance to black refugees but recorded their arrival haphazardly. Consequently only a small fraction (perhaps 25 percent) of the slaves and free Negroes who fled Georgia during this early period were mentioned in official documents. The disparity between actual and reported incidents of escape is illustrated by population data from a settlement of black refugees on St. Simons Island near the mouth of the Altamaha River. Established by the Union Navy in March 1862, the St. Simons settlement (officially designated a "colony") was only one of several locations to which escaped slaves from Georgia were taken. In the space of nine months the island's black population grew from none to nearly 600, but during this same period the total number of black escapees reported by military and naval commanders on station off the Georgia coast was only 144, or about a fourth of the black population of St. Simons alone. By the most conservative estimates, then, commanders of individual blockading vessels failed to record some 70 to 80 percent of the Georgia fugitives who passed through their hands.[5]

Whether or not this ratio remained constant throughout the thirty months preceding Sherman's invasion is uncertain. If it did, and if three out of four black escapees went unreported, then the 561 Georgia slaves and free Negroes known to have reached Union lines from December 1861 through October 1864 would represent a total of 2,000 to 2,500 actual escapees (see Table 1). If one assumes, on the other hand, that the volume of escapes declined and the efficiency of reporting increased markedly after 1862, an estimate of 1,000 black refugees for the entire period would still be well within reason.[6]

Whatever the precise number of refugees may have been, enough escape incidents were reported to reveal clear trends in several key areas. For purposes of analysis escape efforts may, at the outset, be separated into two basic categories: (1) those conceived and initiated by blacks without initial Union assistance (hereafter designated "black-initiated" escapes), and (2) those occurring during Union coastal or river raids (hereafter designated "rescues"). Out of a total of 56 reported escape incidents, 42 fall within the first category. These "black-initiated" efforts involved 290 individuals, or roughly 45 percent of the 650 known Georgia fugitives (see Table 1). The volume and frequency of black-initiated escape efforts varied considerably over time. Whereas "rescue" incidents simply mirrored the pace of Union military operations along Georgia's coast, black-initiated efforts were concentrated most heavily during the first nine to twelve months after the arrival of Federal blockading vessels. The number of such incidents declined slowly throughout 1863 and dwindled to almost nothing after the first three months of 1864.

This pattern suggests that logistical factors were of central importance in determining the rate of black escapes. There was, for example, no perceptible increase in black escape attempts following the issuance of the final Emancipation Proclamation in January 1863. To most black Georgians freedom was a condition rather than a theory, and in Georgia as in neighboring South Carolina, Negroes who reached the sea islands were virtually free from the moment of their arrival.[7] What varied in Georgia was not the desire of black people for liberty but their physical opportunity to obtain it. Black-initiated escapes were most numerous in 1862 because the number of blacks near the Georgia seaboard was larger then than at any subsequent period of the war. By 1863 nearly all coastal planters had moved their slaves well inland to areas where escape was difficult if not impossible.[8] The impressment of 1,500 black laborers to work on Savannah's defenses in the summer of 1862 further increased the pool of potential escapees, while the navy's black settlement on St. Simons Island offered tangible proof of Northern willingness to grant fugitives a safe sanctuary.[9]

As the number of black fugitives increased during the war, the nature of their escape efforts also changed dramatically. In antebellum times few Georgia slaves made bids for permanent freedom, and those who did were usually healthy young men traveling alone to remote and uncertain destinations. Apart from dogs and white pursuers, the male runaway's chief physical obstacle was distance, compounded by the psychological pain of abandoning home, friends, and family. To flee northward meant repudiating not merely servitude but a part of oneself as well, and this fact, perhaps even more than the likelihood of punishment and recapture, helped limit most pre-1861 runaway episodes to temporary defections aimed at securing better treatment under slavery.[10]

The arrival of Union warships off Georgia's coast in 1862 altered the entire context of black escape efforts. Running away ceased to be a solitary endeavor as seaboard slaves seized the chance to gain liberty for themselves and their kindred on the Federally controlled sea islands. Adult men continued to lead or participate in most defections, but statistics reveal a clear trend toward collective escape efforts involving family groups and occasionally plantation communities.[11]

Relevant information is available for a total of forty-two separate black-initiated escape incidents involving 290 people. Thirty-two of the escapees fled Georgia alone or in company with one other person. Two hundred and forty-nine of the remaining 258 black fugitives (86 percent of the total) reached or attempted to reach the sea islands in groups of three or more (see Table 1). Although the specific age and sexual makeup of these groups was seldom recorded, surviving evidence suggests that most of the large parties included women and children as well as men. In 1862, for example, the black refugee population on St. Simons Island grew from 26 men, 6 women, and 9 children in late March to 60 men, 16

TABLE 1
Black Flight from Coastal Georgia, 1861–1864*

Blacks Reaching or Attempting to Reach Union Lines	1861	1862	1863	1864	Total
Alone or in pairs	3	13	11	5	32
	(50.0%)	(8.4%)	(13.6%)	(10.2%)	(11.0%)
In groups of three or more	—	141	64	44	249
		(91.6%)	(79.0%)	(89.8%)	(85.8%)
Method unknown	3	—	6	—	9
	(50.0%)		(7.5%)		(3.1%)
TOTAL	6	154	81	49	290
Initiated by blacks	6	154	81	49	290
	(100%)	(45.2%)	(100%)	(22.1%)	(44.6%)
Freed by coastal raids	—	187	—	173	360
		(54.8%)		(77.9%)	(55.4%)
TOTAL	6	341	81	222	650
Captured during escape attempt	—	39	26	24	89
		(11.4%)	(32.1%)	(10.8%)	(13.7%)
Successful escapees	6	302	55	198	561

*This table summarizes a more detailed monthly record of escape incidents, compiled primarily from the *Official Records of the Union and Confederate Navies in the War of the Rebellion*, 30 vols. (Washington, D.C., 1894–1922), ser. 1, vols. 12–15.

73

women, and 13 children by mid-April. When abolitionist clergyman Mansfield French visited the island in July, 52 black children were presented for baptism during one afternoon service. Susie King Taylor, a slave from Savannah, later recalled that by the time she left St. Simons in October of that year a majority of its 600 inhabitants were women and children.[12]

Strict policing made mass escapes more difficult in 1863, but black families continued to flee. In July "two or three families" of free Negroes from Darien reached Union lines together with "four slaves whom they owned." Nineteen blacks from Samuel N. Papot's plantation near Savannah were less successful in October, when their boat was captured by Confederate pickets. Approximately one-third of the would-be escapees in this group were men, the rest women and children.[13] In late December 1863 thirteen black fugitives from McIntosh County were taken aboard the USS *Fernandina* in St. Catherine's Sound. The leader of the party was a twenty-seven-year-old slave named Cain who, like most of the escapees, had formerly belonged to William King. Accompanying Cain was twenty-two-year-old Bella and her six-year-old son Romeo, twenty-five-year-old Lizzie and her four children (Joseph, Sam, Eve, and Martha, aged twelve years, four years, two years, and five months respectively), and thirty-two-year-old Sallie with her four children (Fannie, Joseph, Emma, and Ben, who ranged in age from eleven years to seven months). Early in 1864 Cain left the *Fernandina* to rescue his relatives from the vicinity of Sunbury, Georgia. He returned on January 7, along with ex-slave Sam, bringing the forty-five-year-old woman Grace, her five children (Judy, Elizabeth, Phoebe, Victoria, and James), her son-in-law Charlie, and her grandchildren Arphee, Virginia, Clarissa, and Edward.[14]

Under the best of circumstances black-initiated escape efforts were risky, a fact graphically illustrated by the failure of at least eighty-nine Georgia fugitives to reach Union lines. From a purely pragmatic standpoint the lone young black man probably continued to stand the best chance of escape throughout most of the war. By including women, children, or old people in escape parties, therefore, black Georgians repeatedly showed their willingness to place family and group loyalty above individual self-interest. A typical episode occurred in September 1862 following the successful escape of twenty-three slaves from plantations on both sides of the Savannah River. The main party paddled their way to freedom in a large canoe, but two men, one woman, and a child failed to reach the boat on time and were left behind to face pursuers. A Georgia planter reported the grim outcome in a private letter. Overtaken while fording a creek, the group refused to stop, whereupon "Bob, who was leading, was shot in the leg and immediately taken. Peter was also fired at and fell," but fled deeper into the marshes in a "wounded condition." After a "pursuit of 3 or 4 miles" the woman and child became exhausted and surrendered, but refused to reveal the hiding place of their wounded companion. [15]

More successful escape incidents also underscored the importance of family ties among Georgia's black refugees. An abolitionist officer from Massachusetts recalled four brothers in a black family named Wilson who planned a daring escape from the interior of Georgia. Leaving their youngest brother behind to look after an aged mother, the other men, in company with their sister and her children, fled downriver in a log dugout. Before reaching. the coast the boat came under heavy fire from Confederate pickets, who wounded every male occupant of the open craft. Despite their injuries the men eventually completed the voyage and reached the safety of Federal gunboats. Even more dramatic was the case of a seventy-year-old Georgia black woman who, after failing in one escape attempt, assembled her twenty-two children and grandchildren on an abandoned flatboat and drifted forty miles down the Savannah River to freedom. When rescued by a Union vessel the grandmother "rose to her full height, with her youngest grandchild in her arms, and said only 'My God! are we free?'"[16]

If family commitments shaped the pattern of wartime escape efforts, they also influenced the nature and scope of black support for the Union cause. Nowhere was the importance of family ties more evident than in the realm of actual military service. Northern recruiters discovered early that the prospect of securing the freedom of friends and relatives was a powerful inducement for blacks to join the Union ranks. Or, taking the opposite viewpoint, blacks soon discovered that the Union Army offered an effective vehicle for rescuing family members still held in bondage.

Thomas Wentworth Higginson, who commanded numerous black Georgians in the famous First South Carolina Volunteers, candidly admitted that his soldiers "had more to fight for than [did] the whites. Besides the flag and the Union, they had home and wife and child."[17] A Northern official who spent the summer and fall of 1862 with Georgia blacks on St. Simons Island fully confirmed this judgment. In early October he attended a Negro "war meeting" at St. Helena village where several speakers, including one black man, addressed an assembly of ex-slaves:

> They were asked to enlist for pay, rations and uniforms, to fight for their country, for freedom and so forth, but not a man stirred. But when it was asked them to fight for themselves, to enlist to protect their wives and children from being sold away from them, and told of the little homes which they might secure to themselves and their families in after years, they all rose to their feet, the men came forward and said "I'll go," the women shouted, and the old men said "Amen."[18]

Family considerations were clearly uppermost in the minds of many black Georgians as they embarked on their first combat mission in November 1862. At the staging area on St. Catherines Island the former bondsmen "needed no 'driver's lash'; . . . for they were preparing to go up Sapelo River, along whose banks on the beautiful plantations were their fathers, mothers, brothers, sisters, wives and children. Weeks and months before some of the men had left those loved ones with a promise to return" if the way were opened. A white observer who accompanied the expedition upriver found it "very affecting" to see the soldiers gaze "intensely [at] the colored forms on land," frequently calling out such things as "Oh, massir, my wife and chillen lib dere" or "dere, dere, my brudder." When the ships were unable to take away slaves from certain plantations, the disappointment of relatives on board was acute, and virtually "inexpressible (except by sighs)."[19]

Some black Georgians were unwilling to risk such disappointments and took the business of rescuing friends and relatives into their own hands. One of the first to adopt this self-help philosophy was ex-slave March Haynes, who functioned unofficially within the military command structure of the Department of the South. Described as a "pure, shrewd, brave, efficient man," Haynes was literate and had worked as a stevedore and river pilot in antebellum Savannah. "Comprehending the scope and spirit of the war," he began smuggling Georgia fugitives into Union lines shortly after the fall of Fort Pulaski in April 1862. When white suspicions against him became too great, he fled Savannah with his wife, but continued his rescue efforts from the sea islands. Although the term "commando" did not exist in the military vocabulary of the 1860s, Haynes's activities fit neatly under this modern rubric. General Quincy A. Gillmore of the Tenth Army Corps recognized the value of Haynes's services and "furnished him with whatever he needed in his perilous missions," including a "staunch, swift boat, painted a drab color, like the hue of the Savannah River." Allowed to "select such negroes to assist him as he thought proper," Haynes landed repeatedly in the marshes below Savannah and entered the city under cover of darkness. Sheltered and supplied by local blacks, he sometimes remained for several days collecting "exact and valuable" information on the strength and location of Confederate defenses. He also made nighttime reconnaissances up numerous small creeks along the Savannah, "gathering information and bringing away boat-loads" of black refugees. On one expedition Haynes was shot in the leg by Confederate pickets, and in April 1863 he was apparently arrested and temporarily jailed by Savannah authorities. [20]

Liberating friends and relatives was only one of many motives for black enlistment in Union ranks. Nearly all Negro soldiers shared a hatred of bondage and a desire to strike out directly at the slave system. Undoubtedly some ex-slaves viewed military service as an opportunity both to demonstrate personal courage and to consummate the process of self-emancipation by meeting white Southerners in battle. Yet even the most dedicated abolitionists admitted that black attitudes toward former masters were ambivalent and complex. Upon reaching the sea islands in 1862, for instance, Colonel Higginson expected to find "a good deal of the patriarchal feeling" among local Negroes, but he discovered instead a very different and more discriminating attitude. Many former slaves did indeed claim to have had kind owners, and some even expressed "great gratitude" for "particular favors" received during slavery. To these same black people, however, the central fact of being owned was "a wrong which no special kindness could right." Thus, whatever their feelings toward individual whites, they looked upon the mass of slaveholders as their "natural enemies." Confederate observers like Mrs. James Sanchez of Florida confirmed the existence of a generalized hostility toward slaveholders among black escapees. In early 1863, while traveling to Georgia under a flag of truce, Mrs. Sanchez was detained briefly at Federally occupied Fort Pulaski. "The negroes there were far more insolent than the [white] soldiers," she reported. The blacks "took great pleasure in insulting the whites; cursing the 'd———n rebel secesh women and men' and laughing in their faces."[21]

Black hostility toward white Confederates often went hand in hand with personal grievances against former owners. Higginson himself mentions several black Georgians who seethed with anger over prior slave experiences and whose desire for revenge steeled their courage on the battlefield. For some bondsmen the war was quite literally an extension of earlier rebellious activities. The theory that black defection to Federal lines acted as a "safety valve" against slave uprisings within the Confederacy finds at least partial confirmation in the career of a militant black runaway named Nat. Owned by a planter in Glynn County, Georgia, Nat left his master sometime in 1860 and remained at large for the next four years. By the summer of 1862 he had reached St. Simons Island, where he engaged in operations somewhat similar to those of March Haynes. Described by white Savannahians as a "notorious runaway . . . and rascal," Nat was ultimately accused of killing one white civilian and two Confederate soldiers. In his most daring wartime exploit he led six other black men some thirty miles up the Altamaha River to rescue their wives and children from bondage. In the course of the expedition he fought off white attackers twice and exchanged gunfire with a Confederate river patrol. Even after most black refugees had been moved to Port Royal, Nat remained on St. Simons and soon joined forces with another slave rebel named Harvey. Denounced on the mainland as "spies, murderers, incendiaries, and thieves," the pair survived until June 1864, when both fell victim to a shotgun-wielding Southern soldier. At the time of his death Georgia whites held Nat responsible for the escape of from seventy to one hundred slaves from the coastal counties.[22]

Whether or not they were rebels before the war, Georgia's black soldiers were ready to redress past wrongs if the opportunity arose. During the 1862 Sapelo River expedition, for example, black troops singled out the plantation of Captain William Brailsford for a special retaliatory attack. Brailsford, a wealthy cotton planter known for his flamboyance and his fiery temper, had succeeded Georgia slave trader C. A. L. Lamar as captain of the Savannah Mounted Rifles in 1861. By July of the following year he was actively engaged in a campaign to recapture slaves from the Georgia sea islands. After Union officers refused his request to return black fugitives from St. Simons, Brailsford descended on St. Catherines Island with thirty armed men in October 1862, killing two black refugees and capturing four others. [23]

The memory of this attack was still fresh in the minds of black soldiers as they descended the Sapelo early the next month. Even without the St. Catherines raid Brailsford would probably still have been a marked man, for on board the Union gunboats were several of Brailsford's former slaves, including one Sam Miller, who had been whipped severely by the hot-tempered planter for refusing to betray another escapee. Since Brailsford's plantation was also a major Confederate picket station, Union officers agreed after "full consultation" to destroy the place during their retreat. Landing after sunset the black troops routed a small force of defenders and pushed inland nearly half a mile, burning cabins, outbuildings, and finally the Brailsford mansion itself. When interviewed immediately after the attack, morale among the black soldiers was high. Some spoke of having "grown three inches," while Sam Miller said simply, "I feel a heap more of a man."[24]

If the alliance between Georgia blacks and the Union military was cemented with blood, it was also constructed upon the shifting foundation of pragmatic self-interest. Throughout most of the war the aims and goals of Northern commanders corresponded neatly with individual priorities and racial or group loyalties of black refugees. So long as this community of interest existed, black allegiance to the Stars and Stripes remained strong. When Federal policies ceased to be mutually beneficial, however, black cooperation and white benevolence declined proportionately. The process was visible on St. Simons Island during the spring and summer of

1862 when naval authorities set out to make the black colony self-supporting. Shortly after the first blacks were landed on St. Simons in March, Commander S. W. Godon decided they should "procure their own living from the land" and ordered them also "to plant cotton and thus . . . become of use to themselves." By mid-April eighty acres of corn plus additional fields of potatoes and beans were under cultivation, and in late May Godon reported triumphantly that "thus far the Government has not spent a dollar on those people." Actually the government probably did more than just break even, for by late July St. Simons's black residents had planted three hundred acres of food crops and picked twenty-five thousand pounds of valuable sea island cotton.[25]

The navy's agricultural achievement fell considerably short of being a genuine cooperative effort. Godon quickly discovered that black refugees showed "a great dislike to do the work they have been accustomed to" under slavery. Toiling daily in the abandoned plantation fields seemed "to make their condition the same as before," and appointing an ex-slave to direct the work accomplished little because even the black foreman needed "pushing" and "indulges his men too much away from the care of fields." Ultimately Godon's solution to the problem was simple and direct. "Where work is neglected my rule has been to stop off the ration of beef or something else," he wrote in late June, adding, "I have also placed men in irons for punishment."[26]

If Godon's heavy-handed methods produced results, they did little to build black trust in the motives of the Federal officials. Confidence was further eroded by the navy's inability to shield the St. Simons settlement from Confederate attack. Naval officers did their best to protect the island, but black refugees seemed more impressed by the flintlock muskets they received for self-defense than by the Navy's good intentions. In May 1862 a large Confederate force actually landed on St. Simons but was repulsed at the last moment by fire from a newly arrived Union gunboat.[27] The island's black residents took the lesson to heart, and when a second Confederate attack occurred in August the ex-slaves seized the initiative.

Ironically the second Confederate landing on St. Simons coincided almost exactly with the arrival of thirty-eight black soldiers from Port

Royal, who were all that remained of General David Hunter's recently disbanded Negro regiment. Still lacking any official military status, the troops and their white commander, Charles T. Trowbridge, were eager for a chance to prove themselves in battle. Grabbing their knapsacks and cartridge boxes "with alacrity," the men came ashore only to discover that twenty-five local blacks were already armed and in pursuit of the invaders. According to one writer, the action was "entirely a spontaneous thing." No white man accompanied the local defenders, who were commanded, instead, by two of their own number, John Brown and Edward Gould. Overtaking the invaders in a swamp, the ex-slaves fought a brief engagement and suffered several casualties, including their leader, John Brown, who was killed. [28]

The August encounter was not the end of local defense efforts on St. Simons. When Captain Trowbridge's company left the island in early November, shortly before being mustered into Union service, the seventy or so black men who remained behind took further precautions against attack. "Immediately, they organized a guard on each plantation, appointed their own sergeant or leader, and guarded the island day and night" until its evacuation five weeks later. The men met for drill each afternoon at T. Butler King's plantation, where assignments for nighttime guard duty were also made. Even during this final period the defenders did not rely on government support and received neither clothing nor pay, nor rations. [29]

Elsewhere along the Georgia coast conditions were much the same. When Confederate forces attacked St. Catherines Island in 1862, they were fired on by six black men armed, like the St. Simons defenders, with flintlock muskets. [30] On Cumberland Island during this same period armed blacks clashed with both Confederate raiding parties and unsympathetic Union naval officers who came to the aid of one R. Stafford, a white slaveowner who had remained on the island. The Stafford incident occurred in early September when a number of the planter's former slaves returned from nearby Fernandina, Florida, in company with other escaped bondsmen. Many of the blacks had obtained guns, and they took up residence on Stafford's plantation, "refusing to submit to any control, killing the cattle and overrunning the private dwelling with arms and

81

clubs in their hands." Naval officers declared the blacks in "a state of mutiny" and sent an armed party of marines to Stafford's assistance. Apparently determined to maintain slavery even inside Union lines, Lieutenant Commander W. T. Truxton reported the arrest of nine Negroes "belonging to Mr. Stafford and said to be dangerous." Truxton placed the men in irons but later released them "at their own request and at the desire of their master (who gives up all claim to them)." Significantly, the black prisoners did not actually go free but were retained on board Truxton's vessel as part of the crew. Approximately a month after this brush with the Union Navy, Negroes on Cumberland Island were attacked by a company of Confederate cavalrymen. The encounter was brief but resulted in the capture of twelve blacks who were returned to slavery on the Georgia mainland.[31]

Episodes like that on Cumberland Island make the zealous self-defense efforts of Georgia escapees more readily understandable. They had learned in antebellum days to take freedom where they found it, and to guard it tenaciously. If, as Willie Lee Rose argues, "Getting out of the master's power was the essence of freedom" for most blacks, then preventing the master's return in either actual or surrogate form was a logical response to wartime conditions along Georgia's coast.[32]

There was, of course, a more positive side to black life on the sea islands. One Georgia escapee recalled that the St. Simons colony consisted, in reality, of numerous small settlements "just like little villages." Despite fear of Confederate attack, women and children were free to move about at will and engage in social activities forbidden during slavery.[33] On St. Simons, Sapelo, St. Catherines, Ossabaw, and elsewhere agricultural operations centered around food-crop production, and were apparently conducted on both a collective and an individual basis. The ex-slaves combined subsistence farming with limited cash transactions in ways which harkened back to their previous commercial dealings in the rural South. They frequently sold vegetables and poultry to the crews of nearby warships, and the women took in sailors' washing to earn extra money. On St. Simons schools were conducted for black children and adults during 1862. Both literate fugitives and white naval personnel served as teachers, while navy surgeons treated the sick and elderly on some islands. [34]

Initially, at least, conditions on the sea islands were fairly conducive to stable family life. In July 1862 the Reverend Mansfield French found blacks on St. Simons eager to formalize their marriage vows in the most "public and solemn manner" possible. The abolitionist clergyman performed numerous marriages and also conducted baptismal services for black children. On these occasions the extended kinship patterns evolved during slavery were clearly visible. Candidates for baptism lined up in two rows. On the right stood "a father and mother with five children; then a mother with so many of her children as she could rescue from Slavery; and then, a father with the two or three children, and their grandmother, in the place of the poor mother who had been sold." In the left-hand line were "children presented by [distant] relatives or strangers, the parents being sold" or not yet escaped from slavery. French genuinely wished to protect black family ties, but he was also a leading advocate of Negro military service. During the summer of 1862 the two objectives were not necessarily incompatible. French could not have known that by the latter stages of the war callous Union conscription policies would wrench many black fathers away from their wives and children, thereby achieving what Southern slave markets had failed to accomplish. [35]

Although sea island refugees showed a strong desire for autonomy and independence, open confrontations between blacks and Union forces were rare. From the outset Georgia escapees showed a general willingness to aid the Northern war effort within reasonable limits. Virtually all refugees shared whatever military information they possessed at the time of their escape, and many offered their services in more tangible form. The quality of military intelligence received from ex-slaves was usually high. Black estimates of Confederate troop strength sometimes proved unreliable, but escapees furnished accurate and detailed information on the ironclad warships under construction in Savannah harbor, as well as up-to-date reports on the movements of potential blockade-runners. [36] In the course of the war black defections stripped the Confederate Navy's Savannah Squadron of numerous highly competent river and coastal pilots, while the Union Navy benefited both from the escapees' services and from the Confederate Navy's resulting weakness.

Among the first black pilots to reach Union lines was Isaac Tatnall, who in December 1861 escaped from the packet ship *St. Mary's* in Savannah harbor. Valued at $1,500 and hired by his master for thirty-five dollars per month, Tatnall had piloted vessels along the entire length of the Georgia coast and could navigate the Savannah River even at night. Union naval officers found he could "be perfectly relied upon," and he remained aboard warships off Georgia as late as 1863.[37] Another 1861 escapee was the slave Brutus, who proved to be "quite familiar with the rivers and creeks between Savannah City and Tybee Island." Captain (later General) Quincy A. Gillmore placed "great reliance on Brutus' statement" after learning that "everything he said of Big Tybee Inlet, was verified with remarkable accuracy."[38] Other additions to the navy's pilot force during 1862 and 1863 included the slave Cassius, who claimed to be "a good pilot" by virtue of his experience as "fireman on one of the small steamers used for inland navigation," an unnamed slave who had worked on a Confederate tugboat in the Ogeechee River, and, finally, even the black pilot from the Confederate blockade-runner *Nashville*.[39] "These men risk their lives to serve us . . . [and] make no bargains about their remuneration," wrote Union Admiral Samuel Francis Du Pont early in 1862. The pay differential was amply demonstrated by the fact that two years later black pilots serving under Du Pont earned from thirty to forty dollars per month, only a fraction of the salaries paid their white counterparts in the same squadron and less than half of the one hundred dollars per month received by Moses Dallas, one of the few black pilots serving the Confederate Navy at that time.[40]

Despite equally unattractive pay rates the Union Army also received its full share of Georgia recruits. Particularly valuable were the services of Abraham [or Abram] Murchison, a literate slave preacher from Savannah who helped initiate the first recruiting efforts among black refugees on Hilton Head Island, South Carolina, in early 1862. After a private interview with General David Hunter, Murchison called a meeting of all black males where the prospect of military service was first broached to the former bondsmen. Murchison addressed this meeting, which was held on

April 7, explaining with "clearness and force" the "obligations and interests" that should induce blacks to take up arms for the Union. A New York *Times* correspondent reported that Murchison's language often "rose to eloquence" as he described the "labors, hardships and dangers, as well as the advantages of soldier life." At the conclusion of his address 105 recruits were enrolled, and within a week the number of volunteers had reached 150.[41]

Perhaps because of his age, Murchison did not join the army himself but remained at Hilton Head throughout the war, serving as the chief religious and secular leader of local blacks. Affiliated with the Baptist denomination during slavery, Murchison was formally ordained by Union Army chaplains and he reportedly baptized more than a thousand freedmen in Port Royal harbor during the war.[42] By 1864 he had also become a pivotal figure in the self-governing black village of Mitchelville where, under army auspices, he exercised the powers of magistrate. At night the village was off limits to all whites, and the black soldiers of the provost guard were placed under Murchison's control for the purpose of making disorderly conduct arrests. When Mitchelville residents held their first election in 1865, two black Georgians headed the ticket. March Haynes, the daring spy and commando, was elected marshal, and Abraham Murchison assumed the duties of recorder.[43]

The men whom Murchison had helped recruit in April 1862 formed the nucleus of General Hunter's ill-fated black regiment which, as mentioned earlier, survived only in the form of a 38-man company sent to St. Simons Island. In November 1862 this hardy remnant, augmented by thirty to forty Georgia recruits from St. Simons, was mustered into service as Company A of the First South Carolina Volunteers. Company E was also composed largely of refugees from St. Simons, and black Georgians were scattered throughout the rest of the regiment.[44] The mandatory conscription of sea island Negroes begun in 1863 ensured that Georgia bondsmen would ultimately find their way into all the black regiments raised in the Department of the South. Recruiting for Colonel James Montgomery's Second South Carolina Regiment occurred mostly in Florida, but during June 1863 a special draft for the Third South Carolina Volunteers was conducted at Ossabaw Island and Fort Pulaski, Georgia, as well as at

Fernandina, Florida, near Georgia's southern border. This regiment, which was soon consolidated with the embryonic Fourth and Fifth South Carolina Volunteers to form the Twenty-first United States Colored Troops, numbered slightly over three hundred men until December 1864, when its ranks were augmented by black Georgians who had followed General Sherman to Savannah.[45]

In addition to purely military training, the army provided some blacks with valuable leadership experience and allowed many others to begin or expand their formal education. Much of the educational work was carried on by literate ex-slaves like Sergeant Edward King of Darien and his young wife Susie, who also served the regiment as nurse and laundress.[46] Although involved in no decisive military campaigns, the "First South" nonetheless acquitted itself well in numerous raids and partisan expeditions from the Edisto River to the St. Johns. Perhaps most importantly, the black troops' solid performance under close public scrutiny paved the way for slave enlistments throughout the South.[47]

III

ALL TOLD, more than thirty-five hundred black Georgians served in the Union Army or Navy before hostilities ended in 1865.[48] Seaboard slaves probably accounted for most of the recruits, but bondsmen from the interior also joined Federal ranks in growing numbers during the last eighteen months of the war (see Tables 2, 3, 4, and 5). Enlistments began in Tennessee among the handful of Georgia fugitives who reached Chattanooga in time to be mustered into the newly created Forty-fourth United States Colored Infantry Regiment early in 1864.[49] For several months, however, the number of black soldiers obtained below the Tennessee border remained small. Prior to the Atlanta campaign of May–September 1864, miles of rugged terrain together with a large Confederate army and an alert populace of white civilians stood between northwest Georgia bondsmen and free territory. Under the circumstances few blacks struck out for Yankee lines, and fewer still arrived at their intended destination.

Slaves who decided to make a bid for liberty recognized the futility of

TABLE 2
*Georgia Blacks in the 33rd United States Colored Infantry**
[First South Carolina Volunteers]

	Place of Enlistment				Place of Birth		
	Georgia Sea Islands	South Carolina Sea Islands	Florida	Savannah, Georgia	Coastal Georgia Counties	Interior Georgia Counties	Unknown
1862 (Oct.–Dec.) Total, 174	74	100			155	13	6
1863 Total, 37	2	32	3		28	7	2
1864 Total, 18		17	1		16	2	
1865 (Jan.–May) Total, 177		50		67	41	70	6
TOTAL	76	199	4	67	240	92	14

TOTAL GEORGIA RECRUITS, 1862–1865: 346

*Source: Descriptive Book, 33rd Regiment, United States Colored Infantry, Adjutant General's Office, RG 94, National Archives.

fleeing in conspicuous and slow-moving family groups. When collective escape efforts occurred, the participants were likely to be young, robust men who could travel rapidly and withstand severe physical hardship. In March 1864 a Floyd County woman recorded the details of a fairly typical runaway episode involving five slaves owned by two different masters: "On last saturday night 3 of Mr. Frankses negroes went off[,] each one of them taking a mule with him[.] they are supposed to have started to the Yankees[.] Tom is the only one . . . left at home. . . . 2 of Richard Gainses [slaves]—Will & Finn are also gone[.] they left on saturday night too taking a horse a piece[.] they are all supposed to have gone to gather[.] Gaines [slaves] succeeded in geting 4 pieces of meat from his smokehouse to take with them."[50] The owners pursued their human property diligently and by April 3, 1864, two of the black fugitives had been incarcerated at Dalton, suffering from the effects of prolonged exposure

TABLE 3
*Georgia Blacks in the 34th United States Colored Infantry**
[Second South Carolina Volunteers]

	Place of Enlistment				Place of Birth		
	South Carolina Sea Islands	Florida	Fort Pulaski and St. Simons Island, Georgia	Camp Casey, Virginia	Coastal Georgia Counties	Interior Georgia Counties	Unknown
1863 (Feb.–Dec.) Total, 30	8	15	7		12	9	9
1864 Total, 70	57	11	2		20	41	9
1865 (Jan.–June) Total, 108	96	6		6	12	69	27
TOTAL	161	32	9	6	44	119	45

TOTAL GEORGIA RECRUITS, 1863–1865: 208

Source: Descriptive Book, 34th Regiment, United States Colored Infantry, Adjutant General's Office, RG 94, National Archives.

and severe frostbite. One of the prisoners subsequently died from the ordeal, while the search for the remaining escapees continued.[51]

Unlike their coastal counterparts, up-country runaways needed food, horses, and a calculated willingness to gamble against long odds if they hoped to make good on early escape plans. During the spring and summer of 1864, however, the picture changed markedly as Union forces took control of most counties north and west of Atlanta. Although many bondsmen were removed to secure areas well ahead of the Union Army's southward advance, a substantial number of slaves remained behind to greet the Yankee invaders. Throughout the occupied regions chattel bondage officially ceased to exist, but the speed and finality of emancipation varied.

Liberty sometimes came swiftly and forced blacks to make fundamental choices about the future with a minimum of deliberation. After Southern troops withdrew from Rome in mid-May, for example, Federal occupation

TABLE 4
Georgia Blacks in the 21st United States Colored Infantry*
[Third, Fourth, and Fifth South Carolina Volunteers]

| | Place of Enlistment | | Place of Birth | | |
	South Carolina Sea Islands	Florida	Coastal Georgia Counties	Interior Georgia Counties	Unknown
1863 (April–Nov.) Total, 70	38	32	54	10	6
1864 (March–Dec.) Total, 52	48	4	37	5	10
1865 (January) Total, 1	1		1		
TOTAL	87	36	92	15	16

TOTAL GEORGIA RECRUITS, 1863–1865: 123

*Source: Descriptive Book, 21st Regiment, United States Colored Infantry, Adjutant General's Office, RG 94, National Archives.

forces allowed all civilians a period of free movement into or out of Union lines. Departing slaveowners were forbidden to intervene while their bondsmen decided what course to pursue. Many blacks refused to leave, but to the Yankees' surprise, and occasional disgust, not all bondsmen made the "right" choice. At least one Negro who elected to accompany his master was "cursed for a fool, and then told to go away, but never to look to them [the Federals] again for help or succor."[52]

In reality, of course, the alternatives presented to black Georgians at the moment of Northern conquest were often more complex than outsiders realized. A bondsman's hatred of slavery might be strong, but the prospect of forfeiting material possessions on a distant plantation, or of losing touch indefinitely with family members still in Confederate territory, was a form of silent coercion that Union soldiers were powerless to prevent. Equally troubling to newly liberated blacks was the widespread uncertainty over what fate awaited them at the hands of white North-

TABLE 5

*Georgia Blacks in the 44th United States Colored Infantry**

	Place of Enlistment				Place of Birth		
	Chattanooga, Tennessee	Rome, Georgia	Dalton, Georgia	Ohio	Coastal Georgia Counties	Interior Georgia Counties	Unknown
March 1864	9					9	
April	7					6	1
May	3					2	1
June	30	35			1	56	8
July	22	40			1	56	5
August		83			1	79	3
September		2		1		2	1
October	2		9			11	
November	43					38	5
December							
January 1865	1					1	
TOTAL	117	160	9	1	3	260	24

TOTAL GEORGIA RECRUITS, 1864–1865: 287

Source: Descriptive Book, 44th Regiment, United States Colored Infantry, Adjutant General's Office, RG 94, National Archives.

erners. On this crucial issue the behavior of Union commander William T. Sherman was hardly reassuring. Never an abolitionist, the general protected black refugees at Rome and other points near the battlefront for reasons which had little to do with humanitarian idealism. Destroying slavery might be a military necessity, but helping the freedmen was never a major goal of the brilliant Yankee tactician. What Sherman wanted was the brawn and muscle of ablebodied Negro men, and he obtained their labor with a minimum of formality. As ex-slave Lucy McCullough would later recall, Federal soldiers who passed by her plantation simply "pick[ed] out de stronges' er Marse Ned's slave mens en take 'em 'way wid 'em."[53] Blacks who became nominal employees in Sherman's "pioneer companies" were apt to notice little immediate difference between slavery and free labor. One group of Georgia bondsmen reportedly carried powder and shot for Union forces all the way to Virginia before learning

90

of emancipation. The incident may have been atypical or even untrue but numerous witnesses testified to the exploitive nature of Sherman's labor policies. Union Adjutant General Lorenzo Thomas put the matter succinctly on June 15, 1864, when he predicted that black workers secured during the Atlanta campaign would be kept "at hard labor—in many instances greater than they were subjected to by their former owners."[54]

Acting with "due regard for the prejudice of the races," Sherman excluded blacks from his own army and effectively stymied Negro enlistment efforts by Federal recruiting officers and agents from various Northern states.[55] Eventually, however, the enrollment of ex-slaves for combat service began in occupied areas of northwestern Georgia under authority granted to Colonel Ruben D. Mussey, the Nashville-based commissioner for the organization of U.S. Colored Troops in the Department of the Cumberland.[56] Most activity occurred between July and September 1864, when the Forty-fourth United States Colored Infantry was stationed in Rome for recruiting purposes. Using methods perfected the previous year in Tennessee, the regiment sent racially mixed scouting parties into the countryside on a regular basis, offering protection and assistance to any residents who wished to enter Union lines. One such evacuation in the "Texas Valley" section of Floyd County was described by a local woman in early September. From her vantage point as a loyal Southerner, the departure scene appeared little short of scandalous: "They had a train of 17 wagons & an escort of between 150 to 200—I don't know what to call them[,] though part of them was black and other white[,] but to say the least of them I guess they have black hearts."[57]

By late summer the Forty-fourth USCI contained about eight hundred black enlisted men, approximately three-fourths of whom were doing garrison duty in Dalton on the morning of October 13 when advance elements of the 40,000-man Confederate Army of Tennessee converged unexpectedly on the little village, cutting off all avenues of escape. Initial skirmishing between black troops and Rebels left several Confederates dead and their comrades "over anxious to move upon the 'niggers.'" Impatient to resume his northward advance, General John Bell Hood demanded that the Union garrison capitulate immediately or face annihilation. Hood vowed to take no prisoners if the Federal defenses were

91

carried by assault, and later added that he "could not restrain his men, and would not if he could."[58]

Although the black soldiers displayed the "greatest anxiety to fight," their commander, Colonel Lewis Johnson, surrendered to Hood around 4 P.M., and was released two days later after securing paroles for himself and the one hundred and fifty or so other white troops attached to the garrison. A considerably harsher fate awaited the regiment's six hundred Negro enlisted men, many of whom were native Georgians only a few months out of slavery. All of the nonwhite captives were immediately stripped of their shoes and ordered to begin destroying a nearby section of the Western and Atlantic Railroad. At least six black prisoners were shot for refusing to obey commands or failing to keep pace with the line of march. Near the hamlet of Villanow on October 14 an unspecified number of freedmen were "returned to their former masters," but most of the black troops remained in military custody and eventually labored on fortification projects in Alabama and Mississippi. Some of the Georgia recruits ended the war as prisoners in Columbus and Griffin, where they were released during May 1865 in a "sick, broken down, naked and starved" condition. Fearful of reprisals from embittered Confederates, the black veterans concealed their wartime connection with the Union Army.[59]

The demise of the Forty-fourth U.S. Colored Infantry may have begun with an ethically defensible decision to avoid pointless bloodshed and forestall an impending racial massacre. But the subsequent conduct of Colonel Johnson and other white officers raised questions about the depth of Federal commitment to black welfare. Doubts stemming from the Dalton affair were reinforced a few weeks later in Rome, where departing Union soldiers exhibited callous indifference to the fate of former slaves within their lines. During five months of Yankee occupation the city had become a rendezvous point for Afro-American refugees of all ages and sexes, including, presumably, the families of many black soldiers.[60] By November, however, most of the Negro troops were Confederate prisoners and the remaining women, children, and elderly men had become excess baggage for an army in the process of redeployment. Strictly speaking, Rome's freedpeople were not abandoned during the Union withdrawal, but for many blacks the result was much the same. As the wife of a local slaveowner made clear, the choices presented to recently liberated bondsmen when the Federal Army pulled out were less than ideal. "I have had a hard time for the last two months," the woman declared on November 17, 1864. "The negroes *all* left me and went to the yankees and when the yankees left the negroes all had to foot it to Kingston, Chanie carr[y]ing her cloth[e]s and Bell her baby and Bill carr[y]ing himself the best he could[.] Pagie she got along very well but old Mary she had a hard time walking so far[.] [B]y the time they reached Kingston they were sick of the Yanks and turned and came home. . . . So I have them all here [but] they lost all their bedding and clothing."[61]

The on-again, off-again nature of Yankee biracialism in northwestern Georgia foreshadowed the tenor of Federal conduct toward blacks during the last phase of the Sherman invasion. With the fall of Atlanta in September and the withdrawal into Tennessee of Hood's Confederate forces, Union troops stood poised for a devastating thrust into the heart of Georgia's plantation belt. Savannah was the ultimate target, and Sherman's strategy of living off the land while pressing southeastward across a forty- to sixty-mile front had the effect of placing thousands of rural bondsmen directly in the army's path. Initially many black Georgians wanted to believe that the Yankees came as friends, or perhaps even divinely inspired agents of deliverance. But neither the Union soldiers nor their commander behaved like messianic figures. Despite his role as de facto emancipator, General Sherman showed little interest in forming a cooperative partnership with Georgia slaves. "We have no 'negro allies' in this army," he stated indignantly when responding to Confederate allegations in mid-September.[62] Blacks were close to the general, but only in capacities Southern whites would have deemed appropriate. As Sherman explained to his wife before leaving Atlanta, "I have two Negroes to take care of my horses, one a boy who now makes up my bed, blacks my shoes and sweeps out the room under the mastery of a very good orderly."[63]

During the Atlanta campaign Sherman occasionally paid lip service to the importance of protecting slave families, but then as later his actions belied his rhetoric.[64] Before embarking upon his celebrated "March to the Sea" in November, the general explicitly warned against permitting refugees or "surplus servants . . . to encumber us on the march." Ablebodied Negroes who could "be of service to the several columns" might be taken along, but the welfare of white troops was to have precedence over the needs of ex-slaves.[65] As implemented by Union corps commanders like General Jefferson C. Davis, Sherman's orders ensured that a majority of Georgia bondsmen would remain in the countryside as spectators to the Federal invasion. Blacks who left their plantations to follow the army received little assistance and were sometimes abandoned to face pursuing Confederates while Union forces escaped.[66]

Many of the white enlisted men under Sherman's command surpassed Southern slaveowners in the depth of their anti-Negro sentiments. Reluctant liberators at best, Sherman's Western troops greeted Georgia bondsmen with profane epithets and physical abuse at least as often as they reached out to blacks in a spirit of brotherly concern. In Atlanta a Federal soldier "cursed the 'damned nigger' and said he would like to kill the whole race." On another occasion Union troops stated "that they hated the Negro race, and they would as quickly shoot a negro as a dog." One Western veteran "was willing the war should continue for 7 years longer if only to kill the negroes off."[67]

From Atlanta to Savannah, Union soldiers pillaged mansions and slave cabins with equal disregard for the human consequences of their actions. Inevitably, perhaps, the army's need for food and draft animals took precedence over the future welfare of civilians along the invasion route. But Sherman's foragers often went beyond the legitimate seizure of commissary stores and robbed both blacks and whites of various personal possessions. On many occasions slaves became targets of theft because their dwellings or persons were easily accessible to passing soldiers. During the Northern occupation of Atlanta neither Federal officers nor avowedly Unionist whites could protect former bondsmen from the avarice of Yankee enlisted men. In a typical encounter white soldiers deprived an elderly female house servant of "all her provisions and clothing, even her needles and thread, leaving her nothing but the clothing she had on."[68] Later, when Sherman's troops entered Milledgeville, black enthusiasm for freedom went hand in hand with consternation over the loss of "money, clothing, blankets—everything stealable." Indeed, commented a Southern observer, "Our negroes have cause to remember the enemy quite as feelingly as their masters and mistresses."[69] Theft continued throughout the closing weeks of 1864, and may have increased as Northern armies reached Georgia's wealthier coastal region. In Liberty County, where bondsmen had amassed unusually large amounts of personal property, Northern conduct was hardly reassuring. Accustomed to the natural disasters and afflictions of rural life, local blacks described the Union Army's behavior with appropriate metaphors from the animal kingdom. To some ex-slaves the Yankees resembled "ravenous wolves [that] didn't say howdy," while others compared the invaders to a "flock of blackbirds[,] only you could not scare them."[70] As late as the 1930s elderly black Georgians harbored painful memories of how Union pilferage compounded already acute wartime shortages of food, clothing, and other necessities.[71]

Probably few bondsmen expected egalitarian treatment from whites on either side of the sectional conflict, and a substantial minority of Georgia slaves seemed willing to ignore or endure Yankee exploitation if freedom hung in the balance. According to some estimates, as many as nineteen thousand Negroes followed Sherman's conquering army to Savannah, thereby inflicting a crippling blow upon Confederate agriculture if not on Southern independence itself.[72] For virtually all of the black refugees, however, liberty's initial cost was high. As often as not, following the army meant abandoning at least some family members or risking the health of the very young and old on a debilitating overland journey. By the time most ex-slaves reached the seaboard they were malnourished, destitute, and in dire need of immediate physical assistance.[73] Government rations and private Northern charity helped alleviate the immediate crisis, but the resources available for relief efforts were always inadequate.[74] In the circumstances some freedmen found it expedient to enlist in the Twenty-first United States Colored Infantry or one of several other black regiments then recruiting in the area.[75] Others, including thousands of newly liberated low-country slaves, moved into the thirty-mile-wide strip of coastal and sea island territory reserved for exclusive black settlement by Special Field Order No. 15 in January 1865. Anxious to rid himself of the black refugee problem, General Sherman offered male

95

Negro family heads "possessory title" to as much as forty acres of tillable ground within the designated area and assured prospective settlers that "sole and exclusive management of affairs will be left to the freed people themselves."[76]

Once peace was restored, Sherman's promises were swiftly repudiated—in part, one suspects, because the former bondsmen refused to join the Yankees in equating free labor with the production of staple crops for an external market. Profit as an end in itself apparently had little meaning for most coastal freedmen, who combined hunting, fishing, and subsistence farming with limited commercial agriculture conducted on a modified "task" basis.[77] As the political battles of Reconstruction made clear, much more than the simple issue of land ownership was at stake for blacks in the Sherman reservation. What the ex-slaves sought was a kind of limited self-determination or autonomy that would preclude any whites from controlling their lives or exploiting their labor. Such aspirations were a natural outgrowth of antebellum servitude, but they ran counter to the dominant forces shaping Southern life in the wake of emancipation.

PART TWO

Slavery Stretched Thin: The Limits of Wartime Institutional Change

4. Masters, Slaves, and the Refugee Experience

O NLY a tiny minority of black Georgians participated in wartime escape efforts, but their conduct sent shock waves throughout plantation society. Wartime defections lent substance to white fears about slave disloyalty and helped seal the determination of masters to place bondsmen beyond the reach of corrupting Yankee influence. Less then two weeks after the fall of Port Royal, a resident of Liberty County described the growing consensus among local planters on the wisdom of a precautionary retreat. Initial panic over the Federal invasion threat had abated, leaving many coastal slaveowners convinced that "it would be but an act of prudence to remove all negroes from the seaboard." The object of such a policy, the writer explained, was to reduce the likelihood of escape since "even the best" slaves might run away if given the chance.[1] Other staunch Confederates were considerably more blunt when assessing the potential effect of Union warships off Georgia's coast. "We are going to see hell this winter," predicted one planter in October 1861. "Lincoln & his immense fleets are going to play the devil on our seaboard—this winter will tell the tale."[2]

Apparently most low-country residents agreed. The practice of slave removal, or "refugeeing" as it was usually called, began sporadically during the closing weeks of 1861 and gained momentum throughout the next twelve months. Bondsmen often began their refugee experience with short treks to some temporary residence a few miles inland, only to find themselves later removed to more remote areas deep in the state's interior. As early as December 1861 hundreds of slaves had begun this first stage of

99

"temporary" retreat, and by the end of 1862 a general evacuation of slaves from most seaboard plantations was well on the way toward completion. The conditions described by a Liberty County planter late in 1862 probably give an accurate picture of developments elsewhere on the Georgia coast. "We are having moving times in old Liberty," he asserted, using language that was equally appropriate in either a figurative or a literal context.

> As a matter of prudence and safety large numbers of our Negro population are carried from the lower to the upper parts of the county, and removed also still further from the coast.
> To give you an idea of the extent of these removals, I give you first a list of those who have taken their people from the lower to the upper parts of the county: Dr. Harris, Mrs. J. R. King (from Yellow Bluff and South Hampton both), Thomas J. Dunham, Brother William, Oliver Stevens, Benjamin Screven, B. A. Busby, Edward J. Delegal, Dr. Delegal, R. Cay. And others wish to do so. Second, a list of those who have taken their people up the country, chiefly to Southwest Georgia: H. H. Jones (sold out entirely and removed for good), Estate of J. B. Barnard, Solomon Barnard, Randal Jones, Rufus A. Varnedoe (old Liberty Hall), Mrs. S. M. Cumming and Rev. D. L. Buttolph (White Oak and Lambert), C. C. J[ones] and C. C. J[ones] Jr., Joseph J. and Rev. R. Q. M[allard] (Montevideo and Arcadia), Thomas W. Fleming, Judge Fleming, Estate [of] Joseph Bacon, Estate [of] R. Quarterman, Rev. John Jones, Captain W. Lowndes Walthour, Russell Walthour, Edward Thomas. And others speak of going. Some have concluded to remain—from necessity or choice.[3]

Although no one kept an accurate count, there can be little doubt that by early 1863 a substantial majority of Georgia's thirty-four thousand seaboard slaves had experienced some variant of the mass evacuation process.[4]

Because refugeeing began along the coast and on the sea islands, it touched the lives of some of the state's most isolated and culturally distinctive black residents. During the previous century the same low-country region had greedily absorbed the massive influx of native Africans which began almost as soon as the Georgia trustees lifted their legal ban on slavery in 1750. Now, in the 1860s, countless second, third, and fourth generation descendants of these early black immigrants still lived within a few miles of the ocean which separated them from the land of their forebears. The topography of Georgia's seaboard counties, the steady westward shift of economic and social dominance after 1800, and the very limited interchange of slaves between rice-growing areas and other types of plantations all combined to produce a relatively unique environment in which black culture retained stronger and more distinctly African components than elsewhere in the state.[5] Just as it made possible the growth and development of a vital Afro-American folk culture, the relative isolation of many plantations may also have engendered an inward social focus conducive to strong bonds of group solidarity among slaves.[6] Even the unhealthy climate of the mosquito-infested coastal region became in some ways a positive factor for blacks by helping to reduce the scope and effectiveness of white surveillance, thus permitting bondsmen to maintain a greater degree of personal autonomy than would otherwise have been possible.[7]

Particularly important in shaping the wartime behavior of coastal blacks was the task system of labor organization which prevailed throughout the Georgia low-country. Unlike their fellow bondsmen in the upland cotton belt, seaboard slaves were spared the ordeal of closely supervised dawn-to-dusk gang toil. On both rice and sea island cotton plantations blacks worked at their own pace to complete a fixed amount of daily labor—a task—which could often be finished by early afternoon. The rest of the day belonged to the Negroes, who used the time to raise cotton, rice, livestock, poultry, and a variety of provision crops for sale or domestic consumption. In the course of the antebellum era de facto "ownership," and even inheritance, of personal property became widespread among coastal slaves, and their web of customary privileges expanded to create a form of peasantlike social autonomy that ran counter to the legal theory of chattel servitude.[8]

Often with dramatic abruptness, the refugee process shattered the stable ethos of coastal plantation life. The initial responses of slaves to the prospect of removal varied considerably, but once evacuations began bondsmen were quick to evaluate the situation in terms of what they perceived as their own best interests. While many blacks readily complied with their masters' wishes to move inland, others doggedly resisted any white attempts to evacuate coastal plantations. How a slave responded to the prospect of removal depended largely upon his or her individual circumstances and perception or understanding of the issues involved. Blacks who resisted refugeeing might be influenced by economics, personal ties, a desire for freedom, or any combination of these factors. Writing in the aftermath of Port Royal, a Savannah resident who witnessed the attempts of numerous coastal planters to remove their bondsmen to places of safety concluded that "the negroes generally are very unwilling to go." He attributed this reluctance to fear, "local attachment," and the unwillingness of many blacks to lose their hogs, poultry, or other possessions. One local planter, upon finding his slaves adamant in their opposition to removal, persuaded them to go inland by offering to purchase all of their personal property in advance at "market value."[9] Another refugee slaveowner attempted to neutralize potential black discontent in advance by issuing the following instructions to his father: "You will, of course, think of all that is necessary for the Negroes to do in order to get them in readiness. I would suggest that all their clothing, pots, etc., etc., be thoroughly washed and put up in bundles of convenient sizes. If they have hogs we will purchase them; and we will have to make the best arrangements we can in reference to their little matters of property."[10]

Some whites apparently anticipated special difficulties with skilled or privileged bondsmen. In April 1862 a Chatham County planter voiced considerable relief when Sam, a highly skilled slave shoemaker, gave up "without a single suggestion of difficulties . . . [or] objections" a profitable business in Savannah and accompanied fellow refugee bondsmen into the interior. Such conduct stood in marked contrast to the behavior of the slave woman Cora, who was apparently Sam's wife. Cora "made some difficulty" and "offered some objections" to refugeeing, based chiefly upon a reluctance to leave behind her few "comforts." In reality, however, even Sam's actions may have entailed less personal sacrifice than his master imagined, since Sam took from Savannah his cobbler's tools and over three hundred dollars worth of leather in anticipation of carrying on his trade in the up-country town of Washington.[11]

Another cause of considerable black opposition to refugeeing was con-cern over the possibility of family separation. The apprehension which many bondsmen felt at the prospect of evacuation or removal was not unlike the aura of dread and uncertainty which usually enveloped slave quarters prior to the division of a deceased master's estate in antebellum times. In both situations blacks had rational grounds to fear that they might be summarily parted from friends or loved ones. Wartime circum-stances, however, in conjunction with the marital patterns of the slave community rendered many bondsmen especially vulnerable to separation.

By early 1862 the Union military presence made the prompt evacuation of numerous coastal plantations an absolute necessity. For most white planters, however, the central question soon became not whether to leave but where to go. Theoretically, southwest Georgia offered the nearest, safest, and most agriculturally suitable refuge. Unfortunately for coastal slaveowners, most southwest Georgia residents were keenly aware of this fact and stood ready to reap rich profits at the expense of their neighbors from the seaboard. During 1862 land prices in southwest Georgia sky-rocketed as owners demanded extravagant prices for even "the most ordi-nary land" and often realized profits of several hundred percent on a single transaction. The rapidly growing burdens of inflation added to the finan-cial plight of numerous refugees, and ultimately there were simply not enough plantations in the southwestern part of the state to absorb the massive exodus of whites and Negroes from the coast. [12]

In practical terms all of this meant that no single common destination for refugee planters and slaves ever existed. Indeed, there was scarcely any definable pattern to refugee migrations beyond a general movement "inland," and for a brief period in 1864 a similar movement "southward" to escape advancing Federal armies. Many coastal bondsmen did go to southwest Georgia, but many also went to plantations in the middle or upper piedmont regions or to the small farming and mining areas of northwest Georgia. Many other black refugees did not go to plantations at all, but rather to various interior towns and villages throughout the state, including Thomasville, Bainbridge, Macon, Columbus, Newnan, Milledgeville, Atlanta, Athens, Rome, and Dalton. [13]

The wide geographical dispersion of refugees greatly increased the likelihood that slave families would be separated, especially when black husbands and wives were owned by different masters and resided on different plantations. Even in peacetime the psychological cushion which black men obtained by choosing a wife who lived on a different plantation carried with it considerable risk. In order to avoid the trauma of helplessly witnessing their wives suffer abuse or ill treatment at the hands of whites, many slave husbands willingly jeopardized the stability of their family relationships by involving two masters in the equation rather than only one. In normal times marriages between slaves on different plantations doubled the chances that one of the partners would be sold individually or separated from the other because of a master's death and subsequent estate division. Interplantation marriages by blacks also created the additional possibility that families would be disrupted if either of the masters involved moved his entire slave force to a new locality. However frequent slave family separations may have been before the war, it is clear that wartime refugeeing greatly increased the possibility that disruptions of the latter type would occur. [14]

When faced with the necessity of immediate removal, many planters were forced to weigh genuine humanitarian impulses against the reality of their own economic self-interest. Blacks who relied upon white paternalism to safeguard family ties in such situations often faced brutal disappointment. The disillusionment was perhaps greatest for privileged bondsmen like William, a black foreman or "driver" on the Liberty County plantation of Rufus Varnedoe. As Varnedoe prepared to move his planting operations inland to Thomas County in late 1862, William faced the unhappy prospect of permanent separation from his wife Judy and their seven children (ranging in age from fifteen years to a few days), who were owned by a neighboring planter. William apparently realized his precarious position and took the initiative, for Judy's mistress was soon advised by "the servants" that Varnedoe wished to hire Judy and her entire family. Judy's mistress hesitated. The family was "very valuable," certainly too valuable for an outright sale. Rhina, the fifteen-year-old daughter was a "good worker in the field" and thirteen-year-old Milton was "a great man for managing horses & care of the stable." Even the boy Pulaski at age eleven was "old enough to be useful." Complicating the decision still further was the fact that five of Judy's offspring were grandchildren of the "faithful Driver Pulaski," who had served the white family two generations earlier.

On the other hand, "every day's experience on the coast" convinced Judy's mistress that she herself would soon be forced to remove her slaves. In this context hiring Judy and her children could be viewed as a practical step, a means of facilitating the refugee process in advance. Throughout all of these deliberations one searches in vain for any overriding concern with the marital ties of the black people involved. In any event, the entire question soon became hypothetical when Varnedoe departed for the interior apparently without even inquiring about the possibility of hiring his driver's family.[15]

How William responded to this separation is not recorded, but revealing information does exist for a similar case involving Samuel Varnedoe, brother of the previously mentioned Rufus Varnedoe. Samuel, like his brother, moved to Thomas County during the war, taking with him a number of slaves including the wife of Lancaster, a skilled black carpenter owned by Joseph LeConte. LeConte's bondsman was powerless to prevent the separation, but an incident in 1864 reveals that he did not accept his fate passively. While en route from Columbia, South Carolina, to Liberty County, Georgia, in late December, Joseph LeConte unexpectedly encountered his slave carpenter at a rural station on the Savannah, Albany and Gulf Railroad. Despite Lancaster's best attempts to argue otherwise, LeConte was convinced that the meeting had been wholly unintentional. That it had occurred at all could be attributed largely to Lancaster's resourcefulness, and in spite of himself LeConte was impressed by his bondsman's skill and singular determination to reach his long-departed wife: "After getting all the information I could from Lancaster I gave him a pass and paid his passage to Thomasville, where his wife, a servant of Mr. Sam Varnedoe's, is now living. Lancaster is a shrewd, slippery fellow. I have known him as such all my life. The fact is, he came to Doctortown with the intention of going to Thomasville, but finding me here he begs permission and the passage money. How he expected to get to Thomasville without a pass I cannot imagine."[16]

The limits of white benevolence were defined with unusual clarity and

105

precision in the experiences of another black carpenter, a slave named William owned by Liberty County planter Charles C. Jones, Jr. Prior to the Civil War William had known what was, at least in relative terms, a "mild" form of slavery. The tone of black life for him and for other slaves on the Jones plantations was largely determined by the Reverend Charles C. Jones, a patriarchal Presbyterian minister who had assumed a self-imposed mission of bringing Christianity to Southern bondsmen. Undoubtedly the religious atmosphere on the Jones estates mitigated some of slavery's harsher aspects, and there is evidence that William himself often responded positively to this environment of genuine, if somewhat distant, Christian paternalism.

Positive responses notwithstanding, William's behavior seems always to have reflected at least as much enlightened self-interest as internalized subserviency or devotion. This attitude was particularly apparent where his marriage and family were concerned. When William came to the "big house" on Arcadia plantation during the evening of December 17, 1855, seeking permission to take a wife, he had obviously weighed his options carefully. The woman he wished to marry was Kate, who along with her mother Hannah and her brother, "Driver William," lived on the neighboring plantation of Susan M. Cumming, the aunt of William's master, Charles C. Jones, Jr. By luck or design William had hit upon a rare set of circumstances whereby he could marry a woman who lived on another plantation but was owned by a blood relative of his master, thus reducing the possibility of an arbitrary separation. In seeking the Jones family's permission to marry, William appealed to their religious principles as well as their practical judgment. Kate, William pointed out, was not only "very clever" but also "a member of the church" who lived quite "near home," all of which the Joneses found "worthy considerations" for assenting to the union.

Perhaps partly out of a desire to add some further element of permanence and stability to his marriage, William sought to seal his wedding vows with maximum religious formality in a ceremony which at least gave the appearance of genuine legality. After one false start, the select company of whites and blacks assembled at Montevideo plantation, bound by an unspoken commitment to act out a drama which all knew was ultimately based upon self-deception. The Reverend Charles C. Jones performed the marriage service with due Presbyterian solemnity, consummating in more ways than he cared to admit his mission as "Apostle to the Blacks":

> . . . [Sunday] morning bright and early, before we had left our chamber, the young [slave] couple were announced as below, awaiting the ceremony. We went down and had them brought into the parlor—bride and bridesmaid in *swiss muslins* with white wreaths on their heads, Sam and William in broadcloth and white gloves. A number of witnesses crowded in. The nuptials being over, I invited the bridal party to retire to the kitchen and partake of a hot breakfast. It was a freezing, shivering morning, and I thought they had displayed a great deal of principle in coming over to be married in the proper manner. [17]

Throughout the rest of the antebellum era fortuitous circumstances lent a substantial air of reality to the numerous fictions implicit in William's decorous wedding ceremony. By slave standards Kate and William were, in fact, among the more fortunate of black couples. Their marriage rested upon genuine affection; three children were born to them within six years, and sympathetic owners had given "official" sanction to their family relationships. Undoubtedly Kate's mistress welcomed the new additions to her slave force, and the Jones family's paternalism and goodwill toward William seemed genuine enough when they applauded him as a "good and trusty man." A scant two months after Harpers Ferry, for example, one encounters an apparently reassuring glimpse of William joining the Joneses in a Sunday evening religious service, after offering diplomatic comments such as "The baby looks same like Massa."

One can only speculate as to how much actual confidence Kate and William placed in their owners' benevolence as a meaningful safeguard against the more brutalizing aspects of slavery. To a much greater extent than was usually the case with plantation slaves, Kate's and William's common experiences seemed to offer some valid empirical evidence that white paternalism contained at least a modicum of protective reciprocity. A white clergyman had, after all, officiated at their wedding, while the Jones family strongly approved the black couple's wish to be married in the "proper manner." There was also the tangible reality of an intact family of three children, combined with six years of relative happiness and tranquility—reason enough, perhaps, for a slave couple to feel some limited confidence in the paternalist ethic. Yet beneath this deceptively benign veneer the basic reality of slavery always remained unchanged, and as the swelling tide of refugees swept more and more coastal bondsmen toward the interior during the fall of 1862 the ultimate implications of chattel bondage grew increasingly difficult to sidestep or ignore.

There can, of course, be little question that slavery's harsh reality had regularly impinged upon the consciousness of Kate and William, even in the "good" years of the 1850s. In November 1862, however, the full weight of this reality came crashing in upon them when they suddenly realized that their respective owners were about to seek refuge in different parts of the state. William's master had already transferred most of his slaves to a newly acquired plantation in Burke County some one hundred miles northwest of Savannah. The services of William as well as several other black carpenters were urgently required to construct adequate housing there for the Jones slaves. Kate's mistress, on the other hand, was preparing to evacuate both of her seaboard plantations and send her entire slave force to rural Baker County in extreme southwest Georgia. Under these circumstances the separation of William from his wife and children seemed all but inevitable. For both the Joneses and their "black family" the time had clearly arrived to define the limits and test the meaning of Christian paternalism.

Perhaps partly because of the relatively humane treatment which they had previously received—or, more likely, because of simple common sense—Kate and William eschewed open resistance and sought redress from the Jones family through appeals which blended protest with supplication. William's wife was first to voice her dismay at the impending separation. "Kate . . . begs to go with her husband," Charles C. Jones, Jr., was informed in early December. Before Jones could make any response to this plea, his "Aunt Susan" had sent off her slaves to Baker County, but fortunately she permitted Kate to stay behind and offered to hire her to Jones if he so desired. Jones tentatively agreed and it seemed momentarily that benevolence had triumphed. By January 1863, however, Jones's aunt had shifted her ground and now offered to sell Kate and the children outright if a mutually acceptable price could be agreed upon. Perhaps a group of disinterested parties could be called in to examine the family and "fix their valuation." Once again Jones agreed, suggesting $1,500 as a fair price but offering to let his father be the ultimate judge in the matter. For several weeks Jones waited in vain for an answer. William, he reported, was "most anxious" that the sale take place so his family could be together.

When the long-delayed answer finally came on January 27 it satisfied no one, least of all William. Jones's aunt "on second thought" had "declined selling Kate and her family" and now stated she would "much prefer to hire her at a *moderate* rate." This none-too-subtle attempt at price bargaining was for Jones a source of embarrassment and irritation. He realized, however, that William's reactions might be far more intense than his own. "I regret very much Aunt Susan's determination in reference to *Kate and her family,*" he confided somewhat uneasily to his father. "The last time I was at the plantation William begged me very earnestly to try and purchase his wife and children, for whom he appears to cherish a strong attachment; and I held out to him the hope that I would be able to do so. I . . . still hope—unless Aunt Susan has some special reason to the contrary—that she will agree to sell them to me, in order that they may be with their husband and father."[18]

Unlike many such disputes, this one was ultimately resolved to the relative advantage of the black people involved when, after several weeks of further negotiation, Jones finally persuaded his vacillating aunt to part with William's wife and children. By February 15, 1863, the entire slave family had arrived at Indianola plantation in Burke County where they remained for the duration of the war. There is much to indicate, however, that in spite of this comparatively happy ending the Jones slaves were anything but euphoric over their eleventh-hour reprieve. Kate and William certainly needed no additional reminders that they were held as human chattels, subject to the whim and caprice of ruling whites. Like many other bondsmen involved in wartime refugeeing, they were subjected to a blunt demonstration of both their own vulnerability and the tenuous nature of any alleged reciprocity inherent in white paternalism.

That such a near brush with personal tragedy left a lasting imprint on Kate and William is suggested by the decisive manner in which they severed all ties with the Jones family at the war's end. Not only did they leave the Burke County plantation at the earliest practical moment, but in common with nearly all of Jones's former slaves they chose to return to the familiar surroundings of Liberty County on the Georgia coast. When questioned by their former master concerning their specific plans, "William, Kate and family" were adamant about only one thing. They would not go back to either of the Jones's Liberty County estates.[19]

Although the number of black people who evaluated the consequences of refugeeing in terms of their continuing self-interest *under slavery* was undoubtedly large, it is unlikely that either personal economic interests or imperiled family and kinship ties were ever the principal cause of black resistance to forced removal. Important though these factors may have been, most slaves probably wished to remain in the vicinity of Northern armies for precisely the reason that masters wished to remove them. Proximity to Federal lines greatly increased the possibility of successful escape from slavery. From the very beginning significant numbers of Georgia blacks strove to make contact with Union forces. Perceiving their own opportunity and sensing the fear and vulnerability of whites in areas threatened with invasion, slaves resisted removal both openly and covertly. Writing in the spring of 1862, a white Savannah woman commented on the perceptible shift in black attitudes following the appearance of Union troops off the Georgia coast. "The negroes on some of the places have behaved very badly," she wrote apprehensively to her father. "[They] show a very different face from what they have had heretofore." In one particular case a black driver or "head man" long trusted as a "good and faithful servant" suddenly stepped out of character and declared openly "that after this he had no master but Jesus Christ." Similar reports came from north Georgia as Union armies approached late in 1863. "I have a great deal of trouble with my negroes," wrote a Dalton area planter who attempted to move his slaves southward to Randolph County. "They don't want to go down the country."[20]

Yet no matter how strong their desire for freedom may have been, most bondsmen who resisted refugeeing did so in ways which wisely stopped short of open defiance. Some, like the Jones slaves mentioned earlier, appealed to the paternalism and ethical sensibilities of their masters. Others resisted through the very process of appearing to acquiesce. The strategy of delay and deception employed by many blacks is clearly revealed in the experience of Mrs. H. J. Wayne, who, despite numerous misgivings, remained in Savannah with her slaves during most of the war. When Mrs. Wayne first considered refugeeing in December 1861 she had no fears about the loyalty of her bondsmen. "My negroes . . . are every one very anxious to go away with me," she reported with confidence. "[They] seem all very civil and I think appear faithful." As late as February 1864 her opinion had not changed. Although many people anticipated trouble, her own slaves still appeared "willing and anxious to go" whenever she gave the order. In a letter written shortly before Christmas, however, she told with shock and dismay of her slaves' behavior when the crucial moment finally came.

> We left Savannah in a very great hurry as the Yankees had cut every road and were in force only three miles from the city. . . . every one of my negroes left me the morning I left which was a great shock as they did not even appear unwilling to come with me but they are so artful and have such an idea of freedom. [O]nly three or four families left before me and all of their servants ran away but mine have always appeared so faithful that I had too much confidence in them.[21]

For the majority of slaves in exposed areas, of course, removal proved inevitable and they could do little except acquiesce and bide their time. Yet if moving thousands of bondsmen to the interior had the immediate effect of preventing mass escapes by blacks to Union lines, refugeeing did little to guarantee the long-term survival of chattel servitude. Once plantations were uprooted, the basic norms of a relatively static and immobile rural society became all but impossible to maintain. Both physically and psychologically the entire refugee process served to undermine the traditional authority structure of previously autonomous and self-contained plantation units.

Generally speaking, bondsmen were as ready to exploit this fluid and unstable situation as their masters were powerless to prevent them from doing so. In many cases the logistics of evacuation ensured that slaves would enjoy lengthy periods of idleness while their owners attempted to relocate and begin life anew. As early as December 1861 a soldier reported that hundreds of blacks had been hastily pulled back from the coast and were temporarily "out of employment" along the Brunswick and Florida Railroad, where they could be hired at very low rates. Nine months later, in September 1862, the superintendent of the same railroad noted that many Altamaha River planters had reconciled themselves to a prolonged exile and were growing provision crops until rice cultivation could be resumed. [22] Low-country bondsmen whose owners applied familiar task-labor methods to wartime subsistence farming probably noticed little immediate change in slavery's rigor or regimen once the initial inland trek was completed. Ultimately, however, a cloud of anxiety and mistrust settled over most refugee plantations in the wake of evacuation. Retreat from the seaboard sent a clear message to blacks that slavery was under attack, and few planters even pretended that a fifty-mile buffer zone would restore equilibrium to the peculiar institution. Such temporary stability as relocation afforded had less to do with geography than with six companies of Confederate cavalry stationed between black refugees and free territory. "Should the troops be removed," one observer warned, "the [refugee] planters would be compelled to leave their [food] crops now planted, or run the risk of losing their Negroes. This would ruin them."[23]

Although the early abandonment of Georgia's coastal plantations proved psychologically unsettling for whites, the rice plantation Negroes described above participated in what was probably the least disruptive variety of the refugee phenomenon. Despite the high risks involved, some rice planters did send bondsmen back intermittently during 1863 to cultivate exposed river plantations on a limited scale and thus preserved appreciable elements of continuity in the daily regimen of their slaves. For numerous other black refugees, however, breaks with the past proved considerably sharper and more enduring.

Notwithstanding the atypical experiences of slaveowners who moved to secure areas and continued farming throughout the war, most refugee planters found it impossible to keep a displaced slave force intact for any extended period of time or to restrict the activities of their bondsmen to prewar occupations. With cotton exporting virtually at a standstill, financially hard-pressed planters were forced to seek profitable employment for their refugee slaves wherever jobs were available. Military and industrial pursuits absorbed many surplus bondsmen and kept their owners financially solvent. But the withdrawal of slaves from agriculture and the parceling out of black workers to widely scattered locations involved hidden costs for slavery as an institution.

The slow but inexorable deterioration of the self-contained antebellum plantation community, with its clearly drawn lines of authority and carefully prescribed daily routine, was a central theme in the refugee experience of most blacks. The efforts of white slaveowners to prevent or retard this process ended almost invariably in failure and frustration. When James Postell, for example, made plans to evacuate his sea island estate in late 1861, he obviously hoped to continue the rhythm of plantation activity without serious interruption. In actual fact, the war had already altered the normal routine for some of his slaves when they were diverted from field work earlier in the year to construct palmetto huts for Confederate troops stationed on the island. Interruptions of this sort appear almost inconsequential, however, when contrasted with the changes which followed. Early in 1862 Postell gathered his slaves and abandoned St. Simons to settle amid other refugee planters in Ware County. During the first year he planted his land in food crops and attempted to carry on normal agricultural activity, but the demands of a wartime economy soon made the arrangement unfeasible. By 1863 Postell had drastically shifted his emphasis and personally took "all his prime hands" to Glynn County to engage in salt boiling, leaving the slave women and children in Ware County totally cut off from his direct control or supervision.[24]

A similar fate awaited the more than four hundred blacks who comprised the work force of James Potter's giant Colerain rice plantation on the Savannah River. After Potter's death in January 1862, all the slaves from Colerain were sent to the northeast Georgia town of Greensboro, where they lived in crowded, unhealthy quarters characterized by one observer as "barracks." Surviving records suggest that Potter's executors hired out at least some of the slaves in Greensboro, although no indication is given of the specific type of activity in which any of the blacks engaged. It is possible, however, that most of the blacks simply remained unemployed during this period, since the Potter estate accumulated a deficit of over thirteen thousand dollars by the year's end. Clearly such an arrangement could not long continue, and during 1863 Potter's heirs brought enough slaves back to Colerain to resume rice production on a limited scale and realized a modest profit of slightly over seven thousand dollars. The following year, 1864, witnessed a further parceling out of human chattels as the estate administrators put profit before paternalism and hired numerous bondsmen to railroads or industrial enterprises in the vicinity of Augusta. [25]

An unusually detailed and revealing picture of how refugee life destroyed or undermined the basic stabilizing norms of rural plantation slavery emerges in the wartime letters of the Thomas Butler King family, whose antebellum residence was an isolated St. Simons Island plantation appropriately called Retreat. The Kings began preparations to move inland in the spring of 1861 and like many coastal planters chose Ware County as a place of refuge. By early 1862 they had settled along with their force of over 130 slaves on a plantation near the village of Tebeauville, some sixty-five miles from the seaboard. Despite the sanguine hopes expressed by some family members that the new plantation would be a stable, profit-making enterprise, the more realistic of T. Butler King's children anticipated problems from the beginning. [26]

The land was fertile and the slaves "well housed," but with all the male members of King's family in the army there seemed to be little prospect of making "more than provisions the first year." Even this cautious prediction proved overly optimistic, and it soon became apparent that the Kings could not employ their bondsmen solely in subsistence agriculture without courting economic ruin. In the spring of 1862 the elder King yielded reluctantly to financial pressure and began the slow process of economic diversification which would ultimately alter the entire character of slave life for many of his bondsmen. At first he divided his slaves into two groups. Blacks in the first group continued to raise provisions while the rest worked in the nearby pine forests producing turpentine. The profits from turpentine sales proved pitifully small, however, and by 1863 King was forced to undertake what amounted to the virtual dismemberment of his plantation as a social and economic unit. In order to increase his dwindling cash income, he discontinued turpentine production in August 1863 and like other refugee planters began hiring out a portion of his slaves to the Confederate government. In describing the new arrangements to her brother, King's daughter Georgia made it plain that the disillusionment and economic strains of refugee life had effectively obliterated any sense of patriarchal obligation to the blacks involved. By hiring a slave to the Confederate government, she explained, "we can get $25 pr month & have him fed—& then if he runs to the Yankees get $2500 from the Government."[27]

The attitude of calculated cynicism becomes slightly more understandable if one examines the behavior of those blacks who still remained on the Ware County plantation. In 1862 King's daughter had derived considerable comfort and reassurance from the frequent queries by bondsmen wishing to know "When are we to see Mausa?" A year later the question had assumed a very different significance in light of increasingly open attempts by many blacks to take full advantage of their master's frequent absence and the white overseer's sloth and incompetence. The productivity of King's slaves was obviously low, for during 1863 "nothing came in, and hundreds—indeed several thousands are spent just supporting the plantation." During this same period many of the blacks grew visibly restive, and late in June the slaves Mack and Abram escaped to the Union forces on St. Simons Island, ironically finding freedom by returning to the place of their lifelong enslavement. The cause of most black discontent on King's plantation was allegedly the "intemperate language" of the overseer, but King's daughter realized that problems actually went much deeper. The entire system of plantation discipline had deteriorated under the stress of refugeeing, and the slaves grew steadily more "dissatisfied unless a master is with them."[28]

In the last analysis, of course, King's dilemma was the same one confronted to a greater or lesser extent by all refugee planters. Responding to the immediate economic and military pressures of a wartime environment, King and others like him gave little thought to the potential effect of their actions on such peacetime institutions as chattel slavery. Blacks, on the other hand, pragmatically exploited the breakdown of traditional institutional restraints in order to lighten or throw off the burdens of bondage whenever possible. Thus, in ironic fashion the attempts of numerous refugee slaveowners to wring a profit out of their "planting operations" led to the slow destruction of the very "way of life" which they hoped to preserve. [29]

As the war progressed, the hardships facing all refugees increased tremendously and the disruptive impact of removal upon plantation life became steadily more pronounced. When slaveowners in northern Georgia began fleeing southward en masse during the closing months of 1863, they often made little or no attempt to continue agricultural operations in a new locality. For many planters the termination of farming activity was dictated less by choice than by stern economic necessity. Notwithstanding occasional offers by farmers in southwest Georgia to hire small numbers of surplus slaves, the agricultural economy of the region was totally incapable of absorbing the massive influx of refugee bondsmen which developed during the last eighteen months of the war. Planters who fled to Georgia's southwestern counties with their slaves characteristically treated blacks less as people than as capital investments to be employed in the most profitable (or least unprofitable) way possible. In spite of an unsuccessful attempt by the Georgia legislature "to prevent refugee negroes from being employed in any labor except agriculture," more and more slaves were taken directly from the isolated environment of small farms or plantations and summarily sold or hired out in any convenient town or village. For these black people the impact of refugee life was immediate and profound. Changes which occurred over a period of months or years on refugee plantations were now compressed into days or weeks. Instead of gradually deteriorating or breaking down, many of plantation slavery's coercive or stabilizing elements simply disappeared. [30]

The experiences of blacks owned by Edward Harden, a small planter in Whitfield County, illustrate the abrupt manner in which many bondsmen were thrust into a new environment. Before abandoning his north Georgia home in the fall of 1863, Harden sold some slaves, including a valuable man known as "Big Henry," who was parted from his wife Laura and her child "little Henry." After much difficulty Harden purchased a residence near the town of Cuthbert in Randolph County and moved there in late December. Immediately upon arrival he took steps to relieve himself of the heavy financial burden which a large group of unemployed blacks would have imposed, making clear as he did so that paternalistic obligations took second place to securing a high return on his capital investment. Harden's description of the various jobs at which his slaves were employed bears less resemblance to the language of a benign patriarch than to the rapid-fire cadence of a bourgeois auctioneer: "I have hired Ed at the depot here for $250.00 a year to be fed and clothed. Mary with the Professor at the Baptist College . . . at $30 per month and clothes—Cloe is hired to a clever gentleman at the same [rate] all payable monthly. I have not yet hired out Joel.—Laura will have to do our cooking and washing[,] [she] and little Henry are all that we intend to keep at home except Cloe's two children."[31]

In terms of physical welfare, opportunities to avoid personal control and supervision by whites, and the broader perspectives to be gained through interaction with a large and diverse black community, Harden's slaves may actually have benefited by their forced exodus from northern Georgia. Yet many other slaves completed a similar trek southward only to encounter conditions of extreme hardship. The poignant and sometimes desperate letters of numerous white refugees clearly indicate that many of the black people taken to southwest Georgia late in the war found employment in neither agriculture nor industry, and were left in some cases to face the prospect of literal starvation. Writing to Governor Brown in 1864 a refugee from Cobb County described the Valdosta region as being crowded with black and white exiles for whom food shortages had become critical. "We have not been able to make our provisions," he reported, adding that even when willing to pay "full prices" many refugees could not get sufficient food. The refugees' dilemma was complicated by the fact that although planters were forced to turn over all surplus food crops to Confederate impressing officers or tax-in-kind agents, these officials generally refused to cooperate even to the limited extent of hiring refugee slaves to gather provisions in return for a portion of the food collected. "If something can not be done for us," warned this Valdosta refugee, "we will be in much distress the coming winter."[32]

The same sentiments were echoed in even stronger language by Edward Harden. "We are nearly starving here," he reported after less than a year in Randolph County. "Every body is bonded to furnish the Govt. all their supplies. God only knows what is to become of us all." If life was precarious for middle-class whites, Harden left little doubt that conditions for black refugees were as bad or considerably worse. "Should you come down with your negroes," he cautioned in a letter to his mother, "I will do the best I can for you; but I really fear your negroes will starve here until you can put them out."[33]

Whether they fared well or poorly in a physical sense, most black refugees shared a number of experiences which contributed to the breakdown of slavery's institutional stability. Slaves whose antebellum world had encompassed only a few square miles of Georgia countryside traveled the length and breadth of the state en route to secure areas. Upon reaching their destination they faced new and unfamiliar tasks, altered work routines, or lengthy periods of sheer idleness. The crowded, chaotic environment of such popular refugee meccas as southwest Georgia reduced the effectiveness of white surveillance and control and brought black refugees into contact with bondsmen from all sections of the state as well as other parts of the Confederacy. Previously isolated plantation slaves gained new opportunities to receive news of the war and discuss its meaning with other blacks.

Apart from any of these developments, refugeeing struck an important psychological blow at the myth of planter invincibility. The knowledge that Southern whites were in control of society as actual or potential wielders of ultimate power—that they were in the most basic sense "masters"—had been a key element in the daily equilibrium of peacetime race relations. Throughout the war, however, every military or naval incursion by Union forces produced scenes of pandemonium among Georgia slaveowners. Bondsmen who participated in panicked evacuations or who witnessed the refugee spectacle from the sidelines could hardly continue to look upon masters as omnipotent authority figures. As a Savannah freedman pointed out in January 1865, no amount of Confederate bravado could conceal the deeper meaning of a consistent pattern of wartime retreat. The ex-slave's former master had been an ardent secessionist who was "all the time talking about licking the norf."

> He said you's [Yankees] couldn't fight on land, you's couldn't ride a hoss, and you's was only good on de water. Oh, sah, all dey wanted was for you's to come down yere, and I don't know how many tousand of you's de was gwine to kill. But when you's captured Port Royal . . . he gets skeered. He sends all his folks back in de country, takes all his niggers away. . . . When you's take Fort Pulaski, he gets so skeered; he sends his folks off again. . . . And when you's all come down dis way and takes Atlanty, he gets skeered again. He sends his folks all off a third time and . . . he gets so frightened dat he took sick and died right off. He was afeared of you un's sah.[34]

One need not accept the postmortem diagnosis of death from fright to appreciate the larger truth contained in the foregoing passage. When white slaveowners retreated in disarray before Union armies they revealed that their power was finite and subject to challenge. Refugee planters ceased to be masters in the full sense, and if blacks remained legally in bondage, they also saw evidence that the foundations of the old regime were crumbling.

"Let us have the labor of your negroes . . ."

5. Blacks and Wartime Industrialization

F OR NEARLY all black Georgians the Civil War's sharpest impact occurred at the workplace. In the state's fertile cotton regions bondsmen on farms and plantations saw slavery recede by degrees through gradual alterations in master-slave relationships, disciplinary patterns, and work routines. But the process of change did not stop with plantation agriculture. In the course of the war a substantial minority of Georgia blacks found themselves temporarily or permanently removed from plantations to work as industrial slaves and Confederate military laborers. Together with numerous free Negroes and antebellum industrial bondsmen, these black workers played a vital, if seldom acknowledged, role in the Southern war effort. Simply by virtue of their occupations and places of employment they became active participants in the sectional conflict. Less numerous than agricultural slaves, blacks working for the army or in industry stood closer to the heart of the Confederate revolution. Their experiences underscore the distinctive character of nonagricultural bondage and illuminate the daily reality of black industrial life in the late antebellum era. Replete with human drama, the story of Georgia's black military and industrial workers is at least as significant, and perhaps ultimately more complex and intriguing, than the chronicle of slavery's subtle erosion in rural areas.

In Georgia as elsewhere black labor proved equally vital to Southern armies and the industries that sustained them. While civilian entrepreneurs hired bondsmen to increase production or replace white workers who joined the ranks, Georgia's military commanders assembled slaves on

120

a massive scale to perform basic support services for troops in the field. Hired or impressed for duty with the Confederate Quartermaster, Commissary, and Medical departments as well as the Ordnance, Engineer, and Nitre and Mining bureaus, blacks soon formed the backbone of Georgia's military labor force. Their range of responsibilities increased steadily as the war progressed, and they eventually participated in nearly every military activity short of armsbearing and combat.

Blacks assigned to the Engineer Bureau spent most of their time digging entrenchments, obstructing rivers, and constructing earthworks or field fortifications. Indeed, during the first three years of the war more black laborers were employed on the defenses of Savannah than on any other single military project in the state. Ranging in size from less than two hundred in 1861 to over two thousand in 1863, the slave work force at Savannah included blacks from most of the counties in coastal, southwestern, and middle Georgia (see Tables 6 and 7). After Vicksburg fell to Union forces in July 1863 the defense of Georgia's interior towns and cities received high military priority, with work on fortifications around Atlanta commencing almost at once under the direction of engineer officer Lemuel Pratt Grant. From the outset Captain Grant relied heavily on black labor hired or impressed from planters in neighboring counties.[1] By the year's end Grant's work force had finished some seven miles of Atlanta's outer defense line, and fortifications were also under construction at Columbus, where Captain Theodore Moreno had full power to "impress such negro labor in the State of Georgia as may be required." Hundreds of blacks from Muscogee, Harris, Chattahoochee, and other counties eventually worked on the Columbus defenses.[2]

Defending Georgia's navigable rivers also became a major military objective in 1863. At the request of General P. G. T. Beauregard some three hundred slaves were impressed to help construct fortifications on the Altamaha River, while state commissioners employed blacks from Decatur, Early, and Mitchell counties to obstruct the Flint River in southwest Georgia. At least fifty Florida slaves were impressed to help obstruct the Apalachicola River after several attempts to obtain Georgia slaves for a similar project upstream on the Chattahoochee proved unsuccessful.[3]

During the winter and spring of 1864 the ominous military situation in

TABLE 6
Black Labor on Fortifications in and Around Savannah, January 1861–November 1862*

	Total Slave Blacks at Work	Total Free Blacks at Work	Sent Voluntarily	Impressed
January 1861	"a large force"	"a large force"	Yes	
June 1861		48	Yes	
"Summer" 1861	300		Yes	
September 1861	160		Yes	
February 1862	500			
March 1862	800			
August 1862	1,500		Yes	Yes
September 1862	1,400		Yes	Yes
October 1862	800–1,000		Yes	Yes
November 1862	1,000		Yes	Yes

**Explanation:* In this table, information from a wide array of primary sources is pieced together in an attempt to present a fairly complete profile of the black labor force around Savannah. With the exception of the statistics for the period August through November, the numbers given in the "Total Blacks at Work" column should be viewed as estimates derived from private personal correspondence or diaries and not as precise head counts. Whenever two equally reliable sources have been at variance, the *lower* figure or estimate has been used. It should also be noted that the number of free black laborers is grossly underrepresented because very little specific numerical data is available, although many sources confirm their more or less constant presence on the fortifications. The data in this table are drawn from the following sources: Macon *Daily Telegraph*, July 19, 1862, p. 2; July 31, 1862, p. 2; August 18, 1862, p. 1; August 25, 1862, p. 4; August 26, 1862, p. 2; August 28, 1862, p. 2; Savannah *Daily Morning News*, August 2, 1861, p. 2; October 3, 1861, p. 2; October 7, 1861, p. 2;

TABLE 6—*Continued*

From What Portions of State	Where or How Employed	When Discharged
Chatham and surrounding counties	Digging out moat and ditches at Fort Pulaski	Prior to March 1861
Chatham County	Working in Fort Pulaski	July 1861
Chatham County	Constructing sand battery on Green Island	
Liberty and Bryan counties	Constructing sand battery on St. Catherines Island "Throwing up breastworks near Fort Jackson"	
All counties of middle and southwest Georgia; 20% of "laboring force" of each county requested. Specific data available only for following counties: Sumter, 50; Calhoun, Terrill, Lee, & Stewart, 58; Houston, 75; Monroe, 100; Hancock & Baldwin, "a great number"	"For important works in the neighborhood of Savannah" "On the works at and near Camp Mercer"	November 1862
Same as above	Same as above	November 1862
Same as above	Same as above	November 1862
Same as above	Same as above	November 1862

October 19, 1861, p. 2; June 16, 1862, p. 2; George A. Mercer Diary, January 19, September 4, 1861; August 9, 14, 19, 23, October 12, 1862, SHC; Joseph L. Locke to his wife, March 3, 1862, Bulloch Family Papers, SHC; Sarah Lawton to "My dear friend," January 4, 1861, Alexander Robert Lawton Papers, SHC; Dr. W. C. Daniel to Joseph E. Brown, March 6, 1861, Robert Habersham to Joseph E. Brown, March 6, 1861, John Screven to Joseph E. Brown, March 29, 1861, all in Telamon Cuyler Collection, University of Georgia; Captain John McCrady to Dr. T. A. Parsons, August 12, 1862, George W. Randolph to General H. W. Mercer, August 15, 1862, General H. W. Mercer to George W. Randolph, August 16, 1862, all in Alexander H. Stephens Papers, LC; John W. Bentley to his father, February 8, 1862, quoted in Byrne, "Slavery in Savannah," 74; CRG, 2:311–14; *Acts of Georgia . . . Annual Session . . . 1862*, pp. 54–55, 108–109, 111–12, 117; OR, ser. 1, vol. 14, pp. 612, 633–34; Lawrence, *A Present for Mr. Lincoln*, 21.

TABLE 7

Black Laborers on Fortifications in and Around Savannah,
*December 1862–August 1863**

	Average Number of Slaves Employed	Total Number of Slaves Employed	Number Impressed	Number Hired
December 1862	1,500	3,000	1,500	
January 1863	2,000		2,000	
February 1863	2,000		2,000	
March 1–15, 1863	1,500		1,500	
Week of April 19, 1863		132	102	30
July 1863		150 (approximate)		150
August 1863		2,311	2,005	306

*The data in the above table are drawn from the following sources: OR, ser. 1, vol. 14, pp. 836, 842, 869, 871, 902, 904; CRG, 3:334–38; Georgia House Journal . . . Special Session . . . 1863, pp. 10–11; OR, ser. 1, vol. 28, pp. 215–16; vol. 53, pp. 292, 296; Savannah Daily Morning News, August 3,

TABLE 7—*Continued*

From What Portions of State	Where or How Employed	When Discharged
All sections of state, but northern and western counties fail to furnish full quota		Prior to March 28, 1863
	"Engaged upon earthworks near Savannah"	Prior to April 29 for impressed slaves
Impressment encompasses 1/4 of all male slaves between ages 16 and 50, owned by planters in "Southern, Southwestern and Eastern Georgia"	*Impressed Force* River batteries, 342 Department force, 323 Clearing woods, 46 Interior lines, 321 Isle of Hope, 427 Beaulieu, 115 Springfield, 147 Cutting hurdles, poles, etc., 183 Hewing timber, 39 Loading lumber, etc., 15 Turned over to chief quartermaster for cutting fuel, 44 Surveying parties, 3 TOTAL, 2,005 *Contract and Hired Force employed before impressment:* Spratt and Callahan, 111 Williams & Co., 32 Kneeland, Thompson & Co., 25 Hired, 105 Surveying parties, 33 TOTAL, 306	

1863, p. 2; August 15, 1863, p. 2; August 24, 1863, p. 2; Macon *Daily Telegraph*, August 8, 1863, p. 2; August 16, 1863, p. 2; August 19, 1863, p. 1.

northern Georgia prompted major additions to Atlanta's defensive works. As white laborers were conscripted for combat, Captain Grant replenished his work force with more and more blacks. At various times thousands of slaves were engaged in clearing trees and brush from hills in front of defense lines, or moving tons of earth for trenches and redoubts. By the summer months the Atlanta campaign was well under way and local Confederate commanders were making frantic efforts to fortify strategic points throughout the state. After two months of constant Rebel retreats the perilous movement of hostilities toward Atlanta caused General Joseph E. Johnston to order the impressment in late June of "every able-bodied negro man that can be found" to work for one week on Atlanta's outer defenses. Planters in southern and southwestern Georgia had forty-eight hours in which to furnish slaves voluntarily, but were informed that if the necessary labor was not forthcoming "then . . . every male negro that can possibly be impressed will be sent to the front, regardless of past exemption."[4]

In early August of 1864, as General John Bell Hood ordered still more slave levies for Atlanta, calls also went out for 1,200 black workers to strengthen Savannah's defenses. Some 900 other Negroes impressed from Sumter and surrounding counties were already at work at Andersonville, while several hundred more slaves were building fortifications near Griffin. During the same period military authorities in Macon required planters in Bibb and other nearby counties to furnish 20 percent of all male slaves between eighteen and fifty years of age for work on the city's fortifications. Less than two months later General Howell Cobb authorized immediate impressment of 500 additional slaves for the Macon project, "without reference to the number already furnished by individuals."[5] Slaves also helped fortify the up-country town of Athens, and after the fall of Atlanta in September Captain L. P. Grant began assembling black laborers to fortify the city of Augusta. In late October his work force numbered only 140 bondsmen, but on November 30, 1864, 409 blacks under three white overseers were at work on the city's interior defensive lines.[6] By the end of the year Grant had hired or impressed nearly 600 slaves for the Augusta project. Approximately two-thirds were obtained on the South Carolina side of the Savannah River, with the remainder coming from various counties north and west of Augusta (see Tables 8 and 9).

TABLE 8	
Black Labor Hired or Impressed for Augusta Fortifications, September–December 1864*	
Month	Number
September	22
October	153
November	374
December	47
TOTAL	596

*Source: Data in the above table are compiled from the manuscript "List of Negroes Hired and Impressed for Work on Fortifications of Augusta, Ga.," Lemuel P. Grant Papers, Atlanta Historical Society.

TABLE 9	
Geographical Origins of Black Labor on Augusta Fortifications, September–December 1864*	
Where Obtained	Number
Troup County, Ga.	20
Coweta County, Ga.	2
Morgan County, Ga.	1
Walton County, Ga.	9
Richmond County, Ga.	19
Columbia County, Ga.	16
Wilkes County, Ga.	119
Talliaferro County, Ga.	3
Burke County, Ga.	1
Granite Mills, S.C.	5
Edgefield, S.C.	397
Unknown	4
TOTAL	596

*Source: Compiled from the manuscript "List of Negroes Hired and Impressed for Work on Fortifications of Augusta, Ga.," Lemuel P. Grant Papers, Atlanta Historical Society.

Even General W. T. Sherman's devastating "march to the sea" failed to halt the military mobilization of Georgia's black workers. Unwilling to face the reality of defeat, the Confederate Congress debated the question of enlisting black troops, while the Bureau of Conscription redoubled its efforts to obtain 20,000 black military laborers authorized in legislation a year earlier. A Conscription Bureau circular dated December 12, 1864, ordered generals in the states east of the Mississippi River to enroll a total of 14,500 slaves for immediate service with the Confederate Engineer Corps. Some 2,500 of these bondsmen were to come from Georgia, where the impressment was apportioned among each of the state's nine congressional districts in the following manner: First District, 150; Second, 450; Third, 450; Fourth, 450; Fifth, 325; Sixth, 325; Seventh, 200; Eighth, 100; Ninth, 50. As the new year began, local enrolling officers were once again at work throughout the state ordering planters to send forward one-fifth of all ablebodied male slaves between ages eighteen and fifty or face impressment. Less than a month before Appomattox, Georgia's chief agent for slave impressment, Captain Charles R. Armstrong, reported confidently that enrolling officers in every county were under orders to "press the impressment with all possible dispatch," and officials in counties along major railroad lines had instructions to "consumate the impressment at once."[7]

Altogether at least 10,000 slaves and free Negroes probably labored at various times on Georgia's military defenses. Aggregate estimates, however, can easily obscure the fact that only a fraction of the state's black fortification workers were in the field at any given period. Secured mostly through impressment, the Engineer Bureau's slave work force was large but temporary. That of most other government agencies was smaller but more permanent. The Medical Department, for example, hired hundreds of black Georgians during the war to work in military hospitals throughout the state. Serving primarily as nurses, cooks, and laundresses, Georgia bondsmen soon became the mainstays of daily hospital operations. Their presence gave stability and continuity to an otherwise fluctuating labor force of detailed and convalescent soldiers. Without black attendants the quality of care in Georgia hospitals would almost certainly have declined, Confederate fighting strength would probably have dwindled, and at critical periods of campaigning the army's medical system might simply have been overwhelmed.

By the middle of the war the great majority of Georgia's black medical workers were employed in the extensive hospital network attached to the Army of Tennessee. The origins of the system dated from February 1862 when Surgeon L. T. Pim, assistant medical director of the Western Department, arrived in Atlanta to establish treatment facilities for approximately three thousand sick and wounded soldiers from General Albert Sidney Johnston's ill-fated Army of the Mississippi. "We need quite a number of negroes . . . to serve in our Hospitals," Pim announced on March 6, 1862. Stressing that soldiers were being detailed as hospital attendants, he urged nearby slaveowners to hire out bondsmen to the Medical Department and thereby "return an efficient man to the field."[8]

Information concerning black medical employment during 1862 is sketchy at best. About all that can be said with certainty is that the pace of Georgia hospital activity began accelerating in July when General Braxton Bragg shifted his base of operations eastward to Chattanooga. Under the guidance of Dr. Samuel Hollingsworth Stout, superintendent and later director of hospitals for Bragg's newly constituted Army of Tennessee, twenty-nine military hospitals were established in northwestern Georgia along the line of the Western and Atlantic Railroad. Fully functional by the end of the year, Stout's hospital network remained basically unaltered until just before the Battle of Chickamauga in September 1863, when the northernmost units were moved to safer locations south of Atlanta.[9]

Fragmentary evidence suggests that post surgeons in Georgia employed blacks routinely from at least 1862 onward.[10] Unfortunately, standard Medical Department "Morning Reports" fail to designate the race of hospital attendants, and not until mid-1863 did Stout gather reliable statistics on black employment. Special reports submitted by approximately two-thirds of Stout's hospitals between June and December 1863 present the first detailed picture of the Army of Tennessee's hospital labor force. Since most information was gathered prior to the army's bloody clashes at Chickamauga, Lookout Mountain, and Missionary Ridge, the 1863 profile is probably also indicative of employment patterns late in 1862.

Table 10 summarizes data from nineteen of Stout's twenty-nine Georgia hospitals. Excluding doctors, these units employed a total of 834 people including 355 soldiers, 95 white civilians, and 384 Negro slaves. Comprising 46 percent of all workers and 80 percent of the hired attendants, blacks formed the largest single component of the work force. Although precise statistics are unavailable for ten additional hospitals in the system, a valid estimate of aggregate slave employment can be obtained by assuming that blacks constituted 80 percent, or 463 of the 579 hired attendants (black and white) serving in all Army of Tennessee hospitals as of September 1, 1863.[11] While not a literal head count, the 463 figure is probably accurate and certainly justifies the conclusion that between 450 and 500 blacks worked in northwest Georgia's military hospitals before any major battles occurred inside the state.

Prolonged fighting on Georgia soil during the last eighteen months of the war placed unprecedented demands on the Army of Tennessee's medical resources. Called upon to treat more patients with fewer detailed attendants, and to relocate hospitals on short notice, Director Stout placed

TABLE 10
Labor Force Composition of Selected Georgia Confederate Hospitals, 1863*

Name and Location of Hospital	Date	Total Attendants	Detailed Soldiers	White Civilians	Negroes
Catoosa Springs Hospital Catoosa Springs	June 13, 1863	47	18 (38%)	8 (17%)	21 (45%)
General Hospital Tunnel Hill	June 19, 1863	90	60 (67%)	21 (23%)	9 (10%)
Cannon Hospital La Grange	Dec. 18, 1863	32	9 (28%)	1 (3%)	22 (69%)
St. Mary's Hospital La Grange	Dec. 18, 1863	40	10 (25%)	1 (3%)	29 (72%)
Oliver Hospital La Grange	Dec. 18, 1863	43	14 (32%)	2 (5%)	27 (63%)
Law Hospital La Grange	Dec. 18, 1863	29	7 (24%)	2 (7%)	20 (69%)
Quintard Hospital Rome	June 10, 1863	46	19 (41%)	5 (11%)	22 (48%)
Bell Hospital Rome	June 10, 1863	39	17 (43%)	12 (31%)	10 (26%)
Pim Hospital Rome	June 10, 1863	27	9 (33%)	3 (11%)	15 (56%)
Polk Hospital Rome	June 10, 1863	39	16 (41%)	5 (13%)	18 (46%)
Lumpkin Hospital Rome	June 10, 1863	49	28 (57%)	7 (14%)	14 (29%)
Small Pox Hospital Rome	June 10, 1863	3	2 (67%)	1 (33%)	0 (0%)
Gate City Hospital Atlanta	June 10, 1863	54	19 (35%)	6 (11%)	29 (54%)

(*Continued*)

increasing reliance on black workers. As early as September 22, 1863, while preparing for the flood of Confederate casualties from Chickamauga, Stout announced that 150 additional slaves were needed at various Georgia hospitals. "Let us have the labor of your negroes," he urged, "and we will strengthen the army."[12] Echoing this theme, post surgeons throughout Georgia combined patriotic appeals with monetary inducements and military coercion in order to increase their force of black attendants. As armies changed positions, proximity to black labor became an important factor in choosing new hospital sites.[13] Doctors who could furnish slave workers were eagerly recruited into the medical services, and

TABLE 10—*Continued*

Name and Location of Hospital	Date	Total Attendants	Detailed Soldiers	White Civilians	Negroes
Medical College Hospital Atlanta	June 9, 1863	28	6 (21%)	1 (4%)	21 (75%)
Empire Hospital Atlanta	June 20, 1863	43	15 (35%)	4 (9%)	24 (56%)
Roy Hospital Atlanta	June 10, 1863	22	10 (45%)	5 (23%)	7 (32%)
Fair Ground Hospital No. 1 Atlanta	June 21, 1863	77	29 (38%)	2 (3%)	46 (60%)
Fair Ground Hospital No. 2 Atlanta	June 21, 1863	90	46 (51%)	6 (7%)	38 (42%)
Johnston Receiving and Distributing Hospital Atlanta	Oct. 30, 1863 to Jan. 1, 1864	36	21 (58%)	3 (8%)	12 (33%)
TOTAL		834	355 (43%)	95 (11%)	384 (46%)

Sources: Dr. Robert C. Foster, "List of Hosptl. Attds. at Catoosa Springs, Ga., June 13, 1863"; Dr. B. M. Wimble, "Report of Hospital Attendants at Tunnel Hill, Ga., June 19, 1863"; Dr. F. H. Evans to "Surgeon Johnson," December 18, 1863; Dr. W. L. Nichol to Dr. S. H. Stout, June 10, 1863; Dr. Paul F. Eve to Dr. J. P. Logan, June 10, 1863; Dr. W. T. Westmoreland to Dr. J. P. Logan, June 9, 1863; Dr. William P. Harden, "Report of Hospital Attendants at the Empire Hospital, Atlanta, Ga., June 20, 1863"; Dr. G. G. Roy to Dr. J. P. Logan, June 10, 1863; Dr. W. H. Brown, "Report of Hospital Attendants at Fair Ground Hospital No. 1., Atlanta, Ga., June 21, 1863"; Dr. Robert Battey, "Report of Hospital Attendants at Fair Ground Hospital No. 2, Atlanta, Ga., June 21, 1863"; Muster Roll of Steward, Wardmaster, Cooks, Nurses, Matrons, and Detailed Soldiers . . . in the Receiving and Distributing Hospital, Atlanta, Ga., October 30, 1863–January 1, 1864—all in Samuel Hollingsworth Stout Papers, University of Texas.

in hospitals for state militiamen disabled soldiers were detailed "as a mere matter of form . . . with instructions that they be allowed to substitute a servant in their place."[14]

Local conditions facilitated the shift to black labor in some hospitals and impeded it in others. In Macon, where government installations were numerous and labor competition was intense, black hospital workers were in chronically short supply and could be secured only through temporary impressment to meet the medical emergencies of late 1863. Yet during the same time period La Grange's chief medical officer hired a force of 120 slaves at modest prices, and returned most detailed soldiers to active service.[15] In the hospital system as a whole, black employment kept pace with and often exceeded increases in the number and capacity of treatment units. Statistics from Atlanta, the state's largest medical center until its hospitals were evacuated in June 1864, reveal how the racial composition of Georgia's hospital work force changed over time. At both the Receiving and Distributing Hospital (Table 11) and the larger Fair Ground Hospital No. 1 (Table 12) similar developments occurred between mid-1863 and mid-1864. While maintaining or slightly expanding their aggregate work forces, each institution experienced a sharp drop in the number of soldiers detailed for hospital duty and an even larger increase in the number of slaves hired. White civilian employees also increased, but their numbers remained small. At the Receiving and Distributing Hospital a 75 percent real increase in black employment raised the proportion of slave attendants from 33 percent to 60 percent of the total staff. At Fair Ground Hospital No. 1 a real increase of 74 percent raised the black component from 60 percent to 73 percent of the work force.

The highest level of black employment in Georgia hospitals probably occurred late in the Atlanta campaign and during Sherman's subsequent march to the sea, when detailed statistics are unavailable. At its zenith the Army of Tennessee's network of fifty-odd mobile hospitals sprawled

TABLE 11

Changes in Labor Force Composition of Johnston Receiving
and Distributing Hospital, Atlanta*

| | | | Hired Attendants | |
Date	Total Attendants	Detailed Soldiers	White Civilians	Negroes
Oct. 30, 1863–Jan. 1, 1864	36	21 (58%)	3 (8%)	12 (33%)
Jan. 31–April 30, 1864	42	22 (52%)	9 (21%)	11 (26%)
April 30–June 30, 1864	35	8 (23%)	6 (17%)	21 (60%)

*Sources: Muster Roll of . . . the Receiving and Distributing Hospital, Atlanta (later Macon), Ga., October 30, 1863–January 1, 1864; January 31–April 30, 1864; April 30–June 30, 1864—all in Samuel H. Stout Papers, University of Texas.

TABLE 12

Changes in Labor Force Composition of Fair Ground Hospital No. 1, Atlanta*

Date	Total Attendants	Detailed Soldiers	Hired Attendants	
			White Civilians	Negroes
June 21, 1863	77	29	2	46
		(38%)	(2%)	(60%)
Dec. 1–31, 1863	90	16	23	51
		(18%)	(26%)	(57%)
April 30–Aug. 31, 1864	110	15	15	80
		(14%)	(14%)	(73%)

*Sources: Dr. W. H. Brown, "Report of Hospital Attendants at Fair Ground Hospital No. 1, Atlanta, Ga., June 21, 1863"; Muster Roll of . . . Fair Ground Hospital No. 1 . . . December 1–31, 1863; April 30–August 31, 1864—all in Samuel H. Stout Papers, University of Texas.

through at least eighteen Georgia towns and stretched westward into Alabama and Mississippi.[16] By February 1865 the number of hired civilian employees in the system had risen to 1,099, an increase of over 100 percent in twenty months. If, as in 1863, at least 80 percent of all hired employees were black, the number of slave hospital attendants serving late in the war can be conservatively estimated at 800 to 900. Since 1865 reports fail to include nine additional hospitals still in transit, actual black employment may have been closer to 1,000.[17]

Whatever their precise numbers, the great bulk of Georgia's black hospital attendants labored at one of three basic occupations: cooking, laundry work, or nursing. The first two tasks fell to slaves from the outset, and by 1864 blacks had also replaced most of the detailed soldiers formerly assigned as hospital nurses. As indicated by data from two Atlanta hospitals (Tables 13 and 14), laundry workers were almost exclusively black women; cooks might be male or female, but were also usually black. Nursing, which involved physically strenuous chores like scrubbing and cleaning wards, shaking out bed ticks, and lifting patients, was an overwhelmingly male occupation. Some Georgia hospitals designated adult black nurses "wardboys" and apparently gave them more menial tasks than those assigned to white nurses. This was certainly the case at Tunnel Hill Hospital, where the chief surgeon felt "obliged to require nurses to per-

TABLE 13

Occupational Distribution by Sex and Race at Johnston Receiving and Distributing Hospital, Atlanta, April 30–June 30, 1864*

Occupation	Total Number	Detailed Soldiers	Hired Attendants			
			White Males	White Females	Black Males	Black Females
Nurse	19	7 (37%)			12 (63%)	
Cook	4	1 (25%)		1 (25%)	1 (25%)	1 (25%)
Laundress	10			3 (30%)		7 (70%)
Supervisory positions**	2			2 (100%)		
Total for all occupations	35	8		6	13	8

**Source:* Muster Roll of . . . Receiving and Distributing Hospital, Atlanta, Ga., April 30–June 30, 1864, Samuel H. Stout Papers, University of Texas.
**Matron, Wardmaster, Steward, Apothecary.

form laundry duty—that is[,] negro women who aid in cleaning the wards are also required to wash."[18]

Outside the wards blacks tended hospital livestock, served as messengers and couriers, and accompanied civilian relief associations to Georgia battlefields.[19] In Macon the Medical Purveyor's Office and its subagencies, the Medical Laboratory and Medical Distillery, employed slave carpenters, teamsters, laborers, and free Negro conscripts on a continuing basis.[20] Blacks also played a vital role in providing medical care for government livestock at the Confederate Horse Infirmary in Laurens County, Georgia. Established in mid-1863 by the Quartermaster Department's Office of Field Transportation, the 8,000-acre facility treated sick and injured army horses from Georgia, South Carolina, and Tennessee. Initially the infirmary employed a total of eight whites and fifty Negroes, but in the spring of 1864 one hundred more blacks were recruited to care for two thousand additional horses. Under the supervision of two white veterinarians, experienced black hostlers curried and rubbed the animals daily, washed their legs and feet, and treated particular injuries or diseases. After observing these activities firsthand, the veteran war corre-

TABLE 14

Occupational Distribution by Sex and Race at Fair Ground Hospital No. 1, Atlanta and
Later Macon, April 30–August 31, 1864*

Occupation	Total Number	Detailed Soldiers	Hired Attendants			
			White Males	White Females	Black Males	Black Females
Nurses (including "wardboys")	54	14			37	3
		(26%)			(69%)	(5%)
Cook	18		1		11	6
			(6%)		(61%)	(33%)
Laundress	23				1	22
					(4%)	(96%)
Supervisory positions**	15	1	2	12		
		(7%)	(13%)	(80%)		
Total for all occupations	110	15	3	12	49	31

*Source: Muster Role . . . Fair Ground Hospital No. 1, Atlanta (later Macon) Ga., April 30–
August 31, 1864, Samuel H. Stout Papers, University of Texas.
**Matron, Wardmaster, Steward, Apothecary.

spondent Peter Wellington Alexander praised the operation highly. With more insight than he probably intended, Alexander assured readers that "the horse receives here the same care and attention as the sick or disabled soldier does at the hospital."[21]

In an agency responsible for all aspects of military transportation, black veterinary workers assumed an importance greater than their limited numbers might indicate. One of the groups most directly dependent on their labors was the Quartermaster Department's own force of slave teamsters. The number of slave and free black Georgians who drove government drays, artillery horses, and military supply wagons during the war was undoubtedly large, but in the absence of detailed records any numerical estimate would be little more than a guess. Shrouded in bureaucratic intricacies, quartermaster transportation activities in Georgia are more easily understood if separated into home-front and battlefield components. On the home front operations were extensive but unavoidably decentralized. At numerous military posts and receiving depots across the state local quartermasters relied almost exclusively on black teamsters and laborers to load military supplies and haul them to designated collection points for storage or transshipment. Quartermasters in Georgia's larger towns and cities commonly sought to hire twenty-five to thirty black teamsters at any given time, plus additional laborers and rough carpenters.[22]

During the first two years of the war white soldiers performed the bulk of transportation work for Confederate armies in the field. Initially about two thousand enlisted men served as teamsters in the Army of Tennessee alone.[23] In Georgia as elsewhere discontent with the practice grew vocal as Confederate manpower dwindled, and during the summer of 1863 newspapers in Macon, Columbus, and Atlanta urged that blacks be substituted as wagon drivers so that white soldiers could return to the ranks.[24] General Gideon Pillow, who commanded the Army of Tennessee's semiautonomous Volunteer and Conscript Bureau, had been scouring the Alabama and Tennessee countryside for slave teamsters since early March of that year. But Georgia fell outside Pillow's jurisdiction and his efforts to hire slaves elsewhere through voluntary contracts produced meager results.[25] Not until the last desperate weeks of the Atlanta campaign did Georgia bondsmen assume the burden of transportation labor for General John B. Hood's badly outnumbered forces. In August 1864 Confederate quartermaster officers visited counties along all major railroad lines in central and southwestern Georgia, under orders to obtain two thousand black teamsters for immediate service with the Army of Tennessee. Six months earlier the Confederate Congress had specifically mandated this labor policy, and planters were urged to furnish slaves "without delay" in order to avoid the impressment "which the officers are authorized to make, and will make if necessary."[26] Remaining with the army after the fall of Atlanta, black Georgians subsequently moved Confederate supply trains northwestward across Alabama in support of General Hood's ill-fated drive toward Nashville and final defeat.[27]

From mid-1863 onward quartermaster officials also supervised military transportation on Southern railroads. In Georgia special agents at Americus, Cassville, Columbus, Macon, West Point, and Augusta exercised rather vague jurisdiction over fourteen hundred miles of track which was owned and operated by eighteen largely autonomous railroad companies. The hand of government regulation rested lightly on these local lines—perhaps too lightly in view of their vital importance as supply arteries for troops in Tennessee and Virginia. Despite the precarious logistical situation of Southern armies, Confederate transportation agents refused to impose "through freight" schedules on major railroads or to assist the carriers with maintenance and manpower problems for which the government was largely responsible.[28] Labor shortages developed initially on Georgia lines when unskilled white section hands became subject to conscription in 1862. Since blacks had participated in most facets of antebellum railroad work, the substitution of slaves for drafted white employees posed little problem for most Georgia roads.[29] Typically the state's railways sought to compensate for lost white manpower by diverting black workers away from nonessential tasks and, when necessary, by hiring additional bondsmen. Fragmentary data from approximately half of Georgia's wartime railroads (Table 15) offers some insight into how black occupational patterns shifted between 1861 and 1865.

On the eve of secession the largest single block of nonwhite railroad workers were slaves engaged in grading and new track construction for the South-Western, the Augusta and Macon, and presumably other lines. Construction work did not cease with the outbreak of hostilities. For most of the war period, blacks worked steadily to complete the Augusta and Macon connection, and by March 1863 trains were running as far as Mayfield on the Ogeechee River in Hancock County. The road from that point southwestward toward Milledgeville was "still in rapid course of construction."[30] Sporadic efforts to forge a direct rail link between Macon and the coastal town of Brunswick occurred throughout the war. With approximately sixty to seventy miles of roadbed yet to be graded, the Macon and Brunswick stockholders took "decisive measures" in August 1863 to "put a large additional force on the road and complete the grading in a very short time."[31] Construction activity in extreme southern Georgia was aimed at extending the Savannah, Albany and Gulf from Thomasville to Bainbridge on the Flint River. In January 1864 a planter near Bainbridge reported that more than one hundred Negroes had been grading the line in his neighborhood for the past six months. He estimated that an additional year would be required to complete the work.[32]

Despite the best efforts of contractors and slaveowning stockholders, none of the above-named projects made significant headway during the

TABLE 15

Black Employment on Selected Georgia Railroads, 1859–1865*

Employer and Occupation	1859		1860		1861	
	Sought	Owned or Hired	Sought	Owned or Hired	Sought	Owned or Hired
Savannah, Albany & Gulf RR						
—road repair			20			
—grading for new construction						
Augusta & Macon RR						
—grading for new construction				200		
Macon & Brunswick RR						
—road repair						
—grading for new construction						
South-Western RR Co.						
—grading for new construction		400				
—road repair					200	
—cooks and shovel hands						40
—train hands and firemen						
Macon & Western RR						
—road repair		100				
—laborers in RR shops						
Muscogee RR						
—depot hands and road repair						
Central RR & Banking Co.						
—unspecified				30 (approximate)		
—road repair						
Georgia RR						
—unspecified		16 (approximate)				
—road repair						
Augusta & Savannah RR						
—road repair					50	

*Sources (listed by individual railroad): Savannah, Albany & Gulf: Savannah Republican, Jan. 14, 1860, p. 3; D. Curry to Joseph E. Brown, Jan. 22, 1864, Telamon Cuyler Collection, University of Georgia. Augusta & Macon: Macon Daily Telegraph, July 26, 1860, p. 2; Jan. 15, 1862, p. 1; Feb. 11, 1863, p. 1. Macon & Brunswick: Macon Daily Telegraph, Jan. 8, 1862, p. 2; May 19, 1862, p. 1. South-Western: Ulrich B. Phillips, A History of Transportation in the Eastern Cotton Belt to 1860 (New York, 1908), 295; Macon Daily Telegraph, Dec. 7, 1860, p. 2; Dec. 26, 1864, p. 2. Macon & Western: Ulrich B. Phillips, "The Origin and Growth of the Southern Black-Belts," American Historical

1862		1863		1864		1865	
Sought	Owned or Hired	Sought	Owned or Hired	Sought	Owned or Hired	Sought	Owned or Hired
					100		
50		30					
40							
100							
						50	
						50	
				50	25		
				10			
20		30		25		100	
				100			
					100		

Review 11 (July 1906): 805; Robert C. Black, "The Railroads of Georgia in the Confederate War Effort," *Journal of Southern History* 13 (November 1947): 516; Macon *Daily Telegraph*, Dec. 30, 1863, p. 1; Aug. 26, 1864, p. 2. *Muscogee:* Columbus *Daily Sun*, April 12, 1862, p. 2; Jan. 3, 1863, p. 2; Dec. 31, 1863, p. 2; Oct. 29, 1864, p. 2. *Central:* Black, "Railroads of Georgia," 516; General B. D. Fry to Howell Cobb, Nov. 4, 1864, Howell Cobb Collection, University of Georgia. *Georgia:* Black, "Railroads of Georgia," 516; General B. D. Fry to Howell Cobb, Nov. 18, 1864; Howell Cobb Collection. *Augusta & Savannah:* Augusta *Constitutionalist*, Jan. 4, 1861, p. 2.

latter stages of the war. From 1863 onward most Georgia railroads apparently gave top priority to the maintenance of existing facilities, and as lines deteriorated under constant military use more and more bondsmen were hired to work on track repairs. Several Georgia carriers had employed blacks on train operating crews before the war, and in 1862 a resolution was introduced in the Georgia legislature "allowing the Superintendent of the W[estern] & A[tlantic] . . . to employ negroes on that road." Late in 1864 the South-Western Railroad offered to hire a total of fifty slaves as "train hands and firemen."[33] The latter company also employed blacks in its repair shops at Macon, as did the Macon and Western and the Central of Georgia, which built new repair shops in Macon after its Savannah facilities were taken over as a Confederate arsenal.[34] At the Western and Atlantic car shops in Atlanta black artisans began to fill vital jobs during the summer of 1862, and their removal during the Sherman invasion was a serious blow to the road. "We are short of workmen in the [car] shop," wrote Superintendent George Phillips in May 1864. "Most of the negro mechanics having just been taken away by their owners, . . . [we] cannot lose one man now in the shop without serious loss."[35]

Confederate engineers relied almost exclusively on black labor to build new or duplicate wooden bridges for Georgia railroads. Most wartime bridge construction on the Western and Atlantic, the Central of Georgia, the Georgia Railroad, and other lines was directed by Captain L. P. Grant, whose "efficient and experienced" workers were "all negroes . . . long engaged in this business."[36] Some bridge-building projects apparently involved free black entrepreneurs. When Union forces captured Atlanta, only the absence of a bridge across the Chattahoochee River at Columbus prevented Confederate authorities from establishing a new rail link between the Upper and Lower South. The task of connecting Georgia's Muscogee Railroad with Alabama's Mobile and Girard line fell to Captain George H. Hazlehurst, who immediately sought to hire one hundred black men to work on "track laying and bridging."[37] Noting that Horace Godwin, "the well known negro bridge builder," had also been employed, a local newspaper assured readers that the river would be spanned "in two months at the farthest."[38]

140

Systematic destruction of Georgia's interior rail network during Sherman's march to the sea made the Columbus project pointless. Hazlehurst soon turned his attention to reopening the shattered South-Western and the Atlanta and West Point line, and by February 1865 his work force had finished cutting new crossties for the latter road.[39] When Savannah fell in December 1864, Captain Grant abandoned efforts to fortify Augusta and began the herculean task of repairing the Georgia Railroad. One hundred blacks were assigned to the work as early as November 1864, and by February 1865 a force of 200 slaves had relaid the track as far west as Social Circle.[40] Grant estimated that at least 700 slaves were needed to complete the Augusta–Atlanta connection, but from February through April 1865 impressment agents succeeded in obtaining only 142 additional bondsmen from counties adjoining the railroad (see Table 16). Repairing the state's devastated rail system under these circumstances was a physical impossibility. Hampered by bad weather, sickness, and a lack of materials, slave work crews remained at their tasks for more than a week

TABLE 16

Slave Labor Impressment for Railroad Repair Work in Georgia for Months of February, March, and April 1865, and by Geographical Origin*

Month	Number	Where Obtained	Number
February	89	Franklin County	3
March	39	Wilkes County	8
April	14	Burke County	24
TOTAL	142	Lincoln County	25
		Madison County	8
		Oglethorpe County	32
		Habersham County	6
		Richmond County	12
		Clarke County	17
		Talliaferro County	2
		Hall County	3
		Morgan County	1
		Johnson County	1
		TOTAL	142

*Source: "List of Negroes Impressed Under Act of February 17, 1864—Gen. Orders No. 86, December 5th 1864, A&I Gen's Office, Richmond, Va.," Lemuel P. Grant Papers, Atlanta Historical Society.

after Lee's surrender at Appomattox. Both literally and figuratively, however, they were engaged in a lost cause. During January 1865 food shipments from Georgia to Virginia were briefly reestablished when the Quartermaster Department invoked its regulatory powers under the 1863 Railroad Act.[41] Theoretically quartermaster control of Georgia's rail transportation continued until the war's end, but except for the tenuous rail connection leading northward from Augusta, the department had little to supervise.

Military transportation was not the only phase of quartermaster operations involving black labor. Blacks also played a significant part in provisioning the army. Designated as a general supply agency, the Quartermaster Department made or purchased virtually all articles of military necessity except arms and munitions, which the Ordnance Bureau provided, and foodstuffs, which were secured through the Subsistence Department. All agencies depended upon quartermaster transportation, however, and bureaucratic supply functions frequently overlapped, resulting in jurisdictional conflicts or various ad hoc arrangements. Discerning a clear pattern of black employment in these circumstances is exceedingly difficult. The procurement of farm produce offers a case in point.

Few items were more vital to the Southern war effort than food, yet no government agency had exclusive control of Georgia's agricultural products. Initially subsistence commissaries furnished food for human consumption and quartermasters supplied grain and fodder for military livestock. In 1863 the division of labor grew more confusing when the War Department delegated special "tithe quartermasters" to collect the Confederacy's new "tax-in-kind," a 10 percent share of all staples, food crops, and slaughtered hogs.[42] Black workers helped sustain the food supply network under various official auspices. Squads of ten or more slaves traveled with quartermaster purchasing agents to prepare fodder for shipment. During trips to remote and sparsely settled cattle ranges, Savannah purchasing agent Samuel Harn took as his "immediate helpers" two trusted plantation slaves. Detailed white subagents drove livestock to designated shipping points, while Harn's black assistants guarded large quantities of Confederate currency "worn in a flat padded roll on the person."[43] Commissary officials sought twenty-five black men to work in the government bakery at Macon, and in Albany the district tithe quartermaster borrowed a slave force from the Engineer Bureau to build storage facilities for grain. [44]

Black involvement in light manufacturing enterprises reflected comparable bureaucratic fragmentation. With a logic predicated on abundance rather than scarcity, government leatherwork was divided between two agencies. The Ordnance Bureau made cartridge boxes, saddles, and artillery harnesses, while the Quartermaster Department produced harnesses for draft animals and shoes for the army. Conflicts over hides and leather supplies caused the Atlanta Arsenal to establish its own tanyard, employing 15 slaves, in Coweta County. [45] The majority of Georgia's black leatherworkers were probably shoemakers, however, laboring either for private firms like the Richmond County shop of James W. Burch, whose staff included 10 to 15 Negroes in 1862, or at major shoe factories operated by the Quartermaster Department in Augusta and Columbus, where a total of 250 black workers were required to maintain output in 1864 and 1865. [46]

Weaponry and munitions production accounted for a substantial percentage of Georgia's black industrial employment. Here again, bureaucratic arrangements were anything but tidy. With five Confederate arsenals, two armories, an ordnance laboratory, a large gunpowder factory, a naval shipyard and ironworks, two civilian rolling mills, and numerous private manufacturers of small arms and military implements, Georgia by 1863 rivaled even the more industrialized state of Virginia as a supplier of war matériel. In Georgia as in Virginia, however, military manufacturing lacked central coordination and ordnance officials competed among themselves for men and matériel. Black workers in particular became objects of a logistical tug-of-war between the army's Bureau of Ordnance, the navy's Bureau of Ordnance and Hydrography, and numerous civilian firms at work on government contracts. Inevitably these agencies also competed with government enterprises like quartermaster transportation shops, which hired slave carpenters, wheelwrights, blacksmiths, and other skilled artisans for wagon production. [47] The ultimate effect of this rivalry was to ensure that black labor would be distributed more or less evenly across the entire spectrum of Georgia's burgeoning war industries.

TABLE 17

Black Labor at Selected Georgia Ordnance Facilities, 1862–1865*

Employer	1862		1863		1864		1865	
	Sought	Hired	Sought	Hired	Sought	Hired	Sought	Hired
Confederate gov't ordnance establishments								
C.S. Armory, Macon	30			115	150	142	250	105
C.S. Arsenal, Macon		30				198		190
C.S. Central Laboratory, Macon				120	240		250	127
C.S. Arsenal, Columbus			20		10			
C.S. Naval Iron Works, Columbus			20					
C.S. Navy Yard, Saffold, Early County		84						
C.S. Powder Works, Augusta				43		98		88
C.S. Arsenal, Atlanta		31		19				
C.S. Arsenal and Ordnance Depot, Savannah					40			
Ordnance Depot, Dalton		8		4				
Private armories and mfgrs. of small arms and military implements								
Samuel H. Griswold Pistol Factory, Griswoldville		22				40		
"Dixie Works," V. Werner and Co., Macon			10		40		40	

(Continued)

144

TABLE 17—*Continued*

Employer	1862 Sought	1862 Hired	1863 Sought	1863 Hired	1864 Sought	1864 Hired	1865 Sought	1865 Hired
Louis Haiman and Brother Sword and Pistol Factory, Columbus	25		50		70			
"Columbus Armory," John D. Gray			45				35	

Sources (listed by individual facility in the order of their appearance in table): Macon Armory: James H. Burton to Colonel Jack Brown, July 19, 1862, RG 109, Chap. 4, vols. 20, 29, and 31, National Archives; "Record of Employees, Master Armorer's Office," ibid., vol. 53; "Return of Employees and Articles Manufactured at the Armory, 1864–1865," ibid., vol. 42; Macon *Daily Telegraph*, July 19, 1862, p. 2; December 8, 1863, p. 2; December 14, 1864, p. 2. *Macon Arsenal:* "Record of Work Performed at the Arsenal, 1862," RG 109, chap. 4, vol. 21, NA; "Record of Clothing issued to Detailed Soldiers and Slaves Employed at the Arsenal, 1864–1865," ibid., vol. 60. *Macon Laboratory:* M. B. Meadows to John W. Mallet, March 2(?), 1863, RG 109, chap. 4, vol. 5, NA; W. H. McMain to John W. Mallet, December 20, 1864, ibid., vol. 37; Macon *Daily Telegraph*, December 10, 1863, p. 2; January 26, 1864, p. 1; December 13, 1864, p. 2. *Columbus Arsenal:* Columbus *Daily Sun*, October 10, 1863, p. 2; March 20, 1864, p. 1. *Columbus Naval Iron Works:* Columbus *Daily Sun*, April 17, 1863, p. 2. *Navy Yard, Saffold, Ga.:* Macon *Daily Telegraph*, March 18, 1862, p. 2; Columbus *Daily Sun*, April 11, 1862, p. 3; Maxine Turner, "Naval and River Operations on the Apalachicola and Chattahoochee Rivers, 1861–1865," *Alabama Historical Quarterly* 36 (Fall–Winter, 1974): 214–15. *Augusta Powder Works:* "Reports of Work Performed, Superintendent of the Powder Factory, November 1862–April, 1865," Records of Ordnance Establishments at Augusta, Georgia, RG 109 (no chapter or volume designation), NA. *Atlanta Arsenal:* "Time Books, Atlanta Arsenal, 1862–1863," RG 109, chap. 4, vols. 81 and 84, NA. *Savannah Arsenal and Ordnance Depot:* Savannah *Republican*, April 27, 1864, p. 2; September 19, 1864, p. 2. *Dalton Ordnance Depot:* "Return of Hired Men employed at Ordnance Depot, Dalton, Georgia . . . 1862," and same for 1863, in RG 109, chap. 4, vols. 145 and 133 respectively. *Griswoldville Pistol Factory:* W. C. Hodgkins to R. M. Cuyler, July 19, 1862, RG 109, chap. 4, vol. 3 NA; E. Merton Coulter, *The Confederate States of America, 1861–1865* (Baton Rouge, 1950), 110. *Dixie Works:* Macon *Daily Telegraph*, November 18, 1863, p. 1; December 2, 1863, p. 2; February 17, 1864, p. 2; December 28, 1864, p. 1. *Haiman and Brother:* Columbus *Daily Sun*, June 10, 1862, p. 2; January 1, 1863, p. 2; December 16, 1863, p. 2. *John D. Gray:* Columbus *Daily Sun*, October 27, 1863, p. 2; December 20, 1864, p. 2.

Ordnance establishments in Georgia hired black craftsmen from virtually all branches of the mechanical and building trades, together with hundreds of unskilled or semiskilled slave laborers. Although detailed records survive from only four of the state's major government installations, and for no private arms works, newspaper advertisements and other unofficial documents reveal broad trends in black employment. As indicated in Table 17, both government and civilian ordnance plants hired blacks from 1862 onward. Demand for black workers increased roughly twofold between 1863 and 1865, but actual employment levels rose much more slowly—an indication, perhaps, that slave-based industrial expansion was approaching its practical limits late in the war. At the peak of their operations in mid-1864, Georgia's ordnance facilities employed at least six hundred and perhaps as many as eight hundred to twelve hundred black workers. Statistics from industrial establishments in Augusta and Macon illustrate how the importance of nonwhite labor increased over time.

The South's largest gunpowder factory, the Confederate States Powder Works at Augusta, commenced operation in 1862 with a predominantly white work force. Little change occurred during the first year, and as late as the second half of 1863 only one-third of all Powder Works employees were black. Conversion to black labor occurred principally during the 1864 Sherman invasion, when diversion of white manpower for military purposes threatened to impair ordnance production at various Augusta facilities. [48] Average weekly employment of blacks doubled in 1864, and from February onward the majority of Powder Works employees were Negroes. After the fall of Atlanta in September, Colonel George W. Rains reported that "but few able-bodied [white] men" were involved in Powder Works operations. [49] Black employment reached a peak of ninety-eight during the week of November 8, 1864, and roughly 60 percent of the total work force was nonwhite from January through April 1865 (see Table 18). In all probability, these statistics refer only to slave employees, omitting a group of twenty-seven free Negroes whose names appear separately in official records. [50]

In July 1862 a dozen impressed slaves helped unload thirty railroad cars

TABLE 18

Black Employment at Confederate States Powder Works, Augusta, 1863–1865 *

	Average Weekly Size of Total Work Force	Average Number of Black Employees	Percentage of Blacks in Total Work Force
Aug. 28–Dec. 28, 1863	88	33	37%
Jan. 1–Dec. 31, 1864	118	63	53%
Jan. 7–April 28, 1865	116	69	59%

*Source: "Reports of Work Performed, Superintendent of the Powder Factory, November, 1862–April, 1865" in Records of Ordnance Establishments at Augusta, Georgia, RG 109 (no chapter or volume designations), National Archives.

of machinery consigned to the newly established Confederate Armory at Macon.[51] From that point onward black workers played a steadily expanding role in armory activities. As early as August 1862, when the facility employed only 34 whites, a "considerable number of negro carpenters and laborers" were already at work on armory buildings.[52] By January 1863 the armory's work force consisted of 57 whites and 79 blacks. Twenty-three of the blacks were "Mechanics & Carpenters," and the remaining 56 were laborers.[53] Daily employment apparently hovered at or near the January level of 79 for well over a year. On March 10, 1864, three months after conversion to annual slave-hiring contracts, the armory's black work force still numbered about eighty bondsmen, but that situation was soon to change.[54] Within four months black employment doubled, climbing to 164 in July, only to drop drastically the next month when over half of the armory's slaves were assigned to emergency duty with the Engineer Bureau at the Atlanta front.[55] Although many bondsmen never returned to Ordnance Bureau employ, the armory's slaves were slowly reassembled and by October 1864 blacks again constituted approximately half the total work force, a percentage that remained fairly constant until the end of the war (see Table 19).

As the number of black ordnance workers increased, so too did the

TABLE 19

Black Employment at Confederate States Armory, Macon, July 1864– February 1865 *

	Total Employees	Black Employees	Percentage of Blacks in Total Work Force
June 1864	252	130	52%
July	309	164	53%
August	155	53	34%
September	188	72	38%
October	204	101	50%
November	245	137	56%
December	241	133	55%
January 1865	199	94	47%
February	209	105	50%

*Source: "Return of Employees and Articles Manufactured at the [Macon] Armory, 1864–1865," in RG 109, chap. 4, vol. 42.

range of their duties and responsibilities. Black occupational patterns reflected both the needs of individual ordnance establishments and the skills possessed by slave or free Negro workers. Approximately 10 percent to 20 percent of the blacks at Georgia's major ordnance facilities were skilled craftsmen, while the remaining 70 percent to 90 percent of nonwhite workers were classified simply as general laborers (see Tables 20 and 21). Inevitably, therefore, most skilled manufacturing jobs fell to whites in spite of the fact that ordnance works hired two to three times more black artisans, especially in the building trades, than would have been obtained from a random sample of the state's adult male slave population.[56]

The tasks assigned black workmen varied greatly at different ordnance installations. In Macon, for example, most black employees of the Confederate States Armory, Arsenal, and Central Laboratory helped erect

TABLE 20
Black Occupations at Confederate States Armory, Macon, 1864–1865*

	Total Black Employees	Carpenters	Brickmasons	Laborers
June 1864	130	12 (9%)	7 (5%)	111 (85%)
July	164	13 (8%)	6 (4%)	145 (88%)
August	53	1 (2%)	5 (9%)	47 (89%)
September	72	13 (18%)	5 (7%)	54 (75%)
October	101	9 (9%)	5 (5%)	87 (86%)
November	137	12 (9%)	3 (2%)	122 (89%)
December	133	13 (10%)	4 (3%)	116 (87%)
January 1865	94	13 (14%)	5 (5%)	76 (81%)
February	105	9 (9%)	5 (5%)	91 (87%)

**Source:* "Return of Employees and Articles Manufactured at the [Macon] Armory, 1864–1865," in RG 109, chap. 4, vol. 42, National Archives. Percentages are rounded off and may total slightly more or less than 100.

TABLE 21

Black Occupations at Confederate States Arsenal, Macon, 1864–1865*

	Total Black Employees	Carpenters	Brickmasons	Cooks	Laborers	Unclassified
1864	198	8 (4%)	14 (7%)	5 (3%)	171 (86%)	1 (.5%)
1865	190	3 (2%)	10 (5%)	2 (1%)	123 (65%)	52 (27%)

*Source: "Record of Clothing Issued to Detailed Soldiers and Slaves Employed at the [Macon] Arsenal, 1864–1865," in RG 109, chap. 4, vol. 60, National Archives. Percentages are rounded off and may total slightly more or less than 100.

temporary or permanent buildings to house men and machinery. Nearly all carpenters and brickmasons at the Macon facilities were Negroes, and blacks also bore the brunt of semiskilled construction labor. The Macon Armory's standard slave-hiring contract stipulated that "Employment will be 'in grading land, making & hauling brick, waiting upon bricklayers & carpenters, cutting wood, burning charcoal, and generally upon such work as may be desired.'"[57] Officials at the Central Laboratory were even more specific, explaining that Negro brickyard hands would drive wagons, dig clay for brick machines, tend fires at brick kilns, carry brick molds, wheel bricks, and sort them from the kilns. Other black laborers would grade land, dig foundations, and act as helpers to carpenters or bricklayers.[58] At the Atlanta Arsenal blacks were apparently involved more directly in manufacturing activities. During 1862–63 the arsenal's black work force included at least 23 laborers, 5 carpenters, 2 teamsters, 1 gun cleaner, 2 blacksmiths, and 1 tinner.[59] The Augusta Powder Works employed nonwhite labor in at least fifteen different capacities. Blacks worked in the refinery, the cooling house (for lead shot), and in sulphur processing. They cleaned steam engines; fired boilers and kettles; burned charcoal; cut and stacked cordwood; tended gardens; did grading, road work, and excavation; laid pipe; fabricated iron bolts and other blacksmith articles; shoveled coal; hauled sand, saltpeter, and gunpowder; served as teamsters and stable boys; and did various types of mechanical, carpentry, and repair work.[60]

Black skilled artisans were probably more indispensable to private weapons producers than to the government. Generally unable to secure military details for white workers, civilian entrepreneurs relied on black craftsmen to perform a variety of skilled tasks. Scores of Negro blacksmiths and strikers, for example, could be counted among the four hundred employees at Prussian emigrant Louis Haiman's large sword and pistol factory in Columbus.[61] Antebellum railroad builder John D. Gray received a Confederate contract for Enfield rifles early in the war, and employed Negro carpenters and blacksmiths at his Columbus armory. In 1863 Gray also removed a substantial slave force from the north Georgia manufacturing town of Graysville, where extensive lime kilns and facilities for gunstock production were located.[62] A slave blacksmith named Augustus Thompson worked briefly in the rifle-making operation of Cook & Brother after the firm moved its armory from New Orleans to Athens, Georgia. Detailed to the Augusta Arsenal in 1863, Thompson helped "iron off" gun carriages for the rest of the war.[63] In Macon a "refugee" industry known as the Dixie Works actively recruited Negro blacksmiths to work in its "extensive machine and manufacturing shops" where a variety of military implements were produced.[64]

Most Georgia weapons makers turned to black craftsmen out of necessity, but some industrialists, like Connecticut native Samuel H. Griswold, employed slave workers as a matter of choice. When Griswold's cotton gin factory was converted to military production early in the war, skilled black mechanics had been part of the labor force for at least a decade. In March 1862 Griswold constructed machinery for the manufacture of Colt-pattern repeating pistols, the first specimens of which were submitted for government approval four months later. An Ordnance Bureau official visited the Griswoldville factory on July 15, 1862, and "found twenty-two . . . machines worked by twenty-four . . . hands—twenty-two . . . of whom are Negro Slaves."[65] One hundred pistols were in the process of being manufactured, and production capacity was estimated at five pistols per day. The weapons subsequently passed inspection, and a local newspaper editor marveled that Colt pistols "as well finished as those made by the patentee himself" could be produced by "men who had never seen a pistol shop, or a single tool or piece of machinery for making them." By

1864 Griswold had a total of forty black workmen in his employ, and pistol production continued until the facilities were destroyed by Union forces during the Sherman invasion.[66]

Georgia weapons makers often found vital raw materials to be as scarce as skilled labor. Imported stocks of gunmetal lasted for only a year or so, and by 1862 a serious "iron famine" threatened to halt armaments production unless domestic ore supplies were quickly developed.[67] At the outbreak of hostilities Georgia's embryonic iron industry consisted of approximately seven blast furnaces, most of which operated sporadically, two commercial rolling mills, and a number of small foundries attached to machine shops or other manufacturing establishments.[68] Initially neglected by Confederate authorities, the Georgia facilities assumed new importance after major iron-producing regions of Tennessee and the border states fell into Union hands. Although direct government intervention in the state's iron industry was rare, private efforts to expand pig iron production in northwest Georgia received strong endorsement from the Ordnance Bureau.[69] Before the Atlanta campaign interrupted mining and smelting activities, at least three of the state's six antebellum ironmakers had reactivated or expanded blast furnaces in Bartow County, and four new iron companies had begun operations in Dade County or elsewhere.[70] Restricted by primitive technology, Southern iron production like Southern agriculture was a "labor-intensive" undertaking. And at ironworks no less than on cotton plantations, the people who labored most intensively were probably Negro slaves.

Wartime manpower shortages and production demands accelerated a shift from free to slave labor that had begun in some branches of Georgia's iron industry during the 1850s. Although specific numbers and percentages remain largely conjectural, it is clear that Georgia's principal ironmakers entered the war with a vital nucleus of trained black employees capable of sustaining production under minimal white supervision. After passage of the first Confederate conscription act in April 1862, older Georgia firms like the Alatoona Iron Works lost nearly all of their white workers, but were able to continue blast furnace operations "by using some negroes who are expert in the business."[71] In the summer of 1863 veteran Bartow County ironmaster John W. Lewis had one furnace in blast

151

"worked nearly entirely by negroes," and was anxious to start up a second furnace he had recently constructed. Pleading with the secretary of war for additional military details, Lewis complained that his eight white employees found the blacks "not only awkward, but hard to manage." Still, his original furnace was turning out limited amounts of pig iron for the government and producing considerably larger quantities of military cooking utensils.[72] Another antebellum firm, the Bartow Iron Works, hired twenty male slaves from one owner in January 1864, agreeing to remove the bondsmen southward if Federal troops approached. By the end of June the Bartow Works' slaves had been evacuated to Macon, where the Confederate States Armory provided temporary employment.[73] As late as July 1864 the Athens Iron Manufacturing Company employed about fifty black miners and colliers at an undetermined north Georgia location.[74]

The experiences of the Empire State Coal and Iron Mining Company reveal the importance of black labor for new firms entering Georgia's wartime iron industry. Formed by a group of Macon investors late in 1862, the company purchased a "large iron Estate" in the Wills Valley section of Dade County, where it planned to erect two or more steam-powered "hot blast" furnaces. Hoping to begin actual iron production by mid-summer of 1863, the firm sought to hire three hundred Negroes in January of that year, probably for the purpose of accumulating necessary stockpiles of iron ore, limestone, charcoal, and construction materials. Subsequent newspaper advertisements suggest that approximately two hundred bondsmen were actually employed, a portion of whom had formerly worked as railroad hands.[75] In February 1863 the company sold an additional one thousand shares of stock in order to purchase a permanent slave force, and by April the firm was ready to hire stonecutters, quarrymen, and stonemasons to build its furnaces. How far construction subsequently progressed is unclear, but during late August the company's black workers were hastily sent to Macon as Union troops advanced into northwestern Georgia. At least one of the firm's officers remained in Dade County during September, when the region was briefly occupied by General William S. Rosecrans, and it is possible that iron operations resumed after the Battle of Chickamauga when Federal forces withdrew into Tennessee.[76] If bad weather did not halt the company's activities during the winter of 1863, the commencement of the Atlanta campaign in May 1864 unquestionably did. Yet even during the Sherman invasion, plans for continuing iron production in Wills Valley persisted. As late as November 1864 an optimistic stockholder described the work as only "temporarily suspended" and expressed confidence that the Empire company would "without doubt soon be again in successful operation."[77]

Despite the absence of detailed business records, there can be little question that pig-iron production in Confederate Georgia depended heavily on slave labor. But if most black ironworkers were employed at blast furnaces, a few highly skilled bondsmen also performed vital functions at foundries and rolling mills. The story of Georgia's largest iron producer, the Etowah Manufacturing and Mining Company, helps illuminate the relative importance of free versus slave labor in various branches of the industry. Founded in the mid-1840s by former Georgia Congressman Mark Anthony Cooper, the Etowah company was an integrated industrial enterprise similar in some respects to the much larger Tredegar Iron Works in Virginia. On the eve of secession the company's assets consisted of twelve thousand acres of land in Cass (later Bartow), Cherokee, Whitfield, and Dade counties, two blast furnaces and foundries, a rolling mill, a factory for making nails and railroad spikes, a grist mill, a commercial flour mill, and a privately owned branch railroad intersecting the Western and Atlantic trunk line near Cartersville. These assets were conservatively assessed at $400,000.[78]

All facets of iron work, from mining and smelting to the manufacture and sale of castings and rolling-mill products, were handled directly by Etowah employees, the majority of whom were white. Writing in 1859, Cooper stated that the Etowah "furnaces and other operations in iron" employed "five or six hundred operators and laborers, and afford support to a population of about two thousand people of all ages and sexes. Of these, about one hundred are blacks." Cooper personally owned twenty-two slaves, half of whom were adults in 1860, while the Etowah Manufacturing and Mining Company owned approximately eleven bondsmen some two years earlier.[79] By the beginning of the war, however, nonfree labor had probably assumed greater significance both qualitatively and quantitatively than the preceding statements would suggest. Like other Southern ironmakers, Cooper introduced skilled blacks into his rolling-mill operations during the 1850s. From 1857 onward, for instance, he hired the slave puddler Davy Cobbs from the Tredegar Iron Works in Richmond for $300 per year.[80] By the end of 1859 Cooper had evidently decided upon a further long-term conversion to slave labor, and he sought to hire fifty Negroes "to be employed in the iron business for 1, 2, 3 or 5 years." Among the bondsmen obtained in response to this advertisement were a number of young male laborers at $170 per year and at least two slaves whose hiring rate of $225 was commensurate with the customary price for black skilled workers.[81]

Coal shortages reduced the Etowah Works' output to only one-third of what was anticipated during the war's first year, and this condition led, in turn, to an increased dependence on black labor. By the time coal supplies arrived in the spring of 1862 Cooper complained bitterly that lack of work had forced many of his white rolling-mill operators to join the army and that their absence reduced mill operations by 50 percent.[82] During the next two years black workers were unquestionably involved in making railroad car axles, plate, and other iron products at Etowah. After the works were finally evacuated in July 1864 the company offered to sell all remaining machinery and assets including "15 likely NEGROES—a portion of them skilled Rolling Mill Operatives, unsurpassed by any in the Confederacy[,] . . . the negroes alone being the best property now offered [for sale] in the country."[83]

At least one of the Etowah slaves, a rolling-mill heater named William Kuhn, was acquired by the Naval Iron Works in Columbus. The facility's chief engineer valued Kuhn's services enough to offer a $1,000 reward when the artisan escaped in September 1864.[84] The fate of other Etowah bondsmen remains in doubt, but some may have gone to Columbia, South Carolina, where machinery from Atlanta's important Gate City Rolling Mill had been sent prior to the Georgia city's capture. Whether or not the Atlanta mill employed slaves earlier in the war is unclear, but late in 1860 the firm had considered purchasing the slave puddler Davy Cobbs, and in 1863 one of the mill's proprietors listed an unspecified number of Negroes among his $500,000 assets.[85] Fragmentary evidence suggests that black laborers and skilled workers played at least a minor role in Georgia's numerous smaller foundries and iron establishments. The presence in 1862 of one slave molder, one blacksmith, and one engineer out of a skilled work force of nine at Macon's Findlay Iron Works may be taken as suggestive of employment patterns elsewhere in the state.[86]

Iron, of course, was not the only mineral resource mined and processed in Confederate Georgia. Equally vital to the Southern war effort were the rich nitre deposits found in natural limestone caves throughout the state's iron-producing region. The basic ingredient of gunpowder, nitre (or salt-peter) was obtained by digging earth from nitre caves, puddling it for several days, and treating the leach-water with potash to produce potassium nitrate. "It was no holiday duty, this nitre digging," Confederate Ordnance Chief Josiah Gorgas later recalled. "It was a rude, wild sort of service."[87] It was also, in Georgia as elsewhere, a service employing substantial numbers of Negro slaves.

Nitre production began under private auspices in northwestern Georgia during late 1861 or early 1862. Although a half dozen or more sites were eventually developed, activity centered around the Bartow County Salt-petre Works, located near Kingston. Initially owned and operated by two Atlanta druggists, the works were seized by the government in June 1862 and placed under the control of the newly created Nitre and Mining Bureau. Considered "one of the most important single saltpetre production units in the entire Confederacy," the Bartow Cave quickly increased its output from eighty to four hundred pounds of nitre per day, and by August 1862 employed a total of 66 slaves. Most of the blacks worked as laborers, teamsters, and cooks, although one slave carpenter helped construct the tanks and hoppers used in leaching. During the next twelve months Nitre and Mining Bureau operations continued to expand. Georgia was divided into at least two administrative subunits, and in July 1863 the superintendent of Nitre District 14, which included Bartow County, sought to hire 100 slaves to work "at points in the State of Georgia."[88] By May 1864 most of Georgia's nitre deposits were behind Union lines, but there is some evidence that production relying heavily on black labor was resumed during the closing months of the war. According to a report submitted in 1865, Captain Henry Pattillo Farrow, in charge of Georgia's Nitre District 14, employed a total of nine white "exempts," 26 conscripts, and 185 Negroes, while Professor Nathaniel Alpheus Pratt, Nitre Bureau chemist and superintendent at Augusta, controlled 64 conscripts and 190 Negroes.[89] Viewed in the aggregate, nearly 80 percent of the Nitre and Mining Bureau's Georgia work force was black.

Georgia bondsmen were the pillars of at least one other wartime extractive industry: saltmaking. During antebellum times the vast quantities of salt needed for meat preservation and other purposes came mainly from England, but British imports ceased abruptly in 1862 when Union blockading vessels closed Southern ports. In an effort to stave off potentially disastrous shortages of the mineral, Governor Joseph E. Brown purchased salt for his state from firms in Virginia and Louisiana, while the Georgia legislature passed measures to stimulate domestic production. Within months, dozens of Georgia-owned saltworks dotted the seaboard from Savannah to the Florida gulf coast, and evaporating facilities were proliferating at saline wells or springs in the interior.[90]

Typical of the many coastal enterprises conducted by Georgia residents was the Empire Salt Company, located three miles west of St. Marks, Florida. Organized by nine Richmond County, Georgia, stockholders during October 1862, the company started out with $8,000 capital and high commercial expectations. By early 1863 salt production from four 500-gallon boilers and six salting kettles stood at twenty bushels per day. The company's fifteen-man labor force consisted of one white superintendent, two stockholders, and twelve blacks who worked as woodchoppers, teamsters, firemen, and laborers. "We run our Boilers & Kettles day & night," the superintendent explained, stressing that except for himself and the two previously mentioned stockholders the firm had "no white men employed at all in any capacity."[91] Similar patterns of labor distribution prevailed at most other saltworks regardless of type or location. The firm of Denmead and Johnson, which leased a salt spring in Cobb County during 1862, employed only one white supervisor who was given "the entire management of the laborers engaged in said business . . . who are slaves (negroes)."[92] Wealthy Georgia planters like Howell Cobb and

David Crenshaw Barrow pooled their resources by furnishing overseers and squads of slaves for a saltworks which Barrow operated in Florida. Confederate commissary officers needed thirty bondsmen in 1863 for a government saltworks near Savannah, and offered wages of $20 per month plus "rations, medecine [sic], and proper medical attention," together with financial compensation to owners whose slaves were lost to the enemy.[93]

These last inducements attest to the precarious labor situation in which many Georgia salt producers found themselves. Few salt companies could have functioned without black workers, but persuading skeptical masters to hire out slaves for debilitating labor in close proximity to Union lines was no easy matter. In January 1863, for example, the Macon Salt Association's "inability to hire negro labor" led to a formal dissolution of the company. Stockholders "agreed to give up the concern to a new Association that will furnish the negroes themselves." Any original stockholders could join the new firm by appearing at a stipulated time with a designated portion of the required slave force "ready to be sent to the works."[94] Engineer Captain Lemuel P. Grant encountered even greater obstacles in his efforts to establish a Confederate saltworks at the saline wells of Clarke County, Alabama. Hoping eventually to provide salt for government agencies throughout Georgia, Grant dispatched agents from Atlanta to hire two hundred black laborers for preliminary grading and excavation at the Alabama site. The missions all proved futile, however, and during the spring and summer of 1863 the government employed an average of only thirty-five bondsmen at the Clarke County salines, most of whom Grant obtained from an Atlanta party in exchange for a contract to build duplicate railroad bridges. No salt was ever produced at the government works, and in August 1863 the project was abandoned.[95] Other salt companies succeeded in hiring black workers, only to lose them once operations began. During 1862 the Columbus Salt Association suffered a serious setback when eleven of its slaves defected to a Union blockading vessel off St. Joseph's Bay, Florida. Saltworks quickly became prime targets of naval attack, and throughout the war Georgia slaves availed themselves of the escape opportunities offered by Federal raiders. Black flight from saltworks along Georgia's coast peaked during the summer of 1864 when over one hundred bondsmen reached Union lines in a two-month period.[96]

Mineral processing and weaponry production accounted for only a portion of Georgia's black industrial employment. Afro-Americans participated in a host of additional manufacturing activities which supported Southern armies and sustained the Confederacy as a nation at war. Blacks were recruited for tasks as peripheral as button making, as transitory as the fabrication of makeshift moss blankets, and as indispensable as textile production and lumbering. In the absence of manuscript records from the bulk of individual business firms, one can do little more than speculate as to the extent of black involvement in various occupations. Lumbering, a pursuit which employed the largest aggregate work force of any Southern industry, offers a case in point. Throughout most of the antebellum era Georgia was the South's chief lumber-producing state, and Savannah's sawmills alone employed over two hundred people, a "large proportion" of whom were black. According to the most careful student of the subject, "Free Negroes and slaves made up a large share of the unskilled and semi-skilled labor force employed" in Georgia lumbering. Serving on racially mixed rafting crews, and frequently trained as sawyers and engineers, blacks also performed a number of less glamorous jobs. "As axemen, hewers, stackers, and in other capacities, they provided the bulk of the labor in the antebellum Georgia lumber industry."[97] Wartime lumber production was no doubt equally dependent on black skill and brawn, as numerous small firms struggled to fill huge government orders. Regrettably, however, records for this segment of the state's economy are apparently nonexistent.

With thirty-three cotton and eleven woolen mills in 1860, Georgia led the South in textile manufacturing as well as lumbering. Although a number of the state's early textile mills employed black workers, slave labor had diminished in importance during late antebellum times as more and more poor whites entered the factories. Some firms considered hired bondsmen too expensive, while other companies feared slavery would make mill work unattractive to whites.[98] There is reason to believe that racially exclusionist labor policies were modified and gradually abandoned during the war, but evidence on the point is largely impressionistic. Textile firms like the Columbus Factory Company counted some thirty blacks among their 110 employees as early as the spring of 1861, but this figure is potentially misleading since it includes bondsmen who worked in the company's sawmill, shoe shop, tanyard, and grist mill as well as in the textile industry itself.[99] Another Muscogee County firm, the Grant Factory, employed an all-white and predominantly female work force of 80 at its Columbus cotton mill in 1861. By 1864, however, racial barriers had apparently fallen and the company was offering a cash reward for the return of a runaway slave named George.[100] One of Georgia's oldest and largest mills, the Eagle Manufacturing Company, wanted to hire a half-dozen slaves as early as 1862, and advertised two bondsmen as runaways the following year. In July 1864 the company offered "good wages and steady employment" to twenty black workers.[101] Even the Roswell Cotton Mills, which sold a valuable slave in 1860 and employed only three bondsmen in its 1861 work force of 350, apparently hired a few black workers as the war progressed. In any event, the mill's quarterly and semiannual payments for "negro hire" rose dramatically in 1863, far surpassing the level of increase which could plausibly be attributed to monetary inflation.[102]

Although highly suggestive, these examples are too few in number to constitute a reliable barometer of trends in the textile industry as a whole. Similar evidentiary gaps preclude analysis of black employment in most other areas of wartime manufacturing. At the Rock Island Paper Mill near Columbus, for example, blacks comprised at least half of a forty-person work force between 1861 and 1864.[103] This information points toward a major role for bondsmen in wartime paper production, but without comparable evidence from the larger Marietta Paper Mill and the smaller Pioneer Mill near Athens any judgment remains tentative.[104] On balance, it seems reasonable to conclude that white manpower shortages affected Georgia's government agencies and private entrepreneurs in roughly equal proportion during the war, and that most types of industrial activity grew increasingly dependent on black labor with the passage of time.

159

II

ALTHOUGH BLACK EMPLOYMENT DATA is fragmentary, surviving records shed considerable light on the relationship between wartime industrial expansion and the declining institutional stability of chattel slavery. To assess the impact of wartime occupational changes, one must consider both the size and the internal composition of Georgia's nonagricultural black labor force. Aggregate employment must be treated as one factor in a larger equation which takes account of the previous occupational background of black military and industrial laborers, the method by which their services were obtained, the duration of their employment, and the geographical location of their work. The first of these considerations—previous employment status—deserves far more rigorous analysis than is possible in the present state of the evidence. Enough is known about slave employment patterns during the late antebellum era, however, to permit at least a speculative assessment of the character, magnitude, and significance of wartime occupational trends.

On the eve of secession a total of twelve thousand to twenty-four thousand slave and free black Georgians were probably engaged in "industrial" activity, defined here as any nonagricultural pursuit except household and domestic service. Of this number, perhaps eight thousand could legitimately be called artisans, mostly plantation carpenters or blacksmiths with rudimentary skills, but also including a nucleus of highly trained industrial workers.[105] Viewed collectively, nonagricultural slaves constituted a heterogeneous amalgam of unskilled factory and construction laborers, plantation craftsmen, urban artisans, and workers in crop-processing or extractive enterprises. Both qualitatively and numerically, however, Georgia's black industrial work force was adequate to meet the modest needs of a planting society. Although mechanical labor was never plentiful, enough black workers existed even during the cotton boom of the 1850s to sustain a respectable industrial growth rate in Dixie's aspiring "Empire State."[106]

In Georgia as elsewhere the guns of Fort Sumter shattered the fragile equilibrium of local labor supplies. With much of the white male work force diverted to combat service, securing black labor for burgeoning war industries and military support activities became an urgent necessity. But altering established patterns of slave employment was seldom a simple matter. Skill disparities between bond and free workers, white hostility to black competition, continuing demands for plantation labor, and skepticism over the morale, health, and physical security of industrial bondsmen all impeded efforts to redirect Georgia slaves into wartime pursuits. In the face of such obstacles, mobilizing black industrial labor constituted both a benchmark of official resolve and a test of the slave system's institutional flexibility. The question ultimately at issue was not the feasibility of slave-based industrial expansion (something most Confederates took for granted) but rather the capacity of slavery as an institution to absorb the shocks of rapid occupational change.

Wartime employment which transferred plantation slaves directly into nonagricultural jobs placed particular stress on the slave system's internal stability. Black fortification labor, for example, struck directly at the legal and institutional foundations of rural bondage. The typical bondsman who worked on Georgia's military defenses was not an urban or industrial slave, but rather an unskilled adult male field hand impressed from an interior agricultural district. Inevitably his stint as a military laborer involved radical breaks with the regimen of rural plantation life, changes that were similar in many ways to those experienced by slaves involved in the refugee process. Like refugeeing, fortification work meant an end to the plantation's cultural insularity and physical isolation. When assembled by the hundreds or thousands to help fortify strategic points near major urban areas, black military laborers mingled with slaves and free Negroes from all parts of Georgia, exchanging information and forming firsthand impressions about the meaning and progress of the war. Confederate labor policies ensured that the impact of such experiences would extend well beyond the bondsmen immediately involved. In contrast to other types of nonagricultural employment, fortification building was nearly always a short-term, temporary assignment for blacks. Within a few weeks or months a given project was usually finished, or else fresh squads of slaves were brought in to continue the work. In the ongoing labor exchange dictated by impressment schedules, black workers became the living links connecting front-line areas with remote plantations. The frequent labor drafts imposed on central and southwestern Georgia left few plantations untouched and kept many slave quarters in regular contact with the outside world. Masters generally considered the repeated coming and going of black military laborers to be an unsettling process even when it posed no direct challenge to white authority. In the minds of many planters, eagerness to regain possession of valuable slave property was tempered by a brooding suspicion that impressed bondsmen would return to "demoralize" blacks who had remained at home. [107]

Some masters worried less about a slave's impending return than about the circumstances that had surrounded his departure. Planters who traditionally tried to cloak themselves in an aura of paternalistic omnipotence feared that the impressment process itself might undermine their authority. When Confederate enrolling officers encountered widespread hostility from slaveowners in southwestern Georgia during the summer of 1862, a local newspaper editor summed up prevailing white sentiment on the subject. Even the most patriotic planter, he felt, would be deeply disturbed by "an arbitrary young officer, coming into his premises and violently seizing his servants before his eyes, and he unable to protect them." Among the many evils of impressment this was the "worst hurt of all," since a master's ability to protect his slaves from "external violence" formed the "great basis of subordination" and was the "grand substratum of the whole system."[108]

Although military labor drafts ran counter to established norms of plantation authority, impressment probably posed less real danger to slave discipline than most masters claimed. Debates over government labor policy involved a variety of issues, and as often as not paternalist rhetoric was the handmaiden of economic self-interest. Protecting one's dependents from "external violence" had a noble ring, while refusing to part with valuable field hands during the growing season could be construed as selfish or even unpatriotic. In any event, the bitter public controversy surrounding slave impressment should not be allowed to obscure the dominant role of laissez-faire capitalism in shaping wartime patterns of black employment. Even the most genuine protests against government intrusion into plantation affairs revealed a significant gap between planter perception and objective reality. When compared to the control exerted over white workers through military conscription, the Confederacy's efforts at mobilizing black labor seem minuscule. Caution, if not actual timidity, marked most official actions touching the property rights of Southern slaveholders. At one time or another nearly every government agency in Georgia sought impressment authority, but during most of the war slave levies were imposed only for work on fortifications. Not until February 1864 did the Confederate Congress authorize conscripting blacks for other essential jobs, and as a practical matter the Engineer Bureau continued to receive the majority of bondsmen impressed during the latter stages of the war. Despite the Army of Tennessee's enrollment of slave teamsters after the fall of Atlanta, and notwithstanding the presence of occasional free Negro conscripts in Ordnance Bureau facilities, the bulk of Georgia's black industrial workers were always secured through voluntary hiring agreements with individual slaveowners. In both the public and private sector, persuasion remained the rule and coercion the exception. [109]

The government's refusal to adopt heavy-handed methods for obtaining black workers minimized the institutional disruption associated with military and industrial employment. In the absence of central planning, market mechanisms continued to determine the size and character of black labor supplies, leaving the state's agricultural interests secure and placing the planting class in a position to dictate the scope and conditions of wartime industrial expansion. The result was predictable. Antebellum economic relationships were modified, and sometimes stretched almost to the breaking point, but were never really abandoned. Or, to state the matter more concretely, the war years saw a major redistribution of Georgia's preexisting industrial slave force, but only a limited transfer of bondsmen directly from farms to factories. Available evidence suggests that slave field hands were recruited primarily by mining and extractive industries, or hired for work in nonmanufacturing activities like fortification building, wagon driving, railroad construction, and hospital service, all of which required large amounts of unskilled labor.

Instead of depleting the state's agricultural work force, these wartime pursuits seem to have absorbed a major portion of the displaced plantation slaves who accompanied "refugee" masters to Georgia's interior counties. Hospital and transportation officials addressed slave-hiring advertisements specifically to "Refugees and Others" during the latter part of the war, and as early as April 1862 planters who had fled the Georgia coast signed a major contract for railroad grading in the state's southern counties. [110] Noting that the bondsmen engaged in the work had previously been "without locality or employment," a local newspaper praised the arrangement as beneficial to all concerned. While "consulting its own advancement," the railroad had also acted in "highly patriotic" fashion by employing a large slave force which would otherwise have remained idle. [111] As Union military victories drove planters deeper into the Confederate interior, refugee bondsmen became "entirely too densely crowded" in many rural Georgia locales. "We have not arable land enough to give them employment," the Columbus *Enquirer* stated flatly in October 1863. Warning that "idle negroes are public curses," the *Enquirer* urged government employment of black refugees on a grand scale. "There ought not to be a white orderly in the army, a white porter in the quartermaster's office, . . . a white laborer in a Government warehouse or fortification, or a white teamster in a camp," the paper editorialized. [112] At almost the same time the Macon and Brunswick Railroad published a special "Notice to Refugees" urging "planters and others driven away from their homes" to hire out unemployed bondsmen for additional work on new roadbeds. [113]

Some black refugees also labored in Georgia's factories and industrial establishments. Late in 1862, for example, the Confederate Ordnance Laboratory in Macon hired a group of eleven slaves owned by Confederate Senator Gustavas Adolphus Henry of Tennessee but temporarily quartered near La Grange, Georgia. "I was forced to run these negroes hastily from my plantation on the Mississippi River, which has been litterally [*sic*] despoiled by the Yankees," Henry explained. Reeling from heavy financial losses, the senator was anxious to find quick employment for his slaves, and even agreed to forfeit a portion of the first month's hire while the unacclimated bondsmen recovered their health. [114] Most Georgia employers could only dream about windfalls like the above. Refugee slave-owners usually extracted top dollar when hiring their human chattels, and local planters were equally hard-nosed in dealings involving no threat of impressment. Not infrequently manufacturers saturated local newspapers with labor advertisements, only to find rural residents "unwilling to send their slaves from the country at any price."[115] In the face of such obstacles many Confederate industrialists concluded that hiring bondsmen already employed outside the agricultural realm offered the most promising solution to the problem of chronic labor shortages.

The most readily available source of seasoned industrial bondsmen was neither the commercial slave trader nor the professional hiring broker. Nor, in all likelihood, was it the large plantation owner. If Ordnance Bureau experiences are any gauge, the crucial middlemen in Georgia's industrial hiring system were small proprietors like A. C. Rogers, who owned slave property for what amounted to rental purposes. A man of "moderate circumstances," Rogers, by his own admission, depended on slave-hiring revenues to support a large family. Barely two weeks before the refugee transaction already described, he hired to the Ordnance Laboratory an even larger group of slaves than those furnished by Senator Henry. The tone of his correspondence was crisp and businesslike. "I will now offer you 13 first rate hands for $160.00 per hand[,] you feeding, clothing, and giving them medical attention," Rogers informed laboratory officials on December 10, 1862. Market conditions rendered quick acceptance of the proposal essential. Rogers stressed that he was "receiving daily propositions" for the slaves, all of whom had "been hired for years" and could thus be warranted as "good grading hands."[116]

Like thousands of other black Georgians, Rogers's slaves probably acquired their grading experience while engaged in railroad construction during the 1850s. Railroad contractors had been among the state's largest antebellum employers of unskilled black labor, but with the outbreak of hostilities the picture changed drastically. As previously noted, new track construction declined sharply from prewar levels, thereby releasing a steady flow of surplus slaves who were channeled into other industrial pursuits. Railroad labor seems, in fact, to have been the most frequently shared occupational background of the state's unskilled industrial bondsmen. Evidence on the point is impressionistic but plentiful. Former railroad hands were found in north Georgia ironworks, in government salt-making operations, in most Ordnance Bureau establishments, and in private weaponry facilities. Initially they were also hired to work on Savannah's defenses, usually at higher prices than those paid for agricultural slaves. Once impressment began, many masters argued that railroad slaves rather than field hands should be responsible for building fortifications. "Our planters very naturally say that we ought to take the negroes working upon railroads, accustomed therefore to such work, and besides the railroads can wait," Howell Cobb told the secretary of war in August 1862.[117]

As black railroad workers penetrated more and more industries, railroad policies became benchmarks of acceptable procedure. In 1862 a Savannah brick maker promised to feed and clothe hired bondsmen "as well as any railroad company hands," and early the next year an Ordnance Bureau official decided to "follow the example of the railroad companies" in making cooking arrangements for industrial slaves.[118] When disputes arose over the meaning of hiring contracts, railroad precedents were invoked with almost canonical authority. A typical exchange involved an owner's decision to furnish his slaves with shoes only once a year rather than twice as previously stipulated. "This I learn from one of the best rail Road contractors in this state is all that he is doing, and all that is necessary," the owner declared adamantly.[119]

The relationship between railroads and other Confederate industries was not always an amicable one. Many manufacturing jobs required the talents of skilled mechanics or craftsmen, and at this level railroads were more often consumers than suppliers of black manpower. Competition for black craftsmen was intense during the war, and railroads, like other private firms, derived considerable advantage from their freedom to exceed the wage scales mandated for government establishments. Ultimately, however, the role of skilled slaves in war production had relatively little to do with the ability of particular industries to outbid their competitors in the hiring market. No matter how labor was allocated or redistributed, the force of slave artisans employed in Georgia's industrial sector as of 1860 was grossly inadequate to sustain the productive capacity of an expanding war economy. Only by training additional slave workmen or by recruiting plantation craftsmen could most industrialists hope to enlarge their staff of skilled blacks. Although pressures for immediate production made the first alternative unappealing, some bondsmen did acquire new skills during the war. Thomas Goosby, an antebellum slave carpenter from Oglethorpe County, became a Confederate shoemaker, as did the Liberty County slave Tom, who spent the summer of 1863 in a rural shoe shop, emerging in September with "quite the air of a *graduated tradesman*."[120] The time required to learn more complex occupations in the mechanical and building trades precluded large-scale transfers of agricultural slaves into skilled industrial jobs. Even shoemakers normally required bondsmen to serve a three-year apprenticeship, and most weapons manufacturers had neither the time nor the inclination to instruct untutored blacks in skilled crafts. A Columbus swordmaker's 1864 offer to hire "six good Negro Blacksmiths . . . [and] six young likely Negro boys, to put at the Forge to learn" was a rare departure from conventional employment practice.[121] Such occupational training as most slaves received during the war was necessarily superficial and thus of little value after emancipation.

The blacks best situated to benefit from wartime industrial training were country craftsmen who had mastered the rudiments of a trade but who lacked the skill and experience to work independently at complicated tasks. Most rural slave artisans probably fell into this category, and the skill gap between bond and free workers constituted a major obstacle to the rapid industrial mobilization of plantation craftsmen. Throughout the war Georgia industries were in great need of accomplished mechanical and building-trades workers, regardless of race. Typically, however, local slaveowners responded to hiring appeals in what became a familiar litany of equivocation. A Dougherty County resident offered to furnish three "excellent country carpenters" who nonetheless could not "be called finished city workmen."[122] The owner of two slave brickmasons recommended one as being "among the best on all jobs" while characterizing the other as simply "a good workman on plain work."[123] An Alabama man sought employment for four black carpenters, "two of whom are first rate hands—the other two not so good, but will . . . work with the others."[124] Still another master noted that his slave Robert had "worked some at the carpenter's trade" and that the bondsman Isaac had "assisted him in covering houses."[125]

The above statements, which could readily be multiplied, lend credence to the view that slave craftsmanship deteriorated significantly in the course of the antebellum era. Highly skilled black artisans were certainly present in Confederate Georgia, but their attainments were recognized as exceptional. The commander of the Macon Armory, for example, hired three slave brickmasons who were also "excellent plasterers, . . . superior in every respect to the ordinary run of negro mechanics."[126] The Macon Arsenal was offered a slave blacksmith who had served a full apprenticeship with the Savannah firm of R & J Lacklison, earning a reputation as "one of Lacklison's best workmen."[127] In the majority of cases slave craftsmen were simply assumed to possess inferior skills unless otherwise specified. "Most of the bricklayers I have now employed are negroes, but I have not been able to obtain others," wrote an Ordnance Bureau official in 1863."[128] The same officer found slave carpenters "very satisfactory indeed" for framing temporary buildings, but refused to hire slave blacksmiths.[129] A slate and granite company near Stone Mountain did hire two Negro smiths, but found them "unable to sharpen tools with as much dispatch as is required."[130]

The sea island planter who described his bondsman as "a good ship builder & joiner & house carpenter" and a "remarkably smart mechanic at almost anything" accurately pinpointed both the strengths and limitations of black skilled workers during the Civil War.[131] Flexibility and lack of specialization were opposite sides of the same coin. Perhaps W. E. B. DuBois, while teaching at Atlanta University in 1902, came closest to capturing the overall character and significance of Confederate Georgia's rural slave craftsmen. "The slave artisan," according to DuBois, "was rather a jack-of-all-trades than a mechanic in the modern sense of the term—he could build a barn, make a barrel, mend an umbrella or shoe a horse. Exceptional slaves did the work exceptionally well, but the average workman was poor, careless and ill-trained, and could not have earned living wages under modern competitive conditions."[132]

Most scholars agree that the apparent antebellum decline in slave skill levels can be attributed largely to growing Southern dependence on Northern manufactures, together with political agitation by native white artisans who sought to eliminate black competition.[133] During the 1840s and 1850s white mechanics in Georgia's major industrial towns grew increasingly hostile to slave craftsmen. The white workers' demands for racially exclusionist legislation blended hatred for blacks with economic

The arrival of Union warships off Georgia's coast during the winter of 1861–62 made war a reality for both masters and slaves. Confederates promptly abandoned most offshore outposts, and when Fort Pulaski fell to the Yankees on April 11, 1862, Cockspur Island became a haven for black refugees like those pictured above. (Courtesy of USAMHI.)

During the next two years black Georgians fled slavery by the hundreds to seek sanctuary on the Federally controlled sea islands. Among the first to escape was Susie King Taylor, whose husband Edward King took up arms for liberty in the First South Carolina Volunteers. Mrs. King served the black regiment as a nurse and laundress. (From Susie King Taylor, *Reminiscences of My Life in Camp* [1902; reprint New York, 1968], frontispiece.)

Later, during the 1864 Sherman Invasion, hundreds of upcountry slaves exchanged tattered plantation garments for blue uniforms in the Forty-fourth United States Colored Infantry. One Georgia recruit was Hubbard Pryor of Polk County, who was captured by Confederates at Dalton shortly after the above pictures were made. (Courtesy of the National Archives.)

Overleaf: Other Georgia bondsmen received their first taste of military life in Confederate ranks. As early as April 1861, slave fifers and percussionists like the three shown above provided spirited accompaniment for the parade ground maneuvers of the Sumter Light Guards. Whites called the tune, but inwardly, perhaps, black musicians stepped to the beat of a different drummer. (Courtesy of the Georgia Department of Archives and History.)

Less visible on ceremonial occasions, but far more numerous than the musicians were the thousands of slave cooks and personal attendants who eased the burdens of army life for white soldiers. Standing inconspicuously in the background of this May 10, 1861, image is an unnamed black servant with the newly mobilized "Clinch Rifles" of the Fifth Georgia Regiment. Eventually the terrible carnage of war would thrust blacks closer to the forefront of battlefield endeavors. (Courtesy of Joseph Canole, Jr.)

In 1863, however, little appeared to have changed when the slave Scott took time out from cooking to pose with members of Company H, Fifty-seventh Georgia Regiment. Or could a close observer have detected a faint undercurrent of pragmatic biracialism in the army of Tennessee? (From James C. Bonner, *Milledgeville: Georgia's Antebellum Capital* [Athens, 1978], p. 185.)

On the home front black labor helped sustain nearly all aspects of the Southern war effort. With weapons and workers in equally short supply, racial integration of a sort took place in many industries. The slave blacksmith Augustus Thompson, for example, divided his time between Cook and Brother's Armory in Athens and the Augusta Arsenal where he "ironed off" gun carriages. (Courtesy of Charles J. Brockman, Jr.; Rev. E. R. Carter, *The Black Side: A Partial History of the Business, Religious, and Educational Side of the Negro in Atlanta* [Atlanta, 1894].)

Throughout the state black train crews and section hands kept Georgia's railroads working—until Sherman destroyed them. (Courtesy of the Georgia Department of Archives
and History.)

In Macon slave workers made bricks by the thousands to build the Confederate States Armory and Central Ordnance Laboratory. When this photograph was taken in the 1870s, the work had changed very little, but the pay was better. (Courtesy of the Georgia Department of Archives and History.)

Antebellum industrial facilities like Macon's Schofield Iron Works had need of slave labor even before converting to military production. In this prewar photograph blacks are visible on the delivery wagon at the left. The Findlay Iron Works, another small Macon firm, counted three skilled blacks among its nine workers in 1862. (Courtesy of the Georgia Department of Archives and History.)

At Mark A. Cooper's larger Etowah Iron Works near Cartersville wartime slave occupations ranged from manual labor to such highly skilled jobs as puddlers and heaters. The factory's importance as a potential source of Confederate weaponry and railroad iron marked it for destruction by Federal forces in 1864. (Courtesy of the Georgia Department of Archives and History.)

Most black Georgians, however, stayed in the countryside throughout the war years. Concerned with tangible matters of family security and physical survival, they faced the future in 1865 with a mixture of hope and sober realism. (Courtesy of the New-York Historical Society.)

grievances against large slaveowners in a way which underscored the latent class tensions in Southern society.[134] Although class hostility was never the central driving force behind Southern emancipationist sentiment, thoughtful observers recognized the antislavery implications of white labor unrest.[135] Writing from Washington, D.C., in 1860, Georgia journalist J. Henly Smith presented an unusually militant formulation of doubts and apprehensions which many Southern planters shared. "It seems to me," Smith confided to Alexander H. Stephens, "that the South should be almost exclusively agricultural, and not manufacturing. I think our safety, greatness and progress all depend on this one policy. . . . [I]f we ever become a manufacturing people, it will introduce a system of *free labor* which will extinguish Slavery. . . . I believe every thread of cotton that is spun in the South, is that much ready antagonism to the interest and permanence of African Slavery; and it ought to be resisted the same as we would so many bristling bayonets in the hands of old John Brown's followers."[136]

Wartime industrial expansion did little to allay the fears of either diehard agrarians or the more typically pragmatic planter-capitalists who participated in manufacturing ventures. By 1863 Georgia was rife with labor unrest as runaway inflation threatened to place even the necessities of life beyond the reach of workingmen. At government ordnance plants, where wages were low and pay increases slow, white skilled workers complained, drafted petitions, staged spontaneous walkouts, threatened general strikes, and, eventually, began to organize.[137] The central issue in nearly all disputes was money, but as slave craftsmen entered the work force in ever increasing numbers white economic grievances took on racial and class overtones. In Macon, where a local Mechanics Society had actively opposed black artisans since the 1840s, free labor confronted the slavocracy with unusual forthrightness during the war. Months of simmering labor disputes in the town's Ordnance Bureau establishments were brought to a head in April 1863 by the Georgia legislature's consideration of a bill prohibiting trade unions. Introduced by state Senator Timothy M. Furlow, a wealthy planter and railroad promoter from Americus, and sponsored in the House by antebellum ironmaster and industrialist B. H. Bigham, the bill ostensibly protected the rights of employers and apprentices, but in reality outlawed any type of effective labor organization.[138]

A group of seventeen white mechanics denounced the measure as class legislation and questioned its sponsors' motives: "We feel that you would have us gravle [sic] in the dust beneath your aristocratic tread," the workers charged, adding that the Confederate Constitution had been "formed solely for the benefit (socially and pecuniarily) of the aristocrats," giving mechanics "no rights that are not guaranteed to the negro."[139] The racial and antislavery dimensions of the dispute became more explicit a few days later. Spokesmen for the mechanics now charged flatly that after passing the bill "the wealthier classes would attempt to apprentice a lot of negroes, and place them in the various machine and workshops (thus placing the negro on an equality with the white man)."[140] Responding to these charges in anticipation of his upcoming election campaign against Governor Joseph E. Brown, Senator Furlow tried to appease both his working-class and his slaveholding constituencies with a classic piece of ideological fence-straddling. While acknowledging that he had presented the anti-union measure to the Senate, Furlow claimed that the "mere act of introducing a bill" did not necessarily imply personal support. What it did imply was even less clear. "I was absent from the Senate and at home, when the bill was reported . . . and did not therefore vote for or against its passage," Furlow observed blandly. Having rendered his position on union organizing as ambiguous as possible, the senator addressed the more volatile issues of racial and class antipathy. On these questions he sought to avoid even the appearance of equivocation. Disavowing any "prejudice against or quarrel with" the state's white mechanics, Furlow vindicated his past conduct in language resembling that of a loyalty oath: "I do not own nor have I ever owned, a negro mechanic, and have no intention or desire to have my negroes become mechanics, to supplant [white workmen] by low wages."[141] Such assurances apparently left many nonslaveholders unmoved, and several months later Furlow ran third in the state's three-man gubernatorial contest.

III

ALTHOUGH PLANTERS were disturbed by wartime labor militancy, slaves had more immediate cause to fear the anger of frustrated white artisans.

However, hostility from white coworkers was something most bondsmen had learned to take in stride. The reactions of black military and industrial laborers to the daily realities of life at the workplace were, in fact, far more subtle and complex than most whites imagined. Cautious skepticism and concern with pragmatic self-interest guided black behavior at every stage of the employment process. When the first large labor drafts for Savannah's defenses occurred in 1862, many rural bondsmen had no clear idea of the fate which awaited them and consequently hesitated to leave their home plantations. Slave motives on such occasions were frequently misinterpreted. There can be little doubt that what masters often construed as manorial fealty on the part of their human chattels was, in reality, a "loyalty" born of expedience. An Athens woman, for example, reported in July 1864 that her slave "old Ben" had returned from a morning errand "in a jiffy[,] saying he met some white men who told him he had better go back if he didn't want to be impressed and put to work on the fortifications—'He didn't want to go.'" In Augusta slaves were "greatly exercised" when Confederate soldiers began impressing hundreds of blacks to work on both local defenses and the fortifications around Atlanta. Some bondsmen feigned illness or physical handicaps, while many others hid during daylight hours and ventured out only under the cover of darkness to swell the audience at local black revival meetings. One of the more extreme cases of master-slave solidarity in resisting impressment was reported by Milton Hammond, a former slave from the vicinity of Griffin. When a detachment of General Joseph Wheeler's cavalry suddenly rode onto his master's property and began impressing the plantation mules, whites as well as blacks were thrown into a state of panic. "My mistress became frightened and locked me in the closet until late in the evening," recalled Hammond.[142]

Evidently most black Georgians shared a strong aversion for the squads of Confederate cavalry assigned to assist impressing officers. In the minds of many bondsmen these cavalrymen must have seemed disturbingly like another group of armed, mounted whites, the detested patrollers who were all too familiar to most slaves. A wartime verse popular among slaves in Warren County suggests that black hostility toward "conscript" officers sometimes embodied broader feelings of resentment toward white authority generally:

On the Threshold of Freedom

I lay down in my bed
I lay down in no dread
Conscript come and took me
And dragged me from my bed

Chorus:

I'll lay ten dollars down
I'll count it one by one
I'll give ten dollars to know the man
Who Struck Peter Butler's son[143]

Resisting impressment usually proved futile, of course, and as the moment of departure approached many bondsmen were haunted by the specter of sale or family separation. Della Briscoe, a former slave in Putnam County, recalled vividly the apprehension which existed when authorities took two adult blacks from each plantation in her neighborhood to work on Savannah's defenses. Nearly all of the men selected had families whom they involuntarily left behind. Upon returning to the quarters after prolonged absences, many of the slave husbands "fell on their knees" to receive the affectionate and enthusiastic welcome of their small children.[144]

Black workers had good reason to fear the prospect of family disruption and to rejoice when it failed to occur. Except for the refugee experience, no wartime phenomenon posed a greater threat to slave domestic ties than did military and industrial employment. The danger resulted less from callousness or indifference on the part of masters than from hard-nosed business policies which placed a premium on the labor of male adults. Seeking to achieve maximum productivity at minimum cost, Georgia's government agencies and civilian firms routinely excluded women and children from slave-hiring agreements. Deviation from this practice was rare, and seldom of sufficient magnitude to alter the basic composition of a slave work force. Outside the iron industry, where age and sex restrictions were either fluid or nonexistent, most major employers of military and industrial bondsmen hired women only in limited numbers to

172

perform cooking and washing chores for slave men. Black male adolescents were sometimes recruited for certain types of unskilled work, but demand for young girls was virtually nonexistent. [145]

For both humanitarian and economic reasons, masters often attempted to hire out bondsmen in family units, but few employers were willing to assume the burden of supporting nonessential or unproductive workers. A Covington, Georgia, medical officer summed up the dilemma facing all parties in 1864 when he found it impossible to hire slave hospital attendants at government prices. "If it were allowable to take men, women & children—there would be no difficulty about" obtaining black workers, the doctor reported. "But, I suppose, the feeding of employees is a considerable item with the government," he conceded. [146] Chronically understaffed agencies like the Nitre and Mining Bureau "did not object to a small proportion of women and boys in a good lot of negroes," but other government departments were much less flexible. [147] Such concessions as masters managed to extract from employers were nearly always accompanied by rigid economic stipulations. When a Columbus slaveowner protested that "Some of my most valuable men have wives," officials at a government ordnance laboratory responded by agreeing to "take five or six women, provided they are able to work with the shovel or spade at grading land" in the same fashion as male hands. [148] The Engineer Bureau made a similar agreement and unceremoniously terminated it when the requisite labor was not performed. Upon ordering a planter to remove his slaves from employment on Atlanta's defenses, an engineer officer observed curtly "that the women and small negroes of both sexes have not earned the rations with which they have been supplied." [149]

The inevitable, if unintended, effect of Civil War slave-hiring practices was to separate husbands from wives and parents from children. Sometimes the blow fell swiftly, as in the case of a Pike County plantation force whose fate was consigned to the Macon slave-auctioning firm of Habersham & Company after a Confederate Ordnance official refused to hire the blacks in families as their master proposed. [150] Other bondsmen preserved family ties when initially hired out, only to be separated later upon changing employers. A typical episode involved thirty-six slave parents and offspring evacuated from the Bartow Iron Works in northern Georgia

173

during the 1864 Sherman invasion and tentatively rehired to the Confederate Armory in Macon. The precariousness of family arrangements in these circumstances became evident when a dispute arose over the ages and sexes of the Bartow slaves who reported to Macon for work. Protesting that the group contained four children and one woman too many, the Armory's commanding officer stated the case with ledger-book precision: "The agreement calls for 13 men [and] 8 women with 13 children—you have sent but 10 men and 9 women with 17 children. I took the 8 women and 13 children for the sake of securing the men. I am unwilling to receive a larger proportion of women and children than agreed to. . . . Please make other arrangements [for the excess women and children] or be charged the cost of maintaining them."[151]

Many employers avoided controversies like the above by hiring black women only when "unencumbered" by offspring. Given the high birthrate among Georgia's late-antebellum slave population, there can be little doubt that a large portion of the women who arrived at Confederate hospitals, ordnance establishments, and private firms "without encumbrance" were mothers who had been separated from their children.[152] Suggestions of the emotional trauma occasioned by this practice appear in the records of employers like Colonel John W. Mallet, who tried to mitigate the harsher aspects of official hiring policy at Macon's Central Ordnance Laboratory. Writing to a local slaveowner in June 1864, Mallet confirmed both the reality and the limitations of his own compassion toward blacks, while also acknowledging the strength of family ties among industrial bondsmen. His brief letter to one W. R. Phillips merits quoting in full:

> Sir:
>
> Your negro woman "Lucy" hired to this establishment, has urgently begged me to let her two small children come up here, as she says both herself and their father are here.
>
> As I have at present more than sufficient house room I am willing to grant her request with the distinct understanding that the children are to be in no way supported from Government Rations (unless from those issued to their parents), and that if the necessity of additional house room should arise the children are to be at once removed on my request.[153]

Other slave couples received similar privileges from Mallet, but most family reunions proved temporary. Several were tragically cut short by a disease outbreak in September 1863. Daphne, the child of Celia belonging to W. R. Phillips, died on the laboratory premises, and two children owned by Mississippi Senator Albert Gallatin Brown were also threatened. After visiting their parents at the laboratory for a few days, one was found "dying . . . and impossible to move" and the other was immediately sent away. [154]

Whether they were hired individually or in families, black military and industrial laborers could anticipate little more than a minimally adequate standard of living. Bondsmen employed by the Ordnance Bureau, the Engineer Corps, and, presumably, other Confederate agencies received a uniform daily food ration which had dwindled by 1863 to one half-pound of bacon or one pound of beef and two pounds of cornmeal, with occasional substitutions of rice or potatoes. [155] At Macon's Central Laboratory this meager diet proved "quite insufficient to support negro laborers at hard work," and bondsmen ran away, complaining of starvation. [156] Fortification laborers employed in isolated areas found that food sometimes ran short due to lack of regular transportation, and in one case a white overseer was arrested after stealing provisions intended for the slaves under his control. [157] Beginning in April 1864 subsistence commissaries stopped issuing rations to slaves, leaving most government agencies to assume the burden of feeding their own workers. Ordnance establishments responded by planting vegetable gardens, purchasing supplies in the open market, and arranging for direct food deliveries from tax-in-kind agents. [158] The system worked well enough to stave off disaster, although conditions fluctuated drastically from one government facility to another, with scarcity and seasonal abundance sometimes occurring simultaneously in the same locale. Contrasts were especially sharp in Macon, where blacks at the Central Laboratory received 7,600 gallons of vegetables and over 3,100 pounds of locally grown beans and corn during the autumn of 1864, while the neighboring Confederate Armory appealed for emergency army rations to feed black workers. [159]

During the first three years of the war most industries followed established antebellum custom and required owners to supply bedding, shoes, and clothing for hired slaves. But as the scarcity and expense of these articles increased, more and more masters began to shirk their responsibilities and renege on contractual obligations.[160] The Confederate Central Laboratory provided clothes for hired bondsmen as early as 1863, and the Macon Armory followed suit the next year, after discovering that some of its black workers were "almost destitute" of garments while virtually all were "becoming infected with vermin on account of not having sufficient clothing to enable them to change and keep themself [sic] in cleanly condition."[161] From 1864 onward, ordnance establishments throughout the state issued bondsmen a more or less standard clothing allotment every six months consisting of one pair of pants, two shirts, two pairs of underdrawers, two pairs of socks, one cap, one jacket, and one blanket. Cheap Osnaburg cloth and "sheeting" provided the fabric for most garments, although wool hats were supplied during cold weather, along with rough "brogan" shoes of local manufacture.[162]

Housing arrangements for military and industrial slaves varied widely. Initially neither government nor civilian employers were prepared to accommodate large numbers of resident laborers, and many industrial bondsmen lived away from the workplace. During the second year of the war, for example, a Columbus sword manufacturer advertised for "someone who will board and lodge 20 to 25 negro men," and a Confederate armory avoided the housing problem entirely by hiring all black workers as day laborers to be fed, clothed, and sheltered by their owners.[163] Gradually, however, this policy was abandoned as blacks assumed a larger role in industrial operations and slaveowners grew increasingly reluctant to bear the expense of maintaining hired-out bondsmen. The change began at Macon's Central Ordnance Laboratory as early as December 1862 when officials sought permission to occupy a plot of railroad land "for the erection of quarters and stables for some negroes and mules."[164] By 1864 virtually all government agencies were housing black workers on institutional premises or at camps near construction work sites.

A charitable observer might have described the living accommodations furnished to Georgia's industrial bondsmen as spartan. Constructed hastily and at minimal cost, industrial slave quarters were usually one-story wooden structures with poor lighting and ventilation. Overcrowding was a constant problem, exacerbated by the necessity to hire black workers faster than housing facilities could be completed. At the Central Laboratory late deliveries of lumber interrupted housing construction in February 1863 and left some hired bondsmen exposed to inclement winter weather.[165] The Macon Armory began building slave quarters late in 1863, but by June of the next year only eight of a projected fifteen units were ready for occupancy.[166] At Atlanta's sprawling Fair Ground Hospital complex a new 30 × 50-foot "building for negro quarters" expanded slave housing accommodations in July 1863, but as late as September 1864 fifteen slave attendants at the Lee Hospital in Columbus were packed into three rented rooms.[167]

Engineer Bureau slaves near Savannah returned each evening to rented buildings in the city where, according to one mistress, the bondsmen were "excellently quartered."[168] But this arrangement, prompted by owners' concerns over poor health conditions, was extremely atypical. Most black fortification workers were shielded from the elements only by crude "plank shelters," a type of accommodation clearly inferior to the rough barracks provided for factory slaves. Even at Savannah, observers acknowledged that impressed bondsmen "are not and cannot be as comfortable as they would be at home," and at other fortification projects slave living conditions went steadily from bad to worse.[169] During the last eighteen months of the war black military laborers bore the brunt of the Confederacy's dwindling resources and deteriorating bureaucratic machinery. An overtaxed domestic economy, an inadequate military supply system, and the general chaos of a continuing army retreat in 1864 all conspired to keep the living standard of Engineer Bureau laborers somewhat below that of most industrial slaves. An emergency impressment of black Ordnance Bureau employees to work on Atlanta's defenses during August 1864 brought the disparity into sharp focus. Given food "of the most inferior character" and deprived of badly needed shoes and clothing, the new workers defected in large numbers. An official investigation revealed that eighty-four bondsmen from the Macon Armory "were taken from comfortable quarters and sent to . . . exposed service in the field," where the work was poorly organized and "very exhausting." Discontent became widespread among the Ordnance Bureau slaves, and even engineer officials eventually conceded that treatment of the workers had been "unsatisfactory & unfortunate."[170]

Harsh living conditions undoubtedly contributed to the serious health problems which plagued military and industrial slaves. Wherever black laborers were concentrated in large numbers, infectious disease made its appearance, sometimes exacting a heavy toll. Around Atlanta the scourge was smallpox, while at Savannah the Engineer Bureau's slave work force was decimated by a prolonged measles epidemic which sometimes incapacitated as many as 150 bondsmen a day.[171] At Ordnance Bureau establishments the most common complaints were vaguely diagnosed fevers, pneumonia, and rheumatism.[172] Illness was especially common among slaves employed at brick making, an occupation requiring heavy labor in damp, low-lying terrain.[173] The inexperience of many black workmen, together with lax supervision and dangerous working conditions, resulted in a number of industrial accidents. Bondsmen fell from scaffolding, were struck by trains, and injured themselves while lifting heavy objects.[174] At Macon's Central Laboratory a slave named Green "came in badly injured in his extremities by the mules running away with him," while in Columbus a black fireman at the Naval Iron Works was hurled some twenty feet when a steam engine boiler exploded. Seriously scalded, the bondsman lived only a few hours after the accident.[175]

Medical care for sick or injured black workers was more institutionalized, but probably no more effective, than that available to plantation slaves. Initially some government agencies contracted with private physicians for annual treatment of an entire slave work force. By 1863, however, most civilian doctors refused to enter into such agreements, and the burden of slave health care fell increasingly upon army surgeons.[176] Eventually the Confederate Medical Department established hospital accommodations for hired bondsmen at major military posts and government industrial facilities throughout the state. Although physical and bureaucratic arrangements were tailored to fit local circumstances, the normal procedure was to place slave medical care in the hands of an army doctor assisted by one or more civilian "contract physicians." Two separate hospitals for Engineer Bureau slaves were operated in this fashion at Savannah, while in Macon the Confederate Arsenal and the Central Laboratory maintained separate slave hospitals with a contract physician residing close to the laboratory premises. The Macon Armory, however, had no slave hospital and called in civilian doctors to treat individual bondsmen as the need arose. [177] Efforts to establish a slave treatment center in Covington failed completely when local whites prevented medical officers from seizing the African Church for hospital purposes. [178]

The mere presence of slave hospital facilities did not, of course, guarantee good medical treatment. Some slaveowners complained bitterly that doctors were too few, their visits too infrequent, and their treatment all but worthless because essential medicines were not supplied. [179] Such charges were not without foundation. In private correspondence with superiors, Ordnance Bureau officials acknowledged that army physicians were badly overworked and frequently unable to secure necessary medical supplies. White overseers made little effort to "check slight cases of disease in the outset" or to "look after the sick and see that they are properly nursed."[180] Even sending slaves to the hospital was sometimes an exercise in futility. In January 1864, for example, a sick bondsman from the Macon Armory was sent to the Confederate Arsenal's nearby hospital where he remained overnight, only to be "turned out" the next morning "tho apparently scarcely able to walk."[181]

No matter how they fared in a purely physical sense, black military and industrial workers derived certain collective advantages from their pivotal role in Georgia's wartime economy. Nonagricultural slaves had always been able to influence white labor policies and disciplinary practices within narrow limits, and as the war progressed the boundaries of slave influence grew wider. Even more than in antebellum days, slave discipline at factories and construction sites became a fluid process in which physical force provided the ultimate sanction for a pragmatic system of day-to-day rewards, incentives, and de facto negotiation between supervisors and bondsmen. The most visible manifestation of black bargaining leverage was the practice of offering incentive payments to slaves for extra work. Indeed, the pervasiveness of the "task system" with its built-in provision for cash bonuses emerges in retrospect as the distinguishing feature of black labor organization outside the agricultural realm.

Adherence to established custom was the reason most often given for

resorting to task-work incentives. Payment for extra work had been standard practice in those prewar occupations which furnished the bulk of
Confederate industrial slaves, and bondsmen expected—even insisted—
that traditional arrangements be continued. Upon converting to the task
system in 1863, the commander of Macon's Central Laboratory stressed
the close relationship between slave occupational backgrounds and the
need for continuity in labor policies. Most of the laboratory's hired
bondsmen had previously worked at jobs like brick making or railroad
construction, where the "general custom" among antebellum employers
was "to assign . . . negroes daily *tasks* of a certain number of cubic yards
of earth work (constituting a fair average day's work) and to allow them to
do some extra work after the completion of these tasks if they are able and
willing . . . , paying for the latter to the negroes themselves at a definite
rate per cubic yard." The system resulted in optimum work output while
also producing "general contentment and cheerfulness" among hired
bondsmen. [182]

In seeking official authority to pay slaves for extra work, the laboratory's commander made it clear that his request grew out of more tangible
considerations than reverence for tradition or abstract concern over efficiency. Much of the impetus for change came from dissatisfied black
workers who "constantly importuned" officials to authorize and pay for
work performed over and above daily tasks. Many of the bondsmen
backed up their pleas with action, or, more precisely, inaction. Rejecting
the "strictly legal assumption" that employers were entitled to the *"whole
time"* of hired slaves, black workmen became frustratingly unproductive
in the absence of cash incentives. In practice, it was simply "impossible to
get from the slaves the same resultant amount of labor by leaving them
without any stimulus in the shape of reward for exertion instead of allowing them the privilege of extra work," a laboratory official concluded. [183]

As the preceding statement suggests, the entire concept of extra work
was rooted in conflicting assumptions about master-slave relations.
Whites, for obvious reasons, preferred to view compensated labor as a
discretionary "privilege," while veteran industrial slaves like those described above had come to regard cash incentives as a customary right.
But like all slave "rights," this one could be safely asserted only through

indirect methods which preserved the outward forms of subservience. Both employers and bondsmen found it advantageous to maintain broad areas of ambiguity in their dealings, and it is only within this context that the wartime actions of Georgia's industrial slaves take on clear meaning.

Black workers at the Central Laboratory were engaging in what amounted to passive resistance. Their behavior was not so much a work slowdown as a failure to speed up, a bargaining tactic calculated to win significant concessions without risking an open challenge to white authority. At Macon and elsewhere the strategy eventually proved successful. By April 1863 slaves at the Central Laboratory were receiving ten to twenty cents for each cubic yard of earth moved in excess of stipulated tasks. [184] Other bondsmen at the same establishment were paid twenty cents for each one thousand bricks wheeled from the kiln and sorted, while slaves who tended kiln fires after dark earned a dollar for each night's work. [185] Macon's Confederate Armory adopted similar arrangements in 1864 with the revealing proviso that blacks "not be permitted to overwork themselves for the purpose of pecuniary gain." Believing that "Justice to owners" could best be served by restraining ambitious bondsmen, armory officials carefully limited the amount of supplemental labor a slave might perform. [186] Blacks digging clay for brick machines were tasked at twenty cubic yards per day, after which they might dig a maximum of five additional yards at twenty cents per yard. All extra labor, however, was to be finished during the standard ten-hour workday. [187]

Restrictive as this policy may have seemed to brickyard hands, it was even less popular among bondsmen whose jobs were excluded from the task system. Armory officials eventually extended incentive payments to other occupations, but, significantly, the action came only after additional pressure from black workers. An illuminating episode in the process occurred early in 1865 when the slave Neely ran away from the armory during a dispute over personal remuneration. "He objects to working at the Armory because he has no opportunity for making money for himself," the master armorer reported at the time of Neely's initial escape. [188] Subsequently recaptured and assigned to a special work detail cutting shingles in rural Georgia, Neely again ran away when financial incentives failed to materialize. Sensing the drift of events, the armory's commander sought to placate the slaves who remained by providing opportunities for extra work. Bondsmen engaged in "drawing" (i.e., using a drawknife to shape roughly split boards into finished shingles) received a dollar for each one hundred shingles produced in excess of the daily quota of one thousand. The foreman was also instructed to determine "if any of the other negroes can be allowed to work extra[,] and explain how and in what terms."[189]

The black workers best situated to make money from wartime employment were probably Engineer Bureau slaves impressed for the defenses of Savannah. Cash incentives seem to have been adopted early at Savannah, and were clearly in force by 1863 when black military laborers helped grade and excavate railway roadbeds near the city. Apparently as a concession to owners, daily tasks for impressed slaves were set at twelve to fifteen cubic yards, or roughly one-third to one-half of the twenty-two cubic yards required of slaves employed by private contractors. Working to the rhythm of slow work chants, with black "headmen" setting a leisurely pace, engineer laborers still finished the assigned task by noontime. They could then spend the rest of the day collecting a government "premium" of fifteen cents for each additional cubic yard of earth excavated.[190] Conceivably a diligent worker in these circumstances might have approached a daily remuneration of two dollars, or roughly twice the maximum earnings of most Ordnance Bureau bondsmen.

Financial gain was not the only stimulus for overtime work by black Georgians. Many industrial slaves performed supplemental labor in order to gain special privileges like the chance to return home for brief visits to spouses and other loved ones. As previously noted, family disruptions were a common occurrence among military and industrial bondsmen. Government hiring policies routinely separated mothers from small children, and even more frequently the black men employed at factories and fortifications were slave husbands with wives and children in distant locales. Although a minority of masters made special efforts to hire out male slaves in close proximity to their spouses, such concessions were rare and seem to have been generally reserved for artisans and skilled craftsmen.[191] Similarly, some employers agreed to hire the wives of black male workers when a particular need arose for female labor.[192] But this practice was, if anything, even more unusual than that of placing spouses in the same town. By far the most common arrangement was for employers to give male bondsmen periodic leaves of absence for the purpose of visiting their families. Slaveowners favored this practice and justified the visits on practical as well as humanitarian grounds. As one master explained to an Ordnance Bureau official in 1863: "[My slave] Isham has a wife and is very anxious to see her[.] I should be glad if he could come home immediately. In fact, I fear he may run away if not permitted to do so."[193]

Employers usually respected owners' wishes on the matter of slave visits, trying in the process to minimize any financial or production losses resulting from a black worker's absence. Some masters agreed to have the value of lost worktime deducted from their monthly hiring payments, but this was only a partial solution which ignored the problem of decreased productivity. Leaves of absence were more easily arranged when blacks worked under the task system, and could perform extra labor without pay in advance of family visits.[194] Although some slaves may have regarded themselves as earning, or even purchasing, released time through this arrangement, white employers took a different view of the subject. Recognizing the importance which black workers attached to visiting spouses and children, employers jealously guarded their prerogative to grant or withhold leaves of absence for disciplinary purposes. "I always hold the discretion . . . in my own hands, in order to use it as a stimulant to industry and good conduct," explained Colonel John W. Mallet of Macon's Central Laboratory.[195]

By linking family visitation privileges to the extra work provisions of the task system, wartime industrialists sought to make the best of the principal concessions which hired bondsmen had secured. In a practical sense, however, the carrot-and-stick approach to slave discipline which prevailed at many industrial establishments probably benefited black workers about as much as employers. Whites, to be sure, remained in ultimate control of the labor system, but their mastery was not absolute. As nonwhite labor assumed an increasingly central role in war production, employers discovered that the ability to enforce racial subordination often counted for less than the ability to enlist blacks' cooperation. Bondsmen, in turn, stood ready to cooperate—up to a point and for a price.

It would, of course, be erroneous to imply that physical force was not used to control and intimidate black workmen. Like all forms of involuntary labor, industrial slavery was rooted in violence. Concessions, rewards, and incentives may have motivated blacks, but only the naked reality of brute force kept them in bondage. For most industrial slaves, however, the *threat* of violence was at least as important as any punishment actually received. Reminders of white coercive power confronted blacks constantly. The whip, whether wielded or simply displayed, was a ubiquitous item at the workplace. Some white supervisors carried guns, and all had access to armed force. Indeed, except for bondsmen employed in certain extractive enterprises, most military and industrial slaves worked and lived in close proximity to Confederate garrisons or armies in the field. Under these circumstances, violence became as much a psychological as a physical weapon. Since the perception of superior power may often have eliminated the necessity for its application, the frequency of whippings or other physical abuse offers little insight into the overall rigor of industrial discipline. Slave punishments ranged in severity from verbal rebukes to potentially lethal assaults with clubs and firearms. The point is not that employers used physical coercion sparingly (although many did), but rather that they directed force against bondsmen in a highly selective fashion.

As a general rule, blacks who worked for the Confederate government ran little risk of physical punishment unless they committed a specific criminal offense like stealing, or openly defied the orders of a white supervisor. Rarely, if ever, were government bondsmen whipped merely for failing to work hard. Private entrepreneurs who owned their work force may have been more inclined to flog slaves for malingering, although evidence on the point is inconclusive. [196] Basically, however, blacks and whites alike seem to have adopted the view that work output was a negotiable commodity to be regulated more through incentives than force.

Wartime labor shortages helped promote moderation in those areas where physical punishment was normally deemed appropriate. Owners received frequent assurances that hired slaves would be treated humanely, and officials at the Atlanta Arsenal went so far as to arrest and court-martial a white blacksmith accused of "beating one of [the] Negro hands."[197] Some employers avoided violent encounters by refusing to hire "unmanageable" slaves, and by summarily dismissing bondsmen who caused trouble.[198] Major government installations established detailed regulations and procedures to prevent serious types of slave misconduct. Following a wave of theft by black carpenters at Macon's Confederate Armory in 1863, officials restricted the personal privacy and physical mobility of all hired bondsmen. Required to enter and leave armory premises through a single gate, black workmen were given to understand that "they are liable to be searched as they leave their work." The master armorer ordered military guards "to search *daily* several negroes as they pass out from work at noon, and at 6 P.M.[,] to be selected promiscuously from the gang according to any suspicion that may exist with reference to any particular individuals."[199] Somewhat less drastic measures were adopted at the Central Ordnance Laboratory in 1864 to prevent the theft of axes, shovels, picks, and cooking utensils. Foremen in charge of black workers were "specially warned that all tools and implements used by or accessible to said negroes must be carefully collected three or four days before Christmas, checked over & counted, and must thenceforward until the negroes leave . . . be recalled into store every night so as to prevent their being stolen."[200] Several months later the laboratory took rather unusual steps to prevent black workers from despoiling nearby public vegetable gardens. Slaves passing through the gardens to or from work were confined to a specially designated "beaten track" and forbidden to use other paths. Watchmen received orders to "exercise a special vigilance to prevent the removal of rails from the garden fence by the negroes." Any bondsman found "carrying off or displacing the fence rails" faced mandatory punishment.[201]

Preventative measures like the above were never wholly effective. Inevitably black workers ignored rules, evaded regulations, and engaged in numerous activities that whites deemed unacceptable. Some bondsmen continually tested the limits of their employer's tolerance, always stopping just short of an open confrontation. At the Central Laboratory, for example, the slave William "behaved very badly—exhibiting positive disobedience to a most reasonable command," and subsequently twice running away. "He has not been whipped . . . although he most thoroughly

deserves it," a frustrated Ordnance Bureau official fumed.[202] Other bondsmen proved less skillful in evading white authority, and several of the
Macon Armory's black carpenters were caught in the act of stealing nails
from a construction site. The slaves' status as nonresident day laborers
saved them from immediate flogging, but the reprieve was only temporary. Apparently reluctant to use force against bondsmen whose services
could be summarily withdrawn, armory officials confined the black offenders in the city jail and requested owners to "have the boys properly
punished before they are again employed."[203]

Although wartime labor shortages helped mitigate harsh disciplinary
methods, the most important deterrent to physical abuse of industrial
slaves was the black worker's own response to mistreatment. Whipping
became a punishment of last resort because, from a white standpoint, it
seldom produced the desired result and was often counterproductive.
Many hired bondsmen simply refused to work for a brutal employer, and
were quick to underscore the point by running away whenever punishment seemed imminent. The slave Austin, a former Etowah Iron Works
employee, fled from the Macon Armory in October 1864. He and two
others had been "caught by . . . [the] overseer, gambling with cards for
money on Sunday in their quarters," all of which violated the armory's
standing regulations on slave conduct. "I assume Austin ran away in order
to escape a whipping which both the other offenders received on Monday
morning," concluded an Ordnance Bureau official.[204]

Comparatively few black workers ran away from employers purely out
of fear. Running away was a favorite bargaining tactic for bondsmen in all
sectors of Georgia's wartime economy, and one which veteran industrial
slaves had reduced to a fine art. By appealing to both the compassion and
the economic self-interest of masters, industrial fugitives could often escape punishment and negotiate concessions from employers as a condition for going back to work. When hiring out his bondsmen in 1864, for
example, one slaveowner offered the less-than-comforting assurance that:
"My negroes never runaway[,] only for a few days at a time; and then
they come home to me: and I always return them."[205] Subsequent events
confirmed all but the last portion of this statement. Among the bondsmen
hired from the owner in question was the previously mentioned slave

William, a confirmed runaway and malcontent described by his master as "an extra fine boy for work under *proper* management, but . . . very intolerant of abuse."[206] William defected from Ordnance Bureau employment twice during 1863, dodging pistol shots from an angry overseer on the first occasion and returning only when offered a different work assignment under a new foreman.[207] William's master also owned a slave named Clinton who was "not a runaway negro, though he is very scarey." Clinton ran away three times in five months, returning each time to his master. Fearing retaliation for earlier acts of theft, Clinton eventually persuaded Macon Armory officials to change the location of his employment, but defected again when his request to become a wagon driver was denied.[208]

A few military and industrial slaves escaped permanently from their wartime employers. Some fugitives sought freedom behind Union lines, while others remained in the state to pass as free and earn money for themselves. Soaring wage scales, the anonymity of burgeoning urban areas, and the general willingness of employers to ask few questions when hiring badly needed workers all contributed to the frequency of slave defections, as did the reluctance of city police to pursue runaways unless substantial rewards were offered.[209] Although there is no real evidence that industrial slaves ran away more frequently than other bondsmen, some black workers were especially well equipped to take advantage of wartime escape opportunities. Black artisans and craftsmen in particular had often traveled widely in antebellum times, gaining valuable knowledge of the state's geography and growing accustomed to face-to-face dealings with whites who engaged their services. Such experiences stood fugitives in good stead once they chose to strike out for freedom.

As early as September 1862 the slave carpenter James led a group of ten Liberty County bondsmen in a daring escape to the Federally controlled sea islands. Fleeing in full view of nearby Confederate soldiers, the blacks added insult to injury by stealing a boat belonging to the troops. Whites viewed James's role in the affair as a consummate act of treachery. At the time of the escape he was actually working for the Confederate picket detachment as "cook, waiter, man of all work & of all confidence." Prior to the war James had been "for a long season employed on the Sav. [annah] [Albany] & G[ulf] R[ail] R[oad] [and] Knows every foot of it." One local

187

planter described the slave as "highly intelligent & one of the most valuable men that has yet gone to the enemy from this county or perhaps from any other."[210] Similar experiences and personal attributes were evident in the thirty-five-year-old slave Jack, who ran away from an interior county early in 1865. Like many rural artisans Jack was "a competent Blacksmith, good Wood Worker, good in repairing old buggies, [and could] do anything in the workmanship line." His skills had been much in demand before the war, causing him to travel extensively. He was "well acquainted at Cuthbert, Randolph County . . . [and had] worked at Cotton Hill, . . . at Starkville, Lee County, and at Abner Howard's . . . in Terrell Co." Self-confidence and sociability were among the distinguishing features of Jack's personality. He was "fond of playing the fiddle, knows everybody, . . . [and] tries to talk very proper." When employed in a blacksmith shop he frequently made a calculated "display" of his skill "by walking around his anvil, first to the right and then to the left." His wardrobe displayed a touch of outright flamboyance. Upon running away he "carried off three pairs of pantaloons, red jeans and grey jeans, and a pair of sattinott pantaloons, a new black satton waistcoat, grey jeans and a black broadcloth coat." His usual attire included "a coarse pair of boots . . . [and] a blue flowered cap or wiregrass hat," together with a silver watch and brass chain which he pointedly wore "in front so that it may be seen." Jack was "full of pride and pomposity," his master explained, as he pondered the fugitive's most likely course of action. "I don't think he will take to the woods but will try to go in a shop, or some Government works, perhaps at Macon, or Albany, or Columbus . . . or he may be making for the Yankee lines," the frustrated owner concluded.[211]

Whatever their previous occupational background, level of skill, or personality traits, a large portion of Georgia's military and industrial slaves were ready to defect when the chances of escape seemed favorable. Federal troops served as catalysts in a number of runaway episodes, although Northern armies seldom liberated black workers directly. As had been true on the seaboard in 1862, logistical factors played a central role in determining the rate of black defections. When military and industrial slaves were in close proximity to Union forces, escape efforts and general black unrest usually increased. Bondsmen at the Georgia-controlled saltworks in Clarke County, Alabama, began making their way to Federal lines after learning of the fall of Vicksburg in July 1863, and by mid-August the thirty-five workers who remained had also grown "rather unmanageable."[212] As previously noted, defections at coastal saltworks peaked during July and August of 1864, when at least 107 blacks escaped from the Georgia seaboard during Union naval expeditions.[213] At almost the same moment, Federal cavalrymen were producing a "demoralizing effect" on black medical attendants in the interior, and in late July the appearance of Yankee raiders "stampeded" the slave work force at a Confederate hospital near Forsyth.[214]

Most black military laborers were kept well out of reach of Northern armies, however, and industrial slaves probably accounted for no more than a small fraction of the ten thousand to twenty thousand bondsmen who joined General Sherman's march to the sea. But despite their limited opportunity to make contact with Union armies, black military and industrial workers frequently managed to escape amid the general chaos which accompanied the Sherman invasion. Many of the bondsmen impressed to help fortify Atlanta during the summer of 1864 simply melted away when Confederate forces retreated late in August. Some blacks returned to their owners, sought out their families, or wound up in county jails, while others remained at large well into 1865.[215] Black Georgians conscripted to serve as teamsters for General John B. Hood's Tennessee Campaign ran away with such regularity that the progress of Confederate supply trains can be charted by slave defections. On a typical journey in October 1864, nine black teamsters deserted en masse at Newnan, Georgia. The slave Alfred continued for some forty additional miles, parting company with the wagon train near his former home of Cedartown in Polk County. A bondsman named Monroe ran away as the wagons were passing through Cave Spring in Floyd County, and two more slaves disappeared near the Coosa River. Still more defections occurred in Jacksonville, Alabama, and some ex-teamsters eventually traveled as far south as Dallas County.[216] For all of these bondsmen, as well as for hundreds of other black fugitives, the Civil War had ended and freedom was at hand.

6. Georgia Blacks and the Urban Revolution

WHITE GEORGIANS left the Union to defend a way of life rooted in agrarian values. Apart from race, few forces were more potent than rural localism in shaping the outlook of Southerners during the 1860s. Whether they owed allegiance to the folk community of self-sufficient yeoman farmers or to the dominant culture of slaveholding planters, most Confederates looked toward a regional destiny based upon agriculture and landed proprietorship. [1]

And yet, as the preceding pages have indicated, the war Georgians launched in the name of tradition and social conservatism became a powerful instrument of domestic institutional change. Rebel soldiers marched off to battle in 1861 determined to stem the tide of Yankee radicalism on the banks of the Potomac. For a time they even appeared to succeed in their impossible quest, but military valor could neither halt nor reverse the clock of history. Prolonged combat, regardless of its outcome, required a sweeping rearrangement of priorities on the Confederate home front, so that, in the end, every headlong charge against Union lines became an indirect assault upon the world Southern soldiers had left behind.

Nothing symbolized the South's departure from antebellum norms more vividly than the development of wartime urban life. Between 1861 and 1865 all of Georgia's major towns and cities increased substantially— often dramatically—in size and importance. Among the principal factors contributing to this rapid growth were the popularity of cities as havens for wartime refugees and "displaced persons," the massive expansion and diversification of Georgia industries to meet the needs of the Confederate war machine, and the key logistical role of cities as military staging areas and supply centers in a war effort largely geared to rail transportation. For reasons which were partly strategic and partly psychological the cities of Atlanta and Savannah also became the focal points of major military campaigns, and as a result large numbers of Confederate soldiers, black military laborers, and attendant civilian entrepreneurs were added to the population of both cities.

Rampant wartime urbanization knew no color line. Black slaves frequently accompanied refugee masters to Georgia's interior towns and cities or were hired out by profit-minded owners to work in urban-based industries. Rural bondsmen were impressed by the thousands to help fortify every significant urban center in the state, and during the latter phases of the war numerous black people came into towns on their own initiative, attracted by many of the same considerations which drew transient whites. Because of general wartime chaos and haphazard or nonexistent record keeping, neither the scope nor the chronology of urban growth in Confederate Georgia can be discussed with any degree of numerical precision. Nevertheless, a cursory examination of conditions in Georgia's major towns and cities strongly suggests that if the state never quite experienced the "urban revolution" which one scholar has described for the Confederacy as a whole, the war years definitely witnessed a termination and major reversal of the "de-urbanization" process which had molded and constricted the lives of many Georgia bondsmen during the last decades of the antebellum era. [2]

Savannah, with its population of over eight thousand blacks and nearly fourteen thousand whites, was Georgia's largest urban center and only real city as of 1860, but, ironically, Savannah stood alone among major Georgia towns in its failure to experience substantial net gains in white or black population during the war. The city's seeming demographic equilibrium was, however, more apparent than real. Substantial population shifts occurred during the war, but they had the effect of altering the composition of the city's population rather than increasing the total number of inhabitants. Numerous whites fled the city out of fear of an invasion or were conscripted for Confederate military service, but their numbers probably did not exceed the average number of Confederate troops stationed in Savannah for defensive purposes. The size of the Savannah garrison, which ranged from a low of about eighteen hundred to a peak of approximately fourteen thousand, increased drastically when Federal attacks were anticipated. It was also during such periods, of course, that the outflow of refugees (particularly women and children) was greatest. Thus, while sex ratios in Savannah's white population may have fluctuated, its overall size remained relatively constant. Where blacks were concerned, a similar pattern developed, but for slightly different reasons. Many slaves, especially female house servants and black children, left the city with refugee mistresses. Beginning in 1862, however, their departure was offset by the periodic impressment of thousands of male adult black military laborers to construct earthworks and fortifications. With blacks as with whites, sex ratios may have shifted toward a heavier concentration of males, but total population size does not appear to have changed significantly. [3]

Demographically nearly all other Georgia towns present a striking contrast to the state's vulnerable seaport. In 1860 Columbus, with some six thousand white and thirty-six hundred black inhabitants, was a prosperous river port and embryonic industrial center. If the presence of three cotton and woolen mills hardly justified the grandiose label "Lowell of the South," the addition of a foundry, paper mill, and cotton gin factory gave Columbus a very respectable list of manufacturing interests. Because of its location at the fall line of the Chattahoochee, the town's prospects for continued industrial growth seemed good, although limited by the modest and narrow demands of a domestic agricultural market. With the coming of the war the picture changed drastically, as industries expanded and converted to military production under the management of private citizens or oftentimes the Confederate government. By 1863 a massive influx of workers had swelled the aggregate population of Columbus to approximately fifteen thousand and unquestionably a substantial portion of the newcomers were black. [4]

No one kept statistics on wartime population growth in Macon, but Confederate officials estimated that local ordnance works would eventually add some nine thousand residents to the city. Subsequent newspaper accounts suggest that the nine thousand figure may well have been reached by the spring of 1864. Since Macon had over five thousand white and nearly three thousand black inhabitants in 1860, there is considerable likelihood that the town matched Columbus's wartime peak of fifteen thousand residents. [5]

If the wartime expansion of Macon and Columbus was impressive, urban growth in Civil War Atlanta was little short of phenomenal. In 1860 Atlanta, with a total of about ninety-five hundred white and black inhabitants, was slightly larger than Macon and almost identical in size to Columbus. During the first year of the war, however, this picture changed rapidly and by July 1862 Atlanta's population had nearly doubled and stood at roughly seventeen thousand including soldiers and assorted government personnel. Over the next eighteen months the city's growth rate declined, but still far exceeded normal peacetime levels. Estimates of the city's population in 1863 ranged between eighteen thousand and twenty thousand. Thus, by the midpoint of the war Atlanta had attained genuine urban status. [6]

As in the cases of Macon and Columbus, much of Atlanta's population growth was related to a rapidly expanding industrial base. Because of its central location and excellent railroad facilities, the city was singled out almost immediately as a key strategic point and major logistical and supply center for the Army of Tennessee. From 1862 onward the Atlanta Arsenal bore the brunt of furnishing ordnance supplies to Confederate troops in northern Georgia as well as in Alabama and Tennessee. The Army of Tennessee's Quartermaster Department was also headquartered in Atlanta, and as already discussed, the city became a major Confederate hospital center—second, perhaps, only to Richmond. In the private sector Atlanta possessed the usual variety of industrial establishments, including the crucial Gate City Rolling Mills, the only Southern firm besides the Tredegar Iron Works in Richmond capable of manufacturing iron rails. [7]

The one factor which did most to push Atlanta's growth rate ahead of other Georgia towns was the city's early and continuing popularity as a haven for refugees from virtually all parts of the Confederacy. The massive refugee influx which began even before the end of 1861 has led one historian to characterize Atlanta as "the most congested city in the state." It is impossible to say how many of the newcomers who poured in from Louisiana, Florida, Alabama, Arkansas, and especially Tennessee were slaves, and adequate data simply does not exist to chart the overall wartime growth of Atlanta's black population. In November 1863 the city tax collector reported that 2,523 slaves and 11 free blacks were listed in the current tax digest, representing an increase of slightly more than 600 slaves, and a decrease of 14 free blacks since the census of 1860. Tax records fail to indicate, however, whether the 2,523 figure included slaves of refugees and other transient residents, and almost certainly the number did not include the hundreds and sometimes thousands of black military laborers employed on the city's fortifications. In view of the dramatic growth of Atlanta's white population during the period, one may logically conclude that the number of slaves listed on municipal tax rolls represented only a portion of the city's total black population. [8]

Augusta, the state's second largest urban center in 1860 with some eight thousand white and four thousand black residents, experienced population gains comparable to other Georgia cities during the war. As in the case of Atlanta, Augusta's population growth resulted from both industrial expansion and periodic infusions of black and white refugees. On the eve of the war Augusta was best known for the large Augusta Cotton Factory, which ranked among the most modern and extensive textile mills in the South. During the war the Augusta Factory employed over 750 workers, a number of whom were slaves. Among the major government agencies based in Augusta were a naval commissary center; the Confederate Clothing Bureau, with more than 1,500 "poor needle-women" on its payrolls; an extensive Confederate States Shoe Manufactory staffed largely by black artisans; the Augusta Arsenal, which assisted Atlanta in supplying the Army of Tennessee and employed some 300 black and white workers as early as the winter of 1861–62; and, of vital importance to the South's war effort, the massive Confederate Powder Works, which began making gunpowder in 1862 and by 1864 employed a large work force of whites and conscripted free blacks. [9]

Some refugees came to Augusta from Savannah and Charleston as early as the autumn of 1861, but their stay proved only temporary, and it was

194

not until New Orleans fell into Union hands during the spring of 1862 that refugees arrived on a "permanent" basis. Beginning prior to the Battle of Chickamauga in the fall of 1863, and continuing for over fifteen months, Augusta absorbed a seemingly endless stream of refugees fleeing Sherman's advance. The homeless exiles came first from north Georgia, then from Atlanta, still later from Savannah, and ultimately from across the river in South Carolina. A substantial portion of the new arrivals were black, and during the winter of 1864–65 a local newspaper editor estimated that the number of Negroes in Augusta had tripled since 1861. Blacks continued to pour into the city throughout the last months of the war, as evidenced by the comments of another Augusta resident who reported in January 1865 that "scarcely a morning passes but a long train of waggons [sic], horses and mules, accompanied by negroes on foot, and followed by their owners in carriages can be seen passing across the bridge coming from South Carolina."[10]

Elsewhere in the state the story was much the same. Along a line running from Rome south to Bainbridge, refugees flocked into Georgia's interior towns and villages, greatly expanding their populations and often severely straining local resources and facilities. Although few statistics are available, it seems reasonably certain that the number of blacks and whites in most country towns increased substantially during the war. In the northeast Georgia town of Athens, for example, the arrival from Louisiana of the Cook and Brother's Armory shortly after the fall of New Orleans in 1862 created several hundred new jobs in the space of a few months. In a single Athens church sixty-six new refugee communicants were added to the membership roles between 1862 and 1864. According to one author, there was also "a considerable increase of the slave population by planters allowing their servants to come to Athens, and very likely a majority of the [nineteen] free persons of color [in Clarke County] moved into Athens" during the war. In extreme southwest Georgia, refugees flocked to the town of Thomasville because of its convenient railroad link with Savannah. By the latter part of the war Thomasville "fairly swarmed with refugees," a great many of whom were slaves who had accompanied their owners to town. The influx of bondsmen was clearly of major proportions, for in 1864 Thomasville Mayor Peter E. Love esti-

195

mated that blacks outnumbered whites in the town by a margin of two to one.[11]

For Georgia's black people the significance of extensive wartime urbanization was basically twofold. First, and most obviously, an increasing number of bondsmen came into contact with an urban environment which by late antebellum times had grown more and more incompatible with the peculiar institution. While the extent of slavery's de-urbanization during the immediate prewar decades remains open to question, the basic distinctions separating urban from rural bondage have been firmly established. In towns and cities bondsmen were subject to institutional rather than personal supervision; they enjoyed substantial autonomy in matters of employment and considerable freedom from white surveillance after working hours, due to the growing trend toward some degree of racial segregation in urban slave housing. If during the 1850s urban living conditions tended to reduce the social distance between slaves and free blacks, the reduction involved benefits for bondsmen as well as social and legal liabilities for black freemen. On the eve of the Civil War, Georgia's towns and cities were places where slaves, free blacks, and occasionally poor whites mingled with unusual social intimacy. Here could be found the highest levels of black literacy, the most extensive and readily available sub-rosa educational opportunities for Negroes, the most sophisticated and articulate of the black community's spokesmen and leaders, the greatest concentrations of black wealth and economic resources, and—in nuclear form—the separate, formally organized, and semiautonomous black church, which served as a focal point for many facets of the black urban experience.[12]

Not only did many thousands of Georgia's rural bondsmen enter into a strange new urban world during the Civil War, but by their very presence the newly arrived blacks contributed to the growing fluidity, instability, and chaos of wartime city life. The net effect in most areas was to speed up and intensify the forces which had slowly transformed and undermined urban slavery during the antebellum era. It was in Georgia's towns and cities that the war's corrosive institutional impact upon chattel bondage appeared first and became most pronounced. For blacks as well as for whites the consequences of large-scale urbanization proved to be socially, economically, and psychologically far-reaching.

By the 1860s white Georgians had gained considerable firsthand knowledge of the problems arising from the extension of a rural-oriented slave system into an urban environment. Since wartime urbanization served to aggravate and intensify these traditional problems, white city dwellers drew heavily upon the antebellum experience in attempting to cope with the many difficulties which arose during the war. In addition, however, white urban dwellers were influenced by the general sentiment supporting stricter slave control during the first months of the Confederacy, as well as by subsequent periods of temporary apprehension over possible black unrest. Thus, throughout 1861 many cities attempted to continue and expand the repressive measures adopted following the John Brown raid and during the secession crisis. [13] Yet almost immediately the demands of the war itself began to impede and frustrate these local efforts.

Central to any attempt at tightening control over urban blacks was the maintenance of an adequate police force, but, ironically, city officials often saw local police forces shrink and lose their effectiveness at the very time when sentiment was strongest to expand them. Early in 1861, for example, the city of Macon greatly increased the size of its police force in response to public pressure. Within a few months, however, the "extraordinary expense" involved, together with the departure of many policemen for the army, had reduced the number of regular night patrolmen to the prewar level of eight. The mayor responded by swearing into municipal service a group of unpaid citizens, known as the "Volunteer City Guards," who agreed to assist regular officers in performing night patrol and police duty. By the middle of 1862 military conscription and volunteering caused the citizen's organization to cease functioning, and by 1863 the city had fallen back upon its volunteer fire brigade as an auxiliary "Police and Patrol Guard" to assist regular officers. [14]

Most other Georgia towns experienced similar manpower problems. In April 1861 John Hull, chairman of the Military Committee of the Augusta City Council, requested Governor Brown to furnish the city from ten to one hundred "heavy revolving pistols" and as many "stand of improved arms" to be used "for the purpose of arming our police . . . in case of emergency." Hull justified this request on the grounds "that in the present excited state of public feeling, it would be well to leave this force fully armed . . . especially in view of the absence of so many of our volunteer companies." By the beginning of 1862 Savannah's entire eighty-man police force was declared subject to military duty, under the terms of an order from state Adjutant General Henry C. Wayne. Savannah Mayor Thomas Purse protested that such an order "would not add to but diminish . . . the defence of the city." Smaller towns and villages seldom commanded the services of more than a handful of law enforcement personnel during the war. In Athens, for example, a force of volunteer policemen briefly assisted authorities in patrolling each of the town's wards in late 1860 and early 1861, but for most of the war the municipal police force consisted solely of a marshal, a deputy marshal (who also doubled as streetlamp lighter), and one night watchman. This force was clearly insufficient, and a local newspaper attributed the noisy nighttime behavior of Athens's black children to the fact that "the police force is so small and the territory so large, that while these sable juvenile riots are being suppressed in one locality, they are in full blast in another." The actions of some fifty to one hundred Athens blacks who celebrated the reelection of Marshal B. B. Moon in January 1862 "by throwing up their caps and hurrahing at the very top of their lungs" suggests that local law enforcement was less than ironclad. [15]

If urban police were often unequal to the task of wartime slave control, local town or city ordinances were also deficient in many cases. Even in peacetime the rules and regulations governing the conduct of urban blacks had been cumbersome, unrealistic, and subject to haphazard enforcement. The war rendered most local statutes even more unworkable, especially the laws relating to slave residency and freedom of movement. Nearly all Georgia towns, for example, revised and modified the so-called pass system during the war. In antebellum times the common, if not universal, practice in urban areas was to allow blacks virtually unrestricted freedom of movement during daylight hours. At most a "general ticket" signed by the owner (or guardian in the case of a free Negro) was required to "pass" the bearer until the curfew bell rang in the evening, an event which occurred as early as 8 P.M. in some places and as late as 10 P.M. in others. Blacks out after curfew needed a "special ticket" with a specific hour of expiration, and in the city of Savannah no black could be out after midnight without a pass stating the specific purpose of his errand, his precise destination, and the time of departure from his owner's or guardian's premises.[16]

In many cases these regulations were undoubtedly ignored, and masters as well as slaves often assumed, correctly, that a "general ticket" would suffice for any occasion. During the first year of the war some city officials decided that such peacetime laxity could no longer be tolerated. In late October 1861 the mayor of Macon deplored the fact that numerous slave passes were "made to cover an indefinite period of time and give permission to visit all parts of the city at any or all hour[s] of the night." If this illegal practice were eliminated, declared the mayor, it would "materially lighten the duties of the citizen and regular police." The City Council responded promptly to these remarks by placing residents on notice that after November 1, 1861, "all passes given to negroes to enable them to be out after the ringing of the bell, shall be legal passes stating the time and place in all cases."[17]

Such declarations were easier to issue than to enforce, and in many cities the war created special difficulties for the regulation of slave movements. The efforts of Atlanta officials to control slave activities were hampered by the frequent overlap of civilian and military authority, as well as by the rapid growth of the city's black population. In 1863, after a year-long influx of slaves employed as military laborers and as workers for various agencies of the Confederate government, the City Council instructed the mayor to give public notice that "passes to slaves from the military authorities alone is [sic] not sufficient to escape such slaves being arrested by the city policemen after nine o'clock at night." In Savannah it was apparently the large-scale impressment of slave military laborers from other parts of the state which led the mayor to declare in December 1862 that "no tickets will be counter-signed at this office for slaves or free negroes leaving the city on either railroad." The city of Macon faced a situation of near chaos in August 1864, as refugees flooded in during the latter phases of the Atlanta campaign. An official announcement to "refu-gee slave-owners" dated August 19 suggests that, amid the widespread pandemonium and confusion of the times, the effectiveness of Macon's pass system may have reached its nadir:

> Office City Council
> Macon, August 19, 1864
>
> Refugees owning slaves are hereby notified that for the purpose of maintain-ing police and detecting runaways, they are requested to furnish each of their Slaves with a certificate, stating ownership and where such slaves are temporarily authorized to reside. All negroes without such certificates will be liable to arrest and imprisonment by the City Marshall.[18]

The same wartime conditions which impeded the operation of the pass system created even more serious problems where slave-housing regula-tions were concerned. During the antebellum era, the practice of allowing urban slaves to live separately from their owners' premises and hire their labor to the highest bidder was firmly established in all of Georgia's towns and cities. By the time of the Civil War these twin arrangements of "work-ing out" and "living out" had given rise to a surprisingly strong and co-hesive urban black subculture, buttressed by an embryonic form of resi-dential segregation which fostered the growth and development of semiautonomous black churches, as well as a crucial, if precariously situ-ated, intelligentsia and propertied class of slave and free Negro artisans and entrepreneurs. To a large extent this glaring urban anomaly survived and grew amid an increasingly constricting system of racial bondage be-cause white slaveholders found the system profitable and were unwilling to sacrifice financial gain to either law or racial dogma. Unquestionably much of what transpired in Georgia's urban black communities was tech-nically against the law, but since these communities were themselves reflec-tions of an unspoken white agreement to ignore state statutes governing slave residency, black urbanites could usually count on white authorities to pursue a hands-off policy concerning minor law violations which oc-curred within this broader framework of illegality.

In all of Georgia's major towns and cities there was apparent by 1860 a discernible trend toward increasingly heavier concentrations of black population in specific areas. In Georgia cities as in urban areas elsewhere in the South the direction of movement was outward, away from the intense white surveillance of the central city toward the privacy and freedom of sparsely settled outlying districts. In Atlanta, Savannah, and Augusta, where accurate statistics are most readily available, significant numbers of blacks resided in every ward during 1860. Yet in each case one or more wards possessed unusually high percentages of black population, and frequently these black wards were located on the urban periphery. Significantly, in Savannah and Augusta four out of a total of six black-controlled African Baptist churches were situated in the same fringe areas. In Atlanta the ward with the largest number of slaves also contained the city's entire population of free blacks. [19]

The war witnessed numerous attempts to reduce the economic independence of urban blacks and to bring their unsupervised living arrangements under tighter control. Surviving evidence indicates not only that such attempts generally failed but, more important, that wartime conditions often brought about substantial increases in the amount of de facto autonomy which black urban dwellers enjoyed. At various times the liberalizing tendency might result from either demographic or economic factors, or from a combination of both. During 1861, for example, the cities of Macon and Athens each revised local ordinances relating to slaves who resided off the premises of their owners or employers. Athens sought to discourage the practice by charging fees of five dollars to twenty-five dollars for each slave "living out," while Macon required owners to obtain joint consent in writing from the mayor and City Council for each slave not residing on the master's property. Several months later the City Council tightened controls still further by issuing a certificate to each local black, "stating the number of the lot and square on which they are registered to sleep." All slaves were categorically forbidden to hire their time or engage in any trade except that of "Barber or Hair Dresser."[20]

As the war proceeded, restrictive ordinances soon became little more than dead letters on local statute books. In Macon, Athens, Atlanta, Augusta, Savannah, and elsewhere blacks continued to "live out" in what appeared to be ever-increasing numbers. Part of the explanation for this trend was simply that most of these towns grew with unplanned rapidity and newly arrived black people were forced to seek living quarters wherever available. In the summer of 1863 the Atlanta City Council vainly attempted to solve the problems of rapid growth and a large transient population by drafting a new ordinance providing that "all negroes (unless they be body servants) who come to our city to stay over night or any length of time and [are] not on special business shall be kept in some negro yard or house, and not permitted to go at large through the city."[21]

During the last two years of the war the influx of refugees into cities like Augusta and Macon created a serious housing shortage and rendered control of slave residency increasingly impracticable. Whites continued to attack local sanction of illegal "living-out" arrangements, but the purpose of the attacks changed drastically. With living space for whites at a premium, critics no longer sought to regulate slave housing, but rather to evict blacks from existing dwellings. "Let the Negro population condense a little," urged an Augusta newspaper in September 1863 during the course of an editorial attack on the City Council's lax attitude toward separate slave housing. The following year law enforcement officers in Macon grew indignant when forced to serve "dispossessary warrants" on white tenants who were unable to pay their rent. The deputy sheriff complained bitterly about the city ordinance allowing numerous blacks to live on "detached" lots. "Now, which ought to suffer most for a residence, a negro or a poor soldier's family—the soldier who is fighting for the liberty of his country, or a negro living in indolence[?]" the sheriff asked rhetorically. A local newspaper editor quickly supplied an answer by declaring it an "outrage that negroes should be permitted to rent houses over the heads of wives and children of soldiers." The fact that many of the houses in question were occupied by "negro families" was to this editor a matter of little consequence.[22]

In most Georgia towns the number of slaves hiring their own time also seems to have increased during the war despite the wishes of local authorities. A number of factors contributed to this increase, including the general growth of urban black populations, war-induced monetary inflation, changing attitudes of refugee masters, and the impact of conscription. Perhaps the most crucial element in this complex equation was the existence of a rapidly expanding urban labor market open to blacks as well as whites. As burgeoning war industries offered higher and higher wages for skilled and unskilled labor, profit-minded masters became increasingly willing to send their slaves to town. "Many negroes have left the field for the workshops of the country," reported a Milledgeville newspaper in the spring of 1863. Near the end of the war a Macon resident provided a graphic assessment of the results produced by steadily rising urban pay scales. "The spirit of speculation has been instilled in the heart of the negro as well as the white man," he asserted in a letter castigating masters for allowing slaves to hire their own time: ". . . hundreds of . . . [slaves], in our city, are engaged in the business, under the auspices of masters, who think of nothing more than the best way to make their slave property pay. In doing this, they are inflicting a great injury upon the community— to say nothing of the tendency of such a course to remove the slave from his proper sphere, and, in the course of time, undermine the very principle which is the supporting prop of the peculiar institution."[23]

Notwithstanding such denunciations as the above, black self-hire probably resulted less from greed and "speculation" than from war-related economic hardships. Throughout the war years a general scarcity of consumer goods combined with the steady depreciation of Confederate currency to produce a drastic escalation in the real cost of life's basic necessities. Cut off from direct sources of supply, urban dwellers were particularly hard hit by rising costs of food and clothing. As landless wage earners in increasingly more crowded towns and cities, they were likewise vulnerable to soaring rental fees and real estate prices. Although the impact of rising costs was probably more direct and immediate for bondsmen who "lived out" and hired their time than for any segment of the urban population, the net result in most cases was to ensure that the number of blacks in this category would increase. In antebellum times white town dwellers who owned surplus slaves permitted or encouraged the practice of self-hire for reasons of both profit and personal convenience. A bondsman who hired his own time could become, for an unconcerned owner, little more than the source of a monthly dividend check. The "nominal master" in such cases was, at least in practice, relieved of all responsibility for feeding, clothing, housing, or directing the daily activities of his slave, while still retaining legal ownership and reaping a healthy profit from his human chattel.

The primacy of economics in shaping the behavior of many urban slaveowners goes far toward explaining why wartime complaints about the social and psychological consequences of black self-hire produced few tangible results. When beset by the dual financial strains of rising prices and spiraling inflation, the last thing most urban masters were likely to do was to encourage the return home of self-supporting, profit-making bondsmen. Evidence of the continuing predominance of economics over ideology is most readily available in the town of Athens, where throughout the war local authorities steadily increased the fees charged masters and guardians for permitting blacks to live separately and hire their time, but failed to achieve any visible results. Fees were doubled in 1862 and again in 1864, and during the early months of 1865 they sometimes soared to a staggering 2,000 percent over 1861 levels. In spite of these periodic increases, however, the number of blacks "living out" and "working out" appears to have remained relatively constant or even to have slightly increased during the first half of the 1860s.[24]

Many urban slaves had no choice but to hire their time if they wished to survive during the war. As white Georgians were conscripted for military service, forced to embark upon a transient refugee existence, or simply saddled with increasingly oppressive economic burdens, their self-imposed paternalistic obligations toward faithful bondsmen were often ignored or forgotten. Enlarging upon a well-established antebellum custom, some masters simply abandoned their slaves in various towns and cities, leaving them to fend for themselves for long periods of time. Such behavior, of course, did not necessarily reflect white malice or even total lack of concern about the personal welfare of the blacks involved. Masters who could not provide their slaves with support or gainful employment had logical reasons to conclude that blacks stood a better chance of finding work in cities than anywhere else. Yet whatever the motives of white masters may have been, their actions in this regard provide striking evidence of the all-but-autonomous existence which many urban black people led during the war, despite the continuing legal restraint of slavery. Surviving evidence also suggests, however, that for most blacks such de facto autonomy carried with it the prospect of considerable physical hardship.

It is impossible to estimate how many slaves were "abandoned" by masters during the war, but the practice was frequent enough to evoke comments throughout the state. Early in 1864 the grand jury of Decatur County reported that "a large number" of blacks in and around the town of Bainbridge were illegally hiring their own time, but the jurors found it "inexpedient" to return true bills because many of the indictable white owners were "in the service." During the same year a number of the newly arrived slaves who thronged the streets of Augusta had reportedly "been released by their masters." Many of the blacks were nearly destitute and their poverty gave rise to frequent allegations that they were responsible for thefts of food and clothing. In Macon the process of institutional breakdown associated with slave "release" and "abandonment" was well advanced by September 1864, as evidenced by a newspaper article entitled "Negroes Running at Large": "Macon is filled to overflowing with negroes, many of whom are here without their owners, and but few, if any, are in possession of 'passes.' They hire their own time—transact business, and demean themselves generally as if they were free people. We think it would be advisable for the Marshall to look after the drove of negroes in our midst and find out by what authority they have located here."[25]

The most revealing examples of how such quasi emancipation came about, and of what it meant to the black people involved, concern bondsmen in the cities of Athens and Savannah. In the former city some four to six slaves of the Howell Cobb family resided on their owner's premises for lengthy periods throughout the war, with no direct white supervision or financial support. Even when Mrs. Cobb was present in 1861, she had difficulty in furnishing her slaves with adequate food and briefly considered sending them to her brother's plantation near Macon, because "the times are hard and they can't get work to support themselves in Athens." Ultimately, however, Mrs. Cobb herself went to Macon, leaving the slaves behind with a small supply of food and a large amount of self-direction. Under the minimal supervision of a literate house servant named Aggy and a slave man named Ben, the blacks either found employment on their own or were hired out by an agent acting on Mrs. Cobb's behalf. After receiving a letter from Aggy in March 1862, Mrs. Cobb described the autonomous but economically precarious life which the slaves were leading during her absence:

> all [the Negroes] on our lot are well & all [is] running on smoothly. The two or three barrels of beef I salted down in Nov. & Dec. are holding out well and Aggy says it is very nice. Aside from this they have to work to buy their meal and wood. Aggy takes in sewing. Ben works out by the day and Vickey was to go out as a washerwoman by the day. All they can save from their support is their own. All I required of them was to take care of the house and lot—and cow & calf and make me a garden in the spring.[26]

The freedom enjoyed by house servants like those in Athens resulted from a typical wartime fusion of white indulgence and opportunistic neglect. Liberal impulses may have determined the fate of Aggy and her companions, but such was not the case with "Old Clarissa," a black woman owned by Terrell County planter William H. Stiles. During the spring of 1864 Stiles in a letter to his wife proposed a course of action which, if not precisely equivalent to abandonment, was certainly a close approximation. "I shall send Old Clarissa down [to Savannah] with the [other] negroes," Stiles informed his wife. "She is of little or no use to me here & she promises to pay wages to you regularly. Viz. $20 the first month & $15 each month after. With us she was not earning her salt. . . . If I am only reimbursed her expense up and down I shall be content to be rid of her support." Upon arriving in Savannah, Clarissa provided her callous master with a sort of *quid pro quo* by promptly repudiating her "solemn promises" to "pay wages regularly" and refusing to remit more than ten dollars per month. Stiles was enraged by this behavior and threatened to sell her or send her to work on the fortifications if she did not pay the full sum. Even as he made these threats, however, he recognized their basic futility. "I do not know that it would do to tell her this as she might run away & go to the Yankees," he confided to his wife. Working in Savannah, Clarissa was now effectively beyond her master's control.[27]

Whether their masters were present or absent, hostile or benevolent, there can be little question that most black Georgians found wartime urban life considerably different from anything they had known before. If most blacks felt the pinch of physical hardships, they also felt the easing of institutional restraints as the structure of urban bondage slowly crumbled under the stress of a war environment. The breakdown of slave discipline was visible in virtually all of Georgia's cities, but nowhere more clearly than in the records of the Savannah Mayor's Court. For the first four years of the war, the records reveal an increase of more than 50 percent in the total number of slaves sent to jail. Given the fact that black population shifts resulting from refugeeing and impressment tended to offset each other, thus keeping the total number of blacks in the area relatively constant, the court records undoubtedly reflect both vigorous law enforcement and an actual increase in slave crime.

When these statistics are considered on an annual basis, certain other trends become apparent. Between late 1862 (after the first large contingent of slaves had been impressed to work on Savannah's defenses) and late 1864 the number of Mayor's Court cases involving blacks increased by a staggering 400 percent. It would, of course, be erroneous to suggest that this increase resulted solely from the reaction of rural plantation slaves to a new urban environment, for in many respects native black Savannahians may have been far better equipped to exploit the city's chaotic wartime atmosphere than newly arrived rural bondsmen. Nevertheless, the periodic arrival and departure of large gangs of impressed black laborers unquestionably hampered the efforts of Savannah whites to enforce slave discipline, just as the rising proportion of men in the black population served to enlarge the pool of potential slave lawbreakers. When city streets were packed with a host of unfamiliar black faces, individual bondsmen automatically achieved relative anonymity and blacks could flaunt local regulations or engage in such crimes as petty theft with increasingly small risk of detection or punishment. [28]

For the city of Atlanta a strikingly different statistical picture emerged during the war when, despite steady growth of the slave population, the number of Mayor's Court cases involving blacks dropped from 37 in 1861 to a mere 12 in 1862, and rose only to 13 in 1863. During the same period the overall case load of the Mayor's Court dropped from 234 in

1861 to approximately 180 in 1862, but then climbed to a record number of 348 in 1863, with the largest increase coming in the area of disorderly conduct violations and public drunkenness. In the Fulton County Superior Court, where more serious crimes were tried, the number of prosecutions rose steadily. Civil offenses increased during 1861 and 1862 but declined in 1863, when the number of violent crimes against property increased sharply. If, as one writer suggests, these constantly rising crime statistics "reflect the increasing instability of an urban society caught in the midst of unprecedented growth and change," then the seeming absence of black offenders can have only one plausible explanation. Assuming that Atlanta's black population was comprised of normal human beings rather than walking zombies, the court records reveal not a low level of black crime but, rather, a high level of tolerance among whites for minor black offenses. In other words, Atlanta, like Savannah, became a city where blacks could violate routine laws and ignore traditional constraints with little danger of incurring white reprisals.[29]

In the last analysis, however, statistics concerning black crime merely point up the significance of those social and psychological aspects of the wartime urban experience which by their very nature do not lend themselves to quantification. Ultimately the breakdown of the urban slave system's complex web of legal and institutional restraints did more than simply free bondsmen from white control. It permitted them to sample an ever increasing variety of the forbidden fruits which flourished covertly but with great abundance throughout the narrow streets and alleyways of Georgia's towns and cities. Here were located the black churches, preachers, schools, entrepreneurs, and even entertainers that formed the constituent elements of a decidedly nonservile black culture. Whites throughout the state complained with growing frequency during the latter phases of the war that their slaves had succumbed to the corrupting influence of this urban environment. Over and over again whites employed similar or even identical language to describe an increasingly uniform pattern of urban black behavior. In Augusta and Macon bondsmen had grown "too free" by 1864 and were also "insolent" and "impudent." In Athens, Macon, and Savannah blacks thronged the streets and sidewalks, refusing to give way to whites, using profane language as white women went by, and often "contending for the right" to "keep the inside walk." Augusta citizens were disturbed by the "pernicious influence" of the "fancy colored refugees" who openly organized slave parties and "canal picnics," while many of Savannah's "best people" found the conduct of the "dressy class of ne-groes" to be "rather obnoxious." In Macon, Augusta, and elsewhere the size and boisterous enthusiasm of black religious revivals seemed to in-crease in direct proportion to the decline of Confederate military fortunes during the summer and fall of 1864.[30]

There is, in fact, much to suggest that the behavior of urban slaves was not unrelated to black knowledge and perceptions of the war. Every city had numerous literate slaves and free blacks who were willing teachers and conveyers of news and information. In Augusta Ned Purdee, a black Methodist preacher, ran a clandestine backyard school for which he was frequently apprehended but seldom whipped. Savannah's black teachers included Mary Beasley, "Mrs. Woodhouse," and a slave named Jim who as late as 1863 was fined fifty dollars for "violating [the] ordinance relative to slaves and free Negroes being taught to read and write." In Atlanta the black shoemaker Harrison Berry authored pamphlets, while in Athens the black Presbyterian preacher Joseph Williams corresponded freely with whites, as did the slave Aggy at the Cobb residence.[31]

Slaves who came in from rural areas had opportunities to receive news of the war and discuss its meaning with these more sophisticated, literate urban bondsmen. In Athens, for example, the Cobb slaves may have met and talked with a literate black woman owned by the John Crawford family. "She would steal the newspapers and read up about the war, and she kept the other slaves posted as to how the war was progressing," the woman's daughter later recalled. If the Cobb slaves attended daytime ser-vices at the First Presbyterian Church they heard the white minister de-clare that "Niggers were born to be slaves" and pray that the Lord would "drive the Yankees back." But, perhaps, like the black woman mentioned above, they prayed silently to themselves a very different prayer: "Oh, Lord, please send the Yankees on and let them set us free."[32]

7. The Transformation of Rural Bondage

Between 1861 and 1865 blacks who left the countryside as runaways, industrial workers, or displaced refugees found increasing freedom in Georgia's cities and towns. Slavery, however, remained a predominantly rural institution which kept most bondsmen isolated on remote farms and plantations throughout the greater part of the war. Change of any sort occurred slowly in the state's agricultural heartland where custom and fixed routine imparted a timeless continuity to the rhythms of daily life. Yet even in Georgia's most secure interior counties the foundations of chattel bondage eventually began to crumble under the pressure of the war environment.

In a purely physical sense, the already meager living standard of most slaves deteriorated even further during the war, particularly after 1861 when the Federal blockade tightened around Southern ports and local merchants exhausted stocks of Northern goods. On many plantations slave clothing decreased in both quality and quantity as the war progressed. Wool was in especially short supply and planters in making winter clothes relied increasingly on lightweight Osnaburg cloth or even makeshift mixtures of cow hair and cotton. The vast amounts of leather used for military purposes created a serious domestic shortage which forced many slaves to patch up cheaply made brogans normally discarded after a season of hard use, or else face the prospect of going barefoot even in cold weather. The fact that most plantations turned largely to food crop production during the war did little to ensure bondsmen of an adequate diet. Large-scale impressment of farm produce by Confederate agents cut into civilian food supplies, as did the reduced amount of salt available for meat-curing purposes. All things considered, it is scarcely surprising that in later years many blacks recalled the war as a period of extreme hardship.[1]

On some farms and plantations, increases in the stringency of daily life led to a gradual modification of the tenor of master-slave relationships. As in the case of the coastal refugees discussed earlier, wartime economic pressures caused many up-country slaveowners to abandon any normal proclivities toward patriarchal benevolence. When local newspapers coupled ominous rhetorical questions such as "WOOL, WOOL, who shall wear it this winter, our negroes or our soldiers?" with equally ominous suggestions that planters return to "old frontier times" by giving slaves Indian moccasins "which will answer all the substantial ends of shoes," the fiction of benign paternalism became increasingly difficult to maintain. On the eve of the Civil War, planters like Adam L. Alexander of Wilkes County derived obvious satisfaction from openly displaying their commitment to the paternalist ethic. "No calicoes [are] wanted for the negroes," he informed his daughter in May 1860. "Their summer garments have been given out a month ago & . . . besides that 4 pieces left over. I never put off these things, where *their* comfort is concerned. . . . The wool for their winter clothes has gone to the factory long ago." A cursory glance at Alexander's wartime plantation records reveals, however, that by 1863 "Osnaburgs" and "Kenseys" had replaced woolen cloth for winter clothing and that the quantity of cloth issued for summer use had been reduced by approximately 50 percent. The slave clothing accounts for 1864 include such revealing comments as "A small allowance, each woman having only one dress" and "Plantation children get no suits, dresses or pants." That many of these cutbacks may have resulted less from choice than necessity was, one suspects, a source of little comfort to Alexander's scantily clad black people. By 1864 Alexander's benevolence was evidently wearing almost as thin as the leather of his slave's worn-out brogans. "My whole shoe business . . . has been so delayed & the winter [is] so near gone, that I shall not think of sending the shoes this winter atall," he wrote his daughter. "Then," he explained, "if any of our people run to the Yankees, we shall save the shoes at least."[2]

Across the entire spectrum of slave life the meager fruits of selectively bestowed paternalistic indulgence withered and died in the arid soil of economic self-interest and racial exploitation. Blacks accustomed to planting small cotton crops after working hours to sell for their own benefit found this privilege abruptly curtailed in 1863 when the state legislature limited cotton acreage on all plantations to three acres per hand. "I cut the negroes crop off one half as theirs has to be included in the amount planted on each place," wrote the son of a wealthy slaveowner with plantations in four Georgia counties. [3] For some blacks the shift from cotton to food crop production simply meant an increased burden of toil and drudgery at the hands of profit-minded planters determined to salvage everything possible from their agricultural endeavors. "I never done much field work till de war come on," recalled Nicey Kinney, a former slave housemaid in Jackson County: "Marster was too old to go to de war, so he had to stay home and he sho seed dat us done our wuk raisin' somepin t'eat He had us plant all our cleared ground, and I sho has done some hard wuk down in dem old bottom lands, plowin', hoein', pullin' corn and fodder, and Ise even cut cordwood and split rails. Dem was hard times."[4]

Numerous blacks found that in addition to heavier work loads the war also brought basic dietary restrictions to the slave quarters. Emma Hurley, who had been a slave in Oglethorpe County during the war, was explicit on this point: "Them wuz the hardest an' saddest days I ever knowed. . . . Times wuz so hard . . . folks couldn't git so much as some plain salt to use on their victuals. The white folks had the dirt dug up from out'n their smokehouses an' hauled it up to Mr. Sisson's an' he run it an' got what salt he could out'n it."[5] If whites were forced to adopt unusual measures in their quest for salt, the task of putting these measures into effect fell largely to the slaves themselves. Here too paternalistic obligations often gave way to economic considerations, as aged black "aunts" and "uncles" were pressed into service so that younger slaves would not be diverted from field work. Late in 1862 Howell Cobb's son John summed up the rationale for this practice in a letter detailing the efforts of an overseer to obtain fifteen bushels of salt from the smokehouse of a plantation in Bibb County. Cobb's son was favorably impressed with the overseer's efforts at salt retrieval because "it does not cost much to make it as he has two old negroes at it who could do very little else."[6]

The salt scarcity also contributed to another wartime deficiency in the diets of many slaves, lack of meat. Even wealthy planters who could afford to pay high prices for salt to be used in the curing process often saw the meat supply on their plantations reduced through seizures by Confederate impressment agents.[7] Less prosperous planters, especially those accustomed to purchasing beef and pork for their slaves in the commercial market, were often unable or unwilling to buy meat at the high wartime prices created by general scarcity and spiraling inflation. Here, as elsewhere, slaves ultimately bore the brunt of their masters' frugality. Physical conditions appear to have been particularly bad for blacks on small farms and plantations where economic pressures often obliterated most of the tangible manifestations of white paternalism before the war had entered its second year. As early as August 1861 a Confederate soldier admonished his wife in Sumter County to "feed the negroes light for I am liveing harder than they are," and the following month he made his instructions still more specific: "Go ahead [and] deal with the Negroes [just as if] they were yours and you had to controll them the balance of your life[.] as for meet [sic] . . . I hardly know what to write you about it[.] I think it best not to buy any bacon[.] get some beef when you can & dont give them [the slaves] as much of it as they can eat[.] everything is so high & money can't be had youl be compelled to live on as little as possible."[8] By the following year it was apparent that this plan for retrenchment had failed to take into account the attitudes of the black people involved. Not only did the slaves fail to acquiesce passively when their food allotment was reduced, but they also retaliated with acts of theft. Coercion seemed to be the only answer. "In reference to your meet difficulty you must do as you think best," the absentee soldier counseled his wife in February 1862. "Have them [the slaves] whiped Severely when they steel [sic] and shorten their [food] allowance for a while[.] I don't know what youl do with them[.]"[9]

In the opinion of one veteran white overseer, the deliberate stinting of slave rations was likely to be no more successful on large plantations than on small ones. Writing to Georgia planter John B. Lamar, the overseer expressed considerable apprehension over how the blacks under his supervision would react if forced to work without adequate food. "I need a better overseer's birth than I have at present," he informed Lamar in December 1861. "I have been overseeing for one man for three years . . . but he is a man that made cotton and bought his meat and now meat is high and he is opposed to paying big prices for meat and intends to work his negroes on dry bread next year, and I think the place too hot for a good man to oversee at." Perhaps the most revealing insight into how Georgia bondsmen perceived masters who reduced slave rations in order to save money came from ex-slave Nancy Boudry, who spent the war on a small farm in Columbia County. "We done de bes' we could," she said, referring to herself and the two other blacks owned by her master. "We et what we could get, sometimes didn' have nothin to eat but piece of cornbread, but de white folks allus had chicken."[10]

Black resentment over Civil War food shortages occurred at a time when the traditional lines of authority in agricultural society had been weakened by demographic change. Prior to secession, masters or overseers resided on virtually all Georgia plantations, secure in the knowledge that neighboring whites stood ready to offer prompt assistance in matters of slave discipline. Bondsmen might enjoy numerical superiority in a particular locale, but night-riding patrol squads of planters and yeomen provided ample proof that slaveowners could, if necessary, marshal overwhelming power in defense of the racial status quo. Secession changed all of that. In Georgia and throughout the South the war years witnessed a wholesale exodus of white adult males from the countryside, as men of all social classes volunteered or, after April 1862, were conscripted into military service.

The Confederacy's massive redeployment of white manpower had both immediate and long-term effects upon the stability of rural bondage. Male absenteeism struck first and most directly at the state's newly revised slave policing system. Grand jury complaints that patrol laws were "entirely neglected" or "utterly disregarded" became commonplace during the last two years of the war and were echoed frequently by apprehensive whites in their private correspondence. "Our County has already been drained of its white male population," reported a Stewart County resident in September 1862. "Our Militia is disorganized & really the new [conscription] law will take most of it. We have no police arrangements & scarcely any men to execute the laws."[11] In June 1863 several citizens of the sixty-sixth militia district of Burke County complained that:

> patriotism and the Conscript Act, have deprived us of all our citizens who were capable of performing military service, . . . thus leaving us with a very sparse population; i.e.—in a scope of country (composed of the 66th, 67th & 68th District) 27 miles in length and twelve miles in breadth, we have now only about 140 white male citizens, between the ages of 16 & 60 years (and many of them are not able to perform any kind of military service) while we have a very large population of negroes.[12]

During this same period similar complaints came from David C. Barrow, a wealthy planter in Oglethorpe County, where over 75 percent of the adult white male population ultimately left to join the army. Barrow deplored the fact that along several miles of the Little River in the southeastern part of the county there were hundreds of slaves supervised by only two white overseers and a few old and crippled men "not effective for police duty." In another section of the county there were "not [white] men enough left liable to militia duty to provide Gov[ernor] Brown with officers." In this region also were hundreds of slaves and Barrow described the ratio of blacks to whites as "a good many to one." When the state militia was mobilized to help defend Atlanta during the summer of 1864, many agricultural districts lost their last remaining white overseers. In mid-July, for example, a woman in rural Columbia County reported that the departure of the militiamen left only one ablebodied white man within a radius of ten miles.[13]

Although wartime slave patrols lost much of their effectiveness, it would be misleading to say that bondsmen went entirely unsupervised. Policing arrangements for blacks in rural districts changed frequently during the war as legislators and other officials sought ways to offset the ongoing drain of civilian manpower. Late in 1862 the upper age limit of persons subject to patrol duty was raised from forty-five to sixty years, and a few months later the legislature passed a comprehensive bill "to suppress insurrection and organize a home guard militia."[14] Governor Brown vetoed the measure because it weakened his ability to fight Confederate conscription, but on May 26, 1863, he issued a proclamation urging the formation of local defense companies in all Georgia counties.[15] Most of the "Home Guard" units organized in response to Brown's call bore a marked resemblance to the vigilante groups of 1859–61 and looked upon slave control as an integral part of their paramilitary responsibilities. At local courthouse meetings in June 1863 citizens of Houston, Dooly, Crawford, Macon, and other counties vowed to resist "Federal or Abolition" incursions like General Abel D. Streight's recent raid into northern Georgia. At the same gatherings special night patrol squads were formed "to prevent our slaves and the free negroes from holding improper meetings and . . . communicating with mischievous or corrupt persons."[16] Many of the June volunteers were subsequently mustered into Confederate service, but continued to perform rural police functions in their new capacity. In July 1864, for example, a captain of the state's reserve forces in Covington reported that besides making several criminal arrests his company had "corrected a great many disobedient Negroes."[17]

The 1864 Atlanta campaign strained conventional methods of slave supervision almost to the breaking point as more and more white Georgians were pressed into emergency combat service. But even in the last desperate weeks before the "Gate City's" surrender, state officials struggled to maintain a semblance of white authority in plantation regions. Having ordered the bulk of Georgia's adult white male population to the front on July 9, Governor Brown issued secret instructions the next week to a group of some 150 militia officers and Executive Department aides-de-camp who had been dispatched to mobilize the state's civilian defenders. After completing their initial task the militiamen and aides were to stay in the countryside and organize the remaining white residents of each senatorial district into a "police & patrol force to . . . keep down any insubordination or attempted insurrection among the negroes."[18] Subsequent orders established a ratio of one policeman for each five hundred blacks and authorized military details in case an adequate force could not be assembled from men over military age. Otherwise, all fifty-five- to sixty-year-old white males "able to ride and carry a gun" were ordered to travel through their counties on a full-time basis in order to "visit the plantations, correct insubordinate negroes, and do all in their power to protect property and preserve order."[19] Broadly implemented by late August, the new system with various local modifications apparently continued to function in unoccupied parts of the state until the war's last months.[20]

Emergency measures like those just described did little to allay white concern over possible slave unrest. Throughout the war, visions of a Yankee-inspired racial uprising haunted the minds of Georgia planters, who saw their coercive power over blacks weakening while the danger of Northern invasion increased. In Calhoun County, where "low white men" had been suspected of spreading abolitionist doctrines in 1861, three local residents were accused of collaborating with the Federals in a scheme to smuggle black recruits into Union lines while supposedly making salt on the Georgia coast during the summer of 1862. Having allegedly promised to lead slaves into a "camp of instruction to be drilled," the men were arrested in June 1862 at virtually the moment when black enlistment was beginning off the Georgia and South Carolina coast.[21] The Lincoln administration's September 1862 decision to support emancipation as a war measure raised new fears of black rebellion and caused Governor Brown to seek extra supplies of gunpowder for the Christmas holidays. No mass uprising took place, but in December three slaves were arrested in Chatham and McIntosh counties "with arms in their hands against their masters."[22] As the new year began, an up-country planter stated flatly that "Lincoln's [Preliminary Emancipation] proclamation is well known by the negroes and is causing some trouble by the bad ones."[23]

Most white Georgians either ignored or ridiculed Lincoln's official announcement of Negro freedom on January 1, 1863, but the presence of armed ex-slaves in Union regiments along the seaboard could not be so easily dismissed. The Savannah *Morning News* wrote ominously of Yankee efforts to "colonize" nearby Florida with black escapees who would plunge the state into a genocidal "war of races." The Georgia newspaper also reprinted articles from the New York *Tribune* advocating that Federal commanders invade South Carolina with a force of five thousand black troops and thereby "surprise the rebels, not with the phantom, but with the reality of servile insurrection."[24] In May 1863 Governor Brown received copies of what purported to be captured military correspondence from North Carolina revealing elaborate plans for inciting slaves throughout the South to rise in rebellion on the night of August 1, 1863. The captured letter urged sympathetic Union officers to send reliable freedmen behind enemy lines to spread word of the revolt's date and purpose. At the appointed time blacks in each state were to "arm themselves with any and every kind of weapon" and "commence operations by burning all railroad and country bridges," tearing up tracks, and destroying telegraph lines. Eventually the slaves could retreat to swamp or mountain regions, emerging "as occasion may offer for provisions and for further depredations."[25]

However implausible so grandiose a scheme may have been, there can be little doubt that Brown and other knowledgeable Georgians took the danger of an externally instigated insurrection seriously. The state's coastal counties had already experienced several unsettling raids by black troops, and antislavery commanders like General David Hunter stood ready to launch more ambitious undertakings in behalf of liberty. Writing from Hilton Head, South Carolina, on May 22, 1863, Hunter outlined a plan of action to President Lincoln that equaled or surpassed anything previously imagined by Georgia's apprehensive slaveholders. If released from the siege of Charleston, Hunter promised immediately to place a "column of ten thousand of the best drilled soldiers in the country . . . in the heart of Georgia, our landing and march being made through those counties in which . . . the slave population is seventy-five percent of the inhabitants." With a flourish worthy of Georgia's own chief executive, Hunter renewed an earlier request for steel pikes, which he considered the "simplest and most effective [weapons] that can be placed in the hands of the slaves who are liberated in our march into the interior."[26]

Had white Georgians learned of Hunter's 1863 letter they would probably have been more frightened than surprised. In the minds of most slaveowners the general's name was indelibly linked with initial efforts to arm and liberate black escapees on the sea islands during the previous year. At that time Georgia newspapers had denounced Hunter as a "cold-

218

blooded abolition miscreant," and the Confederate War Department had directed that, if captured, he should be "held in close confinement for execution as a felon."[27] The simple knowledge that Hunter and other like-minded officers were stationed off Georgia's coast gave substance to Southern fears of slave conspiracy and helped keep alive the crisis mentality of 1859–61. As had been true in antebellum days, racial anxiety culminated in periodic rebellion scares that subjected rural bondsmen to spasms of fierce repression. Well-organized insurrectionary plots were ostensibly discovered among Hancock County Negroes in 1863 and among slaves in Brooks County the following year. Each episode involved allegations of Federal complicity and led to mass arrests, floggings, and the eventual execution of several individuals.[28] Well publicized throughout the state, the panics played an important role in transforming white fear into a weapon of racial intimidation and localized slave control.[29]

By galvanizing public support for campaigns of racial vigilantism, insurrection scares temporarily shored up the structure of rural bondage. On the whole, plantation discipline grew more lax as the war progressed, but slaves received frequent reminders of the lengths to which local communities would go in defense of white supremacy. Even in areas not directly touched by the turmoil of anticipated uprisings, countless acts of violence and terrorism were directed at individual bondsmen. With depressing regularity black Georgians fell victim to the fury of enraged mobs in plantation regions. During a single three-month period of 1862, for example, a runaway slave was beaten to death by pursuers in Thomas County, a bondsman accused of stabbing his overseer was hanged by Washington County citizens who had "called a meeting to consider the case," and five Negroes accused of murdering their master were hanged and burned to death near Columbus.[30]

Particular emotion surrounded the cases of black men accused of sexual offenses against white women. Punishment of alleged rapists was swift, often extralegal, and manifestly aimed at deterring other blacks from what most slaveowners considered the ultimate repudiation of white male authority. Death awaited nearly any male slave believed guilty of an interracial liaison, although the method of execution might vary. Sometimes public anger resulted in a sudden lynching like the one that occurred in

Athens during July 1862 when a Clarke County bondsman was arrested for assaulting an overseer's wife. Despite the objections of prominent local citizens, a mob removed the prisoner from jail, marched him through town with a rope around his neck, and hanged him in a pine tree just outside the city limits.[31] Near Stone Mountain in 1863 a black man accused of violating an eleven-year-old white girl was publicly executed and "his body . . . left hanging on the gallows, there to rot, as a monument of warning to others."[32] Occasionally local tribunals found ways to register their disapproval of black sexual behavior without destroying the life of a valuable chattel. In Bibb County local authorities revived one of Georgia's more barbaric legal penalties by sentencing the slave Melton to be castrated for attempted rape during the war. When two local doctors carried out the order in February 1864, Melton was reportedly "much distressed, and considered the sentence more dreadful than death itself." A local newspaper expressed confidence that Melton's fate would serve as a "terrible warning and example" to other blacks while ensuring that the prisoner would commit no further sexual offenses.[33]

In areas of Georgia that escaped actual invasion, a combination of emergency police arrangements, harsh criminal sentences for black defendants, and intermittent acts of racial terrorism kept most plantations functioning until the war's end. Slaves, however, took frequent advantage of white absenteeism in order to lighten the burden of field work while stopping just short of the kind of open defiance that would result in violent reprisals.

As the war continued, more and more observers became convinced that the efficiency of black agricultural labor was declining.[34] One newspaper editor placed blame on the few remaining white overseers, who since the abandonment of cotton culture had "not yet entered into the new order of things" and seemed "less efficient now than ever before." A correspondent writing under the signature "Agricola" was equally blunt, and agreed that the problem of slave discipline on plantations was crucial to the cause of Southern independence:

Strip the question of all needless appliances, and the truth stares us in the face[,] slave labor must support this war.

 . . . Simplifying [the above] to the understanding of a child, no slave,

male or female, old or young, . . . should be left to idleness, but should be
made to exert every energy to supply food to meet the absolute wants of the
country. . . . There is but one way to do this, and that is, to place the
negro under the immediate control and direction of the white man; . . . In
an observation somewhat extended, I have come to the deliberate conclusion that there is, at least, one-fifth of the negroes at work on the farms who
are not supporting themselves. And why? Because they are not subject to
proper control.[35]

Whether they directed their criticism at negligent overseers or the conscript law itself, nearly all wartime commentators were in agreement upon
one basic point: only white *men* could effectively control Georgia's black
population. "Is it possible," asked one writer, "that Congress thinks
. . . our women can control the slaves and oversee the farms? Do they
suppose that our patriotic mothers, sisters and daughters can assume and
discharge the active duties and drudgery of an overseer? Certainly not.
They know better." A planter from Schley County raised the same issue
more dramatically, in language which was almost certain to strike a responsive chord among his white male audience. "We may *talk* of black
gratitude," he wrote, "but the planters on the coast know of black in-
gratitude. . . . What woman is she whose husband and sons are gone to
the defense of the county [who] cannot testify to the daily augmenting
audacity of her negroes!"[36]

Before dismissing such pronouncements as meaningless effusions of
Southern male chauvinism and sexual anxiety, it is well to ask whether
some shred of historical insight may not lie buried beneath the obvious
hyperbole. An impressive body of surviving evidence confirms that
Southern white women *did* encounter serious difficulties in controlling
slaves during the war, and while much slave recalcitrance, theft, malingering, and absenteeism can be interpreted as a pragmatic exploitation of
weakened institutional controls, there was frequently a dimension of
black behavior which transcended simple opportunism. What took place
on many remote plantations when husbands, sons, and overseers had
gone to war was not, and logically could not be, wholly unrelated to the
traditional status and role of women in Southern society.

Although Southern white women were never the weak, submissive,

221

dependent creatures depicted in cavalier mythology, they were in a very real sense prisoners of a male-dominated society. For better or worse they were products of a culture which reserved aggressive leadership roles for men and demanded that women maintain an outward posture of deferential acquiescence to males. Such a heritage left many women ill-prepared to take control of an isolated agricultural enterprise during the prolonged absence of a spouse. Even women who were psychologically equal to the challenge often found themselves hampered by lack of firsthand knowledge about the day-to-day details of farm work. Professor Anne Firor Scott is undoubtedly correct in stating that antebellum women "knew a good deal more about the planting operation than has generally been supposed," but the fact still remains that the practical accomplishments of most plantation mistresses were largely confined to the realm of domestic tasks and household management. [37]

Here, then, was the partial origin of a broader dilemma. At the very time that many white women were placed in "control" of the slaves on a farm or plantation, they were usually forced to depend upon many of these same bondsmen for crucial knowledge, advice, and assistance on a host of practical matters. Such white dependency, besides providing blacks with a practical bargaining lever, also had more subtle psychological implications.

Although knowledge concerning family structure and sex roles within the slave community remains incomplete, available evidence suggests that when monogamous family relationships existed in the quarters the tendency was toward some degree of male domination. [38] It is, in any event, reasonable to suppose that black men were not unaffected by the overwhelmingly male orientation of white society and that they often defined their roles as husbands and fathers within a social framework somewhat similar to that of their white masters. In this regard, the significance of chattel slavery was doubly ironic, for while the slave system encouraged and reinforced a male-dominated, patriarchal family structure in white society, it acted to prevent the full development of corresponding sets of relationships in slave families by stripping black men of the capacity for autonomous action in domestic matters. At the same time, of course, slavery also placed all white women in a position of dominance over all black men.

With the coming of the war this situation changed appreciably in many remote rural areas. As institutional control and personal supervision of bondsmen lost its effectiveness, blacks experienced greater freedom of action in all areas, including their personal lives. The breakdown of the patrol system made it easier for black men to visit wives and children on other plantations and thus fulfill more effectively their husband and father roles. When white women were left to supervise agricultural units in their husbands' absence, black men often assumed actual control of daily farming operations. And if their role in this regard was something less than that of surrogate master, it was virtually or often literally that of full-fledged overseer. The assumption of these new roles and responsibilities must inevitably have contributed to what W. E. B. DuBois described some four decades ago as a "new undercurrent of independence" among bondsmen in the Confederacy.[39]

One can, at best, offer little more than tentative speculation concerning the psychodynamics of black plantation life during the war. Under slavery blacks unquestionably possessed a major degree of psychological autonomy and exhibited personalities so vital and diverse as to belie any abstract notions of mass "infantalization." Yet the realms in which black people could safely express their true feelings and emotions were clearly delineated and narrowly circumscribed by white society. Surviving evidence suggests that as the war altered traditional power relationships and thrust blacks into new roles on farms and plantations, peacetime barriers of thought and action crumbled, making it possible for many blacks to cast off the psychological chains of bondage, revealing attitudes and personality traits long suppressed or concealed.

Much of the testimony on this subject is fragmentary and indirect, and offers only isolated glimpses of a process of gradual metamorphosis over time. However, numerous white women, whose extant wartime correspondence, if taken separately, consists of only a few disconnected letters, tell strikingly similar stories which suggest tentative outlines for a broader collective portrait of black responses to changing plantation realities. While the specific variations are endless, letters and diaries of Georgia's rural white women contain at least two common themes: personal feelings of inadequacy concerning practical plantation matters and increased reliance upon blacks for knowledge and assistance. The same

223

documents attest to a pattern of growing assertiveness and independence among all blacks, but particularly among male field hands.

As early as February 1862 a woman on a plantation in Habersham County complained to her husband that "I had so much trouble after you left me I hardly felt equal to the undertaking. . . . Samuel [a slave] who had runaway returned. . . . I had to have both Ben and Samuel punished, then there were other annoyances." Throughout 1862 Mrs. Laura B. Comer, a woman living near Columbus, plunged periodically into deep troughs of despair and depression brought on by frequent confrontations with "lazy," "obstinate," "willful," and "indolent" slaves. In a passage which is a superb testament to the constricting effect of the South's patriarchal family structure upon antebellum women, she blamed most discipline problems upon the lenient treatment previously accorded the slaves by her husband (whom she consistently referred to in her diary as "Mr. Comer") and upon lack of male supervision during his lengthy wartime absences:

> I have been able by having no cooking done at all & remaining quietly in my room, to be at peace; but if Mr Comer lives a few years [longer]; I am sure I don't know what anyone can do with his servants about the house; in the field, where a man is with them, whom they fear all the time they will get along but I cannot, nor will not spend all these precious days of my life, following after and watching negroes. It is a terrible life! Who can appreciate or understand anything about such a life, but a *woman* who marries a *Bachelor* who has lived with his negroes as *equals*; at bed and board. [40]

It would be inaccurate to attribute Laura Comer's numerous conflicts with her husband's slaves solely to the unsettling effect of a war environment. In prose laden with color symbolism which differed little from that used by white Englishmen three centuries earlier, she confirmed that even in antebellum days her dealings with bondsmen had been less than harmonious. "May God soften the hearts & enlighten the understanding of these dark, heathen negroes around me," she wrote in a moment of despondency. "I have faithfully taught them for 12 years and it seems to me; with the exception of two or three they are the same; . . . determined, obstinate and dark as midnight." Yet a careful reading of her diary for 1862 indicates that during her husband's prolonged absence relations between Mrs. Comer and the slaves deteriorated steadily. Willis, a black carriage driver, drew a mild rebuke in early January when he drove "awkwardly," giving his mistress an unpleasant ride. During March he committed the more serious offense of breaking the carriage tongue, and in May he overfed one of the carriage horses, causing a near fatal illness. By June, Willis had "very carelessly" broken the carriage tongue again, and in late August he finished the job when he caused a horse to fall and "break the Rockaway very badly," necessitating extensive repairs in a blacksmith shop.[41]

With the other slaves a similar pattern emerged. In March, Fannie, the black cook, refused to prepare breakfast. Several months later Fannie and Lethe, a female house servant, remained "wilful & obstinate" for an extended period, and on September 29 Fannie returned home from a prolonged "frolic." During this same period another bondsman ran away and stayed "out in the woods" for two days, while the slave Tom openly disobeyed his mistress and annoyed her "even to tears." At first Mrs. Comer was perplexed. "It is passing strange that *servants* cannot see it is for their interest to do well!" she mused in late July. "I cannot understand *why* they are so indolent, obstinate & wilful. *I know* I offer servants sufficient inducements to want to do well." Before the year's end, however, her perplexity turned to anger, bitterness, and ultimately despair. The focus of her diary shifted from specific complaints to sweeping indictments. "The *Negro* is a dark, ignorant being," she asserted. None of the blacks were "more than *half civilized*" and many were "lower than the beast." It was, she concluded, a "terrible task . . . to govern these semi-barbarous, half-enlightened beings. How can I endure it. O, God strengthen me."[42]

Most white women, whether mistresses of large plantations or simply wives of small slaveowning farmers, were considerably more pragmatic and less emotional than Laura Comer. But even the most practical and strong-willed women usually experienced some doubts concerning their ability to maintain authority over bondsmen. Sarah A. Gilbert, who managed forty-two slaves on a plantation south of Macon, reported in late 1863, for example, that the slave George would not work without strict supervision and that she despaired "of ever doing anything with him here." Although she never directly analyzed the causes of slave discipline problems, Mrs. Gilbert clearly revealed her own uneasiness when deprived of an overseer and forced to rely upon the skills and knowledge of the blacks to accomplish important tasks about which she knew very little. "We are changing overseers & my hands are full," she wrote in December 1863. "Building is going on too . . . [including] a log kitchen which . . . I today have Solomon & another boy daubing, after the most approved style, learnt by Sol up the country. You ought to see me overseeing the building & looking as if I knew something about it."[43]

Some women, like Mary F. Akin, wife of Confederate Congressman Warren Akin, attempted to augment their limited farming knowledge by seeking detailed instructions by mail from absent husbands. Mrs. Akin went beyond purely agricultural matters, however, and attempted to use what might be termed a "correspondence" approach to slave discipline. After repeated problems with several male field hands whose work output had steadily declined as their open defiance of white authority increased, Mary Akin sought her husband's assistance. She complained especially about a slave named Bob who tended to be more blatant than most of the other blacks in desregarding her instructions. Congressman Akin's response revealed nothing so much as his own failure to comprehend the changes in black attitudes which had occurred during his absence. "I wish you to tell Bob," he solemnly instructed his wife from far-off Richmond, that *"if he leaves the lot day or night, without your permission, I will certainly punish him if I live to get home.* Keep this letter and mark on it the day you tell him, and then keep an account of his going off, and give me this letter, and how often he has left without permission, after I return." If, as the latter sentence indicates, Akin felt some misgivings over the potential effectiveness of threats conveyed by letter, his doubts in this regard were soon confirmed. Less than two weeks after issuing the instructions quoted above, he learned of further problems with Bob, who showed an increasing tendency to be "as mean as possible" about any work assigned him. Although Mrs. Akin never said so directly, her comments clearly reveal that Bob had been given somewhat greater responsibilities than his fellow bondsmen and that he acted as a sort of foreman. His duties included care of the livestock, including two valuable mules, for which purpose he was entrusted with the stable key. The mules were in "tolerably good order" and "if talking will make Bob curry them they will be well curried." Bob also made unsupervised trips with the mules and wagon to haul corn from a neighboring farm. This task, however, remained unfinished because "Bob was determined not to hurry himself before Christmas." He was equally unenthusiastic about hard physical labor like ploughing, and Mrs. Akin was reluctant even to rent new land since Bob "seems to think hauling wood is all he has to do this year." When informed of these and other difficulties, Congressman Akin could scarcely conceal his sense of frustration. Curtly (and rather unrealistically) he admonished his wife to rely on coercion instead of threats. "When you want Bob to do any thing dont *ask* him, but *order* him," Akin fumed. "That is the only way to do Bob. *Make him do just what you want.*"[44]

The interrelationships between weakened institutional controls over plantation slaves, increased white female dependence upon black men, and the assumption of new roles and responsibilities by rural bondsmen emerges with considerable clarity and precision in the experiences of the Pryor family of Sumter County. Early in 1861 Shepard G. Pryor joined the Confederate Army and departed for Virginia, where he remained for most of the war, leaving his wife Penelope in charge of a small farm and thirteen slaves. For the first few months Mrs. Pryor enjoyed the dubious assistance of "Uncle Dick Bass," a profane, drunken, elderly white man who attempted with phenomenal lack of success to act as overseer. Actually there was little or no conflict between "Uncle Dick" and the slaves, for the black people on Pryor's farm usually found it easier simply to ignore the incompetent old man. "They dont hear him at all," Penelope Pryor lamented in October 1861. "I believe they would do better without him, but I cant stay here without some [white] man on the place."[45]

Not surprisingly Mrs. Pryor was plagued with discipline problems from the beginning, as various bondsmen took advantage of their master's absence to engage in unauthorized leisure-time activities and avoid field work. "We had a little Scrumage with your boy George," wrote one Sam-

uel Scrutchin to Shepard Pryor after visiting the latter's farm in July 1861.
According to Scrutchin, the incident occurred when he, along with
Pryor's half-brother, attempted to punish the slave George at Mrs. Pryor's
request:

> "Nep [Penelope Pryor] wanted him whipped for his disobedience to her.
> He asked her for a gun to go hunting and she . . . bid him not to take it but
> he done so without her consent. And other little things that he ought to bin
> whip for. Spencer [Pryor's half-brother] came up at the time I was going to
> whip him. Spencer ordered him to take his mules loos from the wagon. And
> he broke to run, but we picked him up quick. Spencer on bills' horse and I
> on foot. . . . We gave him a good stroping and turned him loos & put him
> to work. [46]

Upon receiving this report in Virginia, Shepard Pryor penned what was
to be the first in an extended series of alternating threats and appeals to
his bondsmen back in Georgia. Using language similar to that of Congressman Warren Akin, Pryor instructed his wife to "tell . . . [George] if I
should be fortunate enough to get home Il reward him according to his
merit & so far he isent meritenting any thing good."[47]

So long as an overseer was present and assistance from nearby white
men was periodically available, a sort of precarious equilibrium existed
between mistress and bondsmen on the Pryor farm. Soon, however, "Uncle Dick" was gone, and in April 1862 his successor also left to join the
army before the conscription law took effect. White mistress and black
slaves were now left alone to explore a new set of realities which became
apparent only gradually. It was during this period, perhaps without anyone clearly perceiving what was happening or why, that a delicate psychological balance began to tip—away from white mastery toward dependence, away from slavery toward freedom.

The process may actually have begun the previous summer when
Shepard Pryor first requested his wife to "speak to the Negroes and try to
make them feel the responsibility to take care & make something." Such a
request was one which a master could make only from a position of

strength, and still remain a master. In the spring of 1862, however, this initial request was superseded by a far more sweeping one. Penelope Pryor could not run the farm alone. Since all the white overseers were gone only one choice seemed to remain, and it was not a choice calculated to strengthen the shackles of racial bondage. With some reluctance Shepard Pryor decided that the overseer's job would fall to a trusted slave named Will: "Say to Will that he is my last overseer and he must try himself farming and take care of every thing[.] You must not make him work as the rest do[.] he must look around and See that every thing goes on right[.] Il write to them [the slaves] as you asked me as soon as I get the chance."[48] True to his word, Pryor soon composed a lengthy message to the black people on his Sumter County farm, seeking their cooperation in a sort of compromise arrangement which would preserve elements of slavery while simultaneously granting them large measures of personal autonomy. He began by repeating his earlier injunction:

> Say to Will that I have confidence in his ability to manage the farm and that he must attend to every thing strictly & [say] to Berry [a field hand] he is old enough to know how to do right[.] Il expect him to assist Will to get along[.] Will must be head[,] the rest must obey him and work for him better than if I was there[.] Say to George that iv heard of his Conduct and regret it verry much[.] he can be a good boy if he will[.] he must do better[.] he can do better[.] I say to him the course he has begun he cant belong to me no longer than I can find a man that will buy him if he doesnt change. . . . as for the women and children I know they will do if the rest does their part. . . . Say to them all that they must not lieve the place without letting you know it before they go[,] then you can know who is at home & who is gone & Will I put the whole under him.[49]

Pryor apparently predicated these unorthodox proposals upon a conviction that his slaves would respond positively to prewar paternalism continued on an absentee basis. To some extent this view may have been correct, for Pryor was apparently a relatively kind and humane master who recognized his slaves' individuality and humanity in some areas even as he denied it in others. Ultimately, of course, the new system which he

229

adopted was destined to fail for it created conditions which destroyed the very bond of paternalism and dependency upon which it was based. As Pryor's bondsmen began to enjoy greater freedom, responsibility, and self-direction, they ceased in many respects to think or act like slaves. For obvious reasons, the transformation was most clearly visible in the case of Will, the black man in whom Pryor placed the highest trust and to whom he assigned the position of greatest authority and independence. Farm work did, to be sure, continue under Will's direction, but as the months passed he became less and less the faithful lieutenant his master had originally envisioned. Indeed, by the spring of 1863, after some ten months in his overseer's post, Will had at least in a metaphorical sense gone over to the enemy. Instead of performing as a dutiful servant and conscientious taskmaster, he was found to be assisting slaves who wished to escape and personally harboring black fugitives. Upon learning of these developments, Will's master reacted with philosophic resignation, displaying a sense of limited disappointment at the betrayal of a trust, but failing to perceive that the paternalism in which that trust was rooted had grown increasingly irrelevant to the new realities of a war environment. "I am truely sorry that it happened with Will for I think a great deal of him," Pryor confided to his wife. "It is true that he did verry wrong in denying the charges after he was caught[,] but Dear I never could blame a negro much for assisting one that was run away[,] that is if he did not steal any thing to do it with[.] he is now to old to be whiped and not to do any thing to deserve it[.] . . . don't have him whiped unless . . . nothing else will do."[50]

We can do little more than speculate concerning the specific details of the transformation which Will experienced while serving as overseer on the Pryor farm, but fortunately such occurrences were sufficiently common to ensure that additional testimony on the subject would survive. Perhaps the most revealing description of the psychological metamorphosis which many rural blacks underwent during the war came from the pen of Mrs. Louticia Jackson, who in 1863 was attempting to supervise a small slave force in rural Clarke County with only the aid of her teenage son Johnny. Writing to an older son in the Confederate Army, she described numerous discipline problems, including the growing recalcitrance of the slave Willes. "We are doing as best we know, or as good as we can get the Servants to do," she reported.

> they seem to feel verry indepenat [sic] as no white man comes to direct or look after them, for Willes speaks shorter to johny and orders *him* about more than any negro on the place. In consequence . . . [Johny] seldom tells him to do anything, so sure as he does . . . Willes will make some insulting reply such as thus[:] whats the matter with you[,] whats the reason you can't do it, and so on, and when I ask him why he has not done certain things he will say John never told him, and says that John will tell a story in a minute. I told him he did not have to tell me so again, but he sayed he did not care what I sayed about it. a few evenings ago I asked him where he had been all the evening; he did not make any reply. John then sayed[:] ma[']s talking to you. he sayed he knew that and she's allways asking some silly question[.] he then commenced in such a loud harangue you might have heard him half a mile or more. It so excited me I left the door[,] went in the room[,] and lay down with the back ache. he does not suffer me to enquire in to anything without giving some insulting reply, though I tell them all together generally what must be done so as to avoid any difficulty with him.
> He done as well as he knew how the first 6 months after you left[.] I was truly proud to see him seem to take such an intrust in the farm[.] but he got his own crop laid by[.] he then helped some in threshing the wheat, he took the fever immediately after[,] which lasted some 5 or 6 weeks in which time i attended him closely day and night[,] bathed and rubed him with my own hands fearing it would not be faithfully done [otherwise.] in 6 mounths he grew w[e]ary in well doing, [and] has been a drag ever since, and we . . . can see his evil influence in most all the others that are large enough to notice him. . . . Some person must have been lecturing him I think, for he runs about a goodeal & but seldom asks for a pass and when he does he will walk up to the door and say some of you write me a pass, rather in a commanding tone. . . . I believe he has got Johny afraid of him. . . . he does seem so wicked [that] if any one was to come upon him about his conduct I do not know what he would do afterwards.[51]

Mrs. Jackson's comments are remarkable for their fulsome detail and straightforward, convincing honesty, but the phenomenon she described was certainly not unique. The experiences of Will and Willes serve to illuminate the inner significance of the war for many rural blacks, as they took the first tentative steps toward an explicit repudiation of white authority. Uncertain of how or when slavery would end, few bondsmen discarded the mask of deference entirely. In growing numbers, however, black Georgians stepped out of the roles assigned them by paternalist etiquette and began laying claim to a larger share of the prerogatives that would accompany legal freedom.

PART THREE

Expedient Moderation: From Ameliorative Reform to Confederate Emancipation

Overleaf: Negro Teamsters, 1864. (Courtesy of the Library of Congress.)

8. Black Bondage and the Climax of Ameliorative Gradualism

THE DEMISE of chattel bondage in Confederate Georgia was a complex social process. Slavery survived on paper until the war's end, but the nature of the institution changed profoundly within the space of four years. Urbanization, refugee life, male absenteeism, military or industrial work assignments, and a host of related developments gradually reshaped the context of black-white interaction, leaving masters and slaves in a kind of psychological limbo as they encountered situations that had no clear peacetime precedent. Uncertainty prevailed on both sides of the color line, and for whites as well as for blacks the war years became a time of tentative adaptation and cautious readjustment. Inevitably members of each race drew upon their prior experiences in a slave society when responding to wartime events. Bondsmen grew more confident and assertive toward whites but continued to push for concessions within the framework of conventional accommodationist etiquette. Planters, on the other hand, vacillated between conciliation and repression, often clinging to the ideology of slavery as they moved grudgingly in the direction of freedom.

Most acts in the drama of Southern independence were played out at least partially in the shadow of the old order. The closing scenes of slavery were no exception. Antebellum rituals and half-truths protected the exterior of Confederate race relations, cushioning the impact of change and often disguising its larger meaning. Beneath the surface, however, important alterations in attitude and behavior were constantly taking place. Sporadically at first, but with growing regularity as the war pro-

235

gressed, white Georgians made conciliatory gestures toward the black men and women whose labor sustained the Southern cause. Racial antipathy did not vanish, but slavery's harshness and brutality declined as whites concealed their loss of mastery beneath a cloak of greater permissiveness. Although full freedom remained a distant dream for most blacks, slave life lost at least some of the nightmarish qualities imparted to it by the crisis of 1859–61.

Probably no single factor did more to hasten the metamorphosis of wartime race relations than the moral conscience of white slaveholders. Generations of Southern apologists had defended slavery as a "civilizing institution" through which benevolent masters could bring about the cultural uplift of a dependent race. For decades such arguments produced more rhetoric than action, but by late antebellum times the doctrine of white responsibility for elevating the bondsman's moral and physical condition had assumed a central place in slavery's religious defense. The war years found advocates of Christian paternalism literally waiting in the wings as hard-pressed slaveowners sought an acceptable rationale for treating blacks more leniently. Religious humanitarianism struck a responsive chord among white Confederates who were already in the process of abandoning rigid norms of racial conduct, and in Georgia and other states long-standing proposals to ameliorate slavery's harsher aspects blossomed into a formal campaign for legal reform.

Compassion and self-interest complemented each other in the Confederacy, as they could never have done before the war, when racial, class, and sectional tensions effectively thwarted the genuine desire of some white Christians to render bondage less oppressive. But while the idea of "reforming" slavery allowed many whites to make a virtue of necessity, the movement cannot be written off as a mere face-saving exercise by beleaguered planters. Fundamental issues were at stake in the campaign for amelioration, issues which transcended immediate arguments over the day-to-day conduct of master-slave relations. By fostering reformist agitation the war served as a catalyst for serious debate over the moral basis and future direction of Southern race relations. Still unresolved in April of 1865, the dispute would return to confound both white and black Americans throughout the next century.

II

FEW GEORGIANS of either race could initially have anticipated the war's liberalizing impact. The panoply of repressive measures adopted in the wake of Harpers Ferry remained in full force after secession as whites continued to guard against possible slave uprisings and passed new laws to meet special contingencies. [1] Georgia's extensive, but futile, effort to strengthen wartime control of bondsmen went hand in hand with a continuing assault on the legal status of nonslave blacks. Hostility toward free Negroes crystalized during the secession crisis, and every Georgia legislative session throughout the first three years of the war saw renewed efforts to enact some version of the compulsory enslavement measure first proposed in 1859. During 1861 state Senator Ralph A. Lane sought to require all nonslave Negroes to leave Georgia within ninety days or "choose an owner." According to Lane's plan, county inferior courts would appoint three people to appraise each free black at a "moderate cash value" not less than two-thirds the "real worth," with the proceeds from all sales going to support indigent families of white soldiers. [2] The Senate rejected this proposal but passed a more moderate bill empowering inferior courts to hear complaints against and, if necessary, enslave any "idle or vicious" free Negroes "so situated as to exercise an improper or mischievous influence" on local bondsmen. [3] Support for forced enslavement, even on a selective basis, failed to materialize in the House of Representatives, where the Senate bill was tabled and allowed to die. [4] Virtually the same sequence of legislative events repeated itself the next year, and finally, in 1863, "an act to sell all free negroes of African descent into slavery" was reported unfavorably by the House Judiciary Committee and soundly defeated. [5]

The General Assembly's rejection of compulsory enslavement marked a turning point in Georgia's wartime political struggle between paternalistic racial moderates and militant white supremacists. Amid the heated atmosphere of the late 1850s and early 1860s doctrinaire Negrophobes gained unprecedented public support for plans to make black bondage universal. The radicals' extensive campaign of racist propaganda eroded the social consensus upon which free Negroes depended for legal and economic survival, and left the group vulnerable to further exploitation. [6] Comprising less than 1 percent of the state's nonwhite population in 1860, free blacks dominated no craft or skilled trade even in the metropolis of Savannah.[7] Economically they were expendable. The combined effect of white hostility and deepening personal poverty did, in fact, cause some black Georgians to enter bondage at their own request. At least seven bills authorizing the voluntary enslavement of individual free Negroes came before the legislature in the course of the war.[8] Most of the measures failed, but a number of blacks became slaves through a simpler petitioning process at the county level.[9]

Although few free Negroes were actually enslaved, the threat to black liberty in Georgia must be judged quite real. All that ultimately stood between nonslave blacks and perpetual bondage was white goodwill, a scarce and unstable commodity in the wake of secession. Had the state's ideological climate remained static throughout the war, there can be little doubt that proponents of forced enslavement would sooner or later have prevailed. But instead of growing stronger, the assault on black freedom lost momentum from 1862 onward, as white moderates seized the initiative. Viewed in its proper context, the preservation of free Negro liberty forms an important opening chapter in the larger story of Confederate humanitarian reform. Georgia's free people of color were lifted up by the same groundswell of white racial liberalism that sustained wartime efforts to ameliorate chattel bondage and eventually brought Southern racial policy to rest on the distant shore of voluntary emancipation. The voyage from slavery to freedom took both races into new and uncharted moral waters which have yet to be mapped in full detail. What made the trip possible was the completion of certain advance preparations prior to 1861 and the conviction of many Southern whites that Christian duty required them to embark, however unclear the final destination.

III

IN 1860 virtually all white Georgians accepted slavery as an integral part of the Southern social order. But while few people were willing to criticize the peculiar institution publicly, many believed from the outset that the new Confederacy's "cornerstone" needed major repair. Efforts to improve the basic conditions of black life began early in the war and continued until Northern victory made emancipation a reality in 1865. Rooted in antebellum religious developments, the Confederate reform movement drew its immediate impetus from the slaveholding ethic of Southern evangelical Protestantism, which, as Donald G. Mathews notes, had a reformist theme at its "very core."[10] But the sources of support for ameliorative change were both broader and deeper than the preceding statement might suggest. Although Georgia lacked a viable antislavery tradition, the state was by no means impervious to the forces that fostered moral ambivalence over bondage elsewhere in the South. During the postrevolutionary generation, rationalistic idealism and natural law doctrines led some white Georgians to manumit bondsmen privately, despite the prevailing hostility to organized abolition societies.[11] From 1800 onward recurring outbreaks of black unrest in Virginia and South Carolina underscored the urgency of slavery as a moral problem and pressing social issue. Proposals for gradual emancipation appeared in Georgia newspapers only months before the Nat Turner insurrection of 1831, and three years later Presbyterian clergyman Charles C. Jones envisioned black religious instruction as an "entering wedge" that would "cause the nation to relax its hold [on slavery], and gradually and peacefully lay it off."[12]

From the outset, however, frontal assaults on the established order were all but unthinkable to Southern white liberals, no matter how genuine their qualms of conscience over black bondage. Georgia's boldest advocate of freedom during the early nineteenth century was probably Judge Jabez Bowen, who was arrested and impeached after an 1804 antislavery speech to the Chatham County grand jury. Yet, for all its drama, the judge's impassioned exhortation contained more shock value than substance. Local whites were enraged by Bowen's prediction of impending black rebellion, but in reality the Rhode Island–born jurist favored nothing more radical than the familiar Jeffersonian era formula of ameliorative reform and eventual emancipation after years of economic, educational, and religious preparation.[13] Most state politicians were, or soon became, still more circumspect. By 1820 slave trade regulation was the only form of antislavery gradualism that prominent officials like Congressman

Robert Raymond Reid and Senator John Alfred Cuthbert would endorse. Of the two, Cuthbert showed greater personal conviction when he proposed the idea of registering all slaves in order to prevent illegal importation. Whatever its stated rationale, the significance of Cuthbert's action lay in the fact that registry had been used by British abolitionists and several Northern states as a preliminary legal step toward general emancipation.[14]

Registry was never adopted by Congress, but moderate elements within Georgia's upper class clung tenaciously to dreams of reducing or ending domestic slave imports, a goal not finally abandoned until 1855.[15] The futility of so passive an approach to the problem of chattel bondage became evident early. By the 1840s gradualism had withered from a concrete program to an abstract philosophical concept so devoid of practical implications that it was frequently incorporated into defenses of the peculiar institution.[16] Individual antislavery convictions continued to find direct outlet through planter participation in the African colonization movement, but few slaveowners were willing or able to incur the financial burden of manumitting and deporting bondsmen.[17] More often, compassionate whites simply made the best of the status quo, easing their consciences with a paternalistic philosophy of Christian stewardship which allowed masters to see themselves as benevolent agents working for the spiritual and cultural uplift of inferior black dependents. The key to this outlook was a belief in reciprocal obligations between masters and servants, including the self-imposed duty of planters to mitigate slavery's exploitive potential by following biblical guidelines. Only through strict adherence to scripture could white Christians ensure that bondage would elevate Southern blacks in the scale of morality and civilization, proslavery churchmen reasoned. In Georgia as elsewhere the religious defense of slavery gradually filled the void created by the stillbirth of Southern abolitionism. Ameliorative doctrines broadened the class appeal of paternalism among whites and provided a "safe" context for internal criticism of slavery's ethical shortcomings. With the rise of sectional hostility and pseudo-scientific racism during the late antebellum era, such criticism took on added moral significance, representing, as it did, a conscious rejection of slave society's most callous and destructive tendencies in favor of a more enlightened humanitarianism.[18]

The picture is complicated by the unavoidable murkiness which surrounded the ultimate purpose of ameliorative reform, as beleagured white moderates found themselves proposing to strengthen bondage by rendering it milder, and thus weaker. Reformist impulses were also subject to conservative manipulation, and in the hands of skillful regional spokesmen ameliorative logic sometimes became a weapon for disarming political opponents. The mixture of strategic calculation and genuine moral concern within reformist ranks is illustrated by the utterances of Senator Robert Toombs, Georgia's outspoken defender of Southern rights. A formidable opponent in platform debate, Toombs championed the cause of amelioration twice before the Civil War, once in an 1853 Georgia speech and more fully three years later during an address at Boston's famous abolitionist meeting hall Tremont Temple.[19] Departing from his normally combative style, Toombs defended the South's overall treatment of blacks but conceded that a true picture of slavery was "not without shade as well as light." Some charges, particularly accusations that bondsmen suffered from inadequate living standards and lack of religious privileges, he dismissed as groundless. Toombs acknowledged, however, that slaves were "debarred from the benefits of education," and this objection he found "well taken,—and not without force." Abolitionist literature had caused Southern states to "take counsel rather of their passions than their reason" in adopting laws against black literacy, the Georgia senator explained, but he assured his listeners that "better counsels will in time prevail, and this evil will be remedied" because education was "useful to . . . [the slave,] his master, and society."[20]

Venturing into an even more sensitive area, Toombs admitted that slave marriages had no legal validity. Abolitionist complaints on this score were "not without foundation," and protecting slave marital and other domestic ties "by laws forbidding, under proper regulations, the separation of families, would be wise, proper, and humane." Having yielded this much ground to his critics, Toombs retreated still further by admitting that the "condition of the slave offers great opportunities for abuse, and these

241

opportunities are frequently used to violate humanity and justice."[21] Conscious that he was straying dangerously close to racial and sectional heresy, the Georgian hastily added a conservative caveat. Slavery reform was predicated on the belief that "the white is the superior race, and the black the inferior," destined to remain subordinate in a mixed society with or without legal bondage. In these premises amelioration rather than emancipation constituted the logical remedy for "the evils of the system." And to Toombs the future looked bright. Northerners could "with hope and confidence" depend upon Southern slaveholders for "the removal of existing abuses, and the adoption of such further ameliorations as may be demanded by justice and humanity."[22]

Other Georgians echoed the reform theme with almost equal conviction. Toombs's close friend, the learned and articulate Alexander H. Stephens, combined religious, scientific, and sociological arguments into a rationale for slave-code amelioration which stressed the doctrine of white supremacist noblesse oblige. Viewing slavery as one aspect of a divinely sanctioned and scientifically verified natural order in the cosmos, Stephens eventually based his entire intellectual defense of bondage on the concept of a static and immutable racial hierarchy But for Stephens as for other white Southerners the liberal heritage of the Revolution remained strong, and the ideal of social justice disturbingly real. To resolve these conflicting impulses reform and improvement of existing institutions became essential. Stephens's position is best captured in a single epigrammatic phrase he repeated almost mechanically from the 1840s onward: "If our system is not the best, or cannot be made the best for both races, it is wrong."[23]

Ambiguity also plagued the utterances of Southern religious leaders, who were the prime movers behind most efforts to ameliorate chattel bondage. Even within the narrow circle of educated proslavery clergymen, advocates of change often seemed to argue at cross-purposes as they tried to avoid confronting contradictions and inconsistencies within their ethical scheme. Evangelical Protestants throughout America and the British Isles could agree that slavery was a flawed system. Antislavery churchmen believed the flaws should be eliminated through emancipation and remonstrated with slaveholding brethren to do their full duty. South-

erners, understandably, saw things differently. Wounded by outside criticism, and increasingly ostracized and isolated, proslavery churchmen
turned inward, proclaiming that bondage was a biblically recognized social relationship which, like any human institution, needed to be improved and perfected, but not abolished. In a properly conducted slave
system, Southern clergymen argued, succeeding generations of blacks
might be gradually lifted out of "sin and depravity" until at some future
day the race as a whole reached a level of civilization compatible with
freedom.[24] During the lengthy but indefinite interim, one Georgian explained, chattel bondage could logically be viewed as "permanent-per-
petual."[25]

If slavery had God's blessing, evangelizing blacks became a sacred duty,
and scores of white clergymen took seriously their obligation to save souls
without regard to race. Throughout the South systematic missionary
work among bondsmen began during the mid-1840s and soon yielded
impressive numerical results. By 1860 Georgia Baptists could claim over
twenty-six thousand black members, while Negro Methodists numbered
in excess of twenty-two thousand. All told, aggregate black church membership within the state probably exceeded sixty thousand.[26] The rapid
influx of slaves into Georgia's leading Protestant denominations provided
additional stimulus for religious programs to humanize chattel bondage.
As black church membership rose, slaves made it clear that they held
definite opinions about what did and did not constitute the "good news."
Proselytizing involved persuasion, and Southern evangelists learned
quickly that blacks had little taste for lengthy proslavery discourses, or,
indeed, for any type of pulpit propaganda that strayed far from Christianity's basic moral tenets.[27] Slaves also demonstrated a general unwillingness to settle for form without substance in spiritual matters. Camp
meetings and emotional preaching enhanced religion's appeal for Georgians of all races, but even the best evangelical showmanship had only a
temporary effect. If white churchmen hoped to attract and retain black
converts they had to meet bondsmen halfway and accord them a reasonable degree of respect as human beings and fellow Christians. It was necessary, that is, to treat the blacks as men if not as brothers.

With twenty-eight semi-independent black churches and two formally recognized church associations composed mainly of blacks, Georgia Baptists represented the best, or in any event the most, that white slaveholders had to offer in the way of biracial Christianity. The key to Baptist success in slave recruitment was the denomination's willingness to see blacks participate in church life with a measure of autonomy. In urban areas, from an early date, this participation took the form of racially separate congregations led by prominent black preachers under what amounted to nominal white supervision. Throughout the antebellum era white Baptists printed the names of "colored ministers" in annual association minutes, and often published obituaries or death notices of black preachers and elders.[28] Around Savannah and Augusta, and to a lesser extent in smaller interior towns, large "colored" or "African" churches provided permanent focal points for slave community life, and also served as power bases for well-known black ministers like Andrew Marshall, James M. Simms, Henry Cunningham, Jacob Walker, and Kelly Low.[29] In the countryside, impulses toward separatism were far less pronounced, usually taking the form of separate business or disciplinary meetings for slave members of "white" churches, together with a pragmatic acceptance of the activities of unordained slave "exhorters."[30] Despite the emergence of some black churches in rural areas, and notwithstanding the high historical profile of urban slave congregations, the bulk of Georgia's black Christians appear to have worshiped with whites in what can best be characterized as an interracial setting.[31]

The status of blacks in racially mixed congregations was always a subordinate one, but the subordination was seldom rigid or total. Unlike labor, a slave's religious faith could not be obtained through coercion, and the bondsman's freedom to accept or reject Christianity acted as a check upon the natural tendency of church discipline to reinforce other methods of slave control. Congregational reprimands for drunkenness, sabbath breaking, profanity, and sexual immorality were meted out routinely with little apparent regard for color.[32] Whites also invested substantial amounts of time and energy investigating cases of unchristianlike conduct between black brethren and mediating the resulting disputes. In part because of these efforts, Southern churchmen were indignant when Yankees accused them of neglecting the slave's spiritual welfare. "I oftener step out to give my hand to a colored disciple than to my white brother," declared Georgia minister Jonathan Davis in 1841.[33]

During twenty years of pastoring to mixed congregations Davis had seen slaves bring complaints against masters in the same church, and knew of whites who were censured on the basis of charges lodged by blacks. To all intents and purposes, Davis believed, Georgia Baptists afforded equal privileges to all members.[34] Nor was he alone in this view. Even in the worsening racial climate of the 1850s another zealous Georgia clergyman could state flatly that "when converted, the negro is as gladly welcomed into our [Baptist] churches as a brother, as if he were of pure Anglo-Saxon blood." To prove his point the minister described how a slave woman and a wealthy white woman "of high social position" received identical treatment when they were simultaneously admitted to church membership. As the closing hymn was being sung, "white and colored, bond and free, came forward and gave the right hand of fellowship to the new sisters. Among them, servants gave the hand to their mistress."[35] Whatever the significance of this particular event may have been, there were many white Georgians who looked upon interracial worship as a serious threat to the slave regime. In an age of strong faith and Christian fundamentalism there would always be those who gave a dangerously literal interpretation to the doctrine of universal brotherhood. A Georgia rice planter discharged his overseer for making precisely this mistake in 1857. The overseer, "elated by a strong" and, in the planter's view, "very false" religious feeling, "began to injure the plantation a vast deal, placing himself on a par with the negroes, by even joining in with them at their prayer meetings, breaking down long established discipline . . . and siding in any difficulty with the people, against the Drivers."[36]

If white churchmen exaggerated the social significance of momentary lapses in racial etiquette during public worship, they also underemphasized the real basis of Southern Protestantism's egalitarian thrust. Once again the determining factor was the black Christian's freedom of choice. Competition for slave converts was intense among Georgia's leading denominations, and serious evangelists understood that pious rhetoric was insufficient to convince blacks of white sincerity in religious matters.

Bondsmen sought a religion that concerned itself with this world as well as the next, and by gravitating toward churches which served their temporal as well as spiritual needs blacks effectively conveyed the message that words should be accompanied by deeds. The slaves' stubborn refusal to separate sacred from secular concerns had the effect of strengthening support among white Christians for various ameliorative measures. In the generation before the Civil War, Georgia clergymen became leading advocates of protecting slave marital and family arrangements.[37] White religious bodies also ignored or evaded a host of legal restrictions in order to give official sanction to black preachers and persuade authorities to tolerate the continued existence of separate Negro churches.[38] A number of devout whites went still further and taught slaves to read the Bible in open defiance of state law.[39] Literacy, religious autonomy, and family stability were, of course, among the most prized objectives of Georgia bondsmen, who correctly looked upon such achievements as tangible attributes of freedom. One suspects that most white evangelists understood this fact, although they often refused to face its implications. Steering a hazardous middle course between expediency and idealism, reformist clergymen braved public hostility throughout the late antebellum era in order to defend the interests of their enslaved co-religionists.

Ameliorative doctrines disguised but could not eliminate the moral quandary facing white Christians in the prewar South. Ultimately the problem lay with the logic of reform itself. Sensitive men like the Reverend Charles C. Jones were never entirely comfortable with the decision to improve a system they had once condemned as wrong, and no amount of soothing rhetoric—even that which postponed the day of emancipation for "ages yet to come"[40]—could mask the troubling implication that slavery was still what most enlightened Southerners had once believed it to be: a necessary evil rather than a positive good. Whether advocates of amelioration acted out of a sense of guilt over black servitude is largely a question of definitions and semantics. Few Southern reformers expressed guilt feelings openly, but most remained keenly sensitive to Northern and transatlantic allegations that slavery fostered heathenism, polygamy, ignorance, and brutality. The element of truth in these charges forced conscientious Southern whites to confront, however reluctantly, the persistent gap between ideals and reality within their domestic social order. Rooted in the contradictions of paternalist ideology, ameliorative doctrines provided the only effective counterweight to the callous scientific racism of the late antebellum era, and constituted an accurate barometer of the moral tension inherent in master-slave relations. As the following pages will show, Southern reform sentiment peaked late in the Civil War when the erosion of white paternalism made the contrast between slaveholding theory and practice especially pronounced.

IV

THROUGHOUT THE SOUTH reform-minded churchmen looked upon Confederate independence as an opportunity to seek modifications of slavery without being branded traitors to their region. Just as North-South denominational schisms had previously freed Georgia clergymen to defend the bondsman's moral personality by preaching the doctrine of reciprocal obligations between masters and servants, reformers now hoped that political separation from the North would make it possible to give their religious and ethical precepts a firm basis in statute law. [41] Clergymen of all denominations participated in Georgia's wartime reform movement, but support for ameliorative measures was strongest among Baptists and Methodists, the churches with the largest black constituencies. Leading reform spokesmen included the Reverend Nathaniel Macon Crawford, son of former Senator William H. Crawford and president of Baptist-supported Mercer University near Penfield, Georgia; the Reverend Henry Holcombe Tucker, a professor at Mercer and a descendant of Baptist reformer Henry Holcombe; the Reverend George Foster Pierce, a native Georgian and Bishop of the Methodist Episcopal Church, South; and the young Methodist Minister Atticus Green Haygood, destined to gain prominence as an exponent of racial moderation during the New South movement of the 1880s.

In a general way, men like Crawford, Tucker, Pierce, and Haygood typified the educated, middle-class "gentlemen preachers" of late antebellum decades who dominated church bureaucracies, staffed denominational colleges, and stood as self-appointed arbiters of Southern theological orthodoxy. Steeped in the philosophical traditions of eighteenth-century Scottish rationalism, Georgia's leading clergymen preferred to think of moral duty as flowing from the specific "relations" which structured life and society, rather than from abstract principles applicable to undifferentiated humanity. The resulting theological belief system reinforced slavery as a legitimate component of the South's existing social hierarchy, but also introduced the potentially subversive doctrine that all men stood on an equal footing relative to their creator. In a somewhat less obvious fashion, Southern theology weakened the moral authority of the plantation regime by upholding behavioral norms such as time-thrift, business success, self-denying labor, and educated citizen participation, all of which ran counter to the values of a traditional agrarian culture. [42] Slavery reform received its impetus from both the reactionary and the modern components of Southern religious thought. Reform ideology combined liberal ideas of universal human progress and spiritual equality with the conservative view that amelioration was an obligation inherent in the master-slave relationship. Sometimes one theme predominated over the others, but each concept cropped up repeatedly in the utterances of Georgia's leading ameliorative spokesmen.

With occasional assistance from other Protestant colleagues, Georgia Baptists and Methodists spearheaded a broad wartime legal offensive against Georgia slavery's most objectionable features. Whether or not they personally initiated ameliorative proposals, reform leaders used their prestige and influence to mobilize denominational support for humanitarian measures. In almost every instance ameliorative agitation was conducted through or in conjunction with established church bureaucracies. Slave code liberalization emerged as a political issue in May 1862 when delegates to northwestern Georgia's Cherokee Baptist Convention voted unanimously to petition the state legislature for repeal of the statute which prohibited teaching slaves to read. [43] Although clearly out of step with the confident proslavery orthodoxy that still prevailed in most parts of the South, the Cherokee Convention's action struck a responsive chord among Georgia churchmen. Within a month the repeal proposal gained public endorsement from the Reverend N. M. Crawford, who praised the idea in a published letter and urged prompt removal of the 1829 anti-literacy law which "for a generation has been a stigma upon our state."[44]

Crawford employed even stronger language during a meeting of Georgia's Central Baptist Association in late August. Declaring that prohibitions against slave education were both needless and unenforceable, he equated Georgia's law with parliamentary enactments under Henry VIII denying the Bible to English yeomenry. In an emotional peroration, Crawford denounced the state statute as "a disgrace to our civilization, to our country, and to the age in which we live."[45] Another visiting dignitary, Marshall J. Wellborn, district judge and former U.S. congressman, supported Crawford's position with equally radical rhetoric. When invited to speak, Wellborn addressed the delegates with "great fervor and animation," urging repeal of the offensive statute and "avowing that if he must retain slaves at such a price, he was willing to let them all go."[46] Perhaps few of Wellborn's listeners placed a literal interpretation on the judge's drastic statement, and certainly no one came forward with a comparable offer. Most delegates, however, seemed receptive to the general line of reasoning advanced by repeal advocates, and at least one previous opponent of slave education "acknowledged that all his objections . . . had vanished, being demolished by the arguments of Dr. Crawford."[47] Before adjourning, the association unanimously concurred with the Cherokee Baptist Convention in memorializing the legislature for repeal of Georgia's 1829 law "so far as it forbids owners from teaching their negroes to read the word of God."[48] Hard on the heels of these official resolutions came a ringing editorial endorsement of repeal from Georgia's influential Baptist newspaper the *Christian Index*. Concerned that even sympathetic legislators might hesitate to act in so controversial a matter, *Index* editor Samuel Boykin assured readers that abolitionist literature could no longer corrupt, or even reach, Southern bondsmen. Secession had removed the pragmatic necessity of keeping slaves illiterate, and to continue withholding the Bible from blacks could only "assist in peopling hell." Such an "enormous offence . . . against [the] inalienable rights of perishing fellow-beings," Boykin warned, would make white Christians "accessory to soul-murder."[49]

Equally vigorous, if less expressly legalistic, moral indictments were soon forthcoming from other leading churchmen. Presbyterians joined the repeal campaign in October 1862 when Oglethorpe University's president, Dr. Samuel Kennedy Talmage, lent his personal and denominational prestige to the cause of slave education. In a letter to the Milledgeville *Confederate Union,* Talmage called upon all Christians as well as nonchurchgoing humanitarians to press for repeal of the law against black literacy. Like his more outspoken Baptist counterparts, Talmage condemned Georgia's statute as an infringement on religious liberty. But he also went on to imply that repeal would facilitate the cultural elevation and spiritual uplift of Southern bondsmen. The Confederacy, Talmage believed, was fighting "a war of humanity in behalf of Africa," where centuries of "heathenism" had debased the condition of all blacks. From their transatlantic ancestors Southern bondsmen had inherited a sad legacy of "indolence, filth, . . . sensuality, . . . ignorance, . . . stupidity, and vice" which could only be erased through prolonged contact with "civilized and christian [white] families." Viewed in this light, anti-education laws made little sense, since their principal effect was to slow even further a recovery process which would already require "generations" to complete.[50]

Fellow churchmen needed little persuading. The Presbytery of Georgia formally endorsed Talmage's letter on November 8, 1862, barely a week after the document's initial publication. But while approving of efforts to legalize slave literacy, most of the body's membership wanted change to go further. Conscious of the moral scrutiny being focused on the South by an "enlightened, discerning, and censorious world," the Georgia Presbytery urged each Confederate state to revise its slave laws until bondsmen obtained "all the rights and privileges guaranteed to them in the Word of God."[51] Wisely, neither Talmage nor his fellow Presbyterians jeopardized ecumenical harmony by offering detailed proposals for slave code revision. In an atmosphere of evolving consensus, elaborate sectarian reform manifestos would probably have been more divisive than useful. Certainly they were unnecessary. Opinions might differ as to the relative importance of various ameliorative measures, but questions of priority aside, there could be little dispute over the major thrust of the reform campaign. Each key point in slaveholding Protestantism's biblical bill of rights had been thoroughly expounded in prewar writings on Christian paternalism, which formed the touchstone of Georgia's liberalization crusade. By 1860 a solid doctrinal foundation had been laid, and no one who sympathized with the basic rationale for slave evangelization could logically question the reformers' basic premises. Even the tactics were familiar. As they had done when promoting slave mission work, wartime reformers cloaked Christianity's libertarian tendencies in a mantle of conservative gradualism, assuring the public (and frequently themselves as well) that they came not to bury slavery but to preserve it.

And, in truth, some reform measures seemed innocuous enough at first glance. One wartime proposal to permit the licensing of black preachers was not an advancement at all but simply an effort to regain the *status quo ante bellum*. Nonwhite clergymen had, of course, been an integral part of Georgia Protestantism for many decades prior to 1860. Extending back to the eighteenth century, the state's tradition of Negro religious leadership gained formal recognition in an 1833 law allowing blacks to preach if first approved by three white ministers and town or county officials.[52] Sanctioning a practice which authorities were powerless to prevent, the face-saving statute remained in force for three decades and was never formally repealed. It was, however, quietly eliminated from the state's first legal code, drafted during the racial panic of 1860 and adopted by the legislature without detailed review. Only after the *Code* actually took effect on January 1, 1863, did most Georgians learn of section 1376, which categorically prohibited granting "any license or other authority to any slave or free person of color, to preach, or exhort, or otherwise officiate in church matters."[53] Reformers were understandably indignant at the unprecedented ban, and almost immediately the Baptists launched a repeal campaign. In early February, with the next legislative session only weeks away, President N. M. Crawford of Mercer denounced the new regulation in a public letter to Governor Joseph E. Brown and five state legislators, all of whom were fellow Baptists. Reaffirming his denomination's historic commitment to strict separation of church and state, Crawford reminded Georgia lawmakers that Baptists were biblically required to ordain anyone whom God "called" to the ministry. Would civil authority presume to intrude in so sacrosanct a matter and thus force churchmen to choose between secular and spiritual obligations? Crawford urged officials to reflect carefully on the practical implications of such a step. The central issue, in his view, was the presence in Georgia Baptist ranks of some thirty thousand black communicants "whom we recognize as brethren in the Lord, and whom, notwithstanding their difference of color and condition, we love as disciples of Jesus and heirs to the common salvation." Citing the careers of black pastors like the late Andrew Marshall of Savannah's First African Baptist Church and Jacob Walker of Augusta, Crawford dismissed the argument that only whites were called to preach. Rather than "ignoring Baptist history," state lawmakers should repeal the *Code's* "obnoxious" provision and thereby "render unto God the things that are God's."[54]

Published conspicuously in the *Christian Index*, Crawford's letter circulated widely among Georgia Baptists.[55] Professor Henry Holcombe Tucker of Mercer generated further denominational interest by drafting a 2,500-word petition for legislative repeal of the ban on slave preaching. Phrased more like an edict than a request, the petition reiterated and expanded upon each of Crawford's major arguments. Tucker's tone, however, was hardly one of supplication. "Soul-liberty," he declared, was the "rightful heritage of all God's moral creatures," and consequently the "sacred right of the black to preach, exhort or pray, if God has called . . . him" should be held inviolable. Reminding readers that the "great majority of the human race are of dark complexion," Tucker rebuked the codifiers for their "heaven-daring impiety" in limiting gospel ministry to the white minority.[56]

There was, moreover, little likelihood that Baptists would capitulate to the *Code's* "intolerant[,] bigoted[,] and persecuting spirit" by obeying a law which carried no specific penalty and which civil authorities were either "afraid or ashamed" to implement. Should enforcement be attempted, Tucker predicted widespread resistance among fellow churchmen. Many congregations could be expected to follow the defiant example of Columbus Baptists who, "with the New Code spread open before their eyes, and with a full knowledge and understanding of . . . section 1376 . . . deliberately violated the same, and ordained two negroes to officiate in church matters in the office of Deacon." For Tucker and his supporters the Columbus episode offered tangible evidence of a "very general and very rapid" growth in ameliorative sentiment among white Georgians. In the wake of secession the South's "long pent-up" humanitarian impulse had finally burst forth, creating a "loud and universal demand for reform."[57] Or so, at least, many churchmen wanted to believe in the hopeful springtime of 1863.

Precisely how loud and how universal reform demands had become was a matter for state lawmakers to assess. They were, however, assisted in their evaluation by two prominent Georgians, neither of whom was an entirely disinterested counselor. First to offer advice was the state's politically astute governor, who took the arguments and, no doubt, the electoral strength of his fellow Baptists seriously enough to endorse at least part of the reform program. In his March 26 message to the new legislature Governor Brown recommended repeal of the controversial section 1376 in Georgia's *Code*. Silently abandoning the opposition to black preaching he had expressed in a legislative vote some thirteen years earlier, Brown now had "no doubt that negroes are sometimes very useful among their own people as preachers and exhorters." Decisions in such matters, the governor argued, properly rested with Georgia's white churches, all of which could "safely be trusted" to support the Confederacy and its institutions.[58]

Last-minute guidance on the sensitive issue of slave literacy was conveyed to legislators through the medium of oral instruction. The fact that Brown's legislative message had passed over the controversial matter in silence probably served to heighten the impact of what lawmakers heard on March 27 when they gathered in Milledgeville's Methodist church for official "fast day" observances. Sharing the pulpit with a Presbyterian colleague, and ultimately dominating the day's activities, was Georgia's outspoken Methodist Bishop George Foster Pierce. In the course of a lengthy sermon on divine influence over national affairs, the bishop condemned Georgia's law against black literacy as palpably unscriptural. "Our Heavenly Father certainly never intended any human mind to be kept in darkness and ignorance," Pierce stated. With rising indignation he admonished legislators that the Negro was an "immortal being" entitled "by the law of creation . . . to read for himself the epistles of his Redeemer's love." The climax of the sermon came in the next sentence when Pierce proclaimed to a stunned audience of dignitaries: "If the institution of slavery cannot be maintained except at the expense of the black man's immortal interests, in the name of heaven, I say—*let it perish.*"⁵⁹ Reported noncommittally in the secular press, Pierce's sermon received unequivocal backing only from the *Christian Index*, whose editor endorsed the bishop's radical language as well as his ameliorative sentiments. Even the *Index* was forced to concede, however, that Pierce's remarks had stirred "no small spirit of controversy" among the members of the legislature.⁶⁰

Events soon gave the latter phrase a prophetic tone. Slavery reform was among the first subjects considered in the special legislative session of 1863, and from the beginning emotions ran high. Something approximating consensus seemed to exist on March 31 when Georgia senators voted almost two to one in favor of repealing *Code* section 1376 and allowing white churches to resume the antebellum practice of licensing black preachers.⁶¹ The next day members of the upper chamber went on to approve legalizing black education, this time by a breathtakingly close vote of 18 to 16.⁶² Legislative battle lines were quickly drawn during the following week as reformers beat back repeated attempts to modify or rescind the two measures. Tempers flared over allegations that literate bondsmen would foment rebellion, and efforts to reimpose bans on black preaching sparked lengthy floor debates with "several Senators taking a hand and pitching in theologically like a 'thousand of brick.'"⁶³ But even while they argued, most lawmakers realized that their disputes would ultimately be resolved in the House of Representatives, where the fate of reform proposals seemed "very questionable" to some observers.⁶⁴ Optimism rose on April 18 when the Senate's bill to permit slave preaching received House endorsement and was promptly signed into law. This, however, was the first and last statutory victory reformers were destined to achieve. With the Senate almost evenly divided over the issue of black education, support for the literacy measure failed to materialize in the lower house. The bill died quietly when the legislature adjourned without further action on the subject.⁶⁵

Having regained lost ground on the question of slave clergymen, reformers were undaunted by the accompanying defeat of literacy legislation. In what may have been regarded as a tactical retreat, Georgia churchmen abandoned the education issue and pressed on with other aspects of their ameliorative campaign. During the last two years of the war reformers gave top priority to securing legal protection for slave marriage and family ties, an issue tentatively broached by Confederate Episcopalians meeting in general council at Augusta late in 1862. Taking their cue from the Right Reverend Stephen Elliott of Georgia, senior prelate of the new Southern church, the Episcopal bishops issued a pastoral letter reminding members that blacks were "not merely so much property," but on the contrary, "a people passing from ignorance to civilization." In addition to giving slaves "that religious and moral instruction which is to elevate them in the scale of being," white Christians had other, more specific, obligations. First among these was modifying slave laws so "as not to necessitate the violation of those sacred relations which God has created, and which man cannot, consistently with Christian duty, annul."[66]

In his 1863 sermon to the Georgia legislature Bishop Pierce reiterated the theme with characteristic Methodist vigor and bluntness. Citing slavery reform as one of the chief "moral ends" of the war, Pierce called for repeal of all laws permitting "arbitrary interference with the connubial relations of slaves." He stressed, however, that the threat to black families came less from hostile legislation than from the absence of protective statutes. As a practical matter Georgia had "no law at all" concerning slave domestic ties. "The whole question is open. Husbands and wives are subject to all the contingencies of time and circumstance—of gain and avarice, of passion and caprice, [and] of the law of inheritance. . . . Verily, 'these things ought not so to be.' It is all wrong. . . . Here, then, upon our knees before High Heaven, let us vow to reform. Yes, my countrymen, let us do right—fear God and keep his commandments."[67]

In condemning official indifference to black family bonds as "a stigma upon our civilization and an offence to our Christianity," Pierce did no more than echo sentiments shared by churchmen of all Protestant denominations. As early as June 1863 a Baptist army chaplain sought guidance from fellow Georgia clergy on the troubling question of whether ministers violated their spiritual office by performing slave "marriages" which lacked legal sanction. Did such mock weddings imply tacit approval of an immoral practice? he asked. "Does not a clergyman officiating become *particips criminis?*"[68] Baptist reform leader N. M. Crawford ridiculed the humanitarian pretense of the state's new legal code, which provided that the "contubernal relation among slaves shall be recognized in public sales whenever possible."[69] After discovering that Webster's dictionary defined contubernal relation as "a species of concubinage," Crawford dismissed the entire matter as a sham. "So far as marriage is concerned," he concluded, Georgia laws simply ignored the slave's existence.

> Or we may vary the proposition, and say that so far as slaves are concerned, our law abolishes the institution of marriage. . . . For what we call the marriage of negroes is subject to be dissolved at any moment by the whim or caprice of a third party. No matter with what solemnities of religion the sacred injunction has sealed the reciprocal vow, ["]What God hath joined together let no man put asunder["]: no matter how fondly and firmly the parties may cleave together, as God has commanded them: no matter what agony and tears and cries the separation may cost, the owner of either of the parties may rend them asunder.[70]

More than any other single issue, the question of slave marriages brought white Christians face-to-face with the inherent contradictions of their ethical system. Trapped by an inescapable moral dilemma, Georgia slaveholders were reduced to selecting the horn on which to be impaled. With a single-mindedness few antislavery critics could have surpassed, Crawford reduced the matter to a stark proposition of logic. "Marriage either exists among the slaves or it does not," he declared. "If the negroes are married, we sin as a people by denying them the rights of marriage: if they are not married, we sin by taking from them the marriage itself. In either case the cry ascends to heaven."[71]

In reality, the problem was even more basic than men like Crawford were willing to admit. The entire reform debate ultimately resolved itself into a series of arguments over the South's conflicting definition of blacks as people and property. To assert the former concept was inevitably to deny the latter—and by implication to attack the morality of chattel bondage, passionate assertions to the contrary notwithstanding. At the practical level, demands for the protection of slave families struck more or less directly at white property rights, making related ideological questions difficult to sidestep. Consequently those who advocated legalizing slave marriages found themselves pressed to take an unequivocal stand on the slave regime's most volatile subject, the question of racial equality.

The racial issue surfaced prominently during the closing months of the war, as reformers prepared for a final political struggle in the special legislative session of February 1865. By the end of 1864 ongoing efforts to rally public support for slave marriage legislation had begun to pay off, and at their October meeting white members of the predominantly black Georgia Baptist Association resolved: "that the institution of marriage was ordained by Almighty God for the benefit of the whole human race, without respect to color; that it ought to be maintained in its original purity among all classes of people, in all countries, and in all ages, till the end of time; and that consequently the law of Georgia in its failure to recognize and protect this relationship between our slaves, is essentially defective and ought to be changed."[72] Adopted in virtually identical form by the Bethel Baptist Association, a body containing over two thousand black members, the resolution received considerable notice in state newspapers.[73] Equally well publicized was the Reverend N. M. Crawford's previously quoted essay on slave marriage. Written for the Baptist *Christian Index*, the article found ready favor among Methodists, who read it on the front page of their own paper, the *Southern Christian Advocate*, during February 1865.[74] In reprinting the lengthy document the *Advocate* simply followed official church policy as enunciated the previous month by the statewide Georgia Methodist Conference. Paraphrasing their Baptist colleagues, the Methodists agreed that marriage was divinely ordained for the "good of the whole human family, without respect to color or race." Conference delegates favored remedial legislation, but urged state lawmakers to attempt the all-but-impossible feat of providing "secure protection" for slave unions without impinging upon the master's legal prerogatives.[75]

The obvious threat which legalized marriage would pose to investments in slave property caused alarm among white conservatives, many of whom were reeling from losses incurred during the recent Sherman invasion. Taking a lesson from their Yankee adversary, those opposed to slavery reform abandoned genteel tactics of argumentation and began stressing naked racism in public debate. The new posture revealed itself with particular clarity in editorial response to a letter from "Many Citizens of Cherokee Georgia" published by the Atlanta *Southern Confederacy.* Reiterating familiar biblical arguments in support of slave marriage, the seemingly innocuous communication touched off a heated debate over the issue of black inferiority. The *Confederacy* printed the letter on March 2, 1865, accompanied by a strong editorial disclaimer challenging reformist assumptions that all races shared a common humanity and potential for improvement. Amelioration, the editor believed, could have no positive impact on Southern bondsmen who were confined by fixed racial traits to a status "but a degree removed from the brute." As members of "the lowest order of creation that walks erect and has the power of articulation," blacks were "totally unfitted for the manners and habits of civilized life," including, of course, marriage. Lest anyone miss the practical implications of his message, the editor assured readers that whites had no moral obligation to respect black domestic ties. "Our negroes," he stated confidently, "are our property—as much so as our horses."[76]

Reformist churchmen were indignant at the Atlanta newspaper's attitude. Besides conflicting with biblical doctrines of a single creation, the *Confederacy*'s unabashed racism placed paternalistic clergymen on the defensive over the issue of white supremacy. Conservative slaveowners had always been dubious of claims that ameliorative laws would strengthen the peculiar institution. To skeptics, the entire idea of "elevating" bondsmen seemed to indicate that blacks would become more like whites and thus less like slaves. So long as slavery remained a stable peacetime institution, the conflict between those who viewed black inferiority as cultural and temporary, rather than biological and permanent, had few practical implications. Both groups could agree that blacks were, for the present, inferior and that seemed to be all that mattered. By early 1865, however, the situation had changed. Slavery now stood on the verge of extinction, making the question of black status in the South's future social order more than a purely theoretical issue. Fearful that the ambiguity which had previously aided their cause might change from an asset to a crippling liability, Confederate reformers exploited the racial vanity of their white critics. Proponents of slave marriage continued to insist that all people were subject to the law of progress, but explained that certain races had a greater capacity for advancement than did others. Whites, predictably, were destined to outstrip blacks in the natural order of things, and reform could thus pose no possible threat to white dominance. On the contrary, ameliorative laws would serve the laudable goal of elevating bondsmen to the most appropriate subordinate niche in the existing racial hierarchy.

Like the reform arguments which had preceded it, the doctrine of limited racial advancement was vague enough to accommodate a wide range of personal interpretations. The more extreme formulations bore a marked resemblance to the pseudo-scientific racial theories of the so-called American School of Ethnology. "That . . . [the Negro] can never equal the Anglo-Saxon, is doubtless demonstrable, from the physiological superiority of the latter," declared Baptist clergyman Ebenezer W. Warren in a letter supporting the legalization of slave marriages.[77] But other reform spokesmen were not so sure. More typical of prevailing ameliorative sentiment were the cautious utterances of the Reverend Atticus G. Haygood, a white Methodist minister who emerged during the next generation as Georgia's leading advocate of black industrial education. Even during the war, elements of the ambiguous racial liberalism expounded in Haygood's famous 1881 volume *Our Brother in Black* were clearly visible. Writing in March 1865, Haygood agreed with the *Southern Confederacy* that blacks were "but one degree removed from the brute." That degree, however, put "an infinite distance" between the two groups. It was, he explained, "the difference between immortal reasoning men, and the mortal, unreasoning, irresponsible brute." If the "endowments" of blacks were inferior to those of whites, Haygood insisted, the condition resulted from a "providential disability" rather than from differing biological origins. The question was largely irrelevant in any case, because marriage was "God's ordinance for Man; not for this class or another, but for Man." Presumably the same doctrine applied to black preaching, Bible reading, and other religious reforms.[78]

No one who advocated liberalizing Georgia's slave code went so far as to repudiate the concept of black inferiority. As a group, reformers displayed ambivalence on the matter, often affirming and denying white supremacy in the same breath. Thus, even while espousing biological racism, the Reverend Ebenezer Warren could applaud the "unparalleled success" with which Southern blacks had "advanced towards the true stature of manhood."[79] In a similar vein, the Reverend N. M. Crawford struggled to reconcile opposing viewpoints in his eleventh-hour defense of slave marriage. Frustrated by lack of progress on the legislative front, Crawford condemned Georgia's clergymen, editors, and political stump speakers for hypocritical posturing over the question of amelioration. But if whites had performed poorly, blacks did not automatically benefit by comparison. Although slaves had "unquestionably been elevated" through residence in the South, their progress, in Crawford's view, was mainly attributable to the natural "imitative propensity" of Negroes and other "barbarians." When pressed, Crawford was even willing to agree that allegedly low standards of "chastity and conjugal fidelity" among bondsmen resulted primarily from the African's inner "nature." But this concession was tempered, if not actually contradicted, by a strong component of environmentalist logic. Noting that slaves received little encouragement to take marriage seriously, Crawford reproached masters for placing their bondsmen in a situation where "temptation is strong, opportunity great, and restraint little." If low moral standards were the result of such arrangements, blacks certainly could not be held solely responsible. It was, Crawford believed, fully appropriate to ask: "In similar circumstances, how much better would be the white?"[80]

Like most rhetorical questions, this one answered itself, but not to the satisfaction of conservative slaveholders. Opponents of reform had little patience with arguments which equated, or even seemed to equate, the responses of blacks and whites. Crawford's line of reasoning left little doubt that slavery reformers were "soft" on the issue of permanent black inferiority, and critics seized upon the fact to help block ameliorative proposals in the final wartime meeting of Georgia's General Assembly, convened on an emergency basis in February 1865. On March 2 the Atlanta *Southern Confederacy* warned reformers to "take care" lest they find themselves "teaching the same doctrines that Garrison, Greeley, Phillips, Sumner and others have always taught."[81] Supporters of amelioration bristled at any suggestion that they were disloyal to slavery, but in at least one respect the Atlanta newspaper's allegation was well founded. Although Southern reformers and Northern Republicans were at war over the issue of immediate emancipation, they had little quarrel about larger racial questions. Not only did abolitionist doctrines of "romantic racialism" borrow heavily from the logic of Southern paternalism, but Confederate slavery reform also incorporated much of the laissez-faire white chauvinism of Northern free labor ideology. Southern reformers saw blacks as culturally inferior human beings capable of advancing morally and intellectually through individual effort and prolonged contact with superior white civilization. Antislavery Northerners held much the same view and agreed with the Southern contention that blacks as a group stood little chance of ever achieving full cultural parity with whites.[82] During subsequent decades these shared assumptions would provide fertile soil for cultivating national reconciliation at the expense of racial equality. But in 1865 any suggestion of ideological affinity with the abolitionist North was anathema to white Georgians, few of whom could divorce the slavery question from the maintenance of white supremacy.

Ignoring charges of racial and sectional disloyalty, reformers helped secure a slave marriage bill from the legislature's House Judiciary Committee, only to have the measure indefinitely postponed on March 10, 1865, as more urgent matters claimed the attention of beleaguered lawmakers.[83] Ending on a note of anticlimax, the campaign to ameliorate Georgia bondage produced abundant rhetoric but meager results. Three years of effort had yielded one legislative victory, two defeats, and no material change in the legal protection afforded to most bondsmen—hardly an impressive record of tangible achievement. But statutory revision is only one, and perhaps ultimately not the most important, measure of the reform campaign's significance. In Georgia and throughout the South there was much to suggest that the *debate* over reform proved at least as important as the success or failure of any particular set of ameliorative proposals. After a thirty-year moratorium on domestic criticism of slavery, few white slaveowners in 1860 were prepared to contemplate basic modi-

fications in Southern racial policy. Reformist agitation changed all of that.
At its deepest level the entire idea of codifying a master's moral obligation
to slaves represented a subtle departure from the inner logic of paternalism and a step away from the aristocratic philosophy of the old regime.[84] The more immediate and visible effect of reform arguments was
to dissolve taboos against critical discussion of bondage and make slavery
once again a debatable issue. Each ameliorative proposal required its own
unique defense, but certain recurrent themes dominated public discussion
of reform, providing focal points for debate and exposing the contradictory moral imperatives within proslavery theology.

Guilt was the chief psychological weapon available to Georgia reformers, and throughout the war they hammered away at the conscience of
slaveholding Christians. To the chorus of voices calling for postponement
of change until the South's permanent separation from Northern abolitionists was assured, the reformers gave a single answer: first things first.
Slave code liberalization, the ministers argued, was a necessary precondi-
tion of Southern independence rather than a consequence. Evidence to
sustain this viewpoint came principally in the form of Confederate military setbacks, which clergymen presented as omens of impending disaster
and defeat, avoidable only if Southerners appeased God's wrath and made
bondage a truly scriptural institution by eliminating the slave system's
"abuses." From the beginning, both the war itself and particular battlefield
reverses were interpreted as Divine punishment, "fatherly chastisement"
of obstinate or indifferent slaveholders in a sinful nation.[85] Some ameliorative spokesmen, of course, chose to emphasize the positive. "O what
a people we might be, with the old patriarchal institution rightly carried
out among us," exclaimed one minister in 1863.[86] But for every preacher
who celebrated the joys of potential salvation, another lamented the prospect of eternal torment. Writing shortly after the bloody Confederate
disaster at Chickamauga in September 1863, *Christian Index* editor Samuel
Boykin saw the "finger of Providence" pointing unmistakably at Southern
blacks who had collectively been victimized by white moral neglect.
"What Christian slaveholder," Boykin asked, "can lay his hand on his heart
and say he has done his *whole duty* to his slaves? Have we not slighted their
moral and religious education? Have we not, by penal statutes, deprived

262

them of God-given rights? Have we not failed, by legislation, to protect them in their marriage relation? Have we not inflicted untold distress in separating families?"[87] Instead of denying responsibility for these failings, Boykin said, Georgia's negligent masters should confess guilt and repent without delay. Borrowing a metaphor from the nearby military hospitals, he urged white Georgians to "apply the knife at any cost" and remove that "gangrenous excrescence . . . whose offensive odors 'go reeking up to heaven.'"[88]

Similar jeremiads appeared regularly during the next eighteen months, intensifying with each Confederate retreat of the 1864 Sherman invasion. Midway through the Atlanta campaign one outspoken reformer even went so far as to berate white Georgians for making slavery "a stumbling block over which men fall into hell." After reiterating the usual catalog of abuses demanding reform, the author declared flatly that "these evils must be speedily corrected or God will blot us out from among the nations of the earth." Masters were pointedly reminded that "the Lord executeth righteousness and judgment for all that are oppressed," and the essay concluded with a somber fourteen-verse quotation from Isaiah containing the famous abolitionist injunction to "loose the bands of wickedness, to undo the heavy burden[s], and to let the oppressed go free."[89] Six months later, when both Atlanta and Savannah had fallen to Union armies, Baptist minister John L. Dagg delivered a last-ditch exhortation to his demoralized co-religionists. Georgians, Dagg believed, could no longer afford the luxury of theoretical debates about amelioration. Experience alone would determine the value of slave code liberalization and shape its subsequent course, but opportunity to implement the reform program was fast receding. Or, as Dagg himself put it, "The rod of God is upon us—disaster staring us in the face—There is no time for delay."[90]

From the vantage point of a more secular age, it is tempting to dismiss the doomsday rhetoric of Georgia reformers as evangelistic hyperbole. Reform propaganda contained its share of exaggeration, to be sure, and Southern clergymen had a long tradition of using theological "fear tactics" during the times of crisis.[91] But despite the element of political calculation evident in reform arguments, the guilt theme underlying ameliorative efforts was more than a contrivance to gain public support. From the

1840s onward proslavery ministers had been increasingly troubled by the gap separating patriarchal ideals from the actual conduct of master-slave relations. The disquieting ease with which numerous planters placed profit ahead of paternalism during the war suggested that slavery retained serious ethical flaws, defects for which whites were responsible and, of course, divinely accountable. Reformist clergymen betrayed their misgivings on the point by drawing a clear distinction between general human sinfulness and the special evils associated with chattel bondage. The *Christian Index*, for example, deplored the wartime increase of sins like pride, sabbath breaking, greed, and extortion, but denied that these evils, either by themselves or collectively, could bring disaster to the Southern republic. God would destroy the Confederacy only for some truly "national sin," an offense of which "we *as a nation*—a mass of people—are generally and individually guilty . . . in a most heaven daring manner."[92] Neglecting the spiritual welfare of a dependent race might constitute just such a fatal misdeed, the reformers believed.

Whatever their political impact on state lawmakers, ameliorative arguments had the inevitable effect of strengthening privately held doubts about the morality of slavery, and by late 1863 the growing undercurrent of doubt and moral uncertainty seemed serious enough to warrant corrective action.[93] Believing the "public mind" to be "not sufficiently convinced that slavery is of God, and that more light on that subject will do good," Georgia's leading Baptist newspaper began publishing the serialized novelette "Nellie Norton," in which a Southern Christian slaveholder refutes the numerous criticisms of black servitude advanced by his naive Northern niece.[94] Among those who turned to the new book for badly needed reassurance was Augusta resident Ella Thomas. Although born into a slaveholding family, reared and educated "wholly under Southern skies," and married to a Georgia planter, Mrs. Thomas "some times doubted on the subject of slavery."[95] In September 1864 she confessed "that what troubles me more than anything else is that I am not certain that *Slavery* is *Right.*"

I have read very few abolition books (Uncle Tom's Cabin making most impression) nor have I read many proslavery books—yet the idea has gradually become more and more fixed in my mind that the institution of slavery is not right. . . . Owning a large number of slaves as we do I might be asked why do I not free them? This if I could, I would not do, but if Mr. Thomas would sell them to a man who would look after their temporal and *spiritual* interest I would gladly do so. Those house servants we have if Mr. Thomas would agree to it I would pay regular wages but this is a subject upon which I do not like to think and taking my stand upon a moral view of the subject, I can but think that to hold men and women in *perpetual* bondage is wrong.[96]

Although she exaggerated in claiming that Southern women were "all at heart abolitionists," Mrs. Thomas was not the only member of her sex to have moral qualms about slavery during the war.[97] Much of the guilt that white women expressed reflected concern over the breakdown of slave discipline and revulsion at the harsh measures being used to keep blacks in subjugation. Near Albany, Georgia, the youthful Eliza Frances Andrews reacted emotionally to the sight of her sister's runaway slave being marched off for punishment with hands tied behind his back. "Such sights sicken me," she wrote, "and I couldn't help crying when I saw the poor wretch, though I know discipline is necessary, especially in these turbulent times." Believing emancipation to be impractical, she favored a law confiscating the slaves of cruel masters if the South won the war.[98] In Thomas County, Mrs. Narcissa Lawton was horrified to learn that the fugitive slave Ben had been apprehended and bludgeoned to death. "No wonder we are punished by a just and avenging god for the injustice and cruelty which is exercised to our poor negroes," she wrote despairingly.[99]

Reform churchmen were also distressed by the wartime harassment and intimidation of Georgia bondsmen. Fearful that white excesses might eventually cause blacks to rebel, leading religious figures pleaded for restraint on practical as well as humanitarian grounds. Moderation, the reformers argued, was in the slaveholder's interest because planters lacked the capacity to control slaves by force. In the face of this reality, masters should seek to cultivate their slaves' goodwill, which, like religious faith, was a sentiment not subject to coercion. Warnings against undue severity were heard frequently during the final weeks of the Atlanta campaign, prompted in most cases by reports of gross misconduct on the part of temporarily detailed rural police squads. In a public letter to the governor, Bishop Pierce revealed that district patrol captains had been ordered to visit plantations and "search negro houses, trunks, chests, [and] corners," whether or not the slaves were suspected of any wrongdoing. Worse still, the special police detachments were disrupting black worship services and undermining the work of white missionaries. [100]

A typical incident occurred in Hancock County near Pierce's home, where bondsmen had assembled at a designated "preaching place" on Sunday, August 21, 1864, to attend the "regular appointment of an old well known preacher." The meeting went off uneventfully until "at the close of the service the patrol appeared and whipped about all [the blacks] they could catch," the only pretext for punishment being that some of the slaves present lacked passes. [101] Bishop Pierce, of course, had a vested interest in guarding the sanctity of religious gatherings, but more neutral observers supported his claim that patrollers were abusing their authority. Writing from Bulloch County some three weeks after the Hancock affair, one L. E. M. Williams urged that the police detail in his region be sent to the battlefront, "as they may do some good their in place of harm hear." One of their number, John Brown by name, was reputedly a "drunkard and Gambler" who "deserted the army and came home and got the appointment." Since then he had "been drunk with a crowd with him in the same fix[,] and [they had] taken a nigra from his wifes house with a pass from his master and beat him until the Doctor says he will die." The folly of such conduct was evident to a practical man like Williams, who ended his account by noting, "There is a greateal of dissatisfaction throughout the County."[102]

Ameliorative spokesmen believed that efforts to inflict a reign of terror on rural blacks could easily produce the opposite result from that intended. Bishop Pierce warned that a policy of indiscriminate violence and repression was "well calculated to produce discontent and insubordination among the colored people . . . whose loyalty at this time demands and deserves a very different treatment."[103] The *Southern Christian Advocate* agreed that whites could bring no greater injury upon their cause than "by undue severity, to alienate our servants, and render them discontented and refractory. . . . Let us so conduct ourselves . . . that, in these times of invasion and peril, they may cling to us for protection and continue loyal to our service," the *Advocate* counseled. [104] An even more direct link between reform sentiment and white insurrectionary fears can be established through the actions of state Senator David A. Vason, a Baptist layman who championed the legalization of slave preaching in 1863. Even as he voted for ameliorative measures in the General Assembly, Vason privately urged state officials to keep as many armed whites as possible on the plantations. There were, he pointed out, roughly thirty blacks for each white male in Dougherty County where he resided. Similar imbalances prevailed elsewhere, and if bondsmen were "corrupted" by enemy influence the state's slave population would constitute not merely a danger but an awesomely powerful "volcano in our midst."[105]

The importance of racial anxiety in shaping white attitudes toward reform might easily be exaggerated. At no time during the war did debates over slave code revision turn solely on the issue of black rebelliousness. Yet statements like those just quoted underscore the pragmatic element present in all ameliorative efforts. As already noted, the wartime reform agenda did more than address specific abolitionist criticisms of bondage. Liberalization measures also expressed the concerns and desires of black Georgians as perceived by white churchmen who had, in a manner of speaking, become prisoners of their own captive clientele. Whatever the immediate origins of particular legislative proposals, the reform campaign's general embodiment of slave aspirations reflected Southern Protestantism's growing tendency to serve the bondsman's secular needs in the interest of successful evangelization. Both before and during the war, "reforming" slavery meant granting blacks expanded areas of personal and institutional autonomy. White clergymen preferred to view the concessions as voluntary acts rooted in the reciprocal obligations of Christian paternalism, but by mid-1864 the war had stripped away enough ideological veneer to expose paternalism's less elegant substructure of biracial expedience. By virtue of their prior experience with slave mission work, reform churchmen were quicker than most whites to discern this reality— and better able to fathom its implications.

Whether or not blacks rose up in rebellion, many reformers eventually came to believe that the end of chattel bondage was near. Predicting slavery's demise early in the war would have been little short of treasonous, but as Confederate military fortunes wavered so did confidence in the peculiar institution. As early as 1862 Baptist spokesman Marshall Wellborn had cautiously raised the prospect "that the relation of 'bond and free'" might prove "a very fluctuating one in this wicked and changeable world."[106] By the end of the following year other observers, including many from outside reformist ranks, were beginning to agree. Indeed, some went considerably further. "I . . . fear the Negro. I tremble for the institution of slavery: it is well nigh done for," one Georgia woman confided to her private journal.[107] Hospital matron Kate Cumming faced the prospect of slavery's demise with considerably more composure. "If the negro should be set free by this war, which I believe he will be, whether we gain [victory] or not, it will be the Lord's doing. The time has come when his mission as a slave has ended," she concluded.[108]

When confronted by the impending reality of emancipation late in the war, few white Georgians were able to take the matter so philosophically. Even during the Confederacy's last months reformers showed understandable reluctance to abandon the cherished vision of a new and benevolent era in Southern race relations, a golden age in which bondage would be sanctioned by God, regulated by scripture, and conducted in the genuine interest of dependent black servants. But as hopes for amelioration faded while black assertiveness grew stronger in the face of sporadic repression, ameliorative spokesmen were increasingly caught in a trap of their own making. Having argued that God would signify approval of a properly conducted slave system by making Confederate armies victorious, reform churchmen now had little choice but to acknowledge the disturbing implications of an ultimate Southern defeat. The subject was a difficult one at best, and so long as a reversal of military fortunes seemed possible most religious leaders carefully avoided any premature rush to judgment. In a typical sermon preached shortly before the fall of Atlanta, a Macon minister staked out a pragmatic middle ground embracing both the old order and any new one that might emerge. As reported by the correspondent "Freeman," the minister's discourse to an interdenominational prayer meeting combined endorsements of white supremacy with speculation that a more elevated status for blacks might soon be at hand. "Perhaps," the speaker suggested, white Southerners were "nearing a crisis" in their connection with slavery.

> Having found us unfaithful to our weighty trust, God may be changing his plan. He may have waited long enough with the barren fig tree, and now the fiat "cut it down" may have gone forth. These poor sons of Africa, so perfectly dependent on us for all social and religious elevation, too stupid to know their own wants, may have cried against us, until His slumbering wrath may have awakened, and He may be about to place them in another political relation, where their moral wants shall press with more effect upon the enlightened Christian sympathy of the world. [109]

Despite the clergyman's stress on black inferiority, it is unlikely that most slaveholders found the message reassuring. A still more penetrating analysis of reform logic came from the pen of Baptist leader N. M. Crawford in a late 1864 essay, republished by the Methodists in 1865. Never one to equivocate, Crawford faced the moral issue squarely by distinguishing between hostile public opinion and a second, more serious, obstacle to slave code liberalization. White sentiment could always be changed through further Divine "chastening," but what if critics were right? What if proposed reforms were, in fact, subversive of chattel bondage? Should that be the case, Crawford conceded, "our system of slavery is in itself, and not in its abuse, irreconcilably opposed to God's law. I do not think it is so; but if it is so, it presents an unanswerable argument against the system itself, for nothing can be right which is opposed to God's law."[110] Bishop Pierce had stated essentially the same premise in his controversial *"Let it Perish"* sermon to Georgia legislators some eighteen months earlier. There was, however, a crucial difference between the two utterances. In offering to give up slavery for the sake of black salvation, Pierce clearly hoped to persuade listeners that reform would make such a sacrifice unnecessary. Crawford, on the other hand, seemed far less confident that the choice would remain hypothetical. Conspicuously absent from his last reform pronouncement was the confident optimism of earlier years, and substituted in its place was a genuine sense of foreboding over the fate of a morally flawed institution.

V

THE SHIFT in attitude among slavery reformers during the war's last months provides a useful clue to the larger meaning of Confederate ameliorative efforts. Reformist churchmen were heirs to a legacy of cautious antislavery gradualism which had flourished throughout America in the postrevolutionary and early national period. By 1860, however, regional factors had effectively obliterated the North-South consensus. Isolated within a traditional society which was largely untouched by the modernizing pressures of rapid industrialization and family freehold market agriculture, Southern clergymen clung to gradualist logic long after it had fallen into disrepute among religious and secular leaders of the more dynamic free states. Conservative in its ultimate social implications at the national level, ameliorative reform nonetheless possessed "liberal" overtones for white Southerners who understood the limits their society placed upon even the mildest forms of antislavery dissent.

The Civil War did for Southern slavery reform what capitalist expansion, evangelicalism, and slave rebelliousness had done for Northern humanitarianism a generation earlier. It wrenched incipient emancipationist impulses out of their well-worn gradualist path and onto the direct route of immediatism. In a sense, therefore, reform churchmen became victims of their own success, overtaken during the war's last months by events which they themselves had set in motion. Having inadvertently prepared the public mind for discussions challenging the fundamental premises of Southern labor and race relations, ameliorative spokesmen saw their legislative program become irrelevant in 1864 when whites began debating Jefferson Davis's plan to emancipate and arm the slaves for Southern defense. At the broadest level enlisting Negro troops and liberalizing the slave regime were complementary endeavors, bound together by a common tendency to enlarge the scope of black freedom. Not all reformers regarded the situation so positively, of course, and those churchmen who genuinely hoped to preserve slavery by liberalizing it had valid reason to view emancipation as a defeat. It seems probable, however, that most of Georgia's hard-pressed ameliorative spokesmen welcomed the appearance of more drastic proposals which would further libertarian ends while deflecting conservative hostility toward new and less vulnerable targets.

"Our whole theory of slavery is wrong."

9. Black Liberty and the Meaning of Confederate Nationalism

SITTING ALONE in a Northern military prison during the summer of 1865, Confederate Vice-President Alexander H. Stephens had ample reason to ponder the history of Southern race relations. As Stephens reflected upon slavery's demise, his thoughts returned to an 1864 conversation with Georgia's Episcopal bishop, the Right Reverend Stephen Elliott. "I told him," Stephens recalled, "that in my judgment abolition was the moving spirit of the war. . . ."

> I did not think the war, end when or how it might, would leave slavery as it found it; while I looked on the institution . . . as sanctioned by God, yet I thought great wrongs had been perpetrated under it; as with all human institutions in accordance with the sanction of the Creator, there were reciprocal duties and obligations; . . . [but] in our system, the superior race had looked too much to the benefits received from the relation, and too little to its obligations to the inferior, and the benefits to which that inferior was entitled; the moral and intellectual culture of the inferior race, to which it was entitled to the extent of its capacity and condition, had been greatly neglected: the Negro had been made to perform his part of the obligation while the white man had failed to fully perform his: this was, in my judgment, one of the great sins for which our people were brought to trial. The status of the Negro would not be left by war where war found it. [1]

In defeat Stephens sought, and occasionally seemed to find, a kind of personal vindication. "God knows my views on slavery never rose from any disposition to lord it over any human being," he protested. Having argued unsuccessfully for laws authorizing black literacy, protecting slave

272

marriages, and facilitating manumission, he now urged white Georgians to provide the former slaves with education and to grant freedmen a limited franchise subject to gradual enlargement. Although convinced that blacks were an inferior race, he acknowledged their right to civil equality and political representation as one of several "antagonistic" interest groups in the postwar South.[2]

Stephens's comments accurately sum up the ambiguous intellectual content of Confederate reform sentiment, but they omit an important chapter in slavery's wartime history. Despite the intense passion that ameliorative efforts aroused, the campaign to liberalize chattel bondage proved to be only the gentle prelude to a fierce storm of racial controversy that raged throughout the South during the war's last months. By that point white Georgians had ceased discussing how to improve slavery and were debating instead whether to abolish the institution and arm liberated bondsmen for Southern defense. Enlisting black soldiers had never been an item on the agenda of Georgia reformers, and not all of them supported the movement to arm and free the slaves. Some advocates of Negro troops did, however, support ameliorative measures as a preliminary step in securing black allegiance to the Confederacy, and there can be little doubt that slave code reformers contributed unwittingly to the emancipation debate that ultimately occurred. By insisting that slavery was no longer above criticism, reform spokesmen helped open the door for criticism of the most fundamental kind. Few white Georgians could have imagined in 1861 that proposals for wholesale, uncompensated emancipation would be seriously debated by Southerners during the winter of 1864–65. That such a discussion took place with the full blessing of the Confederacy's highest civilian and military authorities provides striking evidence of the manner in which wartime circumstances served to undermine bondage and expand the scope of human freedom.

II

Abandoning slavery was never an attractive idea to Confederate leaders, but few could deny that voluntary abolition made sense from the standpoint of international politics. Beginning in 1862 skillful Northern use of the emancipation issue helped frustrate all Southern efforts to gain diplomatic recognition from major European powers. Belatedly accepting the failure of "King Cotton Diplomacy," President Jefferson Davis dispatched special envoy Duncan F. Kenner early in 1865 to seek Anglo-French recognition in exchange for Confederate emancipation.[3] Rumors of the secret mission caused a ripple of speculation in Georgia newspapers, including one self-delusory report that France and England would establish full diplomatic relations with the Confederacy upon its promise to end slavery in fifty years.[4] Most Georgians, however, were too preoccupied with more immediate assaults on chattel bondage to trouble themselves for long over matters of transatlantic diplomacy.

Throughout the South controversy over emancipation had smoldered since the summer of 1863 when spokesmen from war-ravaged states like Louisiana, Alabama, and Mississippi first proposed arming the slaves for combat service. Initially Georgia's leading newspapers rejected the idea out of hand. An Atlanta editor believed that enlisting Negroes to fight would "sacrifice . . . the principle which is the basis of our social system," while the Savannah *Morning News* considered the issue too volatile for public debate.[5] Most private citizens probably shared these sentiments in the beginning, although direct evidence is scant. At the very least, the concept of blacks in gray was something which required considerable getting used to on the part of white Georgians. After listening to an army surgeon argue strongly for slave recruitment during August 1863, the practical-minded nurse Kate Cumming summed up her ambivalent reaction. "Somehow I do not like the idea," she confessed, but then added upon further reflection that the "arguments were, however, very plausible."[6]

A few miles from Miss Cumming's north Georgia hospital hard-pressed military strategists were reaching much the same conclusion as they struggled to protect the state from invasion. Talk of black soldiers became open in the Army of Tennessee during 1863, stimulated by the sixteen thousand Southern casualties incurred during the September fighting at Chickamauga. Eventually the talk led to action. Faced with the prospect of a major spring offensive by General William T. Sherman's numerically superior forces, a group of respected Confederate officers concluded that the time for desperate measures was at hand. At a meeting near Dalton, Georgia, in January 1864 Major General Patrick R. Cleburne unveiled a lengthy proposal for the immediate enlistment and training of "a large reserve of the most courageous of our slaves" who, together with all other bondsmen remaining faithful to the South would be guaranteed freedom at the end of the war.[7] Although Cleburne's memorial was quickly suppressed by Jefferson Davis, the Confederate president's opposition to Negro troops had already begun to soften. During November 1864 Davis himself broached the idea of a biracial army to Southern lawmakers and linked the concept to a program of limited emancipation. Nearly five more months would elapse before slave enlistment received the grudging sanction of a moribund Confederate Congress, time enough for most Georgians to immerse themselves in what has been aptly described as the "fullest and freest discussion of slavery in which the South as a whole ever engaged."[8]

At its deepest level the debate over arming the slaves involved a search for Southern identity and a quest for national purpose. On one side of the controversy stood those traditionalists who looked upon the South's political autonomy as the "armor that encased her peculiar institution." From this vantage point secession became merely a political tactic to defend chattel bondage, and each Confederate battlefield casualty seemed justified as an "offering upon the altar of African slavery."[9] Arrayed against the proslavery conservatives were equally zealous Rebel patriots who reversed the priorities and saw political independence itself as the transcendent war aim. Both groups paid homage to white supremacy, but advocates of black recruitment were prepared, in a sense, to sacrifice slavery upon the altar of Southern nationalism.

Spokesmen for each side in Georgia's eleventh-hour slavery debate employed similar tactics, appealing to the racial prejudices and class interests of white Georgians with an array of overlapping arguments. Proponents of a biracial fighting force brushed aside philosophical objections to black enlistment and sought to persuade slaveholders that Negro troops were an urgent military necessity. If masters refused to arm their bondsmen, the argument ran, they simply ensured defeat and immediate abolition on Yankee terms. Visions of impending disaster dominated arguments aimed at the state's planter elite. "Will two hundred thousand negroes be put into the service?" asked the son of Georgia novelist Richard Malcolm Johnston. "If this . . . is not done & quickly done, we are lost," he concluded.[10] "I have believed for the last two years that we would be compelled to put negroes in the army or go up the spout," another state resident confessed in January 1865.[11] "This has now become a war of extermination on both sides," declared Louisiana's Confederate Governor Henry W. Allen in a letter to Joseph E. Brown. "God has given us the means [to achieve victory, and] if we do not use them, the folly—the blame—the terrible consequences must rest on our heads," Allen warned Georgia's chief executive.[12] Echoing this theme, a correspondent in the Macon *Telegraph* urged Georgians to abandon their scruples and stop wearing "white kid gloves" when battling an opponent who wielded a lethal ebony "sledge hammer."[13] Less colorful but probably more effective appeals to planter self-interest appeared in newspapers like the Augusta *Southern Christian Advocate.* Convinced that failure to arm the slaves would be tantamount to abolition, the *Advocate* urged masters to face reality. "One fact is past argument," the paper observed in February 1865. "The negro will be the future soldier of the war."[14]

Even as they appealed for planter cooperation, advocates of black recruitment openly courted the state's alienated white yeomen, whose resentment against slaveholding aristocrats was intensified by racial hostility toward Negro bondsmen. Arguments directed at Georgia's plain folk promoted black enlistment as a means of equalizing wartime hardships by placing heavier burdens on both slaves and their owners. The Confederacy, according to one writer, had spent four years "driving into a slaughter pen about a million of our white men, the very flower and spirit of our population," while leaving an equal number of blacks at home. The slaves ostensibly did little except pamper wealthy masters who were "ever ready to cry out [']kill the white men but these [blacks] are my property, let the negroes alone[']"[15] Class exploitation received even greater emphasis from the newspaper correspondent "Sidney," who condemned Georgia slaveowners for their indifference to the state's average fighting men, those poor and middling whites who risked death with "nothing but their country to defend," leaving impoverished families to the "cold charities of the world." In contrast, Sidney noted, the "rich planter" remained at home undisturbed, raising greater objections to the arming of a single slave than to the death of a thousand free soldiers. "In God's name," the writer pleaded, "do not sacrifice every white man in the Confederacy in preference to taking a few negroes from their fondling masters."[16]

Planter spokesmen avoided direct discussion of class inequities, but outdid their critics in the use of racial demagoguery. Resorting to black troops, the conservatives claimed, would be an insult to Southern soldiers and would degrade whites at all levels of society. "If white men fighting for liberty, for firesides, for our *lives*—cannot whip the fight—for God's sake, for our own sakes, bend our knee suppliant at the throne of some nobler being—something more like ourselves, than the debased semi-savages, like our negroes," raved one Georgia extremist.[17] Opponents of black troops also urged lawmakers to consider the new policy's revolutionary social implications. Arming the slaves, they warned, would be most significant as "an indication of the future—pointing to a change in the organic structure of society, and giving a new phase to the current of our civilization." Once bondsmen entered Confederate ranks the "old land-marks" would be swept away, and even if the South gained victory on the battlefield, radical changes in the framework of postwar society might well "defeat the object in view," namely the social and political subordination of Southern blacks.[18]

An interlocking concern over white supremacy and the defense of slaveholding ideology lay at the heart of most objections to Negro recruitment. It was possible in theory to advocate black enlistment without repudiating the *status quo ante bellum*, but the idea of docile bondsmen obediently shooting Yankees at the direction of Southern white officer-masters contained too many contradictions to suit most slaveholders. At the beginning of the war conventional wisdom among Southern whites held that blacks were incapable of acquiring the skills and discipline necessary for armed combat. "The negro can never be a soldier," a Savannah editor stated confidently in 1863. Whites alone possessed the "high qualities of courage and honor" essential for military exploits, he said, and to arm a race of childlike dependents would prove "worse than useless."[19]

Incorporating the basic ethnological tenets of proslavery paternalism, such arguments exerted a powerful sway over conservative whites long after former bondsmen had proved their fighting ability in the Union Army. As late as February 1865 Governor Brown could still assure the state legislature that "Providence designed . . . [Negroes] for slavery . . . [and] did not intend that they should be a military people." By conceding that blacks were a "military race," Brown recognized, Southerners jeopardized their entire philosophical defense of chattel servitude.[20] Nor was the governor alone in this view. His political adversary Howell Cobb put the matter succinctly in a letter to Confederate authorities in Richmond. "If slaves will make good soldiers," Cobb protested, "our whole theory of slavery is wrong."[21]

Cobb and other foes of slave enlistment also predicted that efforts at racial integration would backfire. Paraphrasing objections heard two years earlier in the North, the commander of Georgia's reserve forces professed to believe that white soldiers would refuse to serve with Negroes. Instead of strengthening Confederate armies, black recruitment would drive whites from the ranks in massive numbers, leaving Southern commanders "to fight the balance of the war with negro troops." For Cobb such a policy was unthinkable. "You can't keep white and black troops together, and you can't trust negroes by themselves," he warned the secretary of war. To attempt either course would be a "suicidal policy" signaling the "beginning of the end of the revolution."[22]

Many of Georgia's fighting men took a decidedly different view of the matter. From their position near Petersburg, Virginia, in February 1865 the troops of four separate Georgia regiments declared themselves ready to arm and "make soldiers" out of any or all ablebodied Southern slaves.[23] A week later Georgia's celebrated battlefield hero, General John B. Gordon, surveyed his entire Second Corps in the Army of Northern Virginia and found most of the eighty-six hundred officers and men to be "decidedly in favor of the voluntary enlistment of the negroes as soldiers."[24] For skeptics like Cobb, rank-and-file endorsement of black troops represented defeatism in patriotic garb. Most white soldiers, Cobb believed, wanted to extricate themselves from the war at any cost and hoped to gain furloughs or discharges when Negro replacements reached the front. War weariness and disaffection may have influenced the public posture of some army units, but in Virginia, at least, white Georgians showed few traces of weakening resolve. "The army is passing resolutions favoring putting in the negroes & declaring their determination to fight it out," a Georgia officer reported from Richmond in February 1865, as the dying Confederacy experienced a final upsurge of patriotic zeal.[25] Only weeks before stacking their arms at Appomattox, members of the Forty-ninth Georgia Regiment were considering practical measures to mobilize black reinforcements and continue the war. As if responding to those who questioned their motives, the regiment's company officers summed up prevailing sentiment concerning service in a racially integrated army. "When in former years, for pecuniary purposes, we did not consider it disgraceful to labor with negroes in the field or at the same work bench," the Georgia veterans explained, "we certainly will not look upon it in any other light at this time, when an end so glorious as our independence is to be achieved."[26]

The real question facing embattled Confederates was not whether whites would repudiate a biracial army but whether blacks would join one. By the winter of 1864–65 few white Georgians were willing to take the Negro's loyalty for granted. Foes of slave enlistment pointed out that on repeated occasions black "men, women and children" in Georgia had "rushed to the Yankees from every quarter," showing little evidence of the "loyalty for which some gave them credit." Continuing signs of "ill-suppressed discontent" among local bondsmen caused previous escape episodes to take on sinister overtones. "It is evident . . . that . . . [the slaves] made a move against us," concluded one writer who pondered the record of black flight to Union lines.[27] It was equally apparent to other observers that the South had more to fear from black troops than the mere possibility of desertion. By arming the slaves, critics warned, Confederates would risk undermining not only the theory but also the substance of their racial system. Although some whites hoped military life would shore up slave discipline and provide a safety valve for pent-up black unrest, opponents of the plan felt certain that black soldiers would turn against their old masters. Negroes might serve the army in menial positions, a Milledgeville newspaper concluded, but "never, never, we say, with arms in their hands."[28]

The specter of black troops leading a generalized slave revolt haunted white imaginations during the war's last months. From temporary quarters in Georgia, the Memphis *Appeal* warned readers against relying too heavily upon the innate inferiority or pacifism of Southern Negroes. "If there should be any possessing an aptitude for command or war, (and there might be some although incapacitated by nature as a race), they would incite and lead servile insurrections, or incite discontent and insubordination . . . that might entail incalculable troubles," the paper predicted. Compounding the horror of violence inflicted by "Yankees without and negroes within" was a growing anxiety over the tenor of postwar race relations.[29] Predictions that military equality between black and white troops would result in demands for social and political recognition by armed black veterans became a constant refrain among adherents of the old regime. Apparently sensing that chattel bondage was doomed, a few conservative spokesmen began late in the war to distinguish between slavery per se and the larger issue of white supremacy. For writers like "Woodson" in the Macon *Telegraph*, the South's priorities in April 1865 could not have been clearer. "Keep the negroes in their proper places," Woodson urged. "Change, if you will, . . . the relations at present existing between master and slave; but beware how you attempt to change the relations existing between the two races. . . . Destroy, if you will, . . . the right of property in slaves, but keep the negro . . . subordinate and inferior . . . to the white man." If white Georgians hoped to preserve their hegemony over blacks, Woodson advised, slave enlistment must at all costs be avoided. His reasoning was simple. "When you make soldiers of negroes," he warned, "you virtually declare them to be your equals, and if that claim is ignored or denied, they will attempt to establish it by the means which you place in their hands."[30]

Viewed from this perspective, the debate over arming the slaves ceased to be a narrow military question and assumed the character of a strategic dispute about long-range social policy. Although they hesitated to identify themselves openly with Confederate peace sentiment, conservatives like Woodson were making the nominally "defeatist" argument that white Georgians could do more to safeguard the racial status quo by accepting abolition on Northern terms than by securing victory with black aid. Or, put another way, they were suggesting that for those who saw Negro subordination as the essence of Southern life the fruits of a biracial victory might have proven at least as bitter as those of a "lily-white" defeat.[31]

No matter how different their priorities concerning race and regional identity may have been, there was at least one point upon which defenders and critics of slave enlistment could usually agree. Black support for the Confederacy, if it materialized at all, would come at a price. The cost to white Georgians would be high, and whether they settled the debt immediately or postponed payment until after the war, they would eventually discharge their obligation to black soldiers in the currency of freedom. This reality had been clear to General Cleburne as early as January 1864 when he urged Confederates to "make the most" of their opportunity by incorporating universal emancipation into any scheme for black recruitment.[32] Initially few white Southerners were willing to contemplate so drastic a step, preferring like Jefferson Davis to follow legal precedent and offer freedom only as a reward for loyal service.[33] Once they thought about the idea, however, skeptical Georgians were quick to detect shortcomings in the concept of selective postwar manumission. With only white promises to rely on, black soldiers might, in the tactful phrase of one newspaper editor, prove "less efficient" in Confederate gray than in Union blue. The choices presented to most bondsmen would be inherently one-sided.

> The Yankee holds out . . . the inducement of freedom in the event of success, or the triple horrors of slavery in the triumph of the South. The alternative . . . is such that . . . [the Negro] fights willingly and fiendishly [in the Union Army] for his own freedom. With us, stimulated by the certainty of freedom at the end of the war, he still has less to incite him than Cuffy on the other side. After organising him into large [Confederate] armies, to secure immediate freedom, what has he to do but to walk over to the other side, and enjoy all the rights of a freeman. This he would know full well, and, in all probability, this he would do.[34]

The wife of an Augusta planter agreed that by joining the Yankees black Georgians could "*instantly* gain the very reward which Mr. Davis of-

fers . . . after a certain amount of labor rendered and danger incurred."
Taking "a woman's view of the subject," she found it "strangely inconsistent"
to offer some blacks freedom as a reward for helping keep others of their
race in bondage.[35] A male critic of the Davis administration put the case
more bluntly: "The North invokes the aid of negro soldiery for the emancipation of the negro, therefore we will voluntarily emancipate the negro
that he may fight the North against emancipation. . . . How prepos-
terous!"[36]

From the moment white Georgians began talking candidly about black
desires for freedom, the debate over slave enlistment entered a new and
more radical phase. Picking up the gauntlet that conservatives had thrown
down, Georgia liberals admitted that halfway measures were inadequate
to create a biracial army. If Southerners hoped to outbid the North for
black support, they had no choice but to offer bondsmen unconditional
emancipation in advance of military service. Opponents of Negro troops
had already conceded as much. From a logical standpoint the argument
was difficult to fault, but even the boldest and most forward-looking advocates of black recruitment embraced the new radicalism cautiously. Some,
like editor Samuel Boykin of the *Christian Index*, literally backed into the
manumissionist camp.

Although initially opposed to slave enlistment, Boykin was sure from
the outset that no "middle course" concerning freedom would be possible
if blacks joined Southern ranks.[37] Army life, the editor predicted, would
school bondsmen in a curriculum of liberation rather than servitude. Besides firearms training, the Negro soldier would learn "a sense of self-
reliance; irreverence for masters; aspirations for freedom; [and] a vague
perception of equality with the white race." Thus educated, black veterans could not be returned to slavery, and manumitting them would be
only a first step in coping with new social and ethical realities. "The boon
of freedom would be of little value to the man whose wife and children are
slaves," Boykin noted, almost as if thinking out loud. Half forgetting the
original point of his argument, he pursued the unsettling train of thought.
"If it is right to free the parent, it would seem to be a moral obligation to
manumit his wife and their offspring. What would Christians do with
such an obligation—what *could* they do?"[38]

The answer to such questions did not come easily for white reformers who hoped that slavery could still somehow be reconciled with the dictates of religious conscience. Eventually, however, many ameliorative spokesmen, including the editor of the *Index*, faced up to the implications of their own logic. Nearly a month before slave enlistment became official Confederate policy, the Baptists' leading newspaper concluded that Southern nationalism and black liberty were inseparable. "If this measure is really necessary to our success, and will secure it," the paper editorialized, "we say put the slaves into the army, but when you do it, make them freemen at the same time, and give them an interest in the soil they are called upon to defend."[39] Reluctantly, but with unmistakable finality, the *Index* had cast its lot on the side of freedom.

Not all public utterances were so forthright. On March 13, 1865, a timid Confederate Congress authorized the enlistment of up to three hundred thousand black troops, but stipulated that any change in the legal status of slave recruits would require the approval of both state governments and individual owners. The new law effectively sidestepped manumission, leaving the president and his secretary of war to confront the question ten days later when promulgating detailed regulations to implement the legislation. The Confederacy's nearest equivalent to a domestic emancipation proclamation was embodied in the awkward syntax of General Orders No. 14 of the Adjutant and Inspector General's Office which stated, in part: "No slave will be accepted as a recruit unless with his own consent and with the approbation of his master by a written instrument conferring, as far as he may, the rights of a freedman."[40] Black Confederates, in other words, would serve as liberated volunteers.

Word of the government's momentus decision reached Georgia around the first of April, and enlistment efforts began almost at once.[41] Within days the Augusta *Constitutionalist* reported that "quite a number of patriotic negroes" stood ready to volunteer for Confederate service "upon the first call." The paper urged prompt formation of a local *"Corps d' Afrique"* and by April 9 recruiting had apparently begun.[42] At virtually the same moment another Georgia editor was exhorting Columbus residents "to take the matter [of black enlistment] into their own hands, and, by inducements, urge the negroes to volunteer." The Columbus *Enquirer* suggested that each slaveowner act as a recruiting agent and try to persuade one-fourth of his adult black men to enlist. [43] Even as the paper made its proposals, however, Federal cavalrymen under General James H. Wilson were advancing rapidly toward the city from eastern Alabama. Their arrival on April 16 ended slavery and Confederate biracialism with a single stroke. [44]

Black enlistment probably came closest to getting under way in Macon, where at least two white Confederates were actively seeking Negro volunteers during the war's final weeks. One of the men was Private James B. Nelson of the Sixteenth Georgia Battalion, who decided to raise a company of ex-slaves after spending over a year in Northern military captivity. On April 15 Nelson set up recruiting headquarters in a local store. [45] Two days later a more ambitious scheme was launched by Captain Thomas J. Key, whose decimated artillery company had been assigned to Macon's defenses after serving with General Patrick Cleburne the previous year. With a spirit Cleburne would have applauded, Key proposed to assemble a battalion of three hundred to four hundred ex-slaves and employ the remnants of his white command as officers and drill sergeants for the black unit. His approach to recruiting stressed self-interest and revealed a clear appreciation of the difficulties to be overcome in persuading both races to support the government's program. Recognizing the inadequacy of congressional legislation, Key exceeded even the War Department's official instructions by asking slaveowners to "emancipate such negroes as will volunteer in the Confederate service, promising them after we shall gain our independence, and they should desire to return to their old homes, that proper provisions will be made for them and their families and fair wages given." If masters found the prospect of free labor unpalatable, Key urged them to weigh the alternatives. "Better give up half your negroes to defend your homes," he argued, "than let them all fall into the clutches of the North, to be used as spies and guides, and to aid in your utter ruin."[46]

Key's idea of freeing black soldiers and their families while preserving white property rights over other slave noncombatants exposed the contradictory imperatives within wartime race relations. The compromise offered less than most bondsmen wanted but more than their masters were initially willing to concede. Whether Key's formula could have succeeded as a short-term strategy to set the enlistment process in motion remains conjectural. According to one observer, the "holding back of the owners" constituted the chief obstacle to slave recruitment, and there can be little doubt that many Georgia planters greeted the entire scheme with skepticism if not open hostility.[47] Some, however, did respond favorably within the brief time before the South's final surrender. As early as March 8, 1865, a meeting of citizens in Fort Valley assured Confederate leaders that "we are prepared, whenever they shall ask it of us, to devote our slaves to the maintenance of a cause which is already rendered doubly dear by the blood of our kindred."[48] Later the same month Oglethorpe County planter David C. Barrow sought permission from the president to raise a regiment of black troops. Barrow's son agreed that "patriotism required every good citizen to support" the government's slave enlistment policy. He understood his father's "strong desire to see this movement successful" but advised the elder Barrow against abandoning his agricultural interests to accept a military command.[49] Other prominent Georgians showed signs of closing ranks behind the Davis administration's biracial initiative. No less outspoken a critic of black troops than Howell Cobb dutifully helped execute the new law in his capacity as commander of the state's reserve forces. Cobb promised to aid David Barrow in securing command of a Negro regiment, and the general's son, John A. Cobb, offered to furnish a company of black recruits from the family's plantations in southwestern Georgia. If necessary, the Cobbs were even prepared to send their white overseer along to serve as an officer for the former slaves.[50]

III

BY THE END OF THE WAR it seemed clear that at least some white Georgians had begun marching to the beat of a different drummer in racial matters. But where were their footsteps leading? Could the South actually have fielded a new model army composed of white freemen and black freedmen? The answer rested ultimately with thousands of individual bondsmen upon whose voluntary aid Confederate leaders pinned their last desperate hopes. In Georgia and other states the war ended before significant numbers of blacks could be called upon to accept or reject freedom on Confederate terms. Some clue as to the choice black Georgians might have made lies hidden in the events of earlier years, when the alternatives facing Southern slaves were simpler and more clear-cut. Evidence from the pre-1865 period calls into question the entire notion of black "loyalty" to the North or South and underscores the unique moral vantage point from which Southern bondsmen viewed the events of the 1860s.

In early 1865, as Georgians completed their fourth year of life in an independent Southern republic, the idea that emancipated blacks might take up arms for the Confederacy did not seem entirely implausible. Even without the inducement of liberty, bondsmen had been mobilized to produce munitions, erect fortifications, staff hospitals, and perform other types of military labor. Most Negroes who contributed to the war effort had no real choice in the matter, of course, but there were always individuals who did more than the minimum that slavery required. During the Union occupation of St. Simons Island the slave Henry on William Hazzard's estate risked severe punishment in order to give covert assistance to Confederate scouting parties. When the Yankees evacuated the island in December 1862, Henry rejoined his master on the Georgia mainland, bringing detailed military intelligence which would soon be supplemented by the Savannah bondsman David, who returned in February 1863 from a three-month spying mission to Beaufort, South Carolina.[51] A few blacks apparently enlisted in the Confederate Navy's Savannah Squadron, and bondsmen across the state made small contributions to the "Ladies Gunboat Fund" which helped finance construction of the CSS *Georgia*. Gifts normally ranged from twenty-five cents to one dollar, but sometimes included larger amounts such as an offer of twenty dollars from "Old Luke . . . a kind of head man and owner of property in *fee simple* under the care of his master."[52]

Strictly speaking none of the bondsmen mentioned were required to bear arms for the South, although they could hardly be described as neutral noncombatants. Similar ambiguity surrounded the role of black musicians like Camden County native Charles Benger, the "historic fifer of the

2nd Georgia Battalion." A veteran of the Seminole Wars, Benger departed for Virginia with Captain George S. Jones's company of the Macon Volunteers in May 1861. He remained with the unit until July 1862 when, at age sixty-eight, he was "honorably discharged from the Army of the Confederate States" amid glowing tributes from the whites with whom he had served for almost four decades.[53] Lacking the status of full-fledged soldiers, men like Benger nonetheless shared the risks of battle and comprised an integral part of the Confederate Army.

The same was true of hundreds of other black Georgians who went to war as personal attendants of white officers and enlisted men. For the most part slave body servants remained spectators to the military conflict, but occasionally they became active participants. In 1861, for example, the Georgia bondsman Dave won accolades for saving the life of his master's commanding officer and assisting in the capture of several Union soldiers on the battlefield in Virginia. "I was de only one near . . . when . . . de colonel's horse fell and he pitched over his back," Dave later explained.

> One Yankee raised his gun and took aim at de Colonel who said to me: "Davy, are you charged?"
> "Yes Colonel" I replied
> "Then shoot them Yankees"
> I brought my gun to my shoulder . . . when de Yankee laid down his gun and said "I surrender."
> Mars Wright jumps up and says "You are my prisoners."[54]

A similar incident occurred in the trenches outside Savannah during December 1864 when Confederate Marine Lieutenant Henry L. Graves called upon his Negro body servant Lawrence to assist in the city's defense. "Of Lawrence and his conduct I cannot speak too highly," Graves declared on December 28. "He . . . was with me in the trenches and Exposed along with me constantly to a hot, sometimes a terrific fire, from the Enemy's Batteries & Sharp Shooters & his indifference to danger and coolness often put to the blush some of the reserve troops who were around us. I got a Rifle for him & he shot many times at the Yanks, who were at times not over 700 yds from us. I was really quite proud of him."[55]

287

Blacks who proved loyal in combat won high praise in the Confederacy, but no figure evoked a deeper emotional response among paternalistic whites than a slave returning from battle with the corpse of a
fallen master. At the 1862 funeral of Lieutenant James Ware in Columbus
"there was scarcely a dry eye in the house" when the local minister "addressed himself to Phil, the servant who brought . . . his master's body"
home from Virginia. [56] Here, seemingly, was evidence not simply of slave
obedience but of a genuine human bond between owner and chattel, a
kind of individual attachment which might assume collective shape if
bondsmen entered Confederate ranks. There was some rational basis for
such an assumption, although any effort to transform the personal loyalties of slaves into broadly based black political support for the Confederacy would have required a tremendous display of moral alchemy on
the part of white Georgians. Men like Phil, Lawrence, Dave, and Benger
might have provided a small core of loyal recruits but hardly the thousands of replacement troops the South so desperately needed during the
war's last months.

Confederate realists accepted this fact and never predicated their slave-
enlistment plans on the behavior of loyal body servants or trusted household retainers. White strategists looked instead to the thousands of more
typical black Georgians who were "loyal" enough to reap the tangible
benefits that nominally pro-Southern behavior entailed but who also
stood ready to seize their freedom in whatever guise it presented itself,
whether in the midst of Rebel armies or behind Yankee lines. Wartime
experiences proved repeatedly that black allegiance to either side in the
sectional conflict was conditional. Guided by a visceral skepticism concerning the ultimate intentions of all whites, Georgia bondsmen pursued
the substance of liberty with little apparent regard for political theories or
moral abstractions. During most of the war the Unionist or Confederate
sympathies of black Georgians fluctuated with changing circumstances.
For many bondsmen proximity or access to free territory decided the
issue, and white soldiers resigned themselves to the off-again, on-again
behavior of camp servants like Henry, who rendered "great help" during
two years of hard campaigning in Virginia, only to become "very trifling"
after the 1863 Gettysburg invasion. "I think [he] will get better now weev

[sic] got farther away from the free states," Henry's master predicted in late July of that year as the Confederate Army moved southward, but by mid-August it was clear that a complete return to old behavior patterns would be difficult if not impossible. Henry's prolonged sojourn among free Negroes in Martinsburg, West Virginia, had given reality to the concept of an independent life beyond slavery. The memory of such an experience might fade with the passage of time, but its impact could never be fully erased. "He is doing a little better now but isent [sic] the boy he was last year," Henry's master acknowledged reluctantly to relatives back in Georgia.[57]

As Confederate armies advanced and fell back, the pathway to freedom sometimes took unexpected turns. War altered the geography of liberation no less than it changed the physical landscape, and if upheavals occurred suddenly enough the line between loyalty and betrayal became difficult to pinpoint. The problem is illustrated by the case of Prince, a body servant who voluntarily accompanied his master Theodorick W. Montfort into captivity after the Union conquest of Fort Pulaski in 1862. If Prince's initial action grew out of personal regard for Montfort, his subsequent behavior suggested a new set of priorities. "Prince has been emancipated & has left me," Lieutenant Montfort reported shortly after beginning his incarceration at Governor's Island, New York.[58]

An even more striking example of wavering sectional allegiance is provided by Moses Dallas, a twenty-three-year-old Duval County, Florida, slave who joined the Union Navy in 1863 but soon changed sides and became the chief coastal pilot for Georgia's beleaguered Savannah Squadron. It is possible that Dallas was disillusioned by his initial contact with the Yankees, or perhaps he simply followed the path of self-interest. In any event, the Confederacy rewarded him handsomely for his services. On May 31, 1863, barely a week after Dallas's name was officially entered on Union enlistment records, Commander William A. Webb of the CSS *Atlanta* felt "compelled to increase the pay of Moses Dallas from $80 to $100 per month in order to retain him." Considered the "best inland pilot on the coast," Dallas remained in Confederate service for more than a year and apparently enjoyed the full trust of white Southern officers.[59] His loyalty received its greatest test on the night of June 2–3, 1864, when he led a force of 132 Rebel sailors in a daring attack on the Union gunboat *Water Witch*, anchored in Ossabaw Sound near the mouth of the Ogeechee River. Dallas accompanied the expedition's commander, Lieutenant Thomas Pelot, in the first of seven open boats that drifted silently through the darkness on a strong outgoing tide. By taking advantage of a violent thunderstorm, the black pilot was able to bring Confederate seamen within two ship-lengths of the Union vessel before their presence was discovered. Hails from the deck of the *Water Witch* brought defiant Rebel shouts of "Go to hell, you sons of a b———," followed by volleys of gunfire and sharp hand-to-hand fighting as Confederates boarded and subdued the enemy ship. Within minutes the Savannah Squadron had won its only significant combat victory, but in human terms the cost proved high. Combined casualty reports listed twenty-three wounded and eight dead, among them Moses Dallas, who the Confederates believed was killed before his boat reached the *Water Witch's* side. [60]

Union eyewitnesses agreed that the Confederates had "lost" their black pilot in the daring attack, and for once both sides really *were* right. Dallas would serve the Savannah Squadron no more, but obituary notices were somewhat premature. On August 27, 1864, almost three months after the *Water Witch* episode, Moses Dallas's name quietly reappeared on Union Navy enlistment records, and on March 9, 1865, he enlisted in Company E of the 128th United States Colored Infantry at Beaufort, South Carolina. Mustered out with the rank of corporal in October 1866, he rejoined his family in Jacksonville, Florida, where he remained until his death eight years later. Apparently Dallas's wartime career engendered little in the way of permanent racial bitterness. Joseph Haddock, the brother of Dallas's former owner, maintained some contact with the black family and in 1881 described Moses's widow, Delia Dallas, as a "good woman" who deserved a Federal pension because of her husband's Civil War service. [61]

Moses Dallas's capsule biography points up the danger of forcing the wartime experience of black Southerners into a preconceived ethical framework. In affirming their paramount desire for freedom Georgia slaves did not automatically repudiate all ties with the South. On the contrary, there is much to suggest that both before and after 1865 black

Georgians maintained a strong sense of local identity and a bittersweet affinity for the land of their birth. During the war an almost bewildering array of emotions and private considerations influenced the behavior of individual bondsmen. Concern for friends or relatives in slavery, uncertainty over the war's outcome, personal esteem for white owners, disillusioning contacts with racially prejudiced Northerners, awareness of religiously inspired efforts at ameliorative reform, and the actual expansion of slavery's customary prerogatives all served to bind particular Afro-Americans to the Southern cause. Such links were fragile, to be sure, and so long as the North held a monopoly on abolition they were easily severed. With the advent of Confederate emancipation, however, all roads led to liberty for the black recruit and the Southern route promised, in many cases, to be more direct than the Northward passage. Had the war lasted longer, or had the Confederate offer of freedom come sooner, it is reasonable to suppose that a considerable number of Georgia bondsmen would have exited slavery by the shortest and least hazardous thoroughfare.

IV

But what then? To recognize that white Confederates might have fielded a black army in 1864–65 is one thing. To assume that biracial military efforts would have paved the way for postwar cooperation between freedmen and their former masters is quite a different matter. Indeed, it is far from certain that slave enlistment would have constituted a viable long-range military strategy during the war itself. There were simply too many inconsistencies surrounding the plan, too many unanswered questions. Throughout its brief history the campaign for black troops represented an unstable fusion of liberal and reactionary impulses. Support for the measure came from whites on both ends of the Southern ideological spectrum as well as from blacks who saw military service as a way to achieve radical ends through accommodationist means. At one extreme frightened white supremacists like John J. Cheatham of Athens advocated slave conscription as a means of heading off domestic racial violence. Potential black troublemakers, Cheatham reasoned in 1861, could be dispersed through-out existing white military units, "say ten or twenty placed promiscuously in each company . . . [where] there [sic] number would be too small to do our army any injury."[62]

Although Cheatham's logic would be echoed by white Georgians in the Army of Northern Virginia as late as 1865, most state residents eventually came to regard arming and freeing the slaves in a somewhat different light.[63] Tough-minded and resourceful planters often accepted the necessity of emancipation while repudiating the idea of racial equality. Their vision of the future was largely a blueprint for reconstructing the racial hierarchy of the past. Writing from occupied Savannah in late December 1864, planter-aristocrat William B. Hodgson admitted that "slavery as it has existed may be modified," but not to the point of jeopardizing white control of the black work force. In the absence of chattel servitude a "state of serfage or ascription to the soil" seemed inevitable to Hodgson, whose views were probably shared by a significant segment of Georgia's planter elite.[64] Precisely what form postwar race relations might have assumed in an independent Confederacy was revealed by a Confederate surgeon in Columbus during January 1865. Acknowledging that military defeat appeared imminent, the doctor urged Georgians to take steps for ensuring a smooth transition from slavery to freedom. His plan had a familiar ring. "I would suggest that we agree to the emancipation of all [blacks] over thirty years of age, at the expiration of five years, and that all of those under that age, and all the children born, be subject to their masters, both men and women, to the age of thirty, and then be free. The children born of free parents to be bound to serve to the age of thirty." This arrangement, the writer explained, "would pay for the rearing of children and would secure a succession of laborers, by means of whom we can cultivate and retain possession of our plantations."[65]

Statements like those just quoted lend considerable credence to Allan Nevins's contention that enlightened Confederates accepted the inevitability of slavery's demise and "were fighting for the right to deal with the joint problems of slavery and race adjustment in their own time and on their own terms."[66] Those terms, however, appeared to be "serfage" and gradual emancipation at a time when most blacks (and a few liberal whites) anticipated a more rapid and far-reaching program of social democratization. As Reconstruction and its aftermath were soon to demonstrate, nineteenth-century Americans had no magic formula for reconciling these overlapping but ultimately contradictory social agendas.

EPILOGUE

TWENTY-ONE YEARS after Appomattox black Civil War veteran George Washington Williams completed *A History of the Negro Troops in the War of the Rebellion, 1861–1865.* In the preface to that pioneering work the author searched for language and images capable of expressing the inner meaning of Union military service for Southern slaves. By taking up arms in the cause of liberty, Williams wrote, black recruits stepped "from the Egyptian darkness of bondage to the lurid glare of civil war; from clanking chains to clashing arms; from passive submission to the cruel curse of slavery to the brilliant aggressiveness of a free soldier; from a chattel to a person." Altogether, the Afro-American's combat role represented an emotionally climactic historical watershed. "It was midnight and noonday without a space between."[1]

Perhaps unintentionally, Williams adopted a series of metaphors that evoked the duality as well as the drama of black life in the Confederacy. For Georgia's nonwhite population the war presented an abundance of contrasts, not only between the stark alternatives of slavery vs. freedom, but also—and more typically—between the contradictory tendencies within the slave regime itself. With a consistency apropos to a democratic revolution led by slaveowning reactionaries, the struggle for Southern independence pulled domestic race relations in opposite directions. Between 1859 and 1865 campaigns of racial repression and acts of unparalleled barbarity toward blacks went hand in hand with religiously motivated efforts to ameliorate slavery and expand the legal rights of bondsmen. In a similar fashion, the changes associated with wartime urbanization, industrialization, and refugee life produced both benefits and disadvantages for the black people involved. Opportunities to alter plantation routine, to escape white surveillance, and to gain economic bargaining power were often achieved at the expense of family separation

294

and loss of direct access to free territory. Hard-pressed masters became more tolerant of independent behavior among blacks, but they also abandoned an increasing number of paternalism's self-imposed obligations.

For some black Georgians the war did, of course, bring escape from slavery, but the freedom obtained behind Union lines was often less complete and more exploitive than justice would have dictated. Ambiguity also surrounded the triumph of Northern arms during the 1864 Sherman invasion. Blacks had reason to look askance at Yankee liberators who often appeared as hostile to Negroes as to slavery itself. The obvious bigotry displayed by some Northern troops helped dampen the enthusiasm of slaves for the Union cause and may, in the long run, have reinforced the already profound alienation that many freedmen felt toward white society.

When contemplating the events of Reconstruction it is important to bear in mind that the Civil War constituted a cultural bridge as well as a line of historical demarcation. During the late 1860s Georgians of both races frequently found themselves standing astride the boundary of Confederate defeat as they confronted an uncertain future amid vivid reminders of the past. In the realm of domestic race relations the war experience had demonstrated the possibility, indeed the necessity, of change while simultaneously underscoring the organic limits of Southern biracialism. Among former slaveholders the desire to control blacks through violence would continue to find frequent expression, beginning with the Christmas Day insurrection scare of 1865 and broadening into the later exploits of the Ku Klux Klan and related terrorist organizations.[2] But if the popularity of racial vigilantism remained strong after emancipation, so too did the determination of some whites to seek a more just social order. The moderate approach to race relations which characterized the New South movement of the 1880s owed a large debt to churchmen like Atticus Haygood, who reshaped proslavery Christianity to fit the political and economic contours of postemancipation life. Drawing upon the most optimistic and forward-looking elements in prewar theology, Haygood expounded a philosophy of racial tolerance which embraced the laissez-faire realities of the new order without repudiating the paternalist reciprocity of the old regime. Both before and after the war ameliorative gradualism remained central to the strategy of Haygood and other Southern moderates. Conceding the reality but not the immutability of white dominance, postwar religious liberals avoided direct challenges to prevailing racial norms and endorsed segregation as the only practical avenue to black uplift.

Segregation, in the form of a strategic retreat into defensive racial separatism, was also initiated by former slaves during the early years of freedom. Black Georgians emerged from the Confederate experience with a clear understanding of both the humane qualities and the destructive impulses nurtured by the old regime. Thus, the newly liberated Negro's desire for equality was tempered by a sober realism born of antebellum attitudes reshaped in the crucible of war. Instead of seeking revenge, most freedmen seemed anxious to put the past behind them and make a new start. Postwar magnanimity toward former masters grew out of deeply felt religious values, buttressed by the knowledge that Southern whites would probably retain control of local affairs when the Yankees had come and gone.[3] Acutely aware of their long-term vulnerability, black Georgians looked first to obtaining physical security, family stability, economic independence, and, when possible, literacy—tangible elements of freedom that might be preserved in the midst of political defeat and adversity. For future generations these priorities would become a crucial antidote to despair.

NOTES

CHAPTER ONE

1. Savannah *Daily Morning News*, October 18, 1859, pp. 1–2. On erratic law enforcement in Georgia's largest city, see Richard H. Haunton, "Law and Order in Savannah, 1850–1860," *Georgia Historical Quarterly* 56 (Spring 1972): 1–24.

2. Early reports of the Brown raid were very similar in all of the state's leading newspapers. Telegraphic news usually appeared in Augusta and Savannah papers first and was copied by papers in such interior towns as Athens, Columbus, Macon, and Rome a day or so later. These initial reports may be followed in fairly detailed form in the Savannah *Daily Morning News*, October 19, 20, 22, 24, 1859.

3. Columbus *Daily Sun*, October 19, 1859, p. 2.

4. Ibid., October 21, 1859, p. 1.

5. Stephen B. Oates, *To Purge This Land with Blood: A Biography of John Brown* (New York, 1970), 290–306; Allan Nevins, *The Emergence of Lincoln: Prologue to Civil War, 1859–1861* (New York, 1950), 2:78–84.

6. Savannah *Daily Morning News*, October 22, 1859, p. 2.

7. Rev. Charles C. Jones to Charles C. Jones, Jr., November 7, 1859, in Robert Manson Myers, ed., *The Children of Pride: A True Story of Georgia and the Civil War* (New Haven, 1972), 527–28; George A. Mercer Diary, 1855–60, entry of November 4, 1859 (p. 189 of typescript), Southern Historical Collection, University of North Carolina, Chapel Hill, hereinafter cited as SHC; Sarah Frances Hicks Williams to "My dear Parents," November 7, 1859, Sarah Frances Hicks Williams Letters, SHC; same to same, November 11, 1859, Williams Letters.

8. Columbus *Daily Sun*, November 17, 1859, p. 3.

9. Ibid., 2.

10. Ibid., December 3, 1859, p. 3; December 5, 1859, p. 3; December 10, 1859, p. 2.

11. Savannah *Republican*, November 14, 1859, in Columbus *Daily Sun*, November 16, 1859, p. 2. The reports from Talbot County received wide cir-

culation and even appeared in South Carolina newspapers. See Steven A. Channing, *Crisis of Fear: Secession in South Carolina* (New York, 1970), 24.

12. Columbus *Daily Sun*, November 28, 1859, p. 2, quoting Forsyth *Educational Journal*, November 17, 1859; Covington *Times*, November 24, 1859.

13. Elberton *Star of the South* in Columbus *Daily Sun*, November 28, 1859, p. 2;
Wade Banister Gassman, "A History of Rome and Floyd County, Georgia, in the
Civil War" (M.A. thesis, Emory University, 1966), 58–59.

14. Savannah *Daily Morning News*, December 22, 1859, p. 1.

15. Ibid., January 24, 1860, p. 1.

16. Rome *Southerner*, November 24, 1859, in Savannah *Daily Morning News*,
November 29, 1859, p. 1.

17. Savannah *Republican*, January 2, 1860, p. 2.

18. Savannah *Daily Morning News*, February 3, 1860, p. 1.

19. Columbus *Enquirer*, December 5, 1859, in Savannah *Daily Morning News*,
December 7, 1859, p. 1; Eugene Marvin Thomas III, "The Columbus, Georgia
Enquirer, 1855–1865" (M.A. thesis, University of Georgia, 1971), 30; Augusta
Constitutionalist in Savannah *Republican*, January 21, 1860, p. 1; Sumter *Republican* in
Columbus *Daily Sun*, November 28, 1859, p. 2; Savannah *Daily Morning News*,
December 5, 1859, p. 2. See also George A. Mercer Diary, December 15, 1859
(p. 196 of typescript); *Annual Report of the American Anti-Slavery Society, by the Execu-
tive Committee, for the Year Ending May 1, 1860* (New York, 1861), 166–91, 202–206.

20. George A. Mercer Diary, December 26, 1859 (pp. 203–204 of typescript); A. Cuthbert to Rev. W. McLain, January 16, 1860, American Colonization Society Archives, ser. 1, vol. 158, pt. 1, Library of Congress, hereinafter
cited as ACS Archives (the series will not be repeated).

21. Columbus *Daily Sun*, December 19, 1859, p. 1; December 21, 1859, p. 3;
Savannah *Daily Morning News*, January 6, 1860, p. 1; January 11, 1860, p. 1; April
16, 1860, p. 1; Savannah *Republican*, April 18, 1860, p. 1. Clarence L. Mohr,
"Georgia Blacks During Secession and Civil War, 1859–1865" (Ph.D. dissertation, University of Georgia, 1975), 214–15, discusses the content of the above
sources in more detail.

22. Macon *Daily Telegraph*, March 10, 1860, p. 3; Louisville *Gazette* in Savannah *Daily Morning News*, March 15, 1860, p. 1. For additional measures to restrict
black access to alcohol, see *Acts of the General Assembly of the State of Georgia . . .
Annual Session . . . 1859* (Milledgeville, 1860), 140, 167. All Georgia session laws
are hereinafter cited as *Acts of Georgia*.

23. Savannah *Republican*, April 2, 1860, p. 2; July 17, 1860, p. 2; November
13, 1860, p. 2.

24. Rome *Weekly Courier*, January 27, 1860, p. 2.

25. Macon *Daily Telegraph*, March 16, 1860, p. 3; March 13, 1860, p. 2.

26. Ringgold *Express* in Savannah *Daily Morning News*, February 16, 1860, p. 1.

27. The overseer later took Henderson to another Augusta barroom and "treated the Negro in the same brutal way as before . . . (except the hanging)." Anonymous letter (signed "Many German citizens") to "Gov. Hammond" (Senator James H. Hammond of South Carolina), March 20, 1860, Alexander H. Stephens Papers, Library of Congress. For confirmation of the incident and further details, see P. F. Hammond to James H. Hammond, March 28, 1860; James H. Hammond to Alexander H. Stephens, March 31, 1860; same to same, April 19, 1860—all in Stephens Papers.

28. Macon *Daily Telegraph*, June 1, 1860, p. 3; June 3, 1860, p. 3; Savannah *Daily Morning News*, April 19, 1860, p. 1.

29. Vicksburg *Sun* in Macon *Daily Telegraph*, April 15, 1860, p. 2.

30. James A. Spratlin to D. C. Barrow, April 27, 1860, David Crenshaw Barrow Papers, University of Georgia Library.

31. The Oglethorpe affair received notice in several parts of the state. For the most detailed and probably most reliable account, see Augusta *Chronicle and Sentinel*, June 12, 1860, p. 3. See also Savannah *Daily Morning News*, June 12, 1860, p. 1; Ulrich B. Phillips, *American Negro Slavery* (Baton Rouge, 1966), 511, quoting Athens *Southern Banner*, June 14, 1860.

32. William McLain to R. R. Gurley, April 27, 1860, ACS Archives, vol. 159, pt. 1.

33. Savannah *Daily Morning News*, April 2, 1860, p. 1. See also John G. Hottel to Alexander H. Stephens, March 30, 1860, Stephens Papers, for private white reaction to the incident, stressing the financial loss incurred by the master.

34. Macon *Daily Telegraph*, April 25, 1860, p. 2; April 26, 1860, p. 2.

35. William Capers, Sr. to Charles Manigault, June 13, 1860, in James M. Clifton, ed., *Life and Labor on Argyle Island: Letters and Documents of a Savannah River Rice Plantation, 1833–1867* (Savannah, 1978), 300.

36. Savannah *Republican*, July 28, 1860, p. 1.

37. On the infrequency of suicide among antebellum slaves, see Eugene D. Genovese, *Roll, Jordan, Roll: The World the Slaves Made* (New York, 1974), 639–40; Benjamin Quarles, *The Negro in the Making of America*, rev. ed. (New York, 1969), 75–76. The standard account of Georgia's peculiar institution, Ralph B. Flanders, *Plantation Slavery in Georgia* (Chapel Hill, 1933), mentions only four slave suicides, two of which occurred in 1860. See pp. 269–70.

38. Edward Forrest Sweat, "The Free Negro in Antebellum Georgia" (Ph.D.

dissertation, Indiana University, 1957), passim; Whittington B. Johnson, "Free Blacks in Antebellum Savannah: An Economic Profile," *Georgia Historical Quarterly* 64 (Winter 1980): 418–31; Ira Berlin, *Slaves Without Masters: The Free Negro in the Antebellum South* (New York, 1974), 343–80. My assessment of the Georgia situation differs from Professor Berlin's treatment of free Negroes in the Lower South prior to 1850.

39. *Acts of Georgia 1859*, p. 68.

40. Ibid., 68–69.

41. Ibid., 69–70.

42. The towns receiving such powers were Bainbridge, Crawfordville, Warrenton, Hamilton, Griffin, Carnesville, Perry, Louisville, and Augusta. See *Acts of Georgia 1859*, pp. 129–33, 139–41, 146–47, 160–61, 164–68, 182–83, 192–93.

43. Ibid., 141, 146–47. Free blacks in Warrenton and Crawfordville who failed to pay their fines would be sold by the sheriff at public outcry "for the shortest time, [necessary] to pay said sum." This proviso had a dual significance. It provided a convenient avenue for the enslavement of free blacks, and was also an early and primitive form of the practice which evolved into the Southern convict-lease system of the late nineteenth century.

44. Ibid., 132. Other towns with special tax provisions for free blacks were Griffin, Perry, and Louisville.

45. Ibid., 182.

46. In early December 1859, when a great variety of laws hostile to free blacks were pending before the legislatures of Georgia, Alabama, Mississippi, and Tennessee, a Columbus newspaper editor observed: "There seems to be a growing sentiment in favor of the removal of this class of population." Columbus *Daily Sun*, December 7, 1859, p. 1. A scholar who has examined wartime legislation against free blacks throughout the Confederacy concludes that legal repression of free blacks was "greater in volume and more severe" in Georgia than in any other Southern state. See Bernard H. Nelson, "Legislative Control of the Southern Free Negro, 1861–1865," *Catholic Historical Review* 32 (April 1946): 28–46, esp. 40, 45.

47. Savannah *Daily Morning News*, January 21, 1860, p. 1; January 24, 1860, p. 1.

48. Waynesboro *News* in Columbus *Daily Sun*, January 27, 1860, p. 2.

49. Florence Fleming Corley, *Confederate City: Augusta, Georgia, 1860–1865* (Columbia, S.C., 1960), 15; *Acts of Georgia 1859*, pp. 129–30.

50. Campbell's views appear in a letter to the editor of the Augusta *Chronicle and Sentinel*, January 11, 1860, p. 3, and are reprinted in the issue of March 28,

1860, p. 2. An undated newspaper clipping of this letter may also be found in the ACS Archives, vol. 158, pt. 1.

51. Corley, *Confederate City*, 15; Whittington B. Johnson, "Free Blacks in Antebellum Augusta, Georgia: A Demographic and Economic Profile," *Richmond County History 14* (Winter 1982): 13.

52. Several works by James M. Gifford explore the attitudes of black Georgians toward Africa and the colonization movement. Particularly illuminating are: "Anti-Black Bias in Antebellum Source Materials: Lucius J. Gartrell and the Gideon Will Case," *Louisiana Studies* 14 (Summer 1975): 189–97; "Black Hope and Despair in Antebellum Georgia: The William Moss Correspondence," *Prologue* 8 (Fall 1976): 153–62; "Emily Tubman and the African Colonization Movement in Georgia," *Georgia Historical Quarterly 59* (Spring 1975): 10–24. See also Floyd J. Miller, *The Search for a Black Nationality: Black Immigration and Colonization, 1787–1863* (Urbana, 1975).

53. A. Cuthbert to Rev. W[illiam] McLain, February 21, 1860, ACS Archives, vol. 158, pt. 2.

54. James Harper to Rev. W[illiam] McLain, March 8, 1860, ibid.; same to same, March 26, 1860, ibid.

55. For all quotations in the above paragraph, see James Harper to Rev. W[illiam] McLain, April 21, 1860, ibid., vol. 159, pt. 1; William McLain to R. R. Gurley, May 2, 1860, ibid.

CHAPTER TWO

1. Savannah *Republican*, January 18, 1860, p. 1. See also ibid., March 9, 1860, p. 1.

2. The best summary of the presidential campaign in Georgia is Ollinger Crenshaw, *The Slave States in the Presidential Election of 1860* (Baltimore, 1945), 228–41. More detailed but less analytical is I. W. Avery, *The History of the State of Georgia from 1850 to 1881* . . . (New York, 1881), 102–23.

3. The major studies of the role of emotionalism in the press and elsewhere are Ollinger Crenshaw, "The Psychological Background of the Election of 1860 in the South," *North Carolina Historical Review* 19 (July 1942): 260–79, and Donald E. Reynolds, *Editors Make War: Southern Newspapers in the Secession Crisis* (Nashville, 1970). In his treatment of the Georgia campaign Crenshaw further observes that the state's Breckinridge newspapers had assumed a "defiant tone" long before the

Democratic convention in Baltimore. Crenshaw, *The Slave States in the Election of 1860*, 232.

4. The most thoroughly researched accounts of the "Texas Troubles" are Reynolds, *Editors Make War*, 97–117, and Crenshaw, *The Slave States in the Election of 1860*, 92–108. Both authors doubt the existence of any widespread plot. Reynolds is especially skeptical, and while exonerating Breckinridge supporters of "deliberate fraud," he feels that a "tacit" agreement or "conspiracy" existed "among members of the radical Southern rights press to help elect Breckinridge, and, failing that, to prepare the South for secession" (p. 115). On the other side of the debate is William W. White, "The Texas Slave Insurrection of 1860," *Southwestern Historical Quarterly* 52 (January 1949): 259–85. As the title implies, White believes that "a real plot of insurrection existed in 1860 in Texas."

5. Reynolds, *Editors Make War*, 101.

6. For the 1859 fires in cotton gin houses, see Savannah *Republican* in Columbus *Daily Sun*, November 16, 1859, p. 2. For allegations of black involvement in such fires, see Forsyth *Educational Journal*, November 17, 1859, and Covington *Times*, November 24, 1859, both in Columbus *Daily Sun*, November 28, 1859, p. 2.

7. This inward shift in the focus of white concern receives detailed discussion in chapter 1 of this work.

8. Macon *Daily Telegraph*, March 29, 1860, p. 3; March 31, 1860, p. 3; April 6, 1860, p. 3; April 7, 1860, p. 2; April 7, 1860, p. 3; April 9, 1860, p. 3; April 10, 1860, p. 2.

9. Ibid., April 12, 1860, p. 3.

10. Ibid., April 16, 1860, p. 3; April 25, 1860, p. 3.

11. For all quotations on the above incident, see ibid., April 26, 1860, p. 3.

12. For the Montgomery *Mail* quotation, see ibid., June 12, 1860, p. 3. For reports of other fires beginning in late May and continuing through June, see ibid., June 1, 1860, p. 3; June 2, 1860, p. 3; June 4, 1860, p. 3; June 7, 1860, p. 3; June 25, 1860, p. 3; June 28, 1860, p. 3.

13. Ibid., July 6, 1860, p. 3; July 7, 1860, p. 3.

14. For all quotations on the Columbus fires, see Columbus *Daily Sun*, July 25, 1860, p. 3.

15. On Turner's background, see two articles by Lawrence Huff, "The Literary Publications of Joseph Addison Turner," *Georgia Historical Quarterly* 46 (September 1962): 223–36, and "Joseph Addison Turner's Role in Georgia Politics, 1851–1860," ibid., 50 (March 1966): 1–13.

16. For all quotations in the above two paragraphs, see J. A. Turner, "What Are We to Do?" *De Bow's Review* 29 [vol. 4, n.s.] (July 1860): 70–77. Shortly after the Civil War, Turner gave fuller expression to his own racial views in a 41-page poem in heroic couplets entitled *The Nigger: A Satire.* See Huff, "Literary Publications of Turner," 233.

17. Channing, *Crisis of Fear,* 286. Channing uses the phrase quoted above to describe the overall nature of the secession movement.

18. Macon *Daily Telegraph,* July 27, 1860, p. 2; August 2, 1860, p. 2.

19. Savannah *Republican,* July 30, 1860, p. 1.

20. For letters from Charles R. Pryor and other Texas residents, see Savannah *Republican,* July 27, 1860, p. 1; August 4, 1860, p. 1; Columbus *Daily Sun,* August 20, 1860, p. 2. Irrespective of political orientation, all major Georgia newspapers copied numerous stories of suspected insurrections and conspiracies from the Texas press during July and August. An excellent example is the Constitutional Unionist Savannah *Republican,* which, despite its political moderation and frequent skepticism over the veracity of insurrection rumors, still carried a large volume of Texas news. See Savannah *Republican,* August 7, 1860, p. 1; August 8, 1860, p. 1; August 24, 1860, p. 1. For other examples of this same preoccupation with Texas events, see Columbus *Daily Sun,* July 28, 1860, p. 2; August 6, 1860, p. 3; August 13, 1860, p. 2.

21. For reports of actual or anticipated slave revolts in Alabama, Virginia, several areas of Mississippi, Arkansas, and even the Cherokee Nation, see Augusta *Dispatch* in Savannah *Republican,* August 15, 1860, p. 1; Macon *Daily Telegraph,* August 25, 1860, p. 1; Columbus *Daily Sun,* July 18, 1860, p. 2; Macon *Daily Telegraph,* August 27, 1860, p. 1; Savannah *Republican,* July 16, 1860, p. 2; July 30, 1860, p. 1.

22. For all quotations in the above two paragraphs, see Rome *Courier* in Macon *Daily Telegraph,* August 13, 1860, p. 2; August 25, 1860, p. 1. See also Columbus *Daily Sun,* August 11, 1860, p. 2. Writing over a half-century later, Mrs. Rebecca Latimer Felton recalled with surprising clarity how the 1860 Floyd County insurrection panic affected whites attending a camp meeting on her family's plantation some twenty-five miles from Rome, Georgia. As the revival approached its zenith on Sunday evening the Feltons' tent was filled with neighbors "armed to the teeth [and] waiting for midnight to go out quietly to suppress a 'rising' that had been reported to them late in the afternoon." The revolt proved to be a false alarm. Rebecca Latimer Felton, *Country Life in Georgia in the Days of My Youth* (Atlanta, 1919), 87.

23. Ibid.

24. Rome *Courier,* August 14, 1860, in Columbus *Daily Sun,* August 16, 1860, p. 2.

25. Augusta *Dispatch* in Savannah *Republican,* August 15, 1860, p. 1.

26. George A. Mercer Diary, 1860–65, entry of August 22, 1860 (p. 13 of typescript); Columbus *Daily Sun,* August 18, 1860, p. 2.

27. Rome *Courier,* August 28 in Columbus *Daily Sun,* August 30, 1860, p. 3.

28. The "Great Excitement" caused by the wave of robberies in Macon is described in a letter from Young Daniels to J. B. Lamar, July 22, 1860, Howell Cobb Collection, University of Georgia. When a slave carpenter was arrested in one of the robberies, a local cotton merchant named Mr. Wyche "made an attempt to cut his throte [*sic*]." Concerning the beating of a Macon policeman by local Negroes, see Macon *Daily Telegraph,* June 8, 1860, p. 3.

29. Macon *Daily Telegraph,* August 27, 1860, p. 1; Amos W. Brantly to J. B. Lamar, August 30, 1860, Howell Cobb Collection. See also Young Daniels to J. B. Lamar, August 27, 1860, Cobb Collection.

30. Macon *Daily Telegraph,* September 11, 1860, p. 1. According to published reports of this initial hearing, "The only evidence that could be brought to bear on the case was her [i.e., Becky's] own confession, made at different times to different persons in which she acknowledged committing the crime and related the manner in which she proceeded to do the deed in order to revenge herself upon some of the household who had offended her."

31. For a firsthand account of the court proceedings by Becky's lawyer, see Lamar Cobb to his mother [Mrs. Howell Cobb], November 14, 1860, Howell Cobb Collection.

32. For a description of the murdered storekeeper's injuries, see Macon *Daily Telegraph,* August 17, 1860, p. 1. Shortly after Joe's arrest local whites were assured that the evidence against him, although "mostly circumstantial," was "of such a character as to leave no doubt of his being the guilty party." See Columbus *Daily Sun,* July 17, 1860, p. 3.

33. Macon *Daily Telegraph,* August 17, 1860, p. 1.

34. Ibid.

35. Upson *Pilot* in Macon *Daily Telegraph,* October 4, 1860, p. 1; Columbus *Daily Sun,* September 25, 1860, p. 1.

36. Augusta *Dispatch* in Savannah *Republican,* August 13, 1860, p. 1.

37. Macon *Daily Telegraph,* August 15, 1860, p. 1.

38. Ibid., October 3, 1860, p. 1. see also Columbus *Daily Sun,* September 25, 1860, p. 1.

39. Columbus *Daily Sun*, August 29, 1860, p. 2. See also Marietta *Statesman* in Columbus *Daily Sun*, September 3, 1860, p. 2.

40. Columbus *Daily Sun*, August 29, 1860, p. 2.

41. A. C. McKinley to his sister, August 26, 1860, Howell Cobb Collection.

42. Dalton *Times* in Columbus *Daily Sun*, September 4, 1860, p. 3.

43. Savannah *Republican*, September 1, 1860, p. 1; Macon *Daily Telegraph*, August 29, 1860, p. 2; September 1, 1860, p. 2; September 4, 1860, p. 1; September 8, 1860, p. 1; September 27, 1860, p. 1.

44. Rome *Courier* in Columbus *Daily Sun*, August 30, 1860, p. 2; Marietta *Statesman* in Savannah *Republican*, September 12, 1860, p. 1; Macon *Daily Telegraph*, October 8, 1860, p. 1; Waynesboro *News* in Columbus *Daily Sun*, September 15, 1860, p. 1; Waynesboro *Independent South* in Savannah *Republican*, September 17, 1860, p. 1.

45. Gassman, "Rome and Floyd County in the Civil War," 58.

46. Columbus *Daily Sun*, September 27, 1860, p. 3.

47. Macon *Daily Telegraph*, September 8, 1860, p. 1.

48. Ibid., March 10, 1860, p. 3; Anonymous letter signed "A Friend" to Alexander H. Stephens, September 1, 1860, Stephens Papers.

49. On literacy among Georgia's antebellum slaves and free blacks, see Jacqueline Jones, *Soldiers of Light and Love: Northern Teachers and Georgia Blacks, 1865–1873* (Chapel Hill, 1980), 59–61; "History of Schools for the Colored Population" in *Special Report of the Commissioner of Education on the Improvement of Public Schools in the District of Columbia* (Washington, D.C., 1871), 339–41.

50. These accusations appear in the Savannah *Republican*, October 2, 1860, p. 1.

51. On the views of Georgia voters concerning the probability of Lincoln's election, see T. Conn Bryan, "The Secession of Georgia," *Georgia Historical Quarterly* 31 (June 1947): 89; Ulrich B. Phillips, *Georgia and State Rights* (Washington, D.C., 1902), 191.

52. Savannah *Republican*, September 6, 1860, p. 2; Memphis *Avalanche* in Macon *Daily Telegraph*, September 28, 1860, p. 2; Macon *Daily Telegraph*, October 4, 1860, p. 1.

53. John A. Cobb to his mother [Mrs. Howell Cobb], October 1, 1860, Howell Cobb Collection.

54. Jennie Akehurst Lines Diary, November 3, 4, 5, 27, 30, 1860, Akehurst-Lines Collection, University of Georgia.

55. J. R. Sneed to Alexander H. Stephens, November 8, 1860, Stephens Papers.

56. One day after learning of Lincoln's victory an Atlanta man made this point unequivocally: "Lincoln is elected upon a platform the 2nd Resolution of which asserts all men are created equal & endowed with certain inalienable rights amongst which are life *liberty* etc., it is useless for us to deceive ourselves about their including the negro in that[,] if they had not meant to include the negro there would have been no need for the resolution at all." In Athens, Lincoln's election caused "great excitement," public meetings, and talk of "nothing but disunion and war." "I think any Southerner who would accept an office under Lincoln and Hamlin ought to be shot" wrote an Athens woman. "—just to think[,] . . . our President was elected by negroes and the other [Hamlin] half negro—it ought not to be permitted." A woman in Milledgeville was even more blunt in her racial pronouncements: "All the women here are *'right'* but it is strange to say, there are many men quite willing to be ruled by the Yankee and the nigger! I suppose you see that New York has passed the law for *universal suffrage—all* the niggers!" See W. F. Henning to Alexander H. Stephens, November 9, 1860, Stephens Papers; M. Atkinson to [Ella Baber-Blackshear?], November 18, 1860, Baber-Blackshear Collection, University of Georgia; Georgia King to "Tip" [R. Cuyler King], November 13, 1860, Thomas Butler King Papers, SHC.

57. Beginning with Ulrich B. Phillips early in this century, scholars have recognized that a variety of factors influenced white voting behavior in the Georgia secession election. Among these are economics, geography, traditional party loyalties, and the influence of prominent state politicians in specific areas, as well as the density of black population and white racial anxiety. Most recently Michael Paul Johnson's sophisticated statistical study *Toward a Patriarchal Republic* (Baton Rouge, 1977) has interpreted the Georgia secession vote in terms of class divisions between planters and nonslaveowning yeoman farmers. While I do not totally reject Professor Johnson's concept of secession as a "double revolution," I feel that he has pushed his argument far beyond the bounds of plausibility in dismissing white racial fear as a major political factor. For a different view of the role of class factors in the secession election, see Donald Arthur Debats, "Elites and Masses: Political Structure, Communication and Behavior in Ante-Bellum Georgia" (Ph.D. dissertation, University of Wisconsin, 1973), 400–407, 473.

58. Allen D. Candler, comp., *The Confederate Records of the State of Georgia*, 6 vols. (Atlanta, 1909–1911), 1:47, hereinafter cited *CRG*.

59. Georgia King to "Fuddy" [John Floyd King], November 10, 1860; Georgia King to "Tip" [R. Cuyler King], November 13, 1860—both in Thomas Butler King Papers.

60. *CRG*, 1: 163–64.

61. James D. Russ [Athens, Ga.] to Alexander H. Stephens, December 9, 1860, Stephens Papers; (Americus) Sumter *Republican* in Columbus *Daily Sun*, December 19, 1860, p. 2; H. J. Wayne to "My Dear Mama H.," December 3, 1860, Edward Harden Papers, Duke University.

62. Several white residents of Crawford County published surprisingly candid and detailed accounts of their actions during the November insurrection panic. These appear in the Macon *Daily Telegraph*, November 9, 1860, p. 1; November 14, 1860, p. 1; November 15, 1860, p. 2; November 16, 1860, p. 1; November 21, 1860, p. 1. See also Savannah *Republican*, November 12, 1860, p. 1.

63. On the Habersham incident, see Clarksville *Herald* in Macon *Daily Telegraph*, November 21, 1860, p. 3. For details on Joseph W. Ribero, including accounts from the Boston *Courier*, see Savannah *Republican*, November 24, 1860, p. 1; November 27, 1860, p. 1.

64. Sarah Lawton to "My Dear Friend," December 30, 1860, Alexander Robert Lawton Papers, SHC.

65. Concerning restriction of liquor sales in Augusta, see Corley, *Confederate City*, 15. For the Columbus response, see Columbus *Daily Sun*, September 13, 1860, p. 3; September 17, 1860, p. 3. According to one writer, the major source of illegal liquor for Columbus blacks was the area known as "Utah," located on the outskirts of the city. Utah's population was a mixture of free Negroes and poor whites, "some of them rendered low by the indulgence of bad habits." Patrol companies venturing into the area frequently encountered strong resistance from Utah's poor whites, who allegedly encouraged theft and other illegal activities by blacks and then offered them protection from patrollers. See Columbus *Daily Sun*, November 28, 1860, p. 3. Earlier in 1860 a white resident of Columbus had complained about a residence occupied by a black woman named Rachael, who operated "a boarding house where white men and negroes mingle together." Such places were condemned as "dangerous to the institutions of the country" and "bad examples for the negroes." See Columbus *Daily Sun*, August 28, 1860, p. 3.

66. Columbus *Daily Sun*, July 25, 1860, p. 3; March 2, 1861, p. 3.

67. Macon *Daily Telegraph*, February 7, 1861, p. 1; February 22, 1861, p. 1; E. Merton Coulter, "Slavery and Freedom in Athens, Georgia, 1860–1866," *Georgia Historical Quarterly* 49 (September 1965): 264–93, esp. 270; N. C. Barnett [clerk to mayor and council of Milledgeville] to John B. Lamar, October 4, 1860, Howell Cobb Collection. See also Corley, *Confederate City*, 15.

68. Coulter, "Slavery and Freedom in Athens," 266–67; Columbus *Daily Sun*,

December 20, 1860, p. 2; Corley, *Confederate City,* 15. For evidence of similar concern in Atlanta, see Jennie Akehurst Lines Diary, December 27, 1860, Akehurst-Lines Collection.

69. Charles C. Jones, Jr. to Mrs. Mary Jones, October 27, 1860, in Myers, *Children of Pride,* 624.

70. For samplings of local sentiment on this subject, see Macon *Daily Telegraph,* October 27, 1860, p. 1; November 27, 1860, p. 1; Coulter, "Slavery and Freedom in Athens," 267; Gassman, "Rome and Floyd County in the Civil War," 59.

71. In Bryan County a special "Board of Police" was created to organize patrol companies. In McIntosh County a similar five-man Board of Commissioners was to be appointed by Inferior Court justices, while in Effingham County the Inferior Court justices were themselves made patrol commissioners, and in Dougherty County justices of the peace became patrol commissioners. Other affected counties included Dooly and Mitchell. See *Acts of Georgia . . . Annual Session . . . 1860,* pp. 206–10. For general slave patrol legislation in force during the first two years of the war, see *Acts of Georgia . . . Biennial Session . . . 1853–54,* pp. 101–103. For basic patrol laws in force after 1862, see R. H. Clark, Thomas R. R. Cobb, and David Irwin, eds., *The Code of the State of Georgia* (Atlanta, 1861), 263–66, hereinafter cited as *Code of Georgia.* For Bibb County Grand Jury presentments on patrol laws, see Macon *Daily Telegraph,* November 27, 1860, p. 1.

72. Howell Cobb, ed., *A Compilation of the General and Public Statutes of the State of Georgia; with the Forms and Precedents Necessary to Their Practical Use* (New York, 1859), 628; *Acts of Georgia . . . Annual Session . . . 1860,* pp. 54–57; *Code of Georgia,* 369–70, 881–82.

73. See, for example, *Acts of Georgia . . . Annual Session . . . 1860,* p. 154, for a law empowering Inferior Courts in Georgia's coastal counties to levy a $100 fine upon ship captains for each free Negro on their vessels, entering a Georgia "harbor, river, bay or creek" from a nonslaveholding state. This legislation followed an 1859 law (discussed in the preceding chapter), forbidding free blacks to immigrate to Georgia, on penalty of being enslaved, and imposing a minimum $1,000 fine and twelve-month prison term upon anyone aiding a free black to enter the state. The 1860 law also supplemented an 1854 statute limiting the right of free Negro seamen to enter incorporated municipalities. See *Acts of Georgia . . . Biennial Session . . . 1853–54,* pp. 106–107. During the crisis of 1859–61 there is considerable evidence that these laws were enforced and sometimes abused. In March 1860, for example, the British consul in Savannah reported that a black British sailor named Brodie had been arrested on a trumped-up charge of enticing a slave

to run away, tried by the mayor's court in the town of Darien, illegally sold into lifetime slavery, and sent westward beyond the reach of the British government. Later the same year, in October, the mayor of Savannah told of the arrest of an entire crew of free Negro seamen charged with the same offense. See Nevins, *The Emergence of Lincoln*, 2:109–10; Charles C. Jones, Jr. to Mrs. Mary Jones, October 27, 1860, in Myers, *Children of Pride*, 624. For evidence of similar abuse in the antebellum period, see F. N. Boney, ed., *Slave Life in Georgia: A Narrative of the Life, Sufferings and Escape of John Brown, a Fugitive Slave* (Savannah, 1972), 29–39.

74. Corley, *Confederate City*, 15.

75. This development is explored and analyzed in chapter 2 of George M. Fredrickson, *The Black Image in the White Mind: The Debate on Afro-American Character and Destiny, 1817–1914* (New York, 1971). For an opposing view, see Eugene D. Genovese, *The World the Slaveholders Made* (New York, 1971), esp. 118–244.

76. Clement Eaton, *The Freedom of Thought Struggle in the Old South* (New York, 1964), 144–61 passim.

77. Ronald T. Takaki, *A Pro-Slavery Crusade: The Agitation to Reopen the African Slave Trade* (New York, 1971), passim.

78. Columbus *Daily Sun*, August 25, 1860, p. 2; October 3, 1860, p. 3; Macon *Daily Telegraph*, October 27, 1860, p. 1.

79. *Georgia House Journal, 1860*, pp. 74, 188, 246–47; *Georgia Senate Journal, 1860*, p. 322. It is interesting to note that after passage of the bill in the House on December 8 by a vote of 83 to 48, a motion to transmit the bill *immediately* to the Senate for action failed to receive the necessary two-thirds majority vote. Possibly some legislators bowed to strong constituent pressure in voting for the enslavement bill, and then resorted to a clever parliamentary maneuver in order to prevent its becoming law. This explanation is, however, purely conjectural.

80. *Georgia House Journal, 1860*, p. 286; *Georgia State Journal, 1860*, pp. 314, 324. In addition to the petition of Emiline Cole and her two children, the House also acted favorably upon a similar request from Emeline Pearce of Greene County.

81. George A. Mercer Diary, December 19, 1860; Savannah *Republican*, December 13, 1860, p. 1. For a discussion of enslavement pressures on free blacks in the neighboring state of South Carolina during this period, see Marina Wikramanayake, *A World in Shadow: The Free Black in Antebellum South Carolina* (Columbia, S.C., 1973), 168–84, esp. 168–70, 183–84. Professor Wikramanayake points out that between 1859 and 1863 nearly all free blacks who petitioned the South Carolina legislature for "voluntary" enslavement were "women, encumbered with families and having no means of support."

82. Macon *Daily Telegraph*, January 19, 1861, p. 1.

83. Henry Cleveland, *Alexander H. Stephens, in Public and Private, with Letters and Speeches, Before, During, and Since the War* (Philadelphia, 1866), 721–23.

84. On the scope of volunteering in Georgia during 1861 and the difficulty of providing arms for many volunteer companies, see T. Conn Bryan, *Confederate Georgia* (Athens, 1953), 22–23. By May 1861 Georgia had organized 263 volunteer companies, consisting of about 18,000 men. By July the state had sent off some 14,000 soldiers, not including regulars, and in October approximately 25,000 Georgia troops were in Confederate service. Although it is impossible to determine precisely the number of state and Confederate troops in Georgia at any given point, approximately 13,000 soldiers were defending the state's coast by November 1861. See Louise B. Hill, *Joseph E. Brown and the Confederacy* (Chapel Hill, 1939), 61–63, 162–63; Frank L. Owsley, *State Rights in the Confederacy* (Chicago, 1931), 91–94; CRG, 3:96–97, 101–102, 107–108, 109–11, 114, 116–20.

85. For all quotations in the above paragraph, see Louisa Gilmer to Adam Leopold Alexander, May 19, 1861, Alexander and Hillhouse Family Papers, SHC; George A. Mercer Diary, November 13, 1861 (pp. 148–49 of typescript). Whites in various geographical regions of Georgia shared similar views on the importance of armed troops for controlling local slaves. See, for example, D. W. Brandon [Thomasville] to Joseph E. Brown, April 25, 1861, Telamon Cuyler Collection, University of Georgia; John T. Boykin [Antioch, Troup County] to Joseph E. Brown, May 27, 1861, Cuyler Collection; Petition signed by twenty-eight citizens of Albany, Georgia, to Joseph E. Brown, June 17, 1861, Cuyler Collection; W. H. McWhorter [Greene County] to Adjutant General Henry C. Wayne, September 19, 1861, Cuyler Collection. On the army's police and patrol functions, see for example "Instructions for Picket Duty," March 21, 1862, and General Henry C. Wayne to Joseph E. Brown, March 10, 1862, both in Cuyler Collection; Charles C. Jones to Charles C. Jones, Jr., July 30, 1862, Charles C. Jones, Jr. Collection, University of Georgia; Brigadier-General H. W. Mercer to George W. Randolph, August 5, 1862, and accompanying petition from "Committee of Citizens of the 15th District., Liberty County, Ga." in *The War of the Rebellion: A Compilation of the Official Records of the Union and Confederate Armies*, 128 vols. (Washington, D.C., 1880–1901), ser. 4, vol. 2, pp. 33–35, hereinafter cited OR.

86. J. H. Taylor to David C. Barrow, June 16, 1861, Barrow Papers; George H. Davis to David C. Barrow, June 21, 1861, quoted in Bryan, *Confederate Georgia*, 127, 261. By late July the "insurrection mania" had considerably abated in southwest Georgia and, according to one local resident, would "probably settle down

in some stubborn law suits instituted by parties who have been whipped and run from the county." Joseph J. Bradford [Camilla, Ga.] to David C. Barrow, July 24, 1861, Barrow Papers. On earlier insurrection panics in southwest Georgia, see Monday (a slave) vs. The State of Georgia, 33 *Ga.*, 672. This case involved the trial and conviction at the April 1861 term of Sumter County Superior Court of the slave Monday, charged with the assault and attempted murder of a white man named Andrew Bass. In the original trial the Sumter County prosecutor gained a conviction (later overturned) by stressing the danger of a slave revolt as a central point in his closing argument to the jury. The presiding judge turned down a request from Monday's counsel that the jury be officially charged by the court: "That prisoner's rights be considered with the same care and caution as if he were a white man, and the suspicions or apprehensions of insurrection or irrepressible conflict ought and must have nothing to do with this case, unless the evidence showed insurrectionary movements." On insurrection panics in north Georgia, see Cassville *Standard* in Columbus *Daily Sun*, May 21, 1861, p. 1, for reports of the hanging near Kingston of a black man charged with "endeavoring to excite discontent among the negroes." His death was decreed by "a committee of twelve citizens."

87. S. T. Bailey to Howell Cobb, May 4, 1861, Howell Cobb Collection. Even ardent secessionists like George A. Mercer of Savannah often betrayed their own insecurity by the very *manner* in which they proclaimed slave loyalty. "Thank God," wrote Mercer, that abolitionism's "incendiary appeals are no longer addressed to our ignorant and susceptible slaves[.] they are contented and happy, and we feel safer while war is raging than during our mock and hollow peace. No European peasantry could have stood the insidious and dangerous appeals to their passions and avarice to which our negroes have long been subjected." George A. Mercer Diary, August 11, 1861 (p. 101 of transcript). In a similar vein, a planter on Skidaway Island assured his Northern mother-in-law somewhat uneasily, "We believe our negroes as reliable as the mobs of the Northern cities." William W. Gordon to his wife, January 25, 1861, Gordon Family Papers, SHC. For characteristic affirmations of slave loyalty, see Savannah *Daily Morning News*, May 29, 1861, p. 1; September 18, 1861, p. 1; Macon *Daily Telegraph*, April 5, 1861, p. 1.

88. The above quotation is taken from the resolutions of a Committee of Safety formed in the 19th militia district of Bryan County, as reported in Savannah *Daily Morning News*, June 19, 1861, p. 2. Concerning the formation of similar organizations in Floyd, Clarke, Houston, Twiggs, Appling, Tattnall, McIntosh, Bulloch, Clinch, and other counties, see Columbus *Daily Sun*, March 6, 1861, p.

2; Macon *Daily Telegraph*, April 26, 1861, p. 1; April 29, 1861, p. 1; Savannah *Daily Morning News*, June 5, 1861, p. 2; June 8, 1861, p. 1; June 18, 1861, p. 2; July 16, 1861, p. 1; July 17, 1861, p. 1; August 2, 1861, p. 1; August 6, 1861, p. 1; Coulter, "Slavery and Freedom in Athens," 267; Gassman, "Rome and Floyd County in the Civil War," 59. The large black population of southwest Georgia caused many whites to be especially zealous in the matter of slave patrols and other regulations. In Thomas County, for example, four separate home guard organizations were formed between May and July 1861. William Warren Rogers, *Thomas County During the Civil War* (Tallahassee, 1964), 16–17.

89. Charles C. Jones to Charles C. Jones, Jr., August 8, 1861, Charles C. Jones, Jr. Collection; Madison *Visitor* in Macon *Daily Telegraph*, March 20, 1861, p. 1. See also accounts of actual restriction of slave railroad travel in Madison and Augusta as reported in Savannah *Daily Morning News*, June 1, 1863, p. 2; William G. Proctor, Jr., "Slavery in Southwest Georgia," *Georgia Historical Quarterly* 49 (September 1965): 10, 21.

90. Hamilton (Harris County) *Enterprise* in Columbus *Daily Sun*, February 22, 1861, p. 2; March 2, 1861, p. 2; March 29, 1861, p. 3. In abandoning legal proceedings against those responsible for the burning, George's owner, Able Nelson, Sr., cited his "advanced age and infirmities" as reasons for not wishing to undertake "what may result in a long and tedious lawsuit." It seems likely, however, that there may have been other factors involved in his decision, for after the Civil War, in 1866, Nelson undertook a lengthy legal battle with John A. Middlebrook, to whom George was hired at the time of the burning. In a case which ultimately reached the Georgia Supreme Court, Nelson was actually successful in obtaining a judgment against Middlebrook for the amount of a full year's slave hire, although George was burned to death before he had spent two months in Middlebrook's service. See Middlebrook vs. Nelson, 24 *Ga.*, 506 (1866).

91. Savannah *Daily Morning News*, March 4, 1861, p. 1; March 7, 1861, p. 2; March 9, 1861, p. 1.

92. Ibid., July 17, 1861, p. 1. For earlier episodes in the campaign against runaways, see ibid., July 3, 1861, p. 1; June 27, 1861, p. 1. See also Savannah *Republican*, July 26, 1860, p. 2, for the capture of the slave Sampson and another black runaway who were also members of the fugitive group located in the Savannah River swamps.

93. Joseph Williams to William McLain, February 19, 1853, ACS Archives, vol. 129.

94. After the Civil War, Williams's religious posture became more militant when he took the lead in rejecting the second-class status imposed upon blacks

by the white Presbyterian church structure. He vocally protested the inferior treatment accorded him as a black minister, and subsequently led a Negro Presbyterian exodus to the newly organized Knox Presbytery of the Northern church. In 1866 he even voiced black claims for equality in a personal appearance before the General Assembly of the Northern church in St. Louis.

95. Susie King Taylor, *Reminiscences of My Life in Camp* (Boston, 1902), 8.

96. Harrison Berry, *Slavery and Abolitionism as Viewed by a Georgia Slave* (Atlanta, 1861).

97. See Maxwell Whiteman, "Harrison Berry, a Georgia Slave, Defends Slavery: A Bibliographical Note," which precedes a reprint edition of Berry's 1861 pamphlet, in Scholarly Resources' Afro-American History Series Rhistoric publication no. 203, Collection 7, Slave Narratives (Philadelphia, 1969). Whiteman characterizes Berry as "a semi-literate man," describes his "story" as "highly suspect," and discusses the "likelihood that the work was not his own."

98. Berry, *Slavery and Abolitionism*, 34, 17–19.

99. Ibid., 16.

100. Concerning Berry's association with the American Colonization Society, see Harrison Berry to William McLain, May 23, 1854, and same to same, June 27, 1854, ACS Archives, vol. 134. For the Colonization Society's stress on the insurmountable nature of white prejudice, see Fredrickson, *The Black Image in the White Mind*, 20–21.

101. Berry, *Slavery and Abolitionism*, viii, 27.

102. Fredrickson, *The Black Image in the White Mind*, 1–24.

103. Berry, *Slavery and Abolitionism*, 29.

104. Ibid., 38.

105. For a fuller discussion of Berry's antebellum and postwar career, see Clarence L. Mohr, "Harrison Berry: A Black Pamphleteer in Georgia During Slavery and Freedom," *Georgia Historical Quarterly* 67 (Summer 1983): 189–205.

106. Macon *Daily Telegraph*, February 8, 1861, p. 1.

107. Ibid.

108. Benjamin Quarles, *The Negro in the Civil War* (Boston, 1969), 35–41; John W. Blassingame, *Black New Orleans, 1860–1880* (Chicago, 1973), 33–35.

109. Savannah *Daily Morning News*, June 4, 1861, p. 2; June 6, 1861, p. 1.

110. Ibid., June 11, 1861, p. 1.

111. Ibid., July 3, 1861, p. 2; July 26, 1861, p. 2.

112. Columbus *Enquirer* in Macon *Daily Telegraph*, January 29, 1861, p. 2; Milledgeville *Southern Federal Union*, June 11, 1861, p. 3. See also *Southern Federal Union*, July 23, 1861, p. 3.

CHAPTER THREE

1. Charles C. Jones, Jr. to Rev. C. C. Jones, November 8, 1861, and same to Rev. and Mrs. C. C. Jones, November 9, 1861, in Myers, *Children of Pride*, 790–92; Alexander A. Lawrence, *A Present for Mr. Lincoln: The Story of Savannah from Secession to Sherman* (Macon, 1961), 38–39.

2. George A. Mercer Diary, November 13, 15, 1861 (pp. 148–49, 151–52 of typescript); H. J. Wayne to her mother, December 6, 1861, Edward Harden Papers. On the response of sea island blacks to the Port Royal expedition and the subsequent defection of South Carolina slaves to Union lines, see Willie Lee Rose, *Rehearsal for Reconstruction: The Port Royal Experiment* (New York, 1964), 10–11, 103–10 passim; Joel Williamson, *After Slavery: The Negro in South Carolina During Reconstruction, 1861–1877* (Chapel Hill, 1965), 3–31.

3. Georgia newspapers outdid themselves in combing the Union and Confederate press for material which would depict Northern racial attitudes and practices in an unfavorable light. Some stories, like reports that Yankees sold black refugees as slaves in Brazil and Cuba, were complete fabrications. Most reports, however—especially those stressing poor living conditions in contraband camps, exploitive working arrangements, and high black casualty rates in combat—had at least an element of truth. The impact of such propaganda on Georgia blacks is difficult to gauge. Susie King Taylor, the teenage slave girl quoted above, learned from her grandmother "that the white people did not want the slaves to go over to the Yankees, and told them these things to frighten them." Many blacks were unwilling either to accept Confederate warnings at face value or to dismiss them out of hand. As late as 1863 two escaped slaves from Savannah told Union Navy officers that Georgia bondsmen were "still very uncertain as to how they will be treated" by Northerners. One of the escapees was deterred from fleeing sooner by stories "about being sold to Cuba, as we [Yankees] are only fighting to get cotton and niggers." Macon *Daily Telegraph*, January 14, 1862, p. 2; June 17, 1862, p. 3; June 18, 1862, p. 1; August 12, 1862, p. 2; October 16, 1862, p. 2; November 27, 1862, p. 2; February 18, 1863, p. 1; March 2, 1863, p. 4; March 2, 1864, p. 2; Savannah *Daily Morning News*, April 29, 1863, p. 1; September 18, 1863, p. 2; October 31, 1863, p. 1; Taylor, *Reminiscences*, 7–8; *Official Records of the Union and Confederate Navies in the War of the Rebellion*, 30 vols. (Washington, D.C., 1894–1922), ser. 1, vol. 13, pp. 671–72, hereinafter cited as *ORN*.

4. Lawrence, *A Present for Mr. Lincoln*, 40–41, 46–47; Bryan, *Confederate Georgia*, 68–72; *ORN*, ser. 1, vol. 12, pp. 581, 590–92, 612–15, 663–64.

5. The basic facts concerning the St. Simons "colony," at least to the extent

that they are available in the *ORN*, can be found in George Alexander Heard, "St. Simons Island During the War Between the States," *Georgia Historical Quarterly* 22 (September 1938): 249–72. The exact number of blacks on St. Simons at the time of its evacuation in November 1862 was not recorded. Writing from Beaufort, South Carolina, in mid-August 1862, General Rufus Saxton referred to the settlement as "a colony of 400." Charles T. Trowbridge, who was on the island during this period, placed the black population at five hundred, while Susie King Taylor, who left with the other St. Simons refugees in November, gave the number as six hundred. *OR*, ser. 1, vol. 14, p. 375; Thomas Wentworth Higginson, *Army Life in a Black Regiment* (East Lansing, Mich., 1960), 212, 261, 263; Taylor, *Reminiscences*, 14. Unless otherwise indicated, all quantitative references to escape incidents are derived from the table which accompanies the text.

6. Several historians have been misled by a frequently quoted petition from the citizens of Liberty County, Georgia, dated August 1862 and offering twenty thousand as a "low estimate of the number of slaves absconded and enticed from our seaboard." In the context of the document "our seaboard" almost certainly refers to the seaboard of the entire Confederacy. Even if this were not the case, however, the notion that twenty thousand slaves had fled the coast of Georgia, much less Liberty County alone, by August 1862 would still be highly implausible. Significantly, the Reverend Charles C. Jones, who actually wrote the Liberty County petition, made no such claim. On the contrary, his personal letters reveal that black escapees during this period were numbered in scores rather than hundreds or thousands. For the petition itself, see *OR*, ser. 4, vol. 2, pp. 36–38. An unrevised manuscript draft of the document in Jones's handwriting survives in the Charles C. Jones, Jr. Collection.

7. On the irrelevance of Lincoln's Preliminary Emancipation Proclamation to the realities of black life in the South Carolina sea islands, see Williamson, *After Slavery*, 12–13. "Emancipation," Williamson notes, "simply recognized a fact already established."

8. See chapter 4 of the present work for a fuller discussion of slave removal.

9. Statistics on the impressment of slave military laborers are presented in chapter 5 of the present work.

10. Kenneth M. Stampp, *The Peculiar Institution: Slavery in the Ante-Bellum South* (1956; reprint, New York, 1968), 110–11, 117–20; James B. Sellers, *Slavery in Alabama* (University, Ala., 1950), 293; Genovese, *Roll, Jordan, Roll*, 648–49; John W. Blassingame, *The Slave Community: Plantation Life in the Antebellum South* (New York, 1979), 196–202.

11. It should be emphasized that the statements in the text apply only to

blacks seeking refuge behind Union lines. Among other Georgia bondsmen ante-bellum escape patterns continued to manifest themselves during the war years. William A. Byrne found, after examining fugitive slave advertisements in the Savannah *Morning News* from 1861 to 1864, that "the typical runaway was a black male in his twenties. Women were outnumbered by more than two to one. . . . It was the 'prime' hand which ran away, not the old man or young boy." William A. Byrne, "Slavery in Savannah, Georgia During the Civil War" (M. A. thesis, Florida State University, 1971), 119. Several factors help explain the contrast between newspaper runaway advertisements and Union military records of black escapes. For purely economic reasons planters were likely to be more concerned with recovering young adult men than less valuable slaves. Thus, the young black male runaway was perhaps somewhat more visible than women, children, or old people. Data drawn solely from the Savannah area also reflects the abnormally high proportion of young men in the black population, a condition brought about by the large scale impressment of slave military laborers and the simultaneous removal of many female domestic servants. Throughout the war, of course, Savannah itself was also a final destination for lone male fugitives from the up-country. Perhaps more significant than any of these considerations, however, is the likelihood that many of the advertised runaways never attempted to reach Union lines, but simply hid themselves in or near the city for varying periods, as had always been common practice. In other words, while some fugitives sought permanent freedom on the sea islands, others continued to settle for the more limited (and less dangerous) objectives of antebellum times.

12. *ORN*, ser. 1, vol. 12, pp. 727, 756; New York *Daily Tribune*, August 9, 1862, p. 3; Taylor, *Reminiscences*, 14.

13. Savannah *Daily Morning News*, July 22, 1863, p. 2; October 19, 1863, p. 1; Macon *Daily Telegraph*, October 20, 1863, p. 2.

14. Elinor Barnes and James A. Barnes, eds., *Naval Surgeon Blockading the South, 1862–1866: The Diary of Samuel Pellman Boyer* (Bloomington, 1963), 247, 254–55, hereinafter cited as *Samuel P. Boyer Diary*.

15. Port Royal *New South*, September 13, 1862, p. 3; John Screven to Mary Screven, September 12, 1862, in Arnold and Screven Family Papers, SHC. These were not the only slaves who failed to make the rendezvous. The planner of the mass escape, an eighty-year-old slave named Paul on the Daniels plantation in South Carolina, remained behind by choice. Two days later he also reached Union lines, having slipped away while the other Daniels slaves were being moved farther inland. At least one mass escape attempt failed completely in October 1862 when a group of thirty-one runaways were recaptured and con-

fined in the Savannah jail. Boston *Commonwealth*, January 3, 1863, p. 4; Byrne, "Slavery in Civil War Savannah," 123.

16. Higginson, *Army Life in a Black Regiment*, 233–35.

17. Ibid., 194. Ironically, many of the traditional explanations for the superior fighting qualities of white Confederates apply with equal force to the ex-slaves in Union ranks. As Higginson observes, "They were fighting, in a manner, for their own homes and firesides" (p. 200).

18. Article signed "L" in Boston *Commonwealth*, February 21, 1863, p. 2. The article was probably written by Jules S. DeLacroix, the civilian superintendent of plantations on St. Simons Island during the summer and fall of 1862. See Rufus Saxton to Captain [Charles T.] Trowbridge, August 21, September 1, 1862; same to Captain J. E. Thorndike, September 1, 1862; same to Captain J. H. Moore, September 1, 1862; S. Willard Saxton to J[ules] S. DeLacroix, December 23, 1862, January 13, 1863—all in Rufus Saxton Letterbook 1, Rufus and S. Willard Saxton Papers, Yale University.

19. Chicago *Tribune*, November 19, 1862, p. 1.

20. Rev. Frederic Denison, *Shot and Shell: The Third Rhode Island Heavy Artillery Regiment in the Rebellion, 1861–1865* (Providence, 1879), 260–61; Rev. Frederic Denison, "A Chaplain's Experience in the Union Army," in *Personal Narratives of Events in the War of the Rebellion* (Providence, 1893), 32–33. The Savannah *Daily Morning News*, April 28, 1863, p. 2, reported that "a negro man named March, the property of Mr. John C. Rowland, has been arrested and committed to jail, charged with harboring and running off to the Yankees several negroes from this city. . . . He will probably have an examination in a few days."

21. Higginson, *Army Life in a Black Regiment*, 193; Milledgeville *Confederate Union*, February 24, 1863, p. 2.

22. A firsthand account of Nat's activities during the summer and fall of 1862 appears in the Boston *Commonwealth*, February 21, 1863, p. 2. On his earlier and subsequent career as a runaway, as well as the circumstances of his death, see Savannah *Daily Morning News*, June 28, 1864, in Macon *Daily Telegraph*, June 28, 1864, p. 1. For a critical assessment of the "safety valve" thesis as applied to antebellum runaways, see Genovese, *Roll, Jordan, Roll*, 657. The concept was probably more applicable during the early 1860s than at any other period because of the volatile wartime situation.

23. Myers, *Children of Pride*, 1471; Savannah *Morning News*, July 2, 1887, p. 3; ORN, ser. 1, vol. 13, pp. 196–97; George A. Mercer Diary, October 25, 1862 (p. 64 of typescript).

24. Chicago *Tribune*, November 19, 1862, p. 1; Port Royal *New South*, Novem-

ber 15, 1862, p. 3; *OR*, ser. 1, vol. 14, pp. 191–92; George A. Mercer Diary, November 9, 1862 (pp. 69–70 of typescript).

25. *ORN*, ser. 1, vol. 12, pp. 634, 756; ibid., vol. 13, p. 21; New York *Daily Tribune*, August 9, 1862, p. 3.

26. Admiral Samuel F. DuPont to his wife, May 24, 1862, in John D. Hayes, ed., *Samuel Francis DuPont: A Selection from His Civil War Letters*, 3 vols. (Ithaca, 1969), 2:70–71; "Notes on the Colony at St. Simons" in *ORN*, ser. 1, vol. 13, pp. 144–45.

27. Admiral Samuel F. DuPont to his wife, May 11, 1862, in Hayes, *DuPont Letters*, 2:51–52; *ORN*, ser. 1, vol. 12, p. 689.

28. Boston *Commonwealth*, February 21, 1863, p. 2; Higginson, *Army Life in a Black Regiment*, 212–13; Taylor, *Reminiscences*, 12–15; *ORN*, ser. 1, vol. 13, pp. 244–45, 248, 251–52; *OR*, ser. 1, vol. 14, p. 375.

29. Boston *Commonwealth*, February 21, 1863, p. 2.

30. George A. Mercer Diary, October 25, 1862 (p. 64 of typescript).

31. *ORN*, ser. 1, vol. 13, pp. 298–301; George A. Mercer Diary, October 22, 1862 (pp. 61–62 of typescript). For subsequent Confederate activities on Cumberland Island, see *ORN*, ser. 1, vol. 14, p. 186.

32. Rose, *Rehearsal for Reconstruction*, 166.

33. Taylor, *Reminiscences*, 12.

34. Barnes and Barnes, *Samuel P. Boyer Diary*, 15, 73, 181, 189, 203, 217; "Tariff of Prices to be charged to officers' messes and sailors for articles purchased of negroes on the island of St. Simons, Georgia" in *ORN*, ser. 1, vol. 13, p. 159; Taylor, *Reminiscences*, 11.

35. New York *Daily Tribune*, August 9, 1862, p. 3. On most Georgia sea islands the family arrangements of black escapees too old for military service remained largely intact throughout the war. In late November 1863, for example, after most black men of military age had been pressed into Union ranks, some twenty aging ex-slaves still lived on the Waldburg plantation on St. Catherines Island. Included in this group were "Smart and his wife; Young Cudgel, his wife, and grandson Mike (Young Cudgel is . . . 50 years old and his grandson Mike is 4 years old . . . ; Old Cudgel, a widower; Old John, a carpenter . . . ; Old Bob, an old widower . . . ; Old Man Willie who . . . is 110 years old . . . ; Aunt Estrella, a sister to Smart's wife . . . ; and Aunt Mollie." Barnes and Barnes, *Samuel P. Boyer Diary*, 15, 209. On the disruption of black families by military conscription in South Carolina and Louisiana, see Rose, *Rehearsal for Reconstruction*, 265–69; C. Peter Ripley, *Slaves and Freedmen in Civil War Louisiana* (Baton Rouge, 1976), 146–59.

36. For representative examples of the various types of military information furnished by ex-slaves, see *ORN*, ser. 1, vol. 12, pp. 460–61, 664–65, 776–77; ibid., vol. 13, pp. 231, 342, 354, 671–72; ibid., vol. 15, p. 48; Admiral Samuel F. DuPont to his wife, August 6, 1862, and same to Gideon Wells, October 25, 1862, in Hayes, *DuPont Letters*, 2:180, 266–67; New York *Daily Tribune*, August 11, 1862, p. 2; Baltimore *American* in Savannah *Daily Morning News*, March 26, 1863, p. 1. Many Union officers and even some Confederates acknowledged the value of information provided by Georgia's black escapees. For independent confirmation, see the description of the *Fingal* given by an escaped slave in early 1863 (*ORN*, ser. 1, vol. 13, p. 536) and compare it with the detailed description of the *Fingal* (CSS *Atlanta*) in William N. Still, Jr., *Iron Afloat: The Story of the Confederate Armorclads* ([Nashville], 1971), pp. 128–30. As Still notes (p. 136), Union Admiral Samuel F. DuPont's intelligence concerning the Confederate ironclads "was uncanny."

37. *ORN*, ser. 1, vol. 12, pp. 460, 469, 487–88; ibid., vol. 14, pp. 212, 251; ibid., vol. 15, p. 180; John Rodgers to Captain Davis, January 2, 1861 [1862], in Robert Means Thompson and Richard Wainwright, eds., *Confidential Correspondence of Gustavus Vasa Fox, Assistant Secretary of the Navy, 1861–1865*, 2 vols. (New York, 1918), 1:94–96; Admiral Samuel F. DuPont to his wife, January 3, 1862, in Hayes, *DuPont Letters*, 2:306.

38. Captain Quincy A. Gillmore to General Thomas W. Sherman, December 30, 1861, in Thompson and Wainwright, *Fox Correspondence*, 1:90–93.

39. *ORN*, ser. 1, vol. 13, pp. 671–72; Port Royal *New South*, January 31, 1863, p. 2.

40. Admiral Samuel F. DuPont to Gustavus V. Fox, January 4, 1862, in Thompson and Wainwright, *Fox Correspondence*, 1:89–90. On Moses Dallas, see *ORN*, ser. 1, vol. 14, pp. 704, 708, and vol. 15, pp. 478, 481. Pay differentials between black and white pilots, as well as the overall role and status of black sailors, are discussed in Herbert Aptheker, "The Negro in the Union Navy," *Journal of Negro History* 32 (April 1947): 169–200. See also David Lawrence Valuska, "The Negro in the Union Navy, 1861–1865" (Ph.D. dissertation, Lehigh University, 1973).

41. Quarles, *The Negro in the Civil War*, 109–10, contains an accurate summary of Murchison's recruiting activities, apparently drawn from the New York *Times*, April 19, 1862, p. 2; May 1, 1862, p. 2.

42. Denison, *Shot and Shell*, 139; Denison, "A Chaplain's Experience in the Union Army," 28–29; Williamson, *After Slavery*, 194.

43. George L. Hendricks, "Union Army Occupation of the Southern Sea-

board, 1861–1865" (Ph.D. dissertation, Columbia University, 1954), 155–56, 177–78; *American Missionary* 9 (May 1865): 98–99.

44. Higginson, *Army Life in a Black Regiment*, 214; Taylor, *Reminiscences*, 16, 46; Boston *Commonwealth*, February 21, 1863, p. 2.

45. Hendricks, "Union Army Occupation of the Southern Seaboard," 80–89; Dudley Taylor Cornish, *The Sable Arm: Negro Troops in the Union Army, 1861–1865* (New York, 1966), 138.

46. Taylor, *Reminiscences*, 11, 21. While still on St. Simons during the summer of 1862, Mrs. King taught basic reading skills to a group of some forty black children plus a number of adults. Available evidence suggests that she worked in conjunction with New York Marine Edward Herron of the USS *Florida*, who had collected a "school of fifty [black] scholars" on St. Simons by July 1862. New York *Daily Tribune*, August 9, 1862, p. 3. On the desire for education among black troops in Fort Pulaski at the close of the war, see James Leggett Owens, "The Negro in Georgia During Reconstruction, 1864–1872: A Social History" (Ph.D dissertation, University of Georgia, 1975), 152–53.

47. No definitive history of the First South Carolina Volunteers presently exists. See, however, Phyllis M. Cousins, "A History of the 33rd United States Colored Troops" (M.A. thesis, Howard University, 1961), 35–51, 61–64, for an itinerary of the regiment's movements and a description of the principal military actions in which it engaged. The activities of Colonel James Montgomery's Second South Carolina Volunteers (Thirty-fourth United States Colored Troops) are discussed in Rose, *Rehearsal for Reconstruction*, 244–53, and Cornish, *Sable Arm*, 138–42, 148–50, 244.

48. *OR*, ser. 3, vol. 5, p. 138.

49. Bobby Lee Lovett, "The Negro in Tennessee, 1861–1865: A Socio-Military History of the Civil War Era" (Ph.D. dissertation, University of Arkansas, 1978), 301–303; Carded Service Record of Hubbard Pryor, 44th U.S.C.I., Box 41571, #954, Adjutant General's Office, Record Group 94, National Archives, hereinafter cited as RG 94, NA.

50. Margaret Espey to Joseph S. Espey, March 21, 1864, Joseph Espey Papers, SHC.

51. Margaret Espey to Joseph S. Espey, April 3, 1864, ibid. See also J. J. Printup to Daniel S. Printup, April 15, 1864, Daniel S. Printup Papers, Duke University, for the details of a group escape incident involving four northwest Georgia bondsmen fleeing two neighboring masters. Printup confirms widespread defections among blacks in Gordon and Floyd counties.

52. Macon *Daily Telegraph*, May 27, 1864, p. 2.

53. Federal Writers Project Slave Narratives, Georgia, vol. 3, p. 68, quoted in Paul D. Escott, "The Context of Freedom: Georgia Slaves During the Civil War," *Georgia Historical Quarterly* 58 (Spring 1974): 93.

54. Ibid.; Lorenzo Thomas to Edwin M. Stanton, June 15, 1864, *OR*, ser. 3, vol. 4, p. 434.

55. Special Field Orders No. 16, June 3, 1864, *OR*, ser. 3, vol. 4, p. 434; William T. Sherman to Lorenzo Thomas, June 26, 1864, ibid., p. 455 (quotation). See also ibid., pp. 768–69.

56. C. W. Foster to Ruben D. Mussey, May 31, 1864, ibid., p. 416. For a detailed summary of black recruiting efforts in northern Georgia, Alabama, and western Tennessee, see Ruben D. Mussey to C. W. Foster, October 10, 1864, ibid., pp. 762–74.

57. Margaret Espey to Joseph S. Espey, September 6, 1864, Joseph Espey Papers, SHC.

58. Lewis Johnson to Ruben D. Mussey, October 17, 1864, *OR*, ser. 1, vol. 39, pt. 1, pp. 717–21 (all quotations).

59. Ibid., p. 720 (first quotation); Lewis Johnson to William D. Whipple, October 17, 1864, ibid., pp. 721–22; Application for Removal of Charge of Desertion, Case of Hubbard Pryor, December 4, 1889, Record and Pension Division, D90, #80679-83071, Box 22, Adjutant General's Office, RG 94, NA (last quotation).

60. Gassman, "Rome and Floyd County in the Civil War," 118ff. On June 19, 1864, about three hundred black refugees were transported from Rome to Pulaski, Tennessee. The group consisted mainly of women and children, half of whom were estimated to be under twelve years of age. See ibid., 120, n. 43.

61. Martha Battey to Robert Battey, November 17, 1864, Robert Battey Papers, Emory University.

62. William T. Sherman, *Memoirs of General William T. Sherman*, 2d ed., revised and corrected, 2 vols. (New York and London, 1931), 2:127.

63. William T. Sherman to Ellen Sherman, September 17, 1864, in Mills Lane, ed., *Marching Through Georgia* (New York, 1978), 113–14.

64. William T. Sherman to Lorenzo Thomas, June 26, 1864, *OR*, ser. 3, vol. 4, p. 454.

65. Special Field Orders No. 119 and 120, November 8 and 9, 1864, in Sherman, *Memoirs*, 2:174–76.

66. Edmund L. Drago, "How Sherman's March Through Georgia Affected the

Slaves," *Georgia Historical Quarterly* 57 (Fall 1973): 361–75, esp. 369–70. James C. Bonner, "Sherman at Milledgeville in 1864," *Journal of Southern History* 22 (August 1956): 273–91, esp. 285.

67. William King Diary, July 27, 1864 (first quotation), July 24, 1864 (second and third quotations), SHC.

68. Ibid., July 5, 1864 (quotation). See also entries of July 11 and 28, 1864.

69. Milledgeville *Confederate Union*, December 13, 1864, in Macon *Daily Telegraph and Confederate*, December 17, 1864, p. 1.

70. Philip D. Morgan, "The Ownership of Property by Slaves in the Mid-Nineteenth Century Low Country," *Journal of Southern History* 49 (August 1983): 409 (all quotations).

71. *Georgia Narratives*, vol. 12, pt. 1, pp. 7–8, 248; vol. 12, pt. 2, pp. 8, 218, 278–79, in George P. Rawick et al., eds., *The American Slave: A Composite Autobiography*, 31 vols. in three series (Westport, Conn., and London, 1972–1977), ser. 1. Sixty Georgia ex-slaves commented on their contact with Sherman's army when interviewed in the 1930s. "Of those fifty held a negative view of the Federals, with complaints about theft being almost universal." See Escott, "Context of Freedom," 101, n. 7.

72. Drago, "How Sherman's March Affected the Slaves," 363. The 19,000 figure represents the total of rough estimates furnished by Sherman's corps commanders. In a widely quoted statement based upon Southern white observations, the Macon *Daily Telegraph and Confederate*, December 9, 1864, p. 2, estimated that one out of every fifteen ablebodied black men had accompanied Sherman's troops.

73. Rose, *Rehearsal for Reconstruction*, 320–22; Byrne, "Slavery in Savannah," 161–63.

74. Jones, *Soldiers of Light and Love*, 144–48. John W. Blassingame, "Before the Ghetto: The Making of the Black Community in Savannah, Georgia, 1865–1880," *Journal of Social History* 6 (Summer 1973): 463–88, esp. 468–69. See also Jerry Thornberry, "Northerners and the Atlanta Freedmen, 1865–69," *Prologue* 6 (Winter 1974): 236–51, esp. 237–38.

75. Sherman, *Memoirs*, 2:249–51; Williamson, *After Slavery*, 19; Hendricks, "Union Army Occupation of the Southern Seaboard," 88–89; H. K. McCoy to Howell Cobb, January 11, 1865, Howell Cobb Collection.

76. Sherman, *Memoirs*, 2:250–51.

77. The best point of departure for studying postwar developments in the so-called Sherman Reservation is Claude F. Oubre, *Forty Acres and a Mule: The Freedmen's Bureau and Black Land Ownership* (Baton Rouge, 1978), 46–71. On the impor-

tance of the task system and the continuity of black cultural patterns before and after emancipation, see Philip D. Morgan, "Work and Culture: The Task System and the World of Lowcountry Blacks, 1700 to 1880," *William and Mary Quarterly* 39 (October 1982): 563–99.

CHAPTER FOUR

1. William B. Fleming to his son [William O. Fleming], November 19, 1861, William O. Fleming Papers, SHC. See also Louisa N. Brown to her husband, October 19, 1861, Nathan Atkinson Brown Papers, University of Georgia; C. C. Jones to Charles C. Jones, Jr., November 11, 1861, in Myers, *Children of Pride*, 793.

2. Oliver H. Prince to John B. Lamar, October 29, 1861, Howell Cobb Collection.

3. C. C. Jones to Mrs. Eliza G. Robarts, December 13, 1862 in Myers, *Children of Pride*, 998–99. For a similar but less detailed account of the scope of refugeeing by Altamaha River rice planters late in 1862, see Charles L. Schlatter [Superintendent, Brunswick & Albany Railroad] to Joseph E. Brown, September 1, 1862, Telamon Cuyler Collection. Schlatter states that most large Altamaha planters, including the Troups, Dents, Kings, Coupers, and others, had moved their slaves inland. He also stresses the extreme vulnerability of planters along the Satilla River, where a rice crop estimated at 250,000 bushels had been planted in spite of the obvious danger of Union naval expeditions.

4. Rosa Delony to William G. Delony, December 29, 1861, William Gaston Delony Papers, University of Georgia; "1861 Plantation Book, Ossabaw Island," entries of November 18–21, December 16–22, 1861, Kollock Plantation Books, SHC; Georgia King to "Lordy" [Henry Lord Page King], April 19, 1861, Thomas Butler King Papers; same to same, May 4, 1861, King Papers; same to same, May 5, 1861, King Papers; same to same, May 12, 1861, King Papers; Florence King to Henry Lord Page King, July 28, 1861, King Papers; same to same, October 6, 1861, King Papers; Savannah Unit, Federal Writers' Project, Works Progress Administration of Georgia, *Savannah River Plantations*, ed. Mary Granger (Savannah, 1947), 244–47, 323–24; James M. Clifton, ed., *Life and Labor on Argyle Island: Letters and Documents of a Savannah River Rice Plantation, 1833–1867* (Savannah, 1978), xli-xliii; Albert Virgil House, ed., *Planter Management and Capitalism in Ante-Bellum Georgia: The Journal of Hugh Fraser Grant, Ricegrower* (New York, 1954), 14–15; Edward M. Steel, Jr., *T. Butler King of Georgia* (Athens, 1964), 157–58.

Steel provides general information on refugeeing among Altamaha River planters.

5. Darold D. Wax. "'New Negroes are Always in Demand': The Slave Trade in Eighteenth Century Georgia," *Georgia Historical Quarterly* 58 (Summer 1984): 193–220; Savannah Unit, Georgia Writers' Project, Works Projects Administration, *Drums and Shadows: Survival Studies Among the Georgia Coastal Negroes* (Athens, 1940; reprint, Westport, Conn., 1973), xviii–xix passim; Lydia Parrish, *Slave Songs of the Georgia Sea Islands* (reprint, Hatboro, Pa., 1965); Margaret Davis Cate, *Early Days of Coastal Georgia* (St. Simons, 1955), 205–23; Flanders, *Plantation Slavery in Georgia*, 58–64ff; House, *Planter Management and Capitalism*, 52.

6. Peter Kolchin, "Reevaluating the Antebellum Slave Community: A Comparative Perspective," *Journal of American History* 70 (December 1983): 588–91.

7. Peter H. Wood, *Black Majority: Negroes in Colonial South Carolina from 1670 Through the Stono Rebellion* (New York, 1974), 63–91. See also the suggestive article by Philip D. Curtin, "Epidemiology and the Slave Trade," *Political Science Quarterly* 73 (June 1968): 190–216.

8. Morgan, "Work and Culture," 563–99; Morgan, "Ownership of Property by Slaves in the Mid-Nineteenth Century Low Country," 399–420.

9. George A. Mercer Diary, November 13, 1861 [p. 148 of typescript]. Mercer's observations relate mainly to Chatham County planters and slaves, but their accuracy is fully confirmed by the experiences of the Charles C. Jones family in Liberty County. When many of the Jones slaves were moved inland to Burke County in late 1862, Charles C. Jones, Jr., adopted various methods of compensating bondsmen for economic losses resulting from the forced abandonment of personal property. Some slaves prevailed upon Jones to have their hogs, poultry, or farm produce sent inland for their direct use. Other blacks received cash payments for quantities of corn which they were compelled to leave behind. The likelihood exists, however, that Jones may actually have profited from such transactions, especially since he paid bondsmen at customary prewar rates of $1.00 per bushel for corn that was subsequently sold on the coast at inflated wartime prices which had soared to $1.50 per bushel by early 1863. See Charles C. Jones, Jr. to Rev. C. C. Jones, December 15, 1862; Rev. C. C. Jones to Col. Charles C. Jones, Jr., January 23, 1863; same to same, January 27, 1863; Col. Charles C. Jones, Jr. to Rev. C. C. Jones, January 29, 1863—all in Myers, *Children of Pride*, 1000–1001, 1016–17, 1019–20, 1021.

10. Lt. Charles C. Jones, Jr. to Rev. C. C. Jones, November 10, 1862, in Myers, *Children of Pride*, 987.

11. W. Cumming to [Adam Leopold Alexander?], April 24, 1862, Alexander and Hillhouse Family Papers.

12. George A. Mercer Diary, November 4, 1862 [p. 66 of typescript]; Rogers, *Thomas County During the Civil War*, 1, 92–94.

13. Edward R. Harden to his mother, August 9, December 26, 1863, Edward Harden Papers; Mary Elizabeth Massey, *Refugee Life in the Confederacy* (Baton Rouge, 1964), 83–86, 211–15; Corley, *Confederate City*, 70–76; Kenneth Coleman, *Confederate Athens* (Athens, 1967), 154–56; James C. Bonner, ed., *The Journal of a Milledgeville Girl, 1861–1867* (Athens, 1964), 22, esp. n. 43 citing Milledgeville *Southern Recorder*, September 1, 1863; Ralph Benjamin Singer, Jr., "Confederate Atlanta" (Ph.D. dissertation, University of Georgia, 1973), 115–21, 179.

14. Blassingame, *The Slave Community*, 164–65; Herbert G. Gutman, *The Black Family in Slavery and Freedom, 1750–1925* (New York, 1976), 136–38, 141–42 passim.

15. Mrs. Mary Jones to Charles C. Jones, Jr., September 15, 1862, Jones Collection. For information on Rufus Varnedoe, see Myers, *Children of Pride*, 1709.

16. Joseph LeConte, *'Ware Sherman: A Journal of Three Months' Personal Experience in the Last Days of the Confederacy* (Berkeley, 1937), 19–20; Myers, *Children of Pride*, 1709.

17. Mary Jones to Charles C. Jones, Jr., December 18, 1855; same to same, January 31, 1856—both in Myers, *Children of Pride*, 177–78, 185–86.

18. See Mary Jones to Charles C. Jones, Jr., December 19, 1859; Charles C. Jones, Jr. to Rev. C. C. Jones, October 16, 1862; Rev. C. C. Jones to Charles C. Jones, Jr., December 8, 1862; Mary Jones to Charles C. Jones, Jr., December 19, 1862; Rev. C. C. Jones to Charles C. Jones, Jr., January 6, 1863; Charles C. Jones, Jr. to Rev. C. C. Jones, January 8, 1863; Charles C. Jones, Jr. to Rev. and Mrs. C. C. Jones, January 20, 1863; Rev. C. C. Jones to Charles C. Jones, Jr., January 27, 1863; Charles C. Jones, Jr. to Rev. C. C. Jones, January 29, 1863— all in Myers, *Children of Pride*, 549, 976–77, 996–97, 1001, 1008, 1010–11, 1015–16, 1019–20, 1021–22.

19. Rev. C. C. Jones to Charles C. Jones, Jr., February 10, 1863; Charles C. Jones, Jr. to Rev. and Mrs. C. C. Jones, February 14, 1863; Charles C. Jones, Jr. to Mary Jones, November 14, 1865—all in ibid., 1025–26, 1027–28, 1309–10.

20. Louisa Gilmer to Adam Leopold Alexander, May 19, 1861 (internal evidence suggests that the correct date should be 1862 rather than 1861), Alexander and Hillhouse Family Papers; Edward R. Harden to his mother, August 9, 1863, Edward Harden Papers.

21. H. J. Wayne to her mother, December 6, 1861; same to same, February 12, 1864; same to same, December 23, 1864—all in Edward Harden Papers.

22. Anonymous letter signed "Soldier" to Joseph E. Brown, December 1,

1861; Charles L. Schlatter to Joseph E. Brown, September 1, 1862—both in Telamon Cuyler Collection.

23. Charles L. Schlatter to Joseph E. Brown, September 1, 1862, ibid.

24. Letter from correspondent "ENSIGN" of Jackson Artillery, dated February 2, 1861, from "Fort Brown, St. Simons Island," in Macon *Daily Telegraph*, February 7, 1861, p. 2; Julian M. Burnett to Peterson Thweat, May 14, 1863, Telamon Cuyler Collection.

25. Mrs. Phillip Clayton to Mary Ann Cobb, February 20, 1862, Howell Cobb Collection; Savannah Writers' Project, *Savannah River Plantations*, 246–48.

26. Georgia King to Henry Lord Page King, April 19, 1861; same to same, May 5, 1861; Florence King to Henry Lord Page King, October 6, 1861—all in Thomas Butler King Papers.

27. Mallery King to Thomas Butler King, March 16, 1862, ibid.; Henry Lord Page King to Thomas Butler King, April 3, 1862, ibid.; Mallery King to Thomas Butler King, July 1, 1862, ibid.; Georgia King Smith to Thomas Butler King, June 28, 1863, ibid.; Georgia King Smith to John Floyd King, August 25, 1863, in Steel, *T. Butler King*, 158 (quotation).

28. Hannah King Couper to Thomas Butler King, April 8, 1862; Georgia King Smith to Florence B. King, June 16, 1863; Georgia King Smith to Thomas Butler King, June 28, 1863; Georgia King Smith to John Floyd King, August 25, 1863—all in Thomas Butler King Papers.

29. For a perceptive summary of the "breakup of the King menage as an economic unit" during the war years, see Steel, *T. Butler King*, 156–58.

30. *Georgia Senate Journal . . . Annual Session . . . 1863*, pp. 59, 70, 74.

31. Edward R. Harden to his mother, August 9, 1863; same to same, December 26, 1863—both in Edward Harden Papers.

32. Arch Smith to Joseph E. Brown, October 17, 1864, Telamon Cuyler Collection.

33. Edward R. Harden to his mother, July 6, 1864; same to same, September 26, 1864—both in Edward Harden Papers.

34. Samuel Toombs, *Reminiscences of the War, Comprising a Detailed Account of the Thirteenth Regiment New Jersey Volunteers in Camp, on the March, and in Battle* (Orange, N.J., 1878), 196.

CHAPTER FIVE

1. Singer, "Confederate Atlanta," 208–11; L. P. Grant to Col. Jeremy F. Gilmer, August 24, 1863, Lemuel P. Grant Papers, Atlanta Historical Society;

L. P. Grant to John W. Hunt, August 24, 1863, Grant Papers; L. P. Grant to Charles F. Williams, August 24, 1863, Grant Papers; L. P. Grant to Amory Dexter, September 1, 1863, Grant Papers; W. H. Cooper to L. P. Grant, November 10, 1863, Grant Papers.

2. Columbus *Daily Sun,* December 13, 1863, p. 2; Diffie William Standard, *Columbus, Georgia in the Confederacy* (New York, 1954), p. 56. Nearly a year after the first call for black laborers went out, at least ninety impressed slaves were still working on the Columbus fortifications. Major S. L. Bishop to Howell Cobb, December 9, 1864, Howell Cobb Collection.

3. *Georgia House Journal . . . Special Session . . .* 1863, p. 10; *OR,* ser. 1, vol. 14, pp. 493–94, 542–47, 645, 666, 682, 688, 693, 695, 728–32; John A. Davis to General Howell Cobb, May 8, 1863, Howell Cobb Collection; Maxine Turner, "Naval and River Operations on the Apalachicola and Chattahoochee Rivers, 1861–1865," *Alabama Historical Quarterly* 36 (Fall/Winter, 1974): 218–23.

4. Captain L. P. Grant to Sheriff H. K. Allen (Coweta County), December 17, 1863; same to Sheriff W. G. Dewbury (Spalding County), December 17, 1863; same to Sheriff W. H. Cooper (Troup County), December 17, 1863; same to Sheriff John S. Blalock (Meriwether County), February 27, 1864; same to Colonel A. L. Rives, March 8, 1864; same to same, April 4, 1864; same to Major J. J. Clarke, April 16, 1864—all in Lemuel P. Grant Papers. Also Macon *Daily Telegraph,* June 22, 1864, p. 2; June 23, 1864, p. 2; June 24, 1864, p. 2; June 25, 1864, p. 2; Ella Gertrude Thomas Journal, 1861–64, entry of June 29, 1864 (p. 156 of typescript), Duke University; Mrs. Mary S. Mallard to Mary Jones, June 23, 1864, Myers, *Children of Pride,* 1185.

5. Captain John G. Clark to Colonel M. B. McMicken, August 16, 1864; Captain Charles R. Armstrong to Captain John G. Clark, August 26, 1864; Captain John G. Clark to Major W. T. Ayers, October 8, 1864; Captain John G. Clark to General Henry C. Wayne, October 13, 1864—all in Eugenius A. Nisbet Papers, Duke University. Also Macon *Daily Telegraph,* July 29, 1864, p. 2; August 2, 1864, p. 2; August 17, 1864, p. 2; September 6, 1864, pp. 1, 2; September 22, 1864, p. 2; November 12, 1864, p. 1; G. W. Archer to Samuel H. Stout, October 31, 1864, Samuel H. Stout Papers, Emory University.

6. Coleman, *Confederate Athens,* 169; Captain L. P. Grant to Maj. Gen. M. L. Smith, October 18, 1864, Lemuel P. Grant Papers; same to same, October 24, 1864, Grant Papers; Lt. W. A. Hansell to Captain L. P. Grant, November 30, 1864, Grant Papers.

7. *OR,* ser. 4, vol. 3, pp. 897–99, 933–34; Macon *Daily Telegraph and Confederate,* January 25, 1865, p. 2; February 6, 1865, p. 2; February 9, 1865, p. 2;

Captain Charles R. Armstrong to General Howell Cobb, February 13, 1865, Howell Cobb Collection.

8. Atlanta *Southern Confederacy*, April 3, 1862, p. 3.

9. Horace H. Cunningham, *Doctors in Gray* (Baton Rouge, 1962), 55–57; Mildred Jordan, "Georgia's Confederate Hospitals" (M.A. thesis, Emory University, 1942), 56–62.

10. "Special Orders No. 30," May 6, 1862 (authorizing impressment of free Negroes to work in hospitals controlled by S. H. Stout); Contract between Dr. R. D. Spaulding and I. L. P. Powell for hire of four slaves, July 11, 1862; Dr. F. H. Evans to Dr. S. H. Stout, August 29, 1862—all in Samuel H. Stout Papers, Emory University. Also Dr. F. H. Evans to Dr. S. H. Stout, September 13, 23, 1862, Samuel H. Stout Papers, University of Texas; Macon *Daily Telegraph*, September 10, 1862, p. 1; December 11, 1862, p. 2.

11. "Consolidated Weekly Report of Sick & Wounded in Hospitals [of] Genl. Bragg['s] Army, September 1, 1863," Samuel H. Stout Papers, University of Texas.

12. Dr. S. H. Stout to Mrs. Isabel Harmon, September 22, 1863, ibid.

13. Dr. Albert H. Snead to Dr. S. N. Bemiss, December 14, 1863, ibid.

14. Dr. W. L. Nichol to Dr. S. H. Stout, September 14, 1864, ibid.; Dr. Robert J. Massey to Dr. J. R. Bratton, undated [1864], in Samuel H. Stout Papers, Emory University (quotation). See also Dr. W. W. Woodruff to Dr. H. R. Casey, August 7, 1864, in Samuel H. Stout Papers, SHC.

15. Macon *Daily Telegraph*, September 26, 1863, p. 2; October 3, 1863, p. 1; October 8, 1863, p. 2; October 13, 1863, p. 2; December 2, 1863, p. 2; May 26, 1864, p. 2; November 25, 1864, p. 2.

16. James O. Breeden, "A Medical History of the Later Stages of the Atlanta Campaign," *Journal of Southern History* 35 (February 1969): 35–37; Cunningham, *Doctors in Gray*, 66–67.

17. "Consolidated Morning Report of Surgeon S. H. Stout, Medical Director of Hospitals, Army of Tennessee, February 27, 1865," Samuel H. Stout Papers, University of Texas.

18. Dr. B. W. Wimble to Dr. S. H. Stout, March 21, 1863, Samuel H. Stout Papers, SHC.

19. Corley, *Confederate City*, 68–69; Slave "pass" authorizing the "man Jason" to transport hospital bed clothing from Marietta to Atlanta, Georgia (1863), and Dr. F. H. Evans to Dr. S. H. Stout, May 16, 1864, both in Samuel H. Stout Papers, Emory University.

20. Macon *Daily Telegraph*, June 12, 1863, p. 1; March 19, 1864, p. 2; July 7,

1864, p. 2; November 5, 1864, p. 2; November 24, 1864, p. 2; December 13, 1864, p. 2.

21. "P W A" to Savannah *Republican* in Macon *Daily Telegraph*, January 30, 1864, p. 1 (for quotation); ibid., June 10, 1864, p. 1; Columbus *Daily Sun*, December 31, 1863; March 12, 1864, p. 1. Quartermasters of Georgia state troops also employed blacks to care for horses. See Macon *Daily Telegraph*, October 16, 1863, p. 2.

22. Savannah *Daily Morning News*, March 31, 1863, p. 1; Macon *Daily Telegraph*, October 20, 1863, p. 2; Columbus *Daily Sun*, January 14, 1864, p. 2. Most black teamsters were slaves, but in March 1864 Quartermaster Captain Samuel C. Head offered to hire as many as twenty-five free Negroes who wished to avoid conscription. Macon *Daily Telegraph*, March 29, 1864, p. 2.

23. *OR*, ser. 4, vol. 2, p. 421.

24. Memphis *Appeal* in Macon *Daily Telegraph*, August 4, 1863, p. 2; Columbus *Daily Sun*, August 18, 1863, p. 2; Macon *Daily Telegraph*, October 15, 1863, p. 2.

25. Albert B. Moore, *Conscription and Conflict in the Confederacy* (New York, 1924), 192–95, 208–14; General Gideon Pillow to "The Planters of Lauderdale, Lawrence, and Franklin Counties [Alabama]," March 6, 1863, in *OR*, ser. 4, vol. 2, p. 421; Blank contract form for hire of slave teamsters by Volunteer and Conscript Bureau, Army of Tennessee, March 2, 1863, in Cheatham Papers, Tennessee State Library and Archives.

26. Macon *Daily Telegraph*, July 28, 1864, p. 2; August 11, 1864, p. 1 (for quotation); August 12, 1864, p. 2; Columbus *Daily Sun*, July 28, 1864, p. 2; August 14, 1864, p. 2.

27. Major John R. Viley to Captain John G. Clark, October 15, 1864, Captain C. C. Hammock to same, October 16, 1864; Captain M. J. Beanar [?] to same, October 16, 1864—all in Eugenius A. Nisbet Papers.

28. Richard D. Goff, *Confederate Supply* (Durham, 1969), 104–11, 130–31, 195–99; Bryan, *Confederate Georgia*, 112–14; Charles B. Dew, *Ironmaker to the Confederacy: Joseph R. Anderson and the Tredegar Iron Works* (New Haven, 1966), 268–72; Robert C. Black, "The Railroads of Georgia in the Confederate War Effort," *Journal of Southern History* 13 (November 1947): 510–34.

29. Black, "Railroads of Georgia," 520. The role of black labor in constructing Georgia's antebellum railroads has been frequently noted but never systematically explored by scholars. Black employment in railroad shops, on train crews, and as section hands is an even more neglected topic. See, however, Ulrich B. Phillips, *A History of Transportation in the Eastern Cotton Belt to 1860* (New York, 1908), 260–61, 294–95; Flanders, *Plantation Slavery in Georgia*, 197–98; Milton S. Heath,

Constructive Liberalism: The Role of the State in Economic Development in Georgia to 1860 (Cambridge, 1954), 274; Robert S. Starobin, *Industrial Slavery in the Old South* (New York, 1970), 28, 294–95; W. E. B. DuBois and Augustus G. Dill, *The Negro American Artisan* (Atlanta, 1912), 34–36. F. N. Boney presents a lucid and authoritative summary of Georgia railroad development to 1860 in Kenneth Coleman et al., *A History of Georgia* (Athens, 1977), 156–62.

30. Macon *Daily Telegraph*, July 16, 1860, p. 2; July 26, 1860, p. 2; January 15, 1862, p. 1; January 29, 1862, p. 1; February 11, 1863, p. 1; March 19, 1863, p. 2 (quotation).

31. Ibid., April 30, 1862, p. 1; May 19, 1862, p. 1; August 1, 1863, p. 2 (quotation).

32. D. Curry to Joseph E. Brown, January 22, 1864, Telamon Cuyler Collection.

33. Macon *Daily Telegraph*, December 8, 1862, p. 4; Macon *Daily Telegraph and Confederate*, December 26, 1864, p. 2.

34. Macon *Daily Telegraph and Confederate*, August 26, 1864, p. 2; September 17, 1864, p. 2; DuBois and Dill, *The Negro American Artisan*, 36; Black, "Railroads of Georgia," 524.

35. Joseph E. Brown to John S. Rowland, August 29, 1862, Joseph E. Brown Papers, Felix Hargrett Collection, University of Georgia; George D. Phillips to Henry C. Wayne, May 23, 1864, Telamon Cuyler Collection.

36. Howell Cobb to General Braxton Bragg, September 25, 1863, ibid. (quotation); J[eremy] F. Gilmer to L. P. Grant, January 5, 1863, and L. P. Grant to J. T. Sharp (foreman of bridge carpenters, Augusta, Ga.), October 6, 1864, both in Letterbook 9, Lemuel P. Grant Papers; L. P. Grant to Stephen D. Height, March 8, 1865, and John T. Grant to Joseph E. Brown, March 18, 1865, Telamon Cuyler Collection.

37. Columbus *Daily Sun*, September 3, 1864, p. 2.

38. Macon *Daily Telegraph*, August 26, 1864, p. 1. The Negro bridge builder referred to was ex-slave Horace King, who had been emancipated by the Alabama legislature in 1845 upon the petition of John and Ann H. Godwin. See James B. Sellers, *Slavery in Alabama* (University, Ala., 1950), 371–72.

39. L. P. Grant to Major J. H. Alexander, February 3, 1865, Lemuel P. Grant Papers.

40. General B. D. Fry to Howell Cobb, November 18, 1864, Howell Cobb Collection; L. P. Grant to General P. G. T. Beauregard, January 19, 1865, and L. P. Grant to Major J. H. Alexander, February 3, 1865, Lemuel P. Grant Papers.

41. Goff, *Confederate Supply,* 224–26.

42. Ibid., 85–86, 129–31; Richard C. Todd, *Confederate Finance* (Athens, 1954), 141, 145–47.

43. J. T. Pelot to Howell Cobb, September 29, 1863; R. K. Hines to Major Lamar Cobb, December 28, 1864, Howell Cobb Collection; Julia E. Harn, "Old Canoochee-Ogeechee Chronicles," *Georgia Historical Quarterly* 16 (March 1932): 302 (quotation).

44. Macon *Daily Telegraph,* July 1, 1864, p. 2.

45. Clement Eaton, *A History of the Southern Confederacy* (New York, 1954), 139; Colonel Marcus H. Wright to Josiah Gorgas, April 6, 27, 1864, Record Group 109, chap. 4, vol. 16, NA; Colonel Marcus H. Wright to John H. [or A.?] Walker, April 25, May 3, 1864, RG 109, chap. 4, vol. 16; Colonel Marcus H. Wright to W. H. Tracey, June 1, 1864, RG 109, chap. 4, vol. 16. The Macon Arsenal also operated a tanyard and harness shop employing black workers. See Richard M. Cuyler to Joseph E. Brown, July 15, 1865, RG 109, chap. 4, vol. 101.

46. James W. Burch to Joseph E. Brown, February 25, 1862, Telamon Cuyler Collection; Columbus *Daily Sun,* December 20, 1863, p. 2; August 6, 1864, p. 2; December 20, 1864, p. 2; Augusta *Daily Chronicle and Sentinel,* October 15, 1864, p. 4.

47. Columbus *Daily Sun,* December 25, 1864, p. 2.

48. Frank E. Vandiver, *Ploughshares into Swords: Josiah Gorgas and Confederate Ordnance* (Austin, 1952), 217–18.

49. "Reports of Work Performed, Superintendent of the Powder Factory, November, 1862–April, 1865," entry of February 5, 1864, in Records of Ordnance Establishments at Augusta, Georgia, RG 109 (no chapter or volume designations), NA; Vandiver, *Ploughshares into Swords,* 218 (quotation).

50. "List of Free Negroes Employed at Govt. Powder Works" included at back of ledger book entitled "Reports of Work Performed, Superintendent of Powder Factory, November, 1862–April, 1865," RG 109 (no chapter or volume designations), NA.

51. James H. Burton to Colonel Jack Brown, July 19, 1862, ibid., chap. 4, vols. 20, 29, and 31.

52. James H. Burton to Josiah Gorgas, August 15, 1862, ibid., vol. 20.

53. Report of Macon Armory operations prepared by James H. Burton and submitted to General Benjamin Huger, January 1863, ibid.; James H. Burton to Josiah Gorgas, October 23, 1863, ibid., vols. 20, 29, and 31.

54. James H. Burton to Josiah Gorgas, March 10, 1864, ibid.

55. James H. Burton to General John B. Hood, August 3, 19, 1864, ibid.; James H. Burton to Lt. Colonel B. W. Frobel, October 11, 1864, ibid.

56. Recent estimates of slave skill levels during the late antebellum era have varied widely. The most reliable calculations are found in Roger L. Ransom and Richard Sutch, *One Kind of Freedom: The Economic Consequences of Emancipation* (Cambridge, 1977), 223–24, 298–99. Using slave occupational data from the unpublished mortality schedules of the 1860 U.S. Census, Ransom and Sutch found that 6.2 percent of the adult male slave decedents in forty-five rural Georgia counties were skilled artisans.

57. James H. Burton to E. V. Johnson, December 31, 1864, RG 109, chap. 4, vols. 20, 29, and 31, NA.

58. John W. Mallet to Josiah Gorgas, April 10, 1863, ibid., vols. 24 and 28; John W. Mallet to O. R. Singleton, May 18, 1863, ibid.

59. "Time Books, Atlanta Arsenal, 1862–1863," ibid., vols. 81 and 84.

60. "Reports of Work Performed, Superintendent of the Powder Factory, November, 1862–April, 1865," in Records of Ordnance Establishments at Augusta, Georgia, ibid. (no chapter or volume designations).

61. Standard, *Columbus in the Confederacy,* 39; Columbus *Daily Sun,* June 10, 1862, p. 2; January 1, 1863, p. 2; February 24, 1863, p. 2; March 11, 1863, p. 2; December 16, 1863, p. 2; October 28, 1864, p. 2; December 29, 1864, p. 2.

62. Smith Stansbury to Richard M. Cuyler, June 24, 1862, RG 109, chap. 4, vol. 3, NA; Josiah Gorgas to Richard M. Cuyler, July 16, 1862, ibid., vol. 4; Columbus *Daily Sun,* September 15, 1863, p. 2; October 27, 1863, p. 2; December 20, 1864, p. 2; Susie Blaylock McDaniel, *Official History of Catoosa County, Georgia, 1853–1953* (Dalton, Ga., 1953), 106–107; Manuscript U.S. Census, 1860, Catoosa County, Georgia, Schedule II, Slave Inhabitants, p. 373 (microfilm); Colonel B. D. Graves to General Henry C. Wayne, September 10, 1863, Telamon Cuyler Collection.

63. E. R. Carter, *The Black Side: A Partial History of the Business, Religious, and Educational Side of the Negro in Atlanta, Ga.* (Atlanta, 1894), 71–72.

64. Macon *Daily Telegraph,* September 17, 1863, p. 1; October 8, 1863, p. 2; November 16, 1863, p. 1; December 2, 1863, p. 2; February 17, 1864, p. 2; December 28, 1864, p. 1.

65. S. H. Griswold, "The Cotton Gin: An Interesting History of the Gin and Its Maker," in *Jones County News,* April 2, 1908, p. 4; Flanders, *Plantation Slavery in Georgia,* 196–97; W. C. Hodgkins to Richard M. Cuyler, July 16, 1862, RG 109, Chap. 4, vol. 3, NA (quotation).

66. Macon *Daily Telegraph*, August 5, 1862, p. 2 (quotation); October 21, 1864, p. 2; James H. Burton to "Colonel" [Josiah Gorgas?], November 1, 1864, RG 109, chap. 4, vols. 20, 29, and 31, NA; E. Merton Coulter, *The Confederate States of America, 1861–1865* (Baton Rouge, 1950), 110.

67. Bryan, *Confederate Georgia*, 106; Macon *Daily Telegraph*, October 3, 1862, p. 1.

68. For firsthand testimony on the origin and growth of Georgia's antebellum iron industry, see the second installment of Mark A. Cooper's ten-part essay on "The Mineral Resources of Georgia," originally published in the Atlanta *National American* and reprinted in the Augusta *Constitutionalist*, October 29, 1859, p. 1. In addition to his own observations, Cooper relied on data from J. P. Lesley, *The Iron Manufacturer's Guide to the Furnaces, Forges, and Rolling Mills of the United States* (New York, 1859). Lucy Josephine Cunyus, *The History of Bartow County, Formerly Cass* ([Cartersville, Ga.], 1933), 190–98, reprints extracts from both Cooper and Lesley but also contains material not found in either. On the Gate City Rolling Mill and other antebellum Atlanta facilities, see Singer, "Confederate Atlanta," 22–23. On prewar foundries in Columbus, Macon, and Rome, see R. S. Stockton to Captain Richard M. Cuyler, July 28, 1862, RG 109, chap. 4, vol. 4, NA; Macon *Daily Telegraph*, February 22, 1860, p. 2; February 18, 1861, p. 2; May 16, 1863, p. 1; Gassman, "Rome and Floyd County in the Civil War," 77–78.

69. Eaton, *A History of the Southern Confederacy*, 136–37; Dew, *Ironmaker to the Confederacy*, 86–90; Vandiver, *Ploughshares into Swords*, 125.

70. Antebellum ironmakers operating in Bartow County during the war included the Etowah Manufacturing and Mining Company (two prewar furnaces), the Alatoona Iron Works (one furnace), and John W. Lewis (one antebellum furnace and a second constructed during the war). New firms entering the wartime iron business in Dade County included Lowe and Company, refugees from St. Louis and New Orleans; Markham and Schofield, proprietors of Atlanta's Gate City Rolling Mill; and the Empire State Coal and Iron Mining Company of Macon. In December 1863 the Athens Iron Manufacturing Company was organized; it operated until the end of the war at an undetermined north Georgia location. Other firms, like the Noble Brothers foundry in Rome, operated blast furnaces across the state line in northern Alabama.

71. T[?]. C. Moore to George W. Randolph, April 26, 1862, Letters Received, Secretary of War, RG 109, NA.

72. John W. Lewis to James A. Seddon, August 6, 1863, 311-L-1863, Letters Received, Secretary of War, ibid.

73. Ann V. Martin vs. Bartow Iron Works, *35 Ga.*, 320; James H. Burton to

Colonel D. Wyatt Aiken, June 23, 1864, RG 109, chap. 4, vols. 20, 29, and 31, NA.

74. Coleman, *Confederate Athens*, 105.

75. Macon *Daily Telegraph*, October 3, 1862, p. 1; January 14, 1863, p. 1; April 22, 1863, p. 2; Francis Scarlett to E. A. Nisbet, February 25, 1863, Eugenius A. Nisbet Papers.

76. Macon *Daily Telegraph*, February 16, 1863, p. 1; April 16, 1863, p. 2; Francis Scarlett to E. A. Nisbet, August 27, 31, 1863, Eugenius A. Nisbet Papers; Savannah *Daily Morning News*, October 10, 1863, p. 2.

77. Macon *Daily Telegraph and Confederate*, November 7, 1864, p. 2.

78. Augusta *Constitutionalist*, January 4, 1861, p. 2; Cunyus, *History of Bartow County*, 190–95.

79. Augusta *Constitutionalist*, October 29, 1859, p. 1; U.S. Census Returns, Cass County, Georgia, 1860, Schedule II, Slave Inhabitants, p. 368; E. H. Hicks to Eugenius A. Nisbet, February 14, 1860, Eugenius A. Nisbet Papers.

80. Dew, *Ironmaker to the Confederacy*, 22–32; Charles B. Dew, "Black Iron-workers and the Slave Insurrection Panic of 1856," *Journal of Southern History* 41 (August 1975): 324–25; James R. Anderson to Mark A. Cooper, January 21, 1857, December 15, 25, 1860, Tredegar Letterbooks, Tredegar Company Records, Virginia State Library, Richmond. Information on Georgia's iron industry from the Tredegar Company Records, as well as correspondence cited elsewhere to the Confederate secretary of war, was furnished to me through the generosity of Charles B. Dew of Williams College. Professor Dew also guided me to additional primary and secondary material which would otherwise have escaped my notice.

81. Milledgeville *Federal Union*, November 15, 1859, p. 3; E. H. Hicks to Junius Wingfield, December 21, 1859, Eugenius A. Nisbet Papers.

82. Mark A. Cooper to the editors, April 4, 1862, in Atlanta *Southern Confederacy*, April 6, 1862, p. 2. See also Mark A. Cooper to Richard M. Cuyler, May 13, 1862, RG 109, chap. 4, vol. 36, NA.

83. Jesse Osmond to J. W. Mallet, April 16, 1863, and William T. Quimby to J. W. Mallet, April 20, 1863, both in RG 109, chap. 4, vol. 5, NA; Macon *Daily Telegraph and Confederate*, August 2, 1864, p. 2 (quotation).

84. Columbus *Daily Sun*, September 13, 1864, p. 2; September 21, 1864, p. 2.

85. Dew, *Ironmaker to the Confederacy*, 274; Joseph R. Anderson to "Scofield & Markham," December 25, 1860, Tredegar Letterbooks, Tredegar Company Records; Notarized statement of L. Schofield, November 30, 1863, Letters Received, Secretary of War (716-S-1863), RG 109, NA.

86. J. W. and C. D. Findlay to Richard M. Cuyler, April 28, 1862, RG 109, chap. 4, vol. 36, NA.

87. Josiah Gorgas, "Notes on the Ordnance Department of the Confederate Government," *Southern Historical Society Papers* 12 (January–February 1884): 76–77.

88. Ralph W. Donnelly, "The Bartow County Saltpetre Works," *Georgia Historical Quarterly* 54 (Fall 1970): 316 (first quotation), 314 (second quotation).

89. Colonel Isaac M. St. John to James A. Seddon [1865], Letters Received, Secretary of War (14-S-1865), RG 109, NA; N. A. Pratt to Captain W. D. Lanou [name partially illegible], September 8, 1864, Jackson and Prince Family Papers, SHC. In January 1865 Georgia's Conscription Bureau received formal notification that "the slaves under the control of the Nitre & Mining Bureau should be left under their control." C. B. Duffield to General Howell Cobb, January 26, 1865, Howell Cobb Collection.

90. Ella Lonn, *Salt as a Factor in the Confederacy* (1933; University, Ala., 1965), 41, 44, 85–86, 96–97 passim.

91. John P. M. Feller to Howell Cobb, February 25, 1863, Howell Cobb Collection.

92. Notarized Statement of Edward Denmead, October 27, 1862, Letters Received, Secretary of War (614-D-1862), RG 109, NA.

93. Horace Montgomery, *Johnny Cobb: Confederate Aristocrat* (Athens, 1964), 53, 55, 64, 82; Stancel Barwick to Howell Cobb, September 6, 1863, Howell Cobb Collection; David C. Barrow to John A. Cobb, December 16, 1863, Cobb Collection; William Braswell to David C. Barrow, July 10, 1864, Cobb Collection; Savannah *Daily Morning News*, July 4, 1863, p. 2 (quotation).

94. Macon *Daily Telegraph*, February 2, 1863, p. 1. In the summer of 1862 the company had employed slave carpenters in the initial construction of its works. See ibid., June 4, 1862, p. 1.

95. L. P. Grant to Major A. L. Rives, February 10, 1863; L. P. Grant to Colonel Jeremy F. Gilmer, March 12, 1863; L. P. Grant to James J. Colt, March 24, 1863; L. P. Grant to James L. Grant, May 13, 1863; L. P. Grant to Colonel Jeremy F. Gilmer, August 17, 1863—all in Letterbook 9, Lemuel P. Grant Papers.

96. Columbus *Enquirer*, June 11, July 21, September 18, November 26, December 15, 1862, cited in Eugene Marvin Thomas III, "The Columbus, Georgia *Enquirer*, 1855–1865," 81; ORN ser. 1, vol. 15, pp. 584–85, 631, 634, 648–50.

97. John A. Eisterhold, "Savannah: Lumber Center of the South Atlantic," *Georgia Historical Quarterly* 57 (Winter 1973): 533–34 (all quotations). For useful comparative information, see the same author's broader study, "Lumber and

Trade in the Seaboard Cities of the Old South, 1607–1860" (Ph.D. dissertation, University of Mississippi, 1970).

98. Flanders, *Plantation Slavery in Georgia,* 202; Richard W. Griffin, "The Origins of the Industrial Revolution in Georgia: Cotton Textiles, 1810–1865," *Georgia Historical Quarterly* 42 (December 1958): 355–75.

99. Columbus *Daily Sun,* March 5, 1861, p. 3.

100. Ibid., March 16, 1861, p. 3; July 17, 1864, p. 1.

101. Ibid., April 11, 1862, p. 2; September 1, 1863, p. 2; July 10, 1864, p. 2.

102. Ibid., February 16, 1861, p. 2; Barrington King Account Book, 1848–1864, entries of January, June, September, December 1860, March, June, September, December 1861, March, June, October, November, December 1862, June, December 1863, March 1864, microfilm in Georgia Department of Archives and History, Atlanta.

103. Columbus *Daily Sun,* March 9, 1861, p. 2; Macon *Daily Telegraph and Confederate,* November 30, 1864, p. 1.

104. Bryan, *Confederate Georgia,* 107; Coleman, *Confederate Athens,* 105.

105. The numbers given in the text are more in the nature of educated guesses than solid estimates. The smaller figure of 12,000 black industrial workers was derived from the Federal mortality census samples in Ransom and Sutch, *One Kind of Freedom,* 223–24, 298–99. Ransom and Sutch estimate that 10.3 percent of black adult males in Georgia's rural counties were artisans or unskilled non-agricultural laborers in 1860. This percentage was applied to the state's entire male slave and free black population between fifteen and fifty-nine years of age, producing a figure of 11,884, which was adjusted upward to 12,000 in order to compensate for presumably high industrial employment rates among urban blacks. The estimate of 8,000 artisans was obtained in the same manner. The upper estimate of black industrial employment (24,000) is based on the conclusion in Starobin, *Industrial Slavery in the Old South,* 11, that 5 percent of the total Southern slave population was employed in industry. Applying this estimate to Georgia's total black population in 1860 results in a figure of 23,285, which was adjusted to 24,000 to compensate for higher industrial employment rates among free Negroes.

106. Coleman, *A History of Georgia,* 172–73.

107. Richard F. Lyon to Alexander H. Stephens, August 23, 1862, Stephens Papers (quotation); *Acts of Georgia . . . Annual Session . . . 1862,* pp. 108–109. In protesting slave impressment during the war, Georgia planters voiced all of the arguments enumerated in Bell I. Wiley, *Southern Negroes, 1861–1865* (New Haven, 1938), 123–25, and Harrison A. Trexler, "The Opposition of Planters to the

Employment of Slaves as Laborers by the Confederacy," *Mississippi Valley Historical Review* 27 (Setember 1940): 211–24. Such protests were so numerous in Georgia that comprehensive documentation from primary sources is impractical. For representative samplings of the major arguments used, see Macon *Daily Telegraph*, August 16, 1862, p. 2; Howell Cobb to George W. Randolph, August 5, 1862, in OR, ser. 4, vol. 2, pp. 34–35; James Tinsley to Joseph E. Brown, August 8, 1862, Telamon Cuyler Collection.

108. Macon *Daily Telegraph*, July 29, 1862, p. 2.

109. Ordnance establishments in Georgia tried unsuccessfully to impress slave labor both before and after passage of the Confederate slave impressment law of February 17, 1864. See, for example, John McCrady to J. W. Mallet, September 19, 1863, RG 109, chap. 4, vol. 38, NA. Also James H. Burton to Josiah Gorgas, March 10, 23, April 2, June 24, 1864; James H. Burton and J. W. Mallet to Josiah Gorgas, April 12, 1864; James H. Burton to General Sam Jones, June 16, 1864— all in ibid., vols. 20, 29, and 31. Hospital authorities were able to impress slaves only on a short-term basis in medical emergencies. See J. M. Hamilton to Joseph E. Brown, April 20, 1863, Telamon Cuyler Collection; W. J. Burt to Samuel H. Stout, September 21, 1863, and same to "Captain Horback," September 22, 1863, both in Samuel H. Stout Papers, Emory University. On the 1864 impressment law and the instructions for its implementation, see OR, ser. 4, vol. 3, pp. 208–209, 897–99, 933–34.

110. Columbus *Daily Sun*, July 10, 1864, p. 2; Macon *Daily Telegraph*, August 12, 1864, p. 2.

111. Macon *Daily Telegraph*, April 30, 1862, p. 1.

112. Columbus *Enquirer* in Macon *Daily Telegraph*, October 15, 1863, p. 2.

113. Macon *Daily Telegraph*, August 1, 1863, p. 2.

114. G. A. Henry to J. W. Mallet, December 30, 1862 (quotation); same to same, January 17, 1863; same to same, January 28, 1863; same to same, February 8, 1863—all in RG 109, chap. 4, vol. 5, NA.

115. F. O. Rogers to J. W. Mallet, December 23, 1862, ibid.

116. A. C. Rogers to J. W. Mallet, February 15, 1863 (first and fourth quotations), ibid.; same to same, December 10, 1862 (second, third, and fifth quotations), ibid.

117. Francis Scarlett to Eugenius A. Nisbet, February 25, 1863, Eugenius A. Nisbet Papers; Lemuel P. Grant to A. L. Rives, February 10, 1863, Lemuel P. Grant Papers; Columbus *Daily Sun*, December 18, 1863, p. 2. During the summer of 1862 officials in charge of Savannah's defenses offered to hire black railroad hands for thirteen dollars per month, two dollars more than the monthly rate for

field slaves. See Savannah *Daily Morning News,* June 16, 1862, p. 2; *OR,* ser. 4, vol. 2, p. 35 (quotation).

118. Savannah *Daily Morning News,* February 24, 1862, p. 2; J. W. Mallet to Josiah Gorgas, January 6, 1863, RG 109, chap. 4, vols. 24 and 28, NA.

119. A. C. Rogers to George Little, June 16, 1863, RG 109, chap. 4, vol. 38, NA.

120. Carter, *The Black Side,* 166–67; Mary Jones to Charles C. Jones, Jr., September 18, 1863, in Myers, *Children of Pride,* 1100 (quotation).

121. Charles C. Jones, Jr. to Mary Jones, September 1, 1864, Jones Collection; Columbus *Daily Sun,* February 12, 1864, p. 2. (quotation). A more typical kind of black occupational upgrading occurred at the Macon Armory in July 1864 when slave laborers replaced some twenty-five white "helpers" sent to the Atlanta front. James H. Burton to J. Fuss, July 23, 1864, RG 109, chap. 4, vols. 20, 29, and 31, NA.

122. J. P. Graves to J. W. Mallet, December 27, 1862, RG 109, chap. 4, vol. 5, NA.

123. E. H. Walker to [J. W. Mallet?], July 1, 1863, ibid., vol. 38.

124. A. S. Nicolson to J. W. Mallet, June 9, 1863, ibid.

125. A. C. Rogers to J. W. Mallet, December 26, 1862, ibid., vol. 58.

126. James H. Burton to C. P. Bolles, September 21, 1864, ibid., vols. 20, 29, and 31.

127. H. M. Davenport to Richard M. Cuyler, May 21, 1862, ibid., vol. 36.

128. James H. Burton to Josiah Gorgas, November 6, 1863, ibid., vols. 20, 29, and 31.

129. James H. Burton to Josiah Gorgas, August 23, 1862, ibid., vol. 20.

130. Wood, Meador & Co. to J. W. Mallet, June 14, 1863, ibid., vol. 38.

131. William P. White to Richard M. Cuyler, September 25, 1862, ibid., vol. 6.

132. W. E. B. DuBois, *The Negro Artisan: A Social Study* (Atlanta, 1902), 20–21.

133. This argument is presented most convincingly in Eugene D. Genovese, *The Political Economy of Slavery* (New York, 1965), 51–54, and Genovese's *Roll, Jordan, Roll: The World the Slaves Made,* 388–90.

134. Flanders, *Plantation Slavery in Georgia,* 205–207. See especially the documents reprinted in Ulrich B. Phillips, ed., *Plantation and Frontier,* 2 vols. (Cleveland, 1910) [vols. 1 and 2 of John R. Commons et al., eds., *A Documentary History of American Industrial Society,* 14 vols. (Cleveland, 1910)], 2:360–68. Some of the material which Phillips compiled was also reprinted in DuBois and Dill, *The Negro American Artisan,* 30–34.

135. On the limited role of class antipathy in generating Southern antislavery sentiment, see Carl N. Degler, *The Other South: Southern Dissenters in the Nineteenth Century* (New York, 1974), 91–95.

136. J. Henly Smith to Alexander H. Stephens, January 14, 1860, Stephens Papers.

137. On white labor unrest at the Macon Arsenal, see Walter C. Hodgkins to Richard M. Cuyler, June 16, June 18, 1862, RG 109, chap. 4, vol. 36, NA; Richard M. Cuyler to N. F. Cunningham, December 11, 1863, ibid., vol. 101. For problems at the Atlanta Arsenal, see Marcus H. Wright to W. W. Mackall, June 24, 1863, ibid., vol. 10. Concerning workers' petitions at the Macon Armory, see James H. Burton to Josiah Gorgas, May 1, 1863, ibid., vols. 20, 29, and 31. For unrest by "female operatives" at the Confederate Central Laboratory, see Macon *Daily Telegraph and Confederate*, October 19, 1864, p. 2.

138. Flanders, *Plantation Slavery*, 205; Bryan, *Confederate Georgia*, 251; Macon *Daily Telegraph*, April 14, 1863, p. 2; April 17, 1863, p. 2; ibid., April 21, 1863, p. 1.

139. Macon *Daily Telegraph*, April 15, 1863, p. 2.

140. Ibid., April 20, 1863, p. 3.

141. Ibid., May 5, 1863, p. 1 (all quotations).

142. Mary Ann Cobb to Howell Cobb, July 11, 1864, Howell Cobb Collection (first quotation); Ella Gertrude Clanton Thomas Journal, June 29, 1864 (p. 156 of typescript); Julia (Mrs. Irby) Morgan, *How It Was: Four Years Among the Rebels* (Nashville, 1892), 120; Rawick, *The American Slave*, [vols. 12–13 of series 2 constitute the original WPA Georgia Narratives, Parts 1–4 in the Library of Congress, and are hereinafter cited as such], *Georgia Narratives*, pt. 1, p. 130 (second quotation).

143. *Georgia Narratives*, pt. 2, p. 241.

144. Ibid., pt. 1, p. 130.

145. For typical age and sexual stipulations in Ordnance Bureau slave hiring, see Macon *Daily Telegraph*, December 8, 1863, p. 2; December 10, 1863, p. 2; January 13, 1864, p. 2; January 26, 1864, p. 1; March 23, 1864, p. 2; James H. Burton to Mrs. William Duncan Smith, December 30, 1864, RG 109, chap. 4, vols. 20, 29, and 31, NA. On Engineer Bureau policies, see Lemuel P. Grant to Amory Dexter, n.d. [1863], and same to John W. Griffin, August 17, 1863, both in Lemuel P. Grant Papers. On the hiring of slave families in Georgia's iron industry, see Macon *Daily Telegraph*, May 22, 1862, p. 2, and the discussion of black family disruption in the present chapter.

146. Dr. James M. Holloway to Dr. Samuel H. Stout, January 9, 1864, Samuel H. Stout Papers, University of Texas.

147. Donnelly, "Bartow County Saltpetre Works," 314.

148. O. R. Singleton to J. W. Mallet, May 10, 1863, RG 109, chap. 4, vol. 38 (first quotation), NA; J. W. Mallet to O. R. Singleton, ibid., vols. 24 and 28 (second quotation).

149. Lemuel P. Grant to D. M. Haydin, October 19, 1863, Lemuel P. Grant Papers.

150. James H. Burton to George W. Wilne [?], December 28, 1863, RG 109, chap. 4, vols. 20, 29, and 31, NA.

151. James H. Burton to T. J. Hightower, June 23, 1864, ibid.

152. On the hiring of slave women "unencumbered" by children, see Atlanta *Southern Confederacy,* April 3, 1862, p. 3; Macon *Daily Telegraph,* March 16, 1863, p. 1; Columbus *Daily Sun,* November 6, 1864, p. 1; December 17, 1864, p. 2.

153. J. W. Mallet to W. R. Phillips, June 11, 1863, RG 109, chap. 4, vols. 24 and 28, NA.

154. W. H. McMain to "Mr. Stubbs," September 14, 1863 (quotation), and same to W. R. Phillips, September 21, 1863, ibid.

155. John H. McCrady to Charles R. Armstrong, January 26, 1863, Telamon Cuyler Collection; J. W. Mallet to Josiah Gorgas, February 24, 1863, RG 109, chap. 4, vols. 24 and 28, NA. Actually the description of the slave food ration in the letter from McCrady cited above is somewhat inaccurate and misleading, since slaves at Savannah seldom received bacon despite the fact that most preferred it to beef. By using rather evasive language McCrady had simply summarized army regulations, thus leaving the impression that pork was the meat usually issued to slaves. Writing to the commander of the Confederate Laboratory in Macon, however, Joseph L. Locke, chief commissary for Georgia, described the slave diet which existed in reality: "Fresh beef has been issued to the Negroes at work upon the fortifications here almost ever since they began. Bacon is only issued when beef cannot be had. . . . [C]omplaints exist here . . . that the negroes do not get meat enough, but the fact is they would eat 2 pounds each per day if they could get it." Joseph L. Locke to Capt. J. W. Mallet, February 26, 1863, ibid., vol. 5.

156. J. W. Mallet to Josiah Gorgas, February 24, 1863, ibid., vols. 24 and 28.

157. John H. McCrady to Charles R. Armstrong, January 26, 1863, Telamon Cuyler Collection.

158. J. W. Mallet to Josiah Gorgas, December 4, 1863, RG 109, chap. 4, vols. 24 and 28, NA; same to same, April 2, 1864, ibid.; J. W. Mallet to J. L. Locke, April 7, 1864, ibid.; James H. Burton to Josiah Gorgas, April 19, 1864, ibid., vols. 20, 29, and 31; James H. Burton to J. W. Mallet, April 28, 1864,

ibid.; James H. Burton to Josiah Gorgas, November 7, 1864, ibid.; James H. Burton to C. P. Bolles, October 17, 1864, ibid.

159. Records of provisions issued by W. H. McMain, Military Store Keeper, C. S. Central Laboratory, Macon, Georgia, September 20, 1864, September 30, 1864, October 3, 1864, December 31, 1864, ibid., vol. 61; James H. Burton to General Richard A. Taylor, November 26, 1864, ibid., vols. 20, 29, and 31.

160. J. W. Mallet to J. A. McGruder, May 11, 1863; George Little to A. C. Rogers, June 9, July 8, 1863, ibid., vols. 24 and 28; James H. Burton to W. W. Holland, October 29, 1864, ibid., vols. 20, 29, and 31.

161. J. W. Mallet to F. W. Dillard, November 28, 1862, ibid., vols. 24 and 28; J. Fuss to J. H. Burton, February 27, 1864, ibid., vol. 30 (quotation).

162. "Record of Government Stores Received and Issued by the Powder Factory [Augusta, Ga.] 1862–1865," ibid. (no chapter or volume designations); "Record of Articles Issued, Central Laboratory, 1864–1865," ibid., chap. 4, vol. 63; "Record of Clothing Issued to Detailed Soldiers and Slaves Employed at the [Macon] Arsenal, 1864–1865," ibid., vol. 60.

163. Columbus *Daily Sun,* June 10, 1862, p. 2 (quotation); James H. Burton to Josiah Gorgas, October 23, 1863, RG 109, chap. 4, vols. 20, 29, and 31, NA.

164. J. W. Mallet to Virgil Powers, December 1, 1862, RG 109, chap. 4, vols. 24 and 28, NA.

165. J. W. Mallet to J. H. Denson, February 3, 1863, ibid.

166. "Statement of Cost of Public Buildings, Macon Armory, June 30th, 1864," ibid., vol. 30.

167. G. R. Fairbanks to Dr. J. P. Logan, July 15, 1863 (quotation); Dr. W. A. Robinson to Dr. R. R. Spencer, September 1, 1864—both in Samuel H. Stout Papers, University of Texas.

168. Georgia Smith to Floyd King, August 25, 1863, Thomas Butler King Papers.

169. L. P. Grant to Charles F. Williams, August 24, 1863 (first quotation), Lemuel P. Grant Papers; Savannah *Republican* in Macon *Daily Telegraph,* October 15, 1863, p. 1 (second quotation).

170. James H. Burton to General John B. Hood, August 19, 1864, RG 109, chap. 4, vols. 20, 29, and 31, NA; John W. Glenn to J. H. Alexander, January 29, 1865, ibid., vol. 37 (all quotations).

171. Macon *Daily Telegraph and Confederate,* December 6, 1864, p. 2; Charles C. Jones, Jr. to Eva B. Eve, April 8, 1862, Jones Collection; George A. Mercer Diary, August 19, October 12, 1862 (pp. 50, 57 of typescript); Byrne, "Slavery in Savannah During the Civil War," 83.

172. J. W. Mallet to A. C. Rogers, March 23, 31, 1863; J. W. Mallet to H. J. Lamar, May 11, 1863; George Little to J. A. McGruder, June 15, 1863—all in RG 109, chap. 4, vols. 24 and 28, NA.

173. Petition from J. W. Mallet to Mayor and City Council of Macon, Georgia, December 22, 1862 (requesting exemption from municipal tax for brickyard slaves housed within the city of Macon for health reasons), ibid.; J. W. Mallet to James A. Hill, September 3, 1863, ibid.; James A. Hill to J. W. Mallet, August 26, 1863, ibid., vol. 38; A. C. Rogers to J. W. Mallet, February 15, 1863, ibid., vol. 5; James H. Burton to D. Whitaker, January 11, March 15, 1864, ibid., vols. 20, 29, and 31; James H. Burton to James C. Mosby, September 23, October 7, 1864, ibid. Health conditions were also very poor among blacks employed at coastal saltworks. See [William B. Braswell?] to David C. Barrow, November 29, 1863; David C. Barrow to John A. Cobb, December 16, 1863; William Braswell to John A. Cobb, May 29, 1864,—all in Howell Cobb Collection.

174. W. H. McMain to J. W. Mallet, October [21?], 1863, RG 109, chap. 4, vol. 38, NA; A. C. Rogers to J. W. Mallet, February 27, 1863, ibid., vol. 5; William Braswell to David C. Barrow, July 10, 1864, Howell Cobb Collection.

175. A. C. Rogers to J. W. Mallet, March 25, 1863, RG 109, chap. 4, vol. 5, NA (quotation); Columbus *Daily Sun*, April 26, 1864, p. 2; April 27, 1864, p. 2.

176. J. W. Mallet to Josiah Gorgas, January 10, 1863, RG 109, chap. 4, vols. 24 and 28, NA; James H. Burton to Josiah Gorgas, April 20, 1864, ibid., vols. 20, 29, and 31.

177. Dr. R. V. Miller to J. W. Mallet, January 15, 1863, ibid., vol. 5; Dr. Samuel Preston Moore to J. W. Mallet, May 25, 1863, ibid., vol. 38; Savannah *Republican* in Macon *Daily Telegraph*, October 15, 1863, p. 1; J. Fuss to James H. Burton, January 26, 1864, RG 109, chap. 4, vol. 30, NA; J. W. Mallet to A. C. Rogers, February 24, 1863, RG 109, chap. 4, vols. 24 and 28.

178. Dr. Edward M. Donald to E. M. Foster, February 13, 1864; Dr. James M. Holloway to Dr. Samuel H. Stout, February 22, 1864—both in Samuel H. Stout Papers, University of Texas.

179. A. C. Rogers to J. W. Mallet, February 19, March 4, 1864, RG 109, chap. 4, vol. 5, NA.

180. J. W. Mallet to Josiah Gorgas, February 19, 1863, ibid., vols. 24 and 28; J. W. Mallet to A. C. Rogers, February 17, 1863 (quotation), ibid.

181. J. Fuss to James H. Burton, January 26, 1864, ibid., vol. 30.

182. J. W. Mallet to Josiah Gorgas, February 12, 1863, ibid., vols. 24 and 28.

183. Ibid.

184. J. W. Mallet to Josiah Gorgas, February 20, 1863, ibid.

185. Same to same, April 10, 1863, ibid.

186. James H. Burton to J. Fuss, May 18, 1864, ibid., vols. 20, 29, and 31.

187. J. Fuss to H. B. Treadwell, May 18, 1864, ibid. Permission was also given to expand the incentive system to brickmaking per se.

188. J. Fuss to William A. Fort, March 13, 1865, ibid.

189. James H. Burton to James M. Perry, April 5, 1865, ibid.

190. Savannah *Republican* in Macon *Daily Telegraph*, October 15, 1863, p. 1; William Stanley Hoole, *Vizetelly Covers the Confederacy* (Tuscaloosa, 1957), 65–68; *Illustrated London News* 42 (April 18, 1863): 432–33.

191. William P. White to Richard M. Cuyler, September 25, 1862, RG 109, chap. 4, vol. 6, NA; A. Dutenhofer [?] to J. W. Mallet, April 2, 1863, ibid., vol. 5.

192. J. W. Mallet to H. J. Lamar, April 30, 1863, ibid., vols. 24 and 28.

193. James A. Hill to J. W. Mallet, March 16, 1865, ibid., vol. 5.

194. Employers often required hired slaves to perform compensatory labor in advance of family visits. See, for example, John W. Mallet's stipulations to owners on this point in letters to James A. Hill, J. A. Brewer, N. Bass, H. J. Lamar, A. C. Rogers, Samuel F. Beecher, and H. C. Fryer, all dated January 31, 1863, in ibid., vols. 24 and 28.

195. J. W. Mallet to J. C. Barnett, November 12, 1863, ibid.

196. Nearly all evidence is tentative and inferential. Slaveowners complained about mistreatment of bondsmen by employers, but allegations were seldom specific and often arose during contractual disputes. In at least one case, however, a semiliterate Georgia overseer did flog blacks for malingering. The individual in question was supervising plantation slaves who had been sent to a coastal saltworks. William Braswell to John A. Cobb, December 30, 1863, Howell Cobb Collection.

197. Marcus H. Wright to General W. W. Mackall, June 24, 1863, RG 109, chap. 4, vol. 10, NA.

198. Robert Habersham to Richard M. Cuyler, July 15, 1862, ibid., vol. 3; W. H. McMain to Josiah Moody, October 5, 1863, ibid., vols. 24 and 28.

199. James H. Burton to J. Fuss, April 4, 1863, ibid., vol. 29 [?].

200. "Special Orders No. 22," December 15, 1864, ibid., vol. 50.

201. "Special Orders No. 46" [March 5, 1865], ibid.

202. J. W. Mallet to A. C. Rogers, September 15, 1863, ibid., vols. 24 and 28.

203. James H. Burton to William B. Johnston, April 4, 1863 (quotation), ibid., vol. 29 [?]; Burton to T. R. Bloom, April 4, 1863, ibid.; Burton to H. J. Lamar, April 4, 1863, ibid.

204. James H. Burton to L. Toby, October 26, 1864, ibid., vols. 20, 29, and 31.

205. A. C. Rogers to J. W. Mallet, December 18, 1862, ibid., vol. 5.

206. Same to same, September 13, 1863, ibid., vol. 38.

207. J. W. Mallet to A. C. Rogers, September 15, 1863, ibid., vols. 24 and 28; W. H. McMain to A. C. Rogers, November 3, 1863, ibid.

208. A. C. Rogers to J. W. Mallet, May 20, 1863, ibid., vol. 38; Rogers to George Little, May 23, 1863, ibid.; Rogers to J. W. Mallet, June 1, 1863 (quotation), ibid.

209. On the latter point, see George Little to A. C. Rogers, May 27, 1863, ibid., vols. 24 and 28.

210. Charles C. Jones to Charles C. Jones, Jr., September 8, 1862, Jones Collection.

211. Macon *Daily Telegraph and Confederate*, February 24, 1865, p. 2.

212. Amory Dexter to John W. Balfour, July 29, 1863; L. P. Grant to Jeremy F. Gilmer, August 17, 1863 (quotation)—both in Lemuel P. Grant Papers.

213. *ORN*, ser. 1, vol. 15, pp. 584–85, 631, 634, 648–50.

214. Dr. D. D. Launders to [S. H. Stout?], July 31, 1864, Samuel H. Stout Papers, Emory University.

215. John W. Glenn to J. H. Alexander, January 29, 1865, RG 109, chap. 4, vol. 37, NA; James H. Burton to Mrs. L. N. Waddail, October 27, 1864, ibid., vols. 20, 29, and 31.

216. C. C. Hammock to J. G. Clark, October 16, 18, 1864; John R. Viely to J. G. Clark, October 15, 1864; M. J. Beanar [?] to J. G. Clark, October 16, 1864; Augustus Mosley to Eugenius A. Nisbet, November 28, 1864—all in Eugenius A. Nisbet Papers.

CHAPTER SIX

1. James L. Roark, *Masters Without Slaves: Southern Planters in the Civil War and Reconstruction* (New York, 1977), chap. 3 and esp. pp. 98–108; Steven Hahn, *The Roots of Southern Populism: Yeoman Farmers and the Transformation of the Georgia Upcountry, 1850–1890* (New York, 1983) chaps. 1–3. On the general importance of local loyalties, see Lawrence N. Powell and Michael S. Wayne, "Self-Interest and the

Decline of Confederate Nationalism" in *The Old South in the Crucible of War,* edited by Harry P. Owens and James J. Cooke (Jackson, Miss., 1983) 29–45.

2. Emory M. Thomas, *The Confederacy as a Revolutionary Experience* (Englewood Cliffs, N.J., 1971), 93–99; Richard C. Wade, *Slavery in the Cities: The South, 1820–1860* (New York, 1964), 3–27, 258–81.

3. Lawrence, *A Present for Mr. Lincoln,* 71, 103, 168–69; Byrne, "Slavery in Savannah," 108.

4. Standard, *Columbus in the Confederacy,* 11, 34–35, 38–39, 44, 51, 55–56 passim.; Columbus *Daily Sun,* March 5, 1861, p. 3, March 9, 1861, p. 2; Macon *Daily Telegraph,* March 18, 1862, p. 2; September 24, 1864, p. 2; November 30, 1864, p. 1; Turner, "Naval and River Operations on the Apalachicola and Chattahoochee," 214–15, 250–51; Thomas, "The Columbus *Enquirer,* 1855–1865," 86–87, 95.

5. Report of James H. Burton to General Benjamin Huger, dated January 1863, RG 109, chap. 4, vol. 20, NA; Macon *Daily Telegraph,* January 13, 1863, p. 1; April 1, 1864, p. 2.

6. *Eighth Census of the United States, 1860: Population,* 74; Singer, "Confederate Atlanta," 136, 185–86.

7. Singer, "Confederate Atlanta," 102–105, 137–42, 148–52, 158–68; Vandiver, *Ploughshares into Swords,* 148, 155; Goff, *Confederate Supply,* 15, 72, 75, 78, 80, 128, 129, 131, 216–17; Stevens Mitchell, "Atlanta, the Industrial Heart of the Confederacy," *Atlanta Historical Bulletin* 7 (May 1930): 20–28; Robert C. Black III, *The Railroads of the Confederacy* (Chapel Hill, 1952), 23, 193; Dew, *Ironmaker to the Confederacy,* 87, 89, 117, 268. See also the discussion of various Atlanta facilities in chapter 5 of the present work.

8. Massey, *Refugee Life,* 84; Minutes of the Atlanta City Council, November 6, 1863, Atlanta Historical Society; Singer, "Confederate Atlanta," 208–11, 244.

9. Corley, *Confederate City,* 49–60. See also the data on the Confederate Powder Works and other Augusta ordnance and supply installations in chapter 5 of the present work.

10. Corley, *Confederate City,* 70–71, 86; Massey, *Refugee Life,* 85.

11. Massey, *Refugee Life,* 85; Coleman, *Confederate Athens,* 97–99, 154–56; Coulter, "Slavery and Freedom in Athens," 265–66; Rogers, *Thomas County in the Civil War,* 81, 92–93.

12. Wade, *Slavery in the Cities,* passim. Studies which suggest the need for some modification of various aspects of the Wade thesis include Byrne, "Slavery in Savannah," 20–21; Herman Charles Woessner III, "New Orleans, 1840–1860: A Study in Urban Slavery" (M.A. thesis, Louisiana State University, 1967); Terry

L. Seip, "Slaves and Free Negroes in Alexandria, 1850–1860," *Louisiana History* 10 (Spring 1969): 147–65; Claudia D. Goldin, *Urban Slavery in the American South, 1820–1860: A Quantitative Study* (Chicago, 1976).

13. For details on these prewar urban restrictions, see chapters 1 and 2 of the present work.

14. Macon *Daily Telegraph*, April 24, 1861, p. 1; April 26, 1861, p. 1; April 30, 1861, p. 3; May 6, 1861, p. 1; July 6, 1861, p. 2; December 21, 1861, p. 3; December 23, 1862, p. 3; January 21, 1863, p. 4.

15. John H. Hull to Joseph E. Brown, April 15, 1861, and Thomas Purse to Joseph E. Brown, February 20, 1862, Telamon Cuyler Collection; Coleman, *Confederate Athens*, 64–65; Coulter, "Slavery and Freedom in Athens," 275–77.

16. Wade, *Slavery in the Cities*, 80–81, 148; Richard Herbert Haunton, "Savannah in the 1850s" (Ph.D. dissertation, Emory University, 1968), 246; William Warren Rogers, *Ante-Bellum Thomas County, 1825–1861* (Tallahassee, 1963), 67; Ernest C. Hynds, *Antebellum Athens and Clarke County* (Athens, 1974), 15, 50; Corley, *Confederate City*, 15; Coleman, *Confederate Athens*, 71.

17. Taylor, *Reminiscences*, 7; Macon *Daily Telegraph*, October 29, 1861, pp. 2, 3.

18. Minutes of the Atlanta City Council, March 6, 1863, Atlanta Historical Society; Byrne, "Slavery in Savannah," 41, n. 39; Macon *Daily Telegraph*, August 20, 1864, p. 2.

19. Haunton, "Savannah in the 1850s," 76–78 passim.; Byrne, "Slavery in Savannah," 22, 32; Singer, "Confederate Atlanta," 13–16; Corley, *Confederate City*, 16; Wade, *Slavery in the Cities*, 62–79 passim.

20. Coulter, "Slavery and Freedom in Athens," 270; Macon *Daily Telegraph*, February 7, 1861, p. 1; February 22, 1861, p. 1; November 17, 1861, p. 4.

21. Minutes of the Atlanta City Council, August 28, 1863, Atlanta Historical Society.

22. Corley, *Confederate City*, 71; Macon *Daily Telegraph and Confederate*, October 5, 1864, p. 1; October 6, 1864, p. 2.

23. Milledgeville *Southern Federal Union* in Savannah *Daily Morning News*, March 19, 1863, p. 1; Macon *Daily Telegraph and Confederate*, January 14, 1865, p. 1. See also Macon *Daily Telegraph and Confederate*, February 22, 1865, p. 1.

24. Coulter, "Slavery and Freedom in Athens," 270–71. For evidence of similar fee increases in Macon, see Macon *Daily Telegraph*, February 11, 1864, p. 2.

25. Macon *Daily Telegraph*, May 3, 1864, p. 1; September 6, 1864, p. 1 (quotation); Corley, *Confederate City*, p. 86. On the abandonment of elderly slaves in antebellum Southern cities, see Berlin, *Slaves Without Masters*, 152–53.

26. Mary Ann Cobb to "My Dear Brother," November 11, 1861; John B. Lamar to Mary Ann Cobb, December 12, 1861; Thomas Cray to Mary Ann Cobb, December 24, 1861; Mary Ann Cobb to Howell Cobb, March 20, 1862; Aggy to "Dear Mistress," March 7 [?], 1862 [possibly 1865]—all in Howell Cobb Collection.

27. William H. Stiles to his wife, March 30, April 14, May 8, 1864; [Mrs. W. H. Stiles?] to "My dear W^m" [William H. Stiles?], April 5, 1864—all in Mackay and Stiles Family Papers, SHC.

28. The statistical data summarized above is presented in greater detail in Byrne, "Slavery in Savannah," 106–18. Byrne's data takes on even greater significance when considered against the background of black and white crime patterns during the late antebellum era, as described in Haunton, "Law and Order in Savannah, 1850–1860," 1–24.

29. Singer, "Confederate Atlanta," 84–86, 118–20, 186–88. It is, perhaps, significant to note that from January through July 1864—the period immediately preceding the Union capture of Atlanta—a total of fourteen cases involving blacks came before the Mayor's Court, representing an increase of one over the total for the entire year of 1863.

30. Savannah *Daily Morning News*, January 18, 1862, p. 2; May 22, 1863, p. 2; May 23, 1863, p. 2; Savannah *Republican* in Macon *Daily Telegraph*, May 14, 1864, p. 2; Macon *Daily Telegraph*, August 18, 1864, p. 1; Charles C. Jones to Eva B. Jones, August 20, 1864, Jones Collection; Corley, *Confederate City*, p. 72; Coulter, "Slavery and Freedom in Athens," 276. See also Rogers, *Thomas County During the Civil War*, 81–82.

31. Taylor, *Reminiscences*, 5–6; Byrne, "Slavery in Savannah," 30–31, 39–41; *Georgia Narratives*, pt. 4, p. 231.

32. Interview with Mrs. Minnie Davis, former slave house servant of John W. Crawford, in *Georgia Narratives*, pt. 1, pp. 257–58.

CHAPTER SEVEN

1. Concerning the effect of the Federal blockade, see Joseph L. Locke to his wife, October 22, 1862, Bulloch Family Papers, SHC. For details of wartime clothing shortages among plantation slaves, see William H. Stiles to his wife, April 2, 1864, Mackay and Stiles Family Papers; "Book of Plantation Clothing Issued to Negroes—Spring & Autumn, Washington Plantation," Alexander and

Hillhouse Family Papers; Adam L. Alexander to "Dear Child," February 27, 1862, Alexander and Hillhouse Family Papers; Oliver H. Prince to John B. Lamar, October 29, 1861, Howell Cobb Collection; John A. Cobb to Howell Cobb, March 25, 1863, Cobb Collection; John A. Cobb to Mary Ann Cobb, May 14, 1863, Cobb Collection. On the shortage of woolen cloth for slaves, see Savannah *Daily Morning News,* September 19, 1861, p. 1; Macon *Daily Telegraph,* December 11, 1861, p. 1; June 24, 1862, p. 2; Sarah Prince to Mary Ann Cobb, October 22, 1861, Cobb Collection; Charles C. Jones, Jr. to Eva B. Jones, October 5, 1864, Jones Collection. On the wartime scarcity of leather and difficulty in obtaining slave shoes, see Oliver H. Prince to John B. Lamar, October 7, 1861; John A. Cobb to Howell Cobb, Jr., October 6, 1862; John A. Cobb to Howell Cobb, July 6, 1863—all in Cobb Collection. Also see Sarah Gilbert to her father, January 7, 1864, and Adam L. Alexander to "My dear child," January 31, 1864, Alexander and Hillhouse Family Papers.

2. Adam Leopold Alexander to "Minnie," May 3, 1860; same to "My dear child," January 31, 1864; "Book of Plantation Clothing issued to the Negroes—Spring & Autumn, Washington Plantation"—all in Alexander and Hillhouse Family Papers. Also Augusta *Constitutionalist* in Savannah *Daily Morning News,* September 19, 1861, p. 1; Macon *Daily Telegraph,* October 27, 1862, p. 1.

3. John A. Cobb to Howell Cobb, February 11, 1863, Howell Cobb Collection. On the law restricting cotton acreage and Governor Brown's subsequent ruling that plots cultivated by slaves were included in the three-acre allotment, see Macon *Daily Telegraph,* February 26, 1863, p. 2.

4. *Georgia Narratives,* pt. 3, pp. 26–27.

5. Ibid., pt. 2, p. 277.

6. John A. Cobb to Mary Ann Cobb, October 12, 1862, Howell Cobb Collection.

7. Stancel Barwick to Mary Ann Cobb, February 11, 1863, ibid.

8. Shepard Pryor to Penelope T. Pryor, August 30, 1861; same to same, September 24, 1861—both in Shepard Green Pryor Collection, University of Georgia.

9. Shepard Pryor to Penelope Pryor, February 27, 1862, ibid.

10. Thomas H. Stringer to John B. Lamar, December 9, 1861, Howell Cobb Collection; *Georgia Narratives,* pt. 1, p. 115.

11. Macon *Daily Telegraph,* October 15, 1862, p. 1; October 8, 1863, p. 2; William L. Mansfield to Joseph E. Brown, September 1, 1862, Telamon Cuyler Collection.

12. Joseph T. Broome, Seaborn Cox, and Joseph A. Thomas to Joseph E. Brown, June 13, 1863, Telamon Cuyler Collection.

13. David C. Barrow to Col. W. M. Browne, May 3, 1863, Barrow Papers; Clarence L. Mohr, "Slavery in Oglethorpe County, Georgia, 1773–1865," *Phylon* 23 (Spring 1972): 17–20; "Fannie" to "Bec" [Miss Rebecca Richardson], July 19, 1864, Doctor Lindsey Durham Papers, University of Georgia.

14. *Acts of Georgia . . . Regular Session . . . 1862*, p. 45; Savannah *Daily Morning News*, April 23, 1863, p. 1.

15. Savannah *Daily Morning News*, April 25, 1863, p. 1; Macon *Daily Telegraph*, May 29, 1863, p. 1.

16. Macon *Daily Telegraph*, June 3, 1863, p. 2; June 4, 1863, p. 1 (quotations); June 5, 1863, p. 2; June 8, 1863, p. 2; June 10, 1863, p. 2; Joseph T. Broome, Seaborn Cox and Joseph A. Thomas to Joseph E. Brown, June 13, 1863, Telamon Cuyler Collection.

17. General Orders No. 15, Georgia Adjutant and Inspector General's Office, June 22, 1863, as reprinted in Macon *Daily Telegraph*, June 25, 1863, p. 2; William Bailey to Howell Cobb, January 6, 1864 (quotation), Howell Cobb Collection; Andrew Dunn to H. H. Waters, October 17, 1863, Telamon Cuyler Collection.

18. *OR*, ser. 1, vol. 52, pt. 2, pp. 688–91; Circular (Confidential) to the Aides de Camp of the Senatorial Districts and Officers sent home by General Smith to bring up the Reserve Militia, Georgia Adjutant and Inspector General's Office, July 15, 1864, Telamon Cuyler Collection (quotation); G. [Gustavus] W. Smith to Henry C. Wayne, August 13, 1864, Cuyler Collection.

19. Unnumbered Special Orders, Georgia Adjutant and Inspector General's Office, August 1, 1864, as printed in Macon *Daily Telegraph*, August 6, 1864, p. 2.

20. On the implementation of emergency slave patrols at the local level, see Macon *Daily Telegraph*, July 27, 1864, p. 2; E. H. Pottle to Henry C. Wayne, August 31, 1864, Telamon Cuyler Collection. For special policing arrangements along the seaboard, see W. B. Gaulden to Joseph E. Brown, May 25, 1864; L. M. Laws to Joseph E. Brown, July 19, 1864; Joseph E. Brown to L. M. Laws, July 20, 1864; J. Pinckney-Huger to Henry C. Wayne, July 31, 1864—all in Telamon Cuyler Collection.

21. William P. Harrison to Joseph E. Brown, April 29, 1861, Telamon Cuyler Collection (first quotation); *Early County News* in Savannah *Daily Morning News*, June 16, 1862, p. 2 (second quotation).

22. H. W. Mercer to Joseph E. Brown, December 27, 1862, Telamon Cuyler Collection (quotation). See also Joseph E. Brown to H. W. Mercer, December

31, 1862, Governor's Letterbooks, p. 400, Georgia Department of Archives and History, Atlanta; Joseph E. Brown to Jefferson Davis, November 24, 1862, in *OR*, ser. 4, vol. 2, p. 208.

23. Godfrey Barnsley to Thomas C. Gilmour, December 31, 1862, Godfrey Barnsley Papers, University of Georgia.

24. Savannah *Daily Morning News*, March 23, 1863, pp. 1, 2.

25. Augustus S. Montgomery to Maj. Genl. [John Gray] Foster, May 12, 1863, document labeled "A True Copy," Telamon Cuyler Collection. The letter was reportedly obtained following the capture of a Federal steamer off the North Carolina coast, and subsequently forwarded to Jefferson Davis by Governor Zebulon Vance of North Carolina. Bell I. Wiley, *Southern Negroes*, 83.

26. *ORN*, ser. 1, vol. 14, p. 34.

27. Wiley, *Southern Negroes*, 312, n. 55.

28. Milledgeville *Southern Recorder* as quoted in Macon *Daily Telegraph*, October 10, 1863, p. 1; October 30, 1863, p. 1; December 18, 1863, p. 1; Savannah *Morning News* in Macon *Daily Telegraph*, August 26, 1864, p. 2; Augusta *Chronicle and Sentinel* in Macon *Daily Telegraph*, September 1, 1864, p. 1.

29. The psychological significance of prewar insurrection panics and their role in enforcing slave discipline in underpoliced rural areas is explored in Bertram Wyatt-Brown, *Southern Honor* (New York, 1982), a work which appeared in print too late to shape my treatment of similar themes in the present study.

30. Narcissa M. Lawton Diary, March 17, 1862, quoted in Rogers, *Thomas County During the Civil War*, 80; Macon *Daily Telegraph*, April 11, 1862, p. 1 (quotation); April 14, 1862, p. 1; Laura Beecher Comer Diary, vol. 1, entry of June 5, 1862, SHC.

31. Athens *Southern Watchman*, July 23, 1862, p. 2; Athens *Southern Banner*, July 23, 1862, p. 3; Coulter, "Slavery and Freedom in Athens," 278; Coleman, *Confederate Athens*, 158, discusses additional allegations of rape by slaves in 1863 and 1864.

32. Columbus *Daily Sun*, December 5, 1863, p. 2.

33. Macon *Daily Telegraph*, February 4, 1864, p. 2 (all quotations). In 1827, when a Jasper County black was convicted of rape and sentenced to castration and deportation, the Macon *Telegraph* scorned the court for laxity in an editorial entitled "Softening the Law." Flanders, *Plantation Slavery in Georgia*, 267. The incident is also mentioned by Winthrop D. Jordan in his landmark study *White Over Black* (p. 473), and I wish to thank Professor Jordan for initially bringing the information to my attention.

34. Macon *Daily Telegraph*, October 15, 1862, p. 1; B. W. Brown to Eugenius

A. Nesbit, January 4, 1863, Eugenius A. Nesbit Papers; James H. McWhorter to David C. Barrow, December 29, 1863, Barrow Papers.

35. Macon *Daily Telegraph*, December 17, 1863, p. 2; December 19, 1863, p. 2.

36. Ibid., September 1, 1862, p. 1; September 30, 1862, p. 2.

37. Generalizations in this paragraph rest largely upon Anne Firor Scott, *The Southern Lady: From Pedestal to Politics, 1830–1930* (Chicago, 1970), chaps. 1–4. See p. 34 for quotation. Cf. Catherine Clinton, *The Plantation Mistress: Woman's World in the Old South* (New York, 1982), 16–35.

38. Herbert G. Gutman, *The Black Family in Slavery and Freedom, 1750–1925* (New York, 1976), 72–73, 189–91; Jacqueline Jones, "'My Mother Was Much of a Woman': Black Women, Work, and the Family Under Slavery," *Feminist Studies* 8 (Summer 1982): 235–70.

39. W. E. Burghardt DuBois, *Black Reconstruction in America* (1935; New York, 1963), 59.

40. Mrs. George J. Kollock to her husband, February 18, 1862, Kollock Collection, University of Georgia; Laura Beecher Comer Diary, January 5, August 22, 29, 1862, SHC.

41. Laura Beecher Comer Diary, January 4, 5, February 2, March 29, May 7, June 5, August 22, 1862.

42. Ibid., March 9, July 20, August 29, September 4, 23, 29, October 13, 1862.

43. Sarah Gilbert to "Dearest father" [Adam L. Alexander], November 29, 1863; same to same, December 23, 1863—both in Alexander and Hillhouse Family Papers.

44. Warren Akin to Mary F. Akin, January 10, 1865; same to same, January 23, 1865; Mary F. Akin to Warren Akin, January 8, 1865; same to same, January 14, 1865—all in Bell I. Wiley, ed., *Letters of Warren Akin, Confederate Congressman* (Athens, 1959), 74, 94, 118–19, 120, 122.

45. Penelope Pryor to Shepard Pryor, October 8, 1861, and same to same, October 14, 1861, Shepard Green Pryor Collection; Manuscript U.S. Census returns for Sumter County, Georgia, 1860, Schedule 2, Slave Inhabitants, p. 36.

46. Samuel Scrutchin to Shepard Pryor, July 29, 1861, Shepard Green Pryor Collection.

47. Shepard Pryor to Penelope Pryor, August 8, 1861, ibid.

48. Shepard Pryor to Penelope Pryor, August 18, 1861, ibid.; same to same, April 23, 1862, ibid.

49. Shepard Pryor to Penelope Pryor, April 24, 1862, ibid.

50. Shepard Pryor to Penelope Pryor, February 26, 1863, ibid.

51. Mrs. Louticia Jackson to Asbury H. Jackson, August 23, 1863, Edward Harden Papers.

CHAPTER EIGHT

1. See the discussion of wartime slave legislation in the preceding chapter.

2. *Journal of the Senate of the State of Georgia . . . Annual Session . . . 1861*, pp. 130–31.

3. Ibid., 137–38.

4. *Journal of the House of Representatives of the State of Georgia . . . Annual Session . . . 1861*, pp. 205, 352, 387.

5. *Georgia Senate Journal . . . Annual Session . . . 1862*, pp. 100, 115, 142, 150, 155; *Georgia House Journal . . . Annual Session . . . 1862*, pp. 97, 120, 186, 258; *Georgia House Journal . . . Annual Session . . . 1863*, pp. 49, 60, 76.

6. Houston County Grand Jury Presentments in Macon *Daily Telegraph*, October 31, 1862, p. 1; C. D. Mallory to Joseph E. Brown, February 3, 1862, Telamon Cuyler Collection; A. W. Persons to E. A. Nisbet, June 7, 1864, Eugenius A. Nisbet Papers.

7. Sweat, "The Free Negro in Antebellum Georgia," 138–95; Johnson, "Free Blacks in Antebellum Savannah," 418–31. Cf. Blassingame, "Before the Ghetto: The Making of the Black Community in Savannah," 463–88 for evidence that by the 1870s most of Savannah's draymen, porters, bricklayers, coopers, cotton samplers, shoemakers, butchers, and barbers were black. No doubt most skilled Negroes in antebellum Savannah were slaves.

8. *Georgia Senate Journal . . . Annual Session . . . 1861*, pp. 49, 66–67; *Georgia House Journal . . . Annual Session . . . 1861*, pp. 66, 144, 171, 207, 265, 283, 316; *Georgia Senate Journal . . . Annual Session . . . 1862*, pp. 188, 202, 221, 229; *Georgia House Journal . . . Annual Session . . . 1862*, pp. 67, 87, 140, 221; *Georgia House Journal . . . Annual Session . . . 1863*, pp. 47, 53, 137, 167, 170, 184, 206, 233.

9. *Acts of the General Assembly of the State of Georgia . . . Annual Session . . . 1861*, pp. 121–22; ibid., 1862, p. 95. For county-level enslavement petitions from free blacks in Bartow and Clarke counties, see Cunyus, *History of Bartow County*, 273–74, and Coleman, *Confederate Athens*, 158. Such petitions were authorized by *The Code of the State of Georgia*, which took effect on January 1, 1863. An exhaustive search of extant Inferior Court minutes for Georgia's remaining 125 counties would doubtless reveal other instances of voluntary enslavement. Evidence from

Dougherty and Sumter counties suggests that white intermediaries were often the actual initiators of "voluntary" enslavement proceedings. See C. D. Mallory to Joseph E. Brown, February 3, 1862, Telamon Cuyler Collection; A. W. Persons to Eugenius A. Nisbet, June 7, 1864, Eugenius A. Nisbet Papers. For a somewhat different reading of the evidence concerning the late antebellum assault on free Negroes in the south as a whole, see Ira Berlin, *Slaves Without Masters*, 343–80.

10. Donald G. Mathews, *Religion in the Old South* (Chicago, 1977), 179.

11. Sweat, "The Free Negro in Antebellum Georgia," 32–47ff. Ruth Scarborough, *The Opposition to Slavery in Georgia Prior to 1860* (Nashville, 1933), 124–70, overestimates the significance of individual manumissions but compiles valuable documentary evidence on the subject. For additional examples of manumissions prompted by natural rights ideology, see E. Merton Coulter, *Old Petersburg and the Broad River Valley of Georgia* (Athens, 1965), p. 24.

12. Charles Colcock Jones to William Swan Plumer, June 28, 1834, quoted in Donald G. Mathews, "Religion and Slavery: The American South," in *Antislavery, Religion, and Reform: Essays in Memory of Roger Anstey*, edited by Christine Bolt and Seymour Drescher (Folkestone, England, and Hamden, Conn., 1980), 218–19 (quotation); Athens *Athenian*, May 10, 1831, p. 2.

13. Walter G. Charlton, "A Judge and a Grand Jury," in *Report of the Thirty First Annual Session of the Georgia Bar Association, 1914* (Macon, 1914), 209–11; John W. Blassingame, ed., *Slave Testimony: Two Centuries of Letters, Speeches, Interviews and Autobiographies* (Baton Rouge, 1977), 124–28.

14. *Annals of Congress*, 16th Congress, 1st session, pp. 925–26, 1024–26; Betty Fladeland, *Men and Brothers: Anglo-American Antislavery Cooperation* (Urbana, 1972), 122, 152ff. Senator John A. Cuthbert was the uncle of Alfred Cuthbert, Jr., who manumitted and colonized seventy-three Georgia slaves in 1860.

15. Scarborough, *Opposition to Slavery*, chap. 7, esp. pp. 111–21, provides the most detailed summary of state slave trade legislation available in published secondary sources.

16. Flanders, *Plantation Slavery in Georgia*, 297–99. Robert Reid, the Georgia congressman who denounced slavery in 1820 as an "unnatural state; a dark cloud which obscures half of the lustre of our free institutions," took a more conservative stance twenty years later while serving as territorial governor of Florida. In 1840 Reid offered General Zachary Taylor thirty-three newly imported slave-tracking Cuban bloodhounds for use in the Seminole War. James W. Covington, "Cuban Bloodhounds and the Seminoles," *Florida Historical Quarterly* 33 (October 1954): 111–19.

17. The antislavery dimension of Georgia colonizationist activity has been

explored by James M. Gifford in three valuable studies: "Emily Tubman and the African Colonization Movement in Georgia," *Georgia Historical Quarterly* 59 (Spring 1975): 10–24; "The Cuthbert Conspiracy: An Episode in African Colonization," *South Atlantic Quarterly* 79 (Summer 1980): 312–20; and "The African Colonization Movement in Georgia, 1817–1860" (Ph.D. dissertation, University of Georgia, 1977).

18. David Brion Davis, *The Problem of Slavery in the Age of Revolution, 1770–1823* (Ithaca, 1975), 196–212ff., and Winthrop D. Jordan, *White Over Black: American Attitudes Toward the Negro, 1550–1812* (Chapel Hill, 1968), 342–74ff., offer contrasting but not entirely incompatible accounts of the metamorphosis of early Southern antislavery sentiment into paternalistic Christian humanitarianism. On the actual or proposed liberalization of antebellum Georgia slave laws and legal practices, see Flanders, *Plantation Slavery in Georgia,* 261–63; Daniel J. Flanigan, "Criminal Procedure in Slave Trials in the Antebellum South," *Journal of Southern History* 40 (November 1974): 537–64; R. H. Taylor, "Humanizing the Slave Code of North Carolina," *North Carolina Historical Review* 2 (July 1925): 331. The ameliorative content of white proslavery Christianity, which emphasized mutual obligations between masters and slaves, is discussed in Flanders, *Plantation Slavery in Georgia,* 177–81; Mathews, *Religion in the Old South,* 141–42, 180–81; and Blassingame, *The Slave Community,* 82–84, 268–71.

19. Much of the 1853 speech is reprinted in Ulrich B. Phillips, *The Life of Robert Toombs* (New York, 1913), 156ff. The most accessible full text of Toombs's 1856 Tremont Temple address is contained in Alexander H. Stephens, *A Constitutional View of the Late War Between the States,* 2 vols. (Philadelphia, Cincinnati, and Atlanta, 1868), 1:625ff. All quotations are from this source.

20. Stephens, *A Constitutional View of the Late War Between the States,* 1:644 (first quotation), 642 (second, third, fourth, and fifth quotations), 643 (sixth quotation).

21. Ibid., 643 (first and second quotations), 644 (third quotation).

22. Ibid., 625, (first and second quotations), 644 (third quotation).

23. Cleveland, *Alexander H. Stephens,* 125–30.

24. Ernest Trice Thompson, *Presbyterians in the South,* 3 vols. (Richmond, 1963–1973), 2:56 (quotation); Fredrika Bremer, *The Homes of the New World,* 2 vols. (New York, 1853), 1:237; Mathews, *Religion in the Old South,* 174.

25. Howell Cobb, *A Scriptural Examination of the Institution of Slavery in the United States* (Perry, Ga., 1856), 24.

26. *Minutes of the Baptist Convention of the State of Georgia, 1860* (Macon, 1860), 46. Blassingame, *The Slave Community,* Appendix 3, Table 7, contains a convenient

summary of black Methodist membership. See also Henry Thompson Malone, *The Episcopal Church in Georgia, 1733–1957* (Atlanta, 1960), 86–88; Thompson, *Presbyterians in the South,* 1:443. Contemporary estimates placed black Presbyterian membership in Georgia at 577 in 1858. The incomplete statistical returns for 1863 listed a total of 504 black communicants. *Minutes of the Presbyterian Church in the Confederate States of America . . . 1863* (Columbia, S.C., 1863), 190–95.

27. In the *Tenth Annual Report of the Association for the Religious Instruction of the Negroes in Liberty County, Georgia* (Savannah, 1845), Presbyterian minister Charles C. Jones related a striking and probably atypical incident of blacks walking out of and protesting a sermon stressing obedience. The following year Jones's Baptist colleague, the Reverend J. S. Law, unwittingly disclosed the character of his own preaching to slaves by stressing its broad applicability. "It is not necessary that only the Negroes should be at the meeting," Law observed. "It will be convenient for many white people to attend [slave worship services] and though the preaching will be adapted to the capacity of the Negroes, yet I believe the right kind of preaching for them will be likely to prove profitable also to a large portion of white people . . . I do not believe the simplifying of divine truth robs it of any of its intrinsic value." *An Essay on the Religious Oral Instruction of the Colored Race: Prepared in Accordance with a Request of the Georgia Baptist Convention . . .* (Penfield, Ga., 1846), 9. Precisely what most white preachers said to blacks, and what blacks thought of the sermons, can never be known, although further manuscript research may illuminate the question. Suggestive of the facts which may emerge is John Blassingame's discovery that among black WPA interviewees "only 15 percent of the Georgia slaves who had heard antebellum whites preach recalled admonitions to obedience." Blassingame, *The Slave Community,* 89.

28. For listings of black ministers and licentiates, see *Minutes of the Sunbury Baptist Association . . . November . . . 1843* (Savannah, 1843), 9, 13, and all subsequent annual minutes through 1860; *Minutes of the Georgia Baptist Association . . . October . . . 1847* (Penfield, Ga., 1847), 8, and all subsequent annual minutes through 1860. For typical black death notices and obituaries, see *Georgia Association Minutes, 1854,* p. 7; *1856,* p. 6; *1857,* p. 5; *1860,* p. 6; *1861,* p. 5. Black delegates routinely represented their churches at association meetings.

29. The list of antebellum black Baptist preachers could be expanded several-fold on the basis of printed association minutes. For descriptions of black church services and white estimates of individual black ministers, see Charles A. Lyell, *A Second Visit to the United States of North America,* 2 vols. (London, 1849), 2:14–16; Edward A. Pollard, *Black Diamonds, Gathered in the Darkey Homes of the South* (New York, 1859), 36–37; Julia L. Sherwood and Samuel Boykin, *Memoir of Adiel Sher-*

wood (Philadelphia, 1884), 112–13; W. L. Kilpatrick, *The Hephzibah Baptist Association Centennial, 1794–1894* (Augusta, 1894), 109–17, 134–35; H[enry] Lewis Batts, *History of the First Baptist Church of Christ at Macon, Georgia, 1826–1968* (Macon, 1968–69), 52–53. These citations are intended as a more or less representative sampling of pertinent sources, too voluminous for exhaustive listing.

30. A valuable profile of the origin and development of Georgia's preemancipation black Baptist churches is contained in Mechal Sobel, *Trabelin' On: The Slave Journey to an Afro-Baptist Faith* (Westport and London, 1979), 314–31, 355–56. Among the Presbyterians, Charles C. Jones established a tradition of heavy reliance on black exhorters and "watchmen" which persisted along the Georgia coast well into the postwar era. Elsewhere in the state during the late 1830s white Presbyterians in Macon licensed three Negro exhorters who evangelized throughout Georgia for several decades and formed a new black presbytery affiliated with the Northern church during Reconstruction. See Donald G. Mathews, "Charles Colcock Jones and the Southern Evangelical Crusade to Form a Biracial Community," *Journal of Southern History* 41 (August 1975): 312–13; *Presbyterian Monthly Record* 23 (February 1886): 73–76; William Letcher Mitchell to Rev. Dr. S. H. Higgins, July 19, 1859, in "Minutes of the Directors of the Georgia Domestic Missionary Society, 1844–1893," pp. 41–43; Session Minutes, First Presbyterian Church, Athens, Georgia, 1820–61, microfilm copies, Georgia Department of Archives and History, Atlanta. Information on antebellum black Methodist churches and preachers is elusive. See, however, W. P. Harrison, *The Gospel Among the Slaves* (Nashville, 1893), 353–55; Alfred M. Pierce, *A History of Methodism in Georgia* (N. p., 1956), 96–101; *Southern Christian Advocate,* December 15, 1864, p. 2. For examples of slave exhorters in a typical Georgia piedmont county, see Minutes of Millstone Baptist Church (of Oglethorpe County), 1788–1842, entry of September 6, 1823; Minutes of the County Line Baptist Church, 1807–1915, entries of April 1, May 6, 1826; Minutes of the Baptist Church at Clouds Creek, 1826–56, entries of October 13, November 4, 1827—all on microfilm, Georgia Department of Archives and History.

31. Since racial separation takes on fundamentally different meanings in slave and free society there is little to be gained from the semantic quibble over how to designate racially mixed but separately seated congregations. Neither "segregation" nor "integration" is employed as a descriptive term in the present discussion.

32. One example must suffice. During the four-year period 1826–30 the "white" Clouds Creek Baptist Church increased its black membership from forty-two to seventy-six. In the process a total of thirty-one blacks were excommunicated for various moral offenses and fourteen of the bondsmen were later read-

mitted after giving evidence of sorrow and repentance. Disciplinary patterns among white members of Clouds Creek and other nearby churches appear broadly similar, but valid generalizations must await large scale statistical research in manuscript records. See also Rogers, *Antebellum Thomas County*, 82–84ff.; Coleman, *Confederate Athens*, 134–36.

33. *Journal of the American Baptist Anti-Slavery Convention* 1 (July 1841): 93.

34. Ibid., 99, 165.

35. Letter from an anonymous Georgia Baptist clergyman to the New York *Examiner*, reprinted in Rev. John Dixon Long, *Pictures of Slavery in Church and State* (Philadelphia, 1857), 162–63.

36. Ulrich B. Phillips, "The Origin and Growth of the Southern Black Belts," reprinted in Eugene D. Genovese, ed., *The Slave Economy of the Old South* (Baton Rouge, 1968), 105, n. 14.

37. The leading spokesman on this point in Georgia and the South was Charles C. Jones, who addressed the theme repeatedly. His most forceful utterance is contained in the *Thirteenth Annual Report of the Association for the Religious Instruction of the Negroes, in Liberty County, Georgia* (Savannah, 1848), 16. See also Eduard Nuesse Loring, "Charles C. Jones: Missionary to Plantation Slaves, 1831–1847" (Ph.D. dissertation, Vanderbilt University, 1976), 320–27.

38. In addition to the sources in notes 9 and 10 above, see James M. Simms, *The First Colored Baptist Church in North America* (Philadelphia, 1888), 18–28; John W. Davis, "George Liele and Andrew Bryan, Pioneer Negro Baptist Preachers," *Journal of Negro History* 3 (April 1918): 119–27. In 1852 the Rehoboth Baptist Association sent one of Augusta's black ministers, a multilingual native African named Cesar Fraser, to serve as a missionary in Liberia. *Minutes of the Rehoboth Baptist Association . . . September . . . 1852* (Macon, 1852), 5.

39. Several of Charles C. Jones's bondsmen were literate, and Georgia author and Methodist clergyman Augustus Baldwin Longstreet reportedly taught informal classes of black and white children prior to emancipation. See Robert S. Starobin, ed., *Blacks in Bondage: Letters of American Slaves* (New York, 1974), 42–58; John W. Blassingame, *Slave Testimony*, 90–91; John Donald Wade, *Augustus Baldwin Longstreet: A Study in the Development of Culture in the South*, edited with an introduction by M. Thomas Inge (Athens, 1969), 272, 347; Harrison, *The Gospel Among the Slaves*, 393. See also *Journal of the American Baptist Anti-Slavery Convention* 1 (July 1841): 135.

40. Thompson, *Presbyterians in the South*, 2:56, quoting reformist clergyman James A. Lyon of North Carolina.

41. For a pioneering survey of wartime slavery reform in the South as a whole,

see Bell I. Wiley, "The Movement to Humanize the Institution of Slavery During the Confederacy," *Emory University Quarterly* 5 (December 1949): 207–20.

42. My assessment of the theology and social perspective of leading Southern clergymen draws heavily on E. Brooks Holifield's indispensable study *The Gentlemen Theologians: American Theology in Southern Culture, 1795–1860* (Durham, 1978), especially chapters 2 and 6.

43. *Christian Index*, June 3, 1862, p. 3.

44. Ibid., June 17, 1862, p. 3.

45. Ibid., September 2, 1862, p. 2.

46. Ibid.; [Samuel Boykin], *History of the Baptist Denomination in Georgia, with a Biographical Compendium and Portrait Gallery of Baptist Ministers and Other Georgia Baptists* (Atlanta, 1881), 569–75.

47. *Christian Index*, September 2, 1862, p. 2.

48. Ibid. See also ibid., September 23, 1862, p. 2.

49. Ibid., September 9, 1862, p. 2.

50. Milledgeville *Confederate Union*, October 28, 1862, p. 3.

51. "The Presbyterian Church in Georgia on Secession and Slavery," *Georgia Historical Quarterly* 1 (September 1917): 265.

52. Thomas R. R. Cobb, ed., *A Digest of the Statute Laws of the State of Georgia in Force Prior to the Session of the General Assembly of 1851* (Athens, 1851), 1005–1006.

53. Bond Almand, "The Preparation and Adoption of the Code of 1863," *Georgia Bar Journal* 14 (November 1951): 161–70; *Code of Georgia*, section 1376 (quotations).

54. *Christian Index*, February 16, 1863, p. 1.

55. The letter was publicized even among Baptists who could not afford newspaper subscriptions. See, for example, M. J. Wellborn to J. L. M. Burnett, March 6, 1863, in Edmund Cody Burnett, ed., "Some Confederate Letters: Alabama, Georgia, and Tennessee," *Georgia Historical Quarterly* 21 (March 1937): 195–97.

56. *Christian Index*, June 1, 1863, p. 4.

57. Ibid.

58. Joseph H. Parks, *Joseph E. Brown of Georgia* (Baton Rouge, 1977), 10; Savannah *Daily Morning News*, March 30, 1863, p. 2 (quotation).

59. Published initially as the *Sermon of Bishop George F. Pierce Before the General Assembly of Georgia, March 27, 1863* (Milledgeville, 1863), most of the text was later reprinted in George G. Smith, *The Life and Times of George Foster Pierce, D.D., LL.D.* (Sparta, Ga., 1888), 465–77. Quotations are from the latter source, p. 474 (italics in original).

60. Macon *Daily Telegraph*, March 31, 1863, p. 3; Macon *Christian Index*, April 6, 1863, p. 1.

61. Macon *Daily Telegraph,* April 1, 1863, p. 4; Columbus *Daily Sun,* April 9, 1863, p. 2.

62. Savannah *Daily Morning News,* April 8, 1863, p. 2; Columbus *Daily Sun,* April 9, 1863, p. 2.

63. Savannah *Daily Morning News,* April 3, 1863, p. 1 (quotation). See also the speech of state Senator George Anderson Gordon of Chatham County, reprinted in ibid., April 15, 1863, p. 1, and the resolutions of state Senator John M. Jackson in *Georgia Senate Journal . . . Extra Session . . . 1863,* pp. 67, 88.

64. Milledgeville *Southern Recorder,* quoted in Savannah *Daily Morning News,* April 8, 1863, p. 2.

65. Macon *Daily Telegraph,* April 21, 1863, p. 1; *Acts of Georgia . . . Extra Session . . . 1863,* p. 106.

66. *Pastoral Letter From the Bishops of the Protestant Episcopal Church to the Clergy and Laity of the Church in the Confederate States of America; Delivered Before the General Council, in St. Paul's Church, Augusta, Saturday, November 22d, 1862,* in Thomas M. Hanckel, ed., *Sermons of the Right Reverend Stephen Elliott, D.D., Late Bishop of Georgia* (New York, 1867), 576–77.

67. Smith, *Life and Times of George F. Pierce,* 475.

68. Ibid.; *Christian Index,* July 6, 1863, p. 2.

69. *Code of Georgia,* section 1666.

70. *Christian Index,* November 4, 1864, p. 2.

71. Ibid.

72. *Minutes of the Eightieth Anniversary of the Georgia Baptist Association, Held with Pine Grove Church, Columbia County, Georgia, October 7th and 8th, 1864* (Macon, 1864), 8. The resolution was submitted by the Reverend H. H. Tucker of Mercer, who had previously been active in the movement to legalize slave preaching.

73. *Minutes of the Bethel Baptist Association, Held at Cotton Hill, Clay County, Georgia, on Saturday, November 5, 1864* (Macon, 1864), 6; Macon *Daily Telegraph and Confederate,* November 3, 1864, p. 2; *Christian Index,* November 4, 1864, p. 2; Tuskegee (Alabama) *South Western Baptist,* November 10, 1864, p. 1.

74. *Southern Christian Advocate,* February 2, 1865, p. 1.

75. Ibid., January 19, 1865, p. 2. During the same conference a white Methodist preacher was publicly reprimanded for his brutal treatment of a Negro boy.

76. Atlanta *Southern Confederacy,* March 2, 1865, as quoted in Macon *Daily Telegraph and Confederate,* March 10, 1865, p. 1.

77. Macon *Daily Telegraph and Confederate,* March 10, 1865, p. 1.

78. Ibid., March 17, 1865, p. 1.

79. Ibid., March 10, 1865, p. 1.

80. All quotations are from the second installment of Crawford's lengthy

"Thoughts on Government," published in the *Christian Index*, November 4, 1864, p. 1.

81. Atlanta *Southern Confederacy,* as quoted in Macon *Daily Telegraph and Confederate,* March 17, 1865, p. 1.

82. Eric Foner, *Free Soil, Free Labor, Free Men: The Ideology of the Republican Party Before the Civil War* (London, 1970), 295–300; Lawrence N. Powell, *New Masters: Northern Planters in the South During Reconstruction* (New Haven, 1979), 5; George M. Fredrickson, *The Black Image in the White Mind: The Debate on Afro-American Character and Destiny, 1817–1914* (New York, 1971), chaps. 1, 4, 7 passim, esp. p. 128.

83. *Georgia House Journal . . . Extra Session . . . February, 1865,* pp. 148, 149, 222. See also the somewhat fuller reports of legislative proceedings published in the Macon *Daily Telegraph and Confederate* during February and March 1865.

84. In formulating a legislative program Confederate reformers encountered conceptual problems similar to those of antebellum Southern jurists who sought to create a coherent "law of slavery." As a careful student of the latter subject has noted, "There was a fundamental contradiction between the idea of a law of slavery and a social structure that provided the basis for the idea that slave relationships should be regulated by sentiment, not law." Mark Tushnet, *The American Law of Slavery, 1810–1860* (Princeton, 1981), 230.

85. *Christian Index,* January 5, 1865, p. 1 (quotation). The universality of this theme renders comprehensive documentation impractical, but see, for example, typical letters and editorials in ibid., March 23, 1863, p. 2, and November 20, 1863, p. 1, and in *Southern Christian Advocate,* April 17, 1864, p. 3, as well as the citations in subsequent footnotes.

86. *Christian Index,* May 11, 1863, p. 4.

87. Ibid., September 18, 1863, p. 2.

88. Ibid.

89. Ibid., June 10, 1864, p. 1.

90. Ibid., January 5, 1865, p. 1.

91. John B. Boles, *The Great Revival: Origins of the Southern Evangelical Mind, 1787–1805* (Lexington, 1972), 115.

92. *Christian Index,* September 18, 1863, p. 2.

93. Conservatives contributed unwittingly to white guilt feelings by arguing that ameliorative goals were incompatible with slavery. Some critics went even further and claimed that the logic of reform, once accepted, would require Southern Christians to work actively for the destruction of slavery. See, for example, *Christian Index,* October 7, 1862, p. 1.

94. Ibid., December 25, 1863, p. 1.

95. Mary Elizabeth Massey, *Bonnet Brigades* (New York, 1966), 19–20; Ella Gertrude Clanton Thomas Journal, September 17, 1864 (p. 195 of typescript), Duke University (quotation).

96. Thomas Journal, September 23, 1864 (p. 5 of typescript).

97. Massey, *Bonnet Brigades*, 20.

98. Eliza Frances Andrews, *The Wartime Journal of a Georgia Girl, 1864–1865,* edited by Spencer Bidwell King, Jr. (Macon, 1960), 122 (quotation), 127.

99. Narcissa M. Lawton Diary, March 17, 1862, quoted in Rogers, *Thomas County During the Civil War,* 80.

100. Macon *Daily Telegraph,* August 31, 1864, p. 2.

101. Ibid.

102. L. E. M. Williams to Henry C. Wayne, September 13, 1864, Telamon Cuyler Collection.

103. Macon *Daily Telegraph,* August 31, 1864, p. 2. Claiming to be "extremely mortified" by Bishop Pierce's revelations, Governor Brown instructed policemen to "be careful that those [slaves] who act well their part receive just praise and kind treatment as incentives to good conduct in the future." See also Joseph E. Brown to G. F. Pierce, September 5, 1864, Governor's Letterbooks, Georgia Department of Archives and History.

104. *Southern Christian Advocate,* September 8, 1864, p. 4.

105. D. A. Vason to "Col. Whittle," March 29, 1863, Telamon Cuyler Collection. During this same period Vason joined other local whites in petitioning the secretary of war to exempt all Dougherty County overseers from conscription. H. Morgan to Howell Cobb, June 8, 1863, Howell Cobb Collection.

106. *Christian Index,* September 30, 1862, p. 2.

107. Margaret Dailey Journal, December 20, 1863, as quoted in Bell I. Wiley, *Confederate Women* (Westport, Conn., 1975), 154.

108. Kate Cumming, *A Journal of Hospital Life in the Confederate Army of Tennessee, from the Battle of Shilo to the End of the War* (Louisville and New Orleans, 1866), 102.

109. *Southern Christian Advocate,* September 29, 1864, p. 2.

110. Ibid., February 2, 1865, p. 1.

CHAPTER NINE

1. Myrta Lockett Avary, ed., *Recollections of Alexander H. Stephens, His Diary Kept When a Prisoner at Fort Warren, Boston Harbor, 1865; Giving Incidents and Reflections of His Prison Life and Some Letters and Reminiscences* (New York, 1910), 249–50.

2. Ibid., 174–75, 198–99, 208 (first quotation), 272–74 (second quotation), 536–37, 547.

3. Robert F. Durden, *The Gray and the Black: The Confederate Debate on Emancipation* (Baton Rouge, 1972), 147–51.

4. Unidentified Richmond newspapers quoted in Augusta *Constitutionalist* and reprinted in Macon *Daily Telegraph and Confederate,* January 19, 1865, p. 2. See also ibid., January 5, 1865, p. 2.

5. Atlanta *Southern Confederacy,* August 23, 1863, quoted in Bryan, *Confederate Georgia,* 133; Savannah *Daily Morning News,* August 18, 1863, p. 2.

6. Cumming, *Journal of Hospital Life,* 85.

7. Durden, *The Gray and the Black,* 53–67, p. 61 (quotation).

8. Ibid., viii (quotation), 100–106, 202–203, 240ff.

9. Macon *Daily Telegraph and Confederate,* January 6, 1865, p. 2.

10. John M. Johnston to Mary Ann Cobb, February 11, 1865, Howell Cobb Collection.

11. Anonymous letter to Howell Cobb, January 3, 1865, ibid.

12. Henry W. Allen to Joseph E. Brown, December 15, 1864, Telamon Cuyler Collection.

13. Macon *Daily Telegraph and Confederate,* October 21, 1864, p. 2.

14. *Southern Christian Advocate,* February 2, 1865, p. 2.

15. Macon *Daily Telegraph and Confederate,* January 23, 1865, p. 2.

16. Ibid., November 19, 1864, p. 2.

17. Ibid., October 26, 1864, p. 1.

18. Ibid., October 18, 1864, p. 2.

19. Savannah *Daily Morning News,* August 18, 1863, p. 2.

20. Message of Governor Joseph E. Brown to the Georgia legislature, February 15, 1865, in Candler, *Confederate Records of the State of Georgia,* 2:832–35.

21. Howell Cobb to James A. Seddon, January 8, 1865, OR, ser. 4, vol. 3, pp. 1009–10.

22. Ibid.

23. "Resolutions of 'Thomas' Brigade'" (Fourteenth, Thirty-fifth, Forty-fifth, and Forty-ninth Georgia Regiments), February 10, 1865, Telamon Cuyler Collection.

24. John B. Gordon to W. H. Taylor, February 18, 1865, quoted in Durden, *The Gray and the Black,* 217.

25. Edward Porter Alexander to his wife, February 21, 1865, Edward Porter Alexander Papers, SHC.

26. OR, ser. 1, vol. 46, pp. 1315–17. All quotations are on p. 1316.

27. Macon *Daily Telegraph and Confederate,* October 29, 1864, p. 1 (first, second, and fourth quotations); ibid., January 6, 1865, p. 2 (third quotation).

28. Milledgeville *Southern Recorder* quoted in Macon *Daily Telegraph and Confederate*, October 26, 1864, p. 1.

29. Memphis *Appeal* reprinted in Macon *Daily Telegraph and Confederate*, October 31, 1864, p. 1 (first quotation); ibid., January 6, 1865, p. 2 (second quotation).

30. Ibid., April 17, 1865, p. 2. See also ibid., October 29, 1864, p. 2.

31. For the latter phrase, employed with a somewhat different emphasis, I am indebted to Kenneth M. Stampp, "The Southern Road to Appomattox," in the same author's *The Imperiled Union: Essays on the Background of the Civil War* (New York, 1980), 246–69.

32. Durden, *The Gray and the Black*, 61. No disciple of immediatism, Cleburne envisioned freeing Southern blacks within "such reasonable time as will prepare both races for the change."

33. Ibid., 103ff.

34. Macon *Daily Telegraph and Confederate*, October 21, 1864, p. 2.

35. Ella Gertrude Clanton Thomas Journal, November 17, 1864.

36. Macon *Daily Telegraph and Confederate*, October 27, 1864, p. 1.

37. *Christian Index*, November 11, 1864, p. 2.

38. Ibid., November 18, 1864, p. 2.

39. Ibid., February 23, 1865, p. 3.

40. Durden, *The Gray and the Black*, 202–203, 268, 269 (quotation).

41. Macon *Daily Telegraph and Confederate*, April 4, 1865, p. 2.

42. Augusta *Constitutionalist* quoted in Macon *Daily Telegraph and Confederate*, April 12, 1865, p. 2 (quotation); Augusta *Constitutionalist*, April 9, 1865, quoted in Macon *Daily Telegraph and Confederate*, April 14, 1865, p. 2.

43. Columbus *Enquirer* quoted in Macon *Daily Telegraph and Confederate*, April 12, 1865, p. 1.

44. Standard, *Columbus in the Confederacy*, 59–61; James P. Jones, *Yankee Blitzkrieg: Wilson's Raid Through Alabama and Georgia* (Athens, 1976), pp. 134–44.

45. Macon *Daily Telegraph and Confederate*, April 15, 1865, p. 2.

46. Ibid., April 17, 1865, p. 2.

47. Ibid., April 14, 1865, p. 2.

48. Ibid., March 13, 1865, p. 2.

49. William M. Browne to David C. Barrow, March 26, 1865; Pope Barrow to David C. Barrow, March 26, 1865 (quotations)—both in Barrow Papers.

50. James H. McWhorter to David C. Barrow, March 29, 1865, ibid.; John A. Cobb to David C. Barrow, April 15, 1865, ibid.

51. *ORN.*, ser. 1, vol. 13, p. 144; ibid., vol. 14, pp. 727–28; George A. Mercer Diary, February 25, 1863 (p. 85 of typescript).

52. Maurice Kaye Melton, "The Savannah Squadron: A Study in Failure"

(M.A. thesis, University of Georgia, 1971), p. 75, n. 47; Savannah *Daily Morning News*, April 8, 1862, p. 2 (quotation). The black sailors in question—slaves Edward, William, and Charles owned by one R. Ryan—were serving aboard the CSS *Savannah* in July 1864. For additional slave monetary contributions to the Georgia "Ladies Gunboat Fund," see Macon *Daily Telegraph*, March 24, 1862, p. 4; March 27, 1862, p. 3; April 24, 1862, p. 2; April 25, 1862, p. 4; May 12, 1862, p. 4.

53. Macon *Daily Telegraph*, July 28, 1862, p. 4.

54. Savannah *Daily Morning News*, December 7, 1861, p. 1.

55. Henry L. Graves to Mrs. Sarah D. Graves, December 28, 1864, Graves Family Papers, SHC.

56. Laura Beecher Comer Diary, July 4, 1862.

57. Shepard Pryor to Penelope Pryor, January 28, 1862 (first quotation); same to same, July 30, 1863 (second and third quotations); same to same, August 11, 1863 (fourth quotation)—all in Shepard Green Pryor Collection.

58. Spencer B. King Jr., ed., *Rebel Lawyer: Letters of Theodorick W. Montfort, 1861–1862* (Athens, 1965), 68, 77 (quotation).

59. David Lawrence Valuska, "The Negro in the Union Navy: 1861–1865" (Ph.D. dissertation, Lehigh University, 1973), 280; ORN, ser. 1, vol. 14, p. 704 (quotations).

60. ORN, ser. 1, vol. 15, pp. 469–83, 501–502 (quotation p. 469).

61. Notarized statement of Joseph A. Haddock, October 14, 1881 (quotation); George D. Ruggles to the Commissioner of Pensions, February 23, 1881, and various related Pension File documents, Compiled Service Record of Moses Dallas, No. 343-108, Adjutant General's Office. RG 94, NA.

62. John J. Cheatham to Leroy Pope Walker, May 4, 1861, in Ira Berlin, Joseph P. Reidy, and Leslie S. Rowland, eds., *Freedom: A Documentary History of Emancipation, 1861–1867, Selected From the Holdings of the National Archives of the United States*, series 2: *The Black Military Experience* (Cambridge, 1982), 282 (quotation), 283. See also pp. 285–87.

63. Colonel J. T. Jordan and eleven other officers of Thomas's Brigade, Forty-ninth Georgia Regiment, to Colonel W. H. Taylor, March 15, 1865, in OR, ser. 1, vol. 46, pp. 1315–16. The officers sought permission to "fill up their ranks with negroes" after sending one white man from each company back home to Georgia to select local black recruits "suitable to be incorporated in those companies." This arrangement, the officers believed, would "create, or rather cement, a reciprocal attachment between the men now in service and the negroes." Regiments from other states apparently made somewhat similar proposals. In March

1865 President Jefferson Davis stated flatly that "we should draw into our military service that portion of the negroes, which would be most apt to run away and join . . . the enemy." Durden, *The Gray and the Black,* 278 (quotation), 279–83.

64. William B. Hodgson Journal, December 27, 1864, Charles Colcock Jones, Jr. Collection.

65. Columbus *Sun* in Macon *Daily Telegraph,* January 11, 1865, p. 1.

66. Allan Nevins, *The Statesmanship of the Civil War* (New York and London, 1962), 91.

EPILOGUE

1. George Washington Williams, *A History of the Negro Troops in the War of the Rebellion, 1861–1865* (New York, 1888), xiii.

2. Dan T. Carter, "The Anatomy of Fear: The Christmas Day Insurrection Scare of 1865," *Journal of Southern History* 42 (August 1976): 345–64; Allen W. Trelease, *White Terror: The Ku Klux Klan Conspiracy and Southern Reconstruction* (New York, 1971), esp. chaps. 14 and 20; George C. Rable, *But There Was No Peace: The Role of Violence in the Politics of Reconstruction* (Athens, 1984).

3. Edmund L. Drago, *Black Politicians and Reconstruction in Georgia: A Splendid Failure* (Baton Rouge, 1982), chaps. 2 and 3.

BIBLIOGRAPHY

PRIMARY SOURCES

Manuscripts

ATLANTA HISTORICAL SOCIETY
Lemuel P. Grant Papers.
Minutes of the Atlanta City Council, 1860–1865.

DUKE UNIVERSITY
Augusta Arsenal Records, 1863–1864.
Edward Harden Papers.
Eugenius A. Nesbit Papers.
Daniel S. Printup Papers.
Joseph Belknap Smith Papers.
Ella Gertrude Thomas Journal, 1861–1864.

EMORY UNIVERSITY
Robert Battey Papers.
Samuel H. Stout Papers.

GEORGIA DEPARTMENT OF ARCHIVES AND HISTORY
Barrington King Account Book, 1848–1864.
Governor's Letterbooks, 1861–1865.
Minutes of the Baptist Church at Clouds Creek, 1826–1856.
Minutes of the County Line Baptist Church, 1807–1915.
Minutes of the Executive Department, 1861–1865.
Minutes of the Georgia Domestic Missionary Society, 1844–1893.
Minutes of Millstone Baptist Church, 1788–1842.
Session Minutes, First Presbyterian Church, Athens, Ga., 1820–1861.

LIBRARY OF CONGRESS
American Colonization Society Archives.
Alexander H. Stephens Papers.

Bibliography

NATIONAL ARCHIVES
Records of the Adjutant General's Office, 1780s–1917, Record Group 94.
War Department Collection of Confederate Records, Record Group 109.

UNIVERSITY OF GEORGIA
Akehurst-Lines Collection.
Baber-Blackshear Collection.
Godfrey Barnsley Papers.
David Crenshaw Barrow Papers.
Joseph E. Brown Papers, Felix Hargrett Collection.
Nathan Atkinson Brown Papers.
Howell Cobb Collection.
Telamon Cuyler Collection.
William Gaston Delony Papers.
Doctor Lindsey Durham Papers.
Charles Colcock Jones, Jr., Collection.
Shepard Green Pryor Collection.

UNIVERSITY OF NORTH CAROLINA, SOUTHERN HISTORICAL COLLECTION
Alexander and Hillhouse Family Papers.
Arnold and Screven Family Papers.
Bullock Family Papers.
Laura Beecher Comer Diary.
Joseph S. Espey Papers.
William O. Fleming Papers.
William W. Gordon Family Papers.
Graves Family Papers.
Jackson and Prince Family Papers
Thomas Butler King Papers.
William King Diary.
Kollock Collection.
Alexander Robert Lawton Papers.
Mackay and Stiles Family Papers.
George A. Mercer Diaries, 1855–1865.
Samuel H. Stout Papers.
Sarah Frances Hicks Williams Letters.

UNIVERSITY OF TEXAS, BARKER TEXAS HISTORY CENTER
Samuel H. Stout Papers.

Bibliography

VIRGINIA STATE LIBRARY
Tredegar Company Records

YALE UNIVERSITY, STERLING LIBRARY
Rufus and S. Willard Saxton Papers.

Government Documents

UNITED STATES

Official Records of the Union and Confederate Navies in the War of the Rebellion. 30 vols. Washington, D.C.: Government Printing Office, 1894–1922.

The War of the Rebellion: A Compilation of the Official Records of the Union and Confederate Armies. 128 vols. Washington, D.C.: Government Printing Office, 1880–1901.

STATE AND LOCAL

Acts of the General Assembly of the State of Georgia. Places and publishers vary. 1859–1865.

Candler, Allen D., comp. The Confederate Records of the State of Georgia. 6 vols. Atlanta: C. P. Byrd, State Printer, 1909–1911.

Clark, R. H., Thomas R. R. Cobb, and David Irwin, eds. The Code of the State of Georgia. Atlanta: Franklin Steam Printing House, 1861.

Cobb, Howell, ed. A Compilation of the General and Public Statutes of the State of Georgia; with the Forms and Precedents Necessary to Their Practical Use. New York: E. O. Jenkins, 1859.

Cobb, Thomas R. R., ed. A Digest of the Statute Laws of the State of Georgia in Force Prior to the Session of the General Assembly of 1851. Athens: Christy, Kelsea and Burke, 1851.

Journal of the House of Representatives of the State of Georgia. Places and publishers vary, 1859–1865.

Journal of the Senate of the State of Georgia. Places and publishers vary, 1859–1865.

Newspapers

American Missionary.
Athens Southern Banner.
Atlanta Southern Confederacy.
Boston Commonwealth.

Bibliography

Chicago *Tribune.*
Christian Index (Macon, Ga.).
Columbus *Daily Sun.*
Columbus *Enquirer.*
Milledgeville *Southern Federal Union.*
Milledgeville *Southern Recorder.*
New York *Daily Tribune.*
New York *Times.*
Port Royal *New South.*
Rome *True Flag.*
Rome *Weekly Courier.*
Savannah *Daily Morning News.*
Savannah *Republican.*
Southern Christian Advocate (Augusta, Ga.).

Published Records of Religious Bodies

Journal of the American Baptist Anti-Slavery Convention. 1 (July 1841).
Law, J. S. *An Essay on the Religious Oral Instruction of the Colored Race: Prepared in Accordance with a Request of the Georgia Baptist Convention.* Penfield, Ga.: Georgia Baptist Convention, 1846.
Minutes of the Baptist Convention of the State of Georgia, 1860. Macon: Telegraph Steam Printing House, 1860.
Minutes of the Bethel Baptist Association, Held at Cotton Hill, Clay County, Georgia on Saturday, November 5, 1864. Macon: Burke, Boykin and Co., 1864.
Minutes of the Fifteenth Annual Session of the Rehoboth Baptist Association Convened at Spring Creek, Houston County, Ga., Saturday, Sep. 18th, 1852. Macon, Ga.: Benjamin F. Griffin, 1852.
Minutes of the Georgia Baptist Association, 1843–1864. Places and publishers vary.
Minutes of the Presbyterian Church in the Confederate States of America . . . 1863. Columbia, S. C.: Southern Guardian Steam-Power Press, 1863.
Minutes of the Sunbury Baptist Association . . . November . . . 1843. Savannah: Thomas Purse, 1843.
Tenth Annual Report of the Association for the Religious Instruction of the Negroes in Liberty County, Georgia. Savannah: Office of P. G. Thomas, 1845.

370

Bibliography

Thirteenth Annual Report of the Association for the Religious Instruction of the Negroes in Liberty County, Georgia. Savannah: Edward J. Purse, 1848.

Diaries, Memoirs, Reminiscenses, and Other Printed Sources

Andrews, Eliza Frances. *The Wartime Journal of a Georgia Girl, 1864–1865.* Edited by Spencer Bidwell King. Macon: Ardivan Press, 1960.

Annual Report of the American Anti-Slavery Society by the Executive Committee for the Year Ending May, 1, 1860. New York: American Anti-Slavery Society, 1861.

Avary, Myrta Lockett, ed. *Recollections of Alexander H. Stephens, His Diary Kept When a Prisoner at Fort Warren, Boston Harbor, 1865; Giving Incidents and Reflections of His Prison Life and Some Letters and Reminiscences.* New York: Doubleday, Page and Company, 1910.

Barnes, Elinor, and James A. Barnes, eds. *Naval Surgeon: Blockading the South, 1862–1866: The Diary of Samuel Pellman Boyer.* Bloomington: Indiana University Press, 1963.

Berlin, Ira, Joseph P. Reidy, and Leslie S. Rowland, eds. *Freedom: A Documentary History of Emancipation, 1861–1867. Selected from the Holdings of the National Archives of the United States.* Series 2: The Black Military Experience. Cambridge: Cambridge University Press, 1982.

Berry, Harrison. *A Reply to Ariel.* Macon, Ga.: American Union Book and Job Office, 1869.

—————. *Slavery and Abolitionism as Viewed by a Georgia Slave.* Atlanta: Franklin Printing House, 1861.

Blassingame, John W., ed. *Slave Testimony: Two Centuries of Letters, Speeches, Interviews and Autobiographies.* Baton Rouge: Louisiana State University Press, 1977.

Boney, F. N., ed. *Slave Life in Georgia: A Narrative of the Life, Sufferings and Escape of John Brown, A Fugitive Slave.* Savannah: Beehive Press, 1972.

Bonner, James C., ed. *The Journal of a Milledgeville Girl, 1861–1867.* Athens: University of Georgia Press, 1964.

[Boykin, Samuel.] *History of the Baptist Denomination in Georgia, with a Biographical Compendium and Portrait Gallery of Baptist Ministers and Other Georgia Baptists.* Atlanta: Jos. P. Harrison & Co., 1881.

Bremer, Fredrika. *The Homes of the New World.* 2 vols. New York: Harper and Brothers, 1853.

Cleveland, Henry. *Alexander H. Stephens, in Public and Private, with Letters and Speeches,*

Before, During, and Since the War. Philadelphia: National Publishing Company, 1866.

Clifton, James M., ed. *Life and Labor on Argyle Island: Letters and Documents of a Savannah River Rice Plantation, 1833–1867.* Savannah: Beehive Press, 1978.

Cobb, Howell. *A Scriptural Examination of the Institution of Slavery in the United States.* Perry, Ga.: Printed for the author, 1856.

Cumming, Kate. *A Journal of Hospital Life in the Confederate Army of Tennessee, from the Battle of Shilo to the End of the War.* Louisville and New Orleans: J. P. Morton & Co. and W. Evelyn, 1866.

Denison, Rev. Frederic. "A Chaplain's Experience in the Union Army." In *Personal Narratives of Events in the War of the Rebellion.* 4th ser., No. 20. Providence: Soldiers' and Sailors' Historical Society of Rhode Island, 1893.

———. *Shot and Shell: The Third Rhode Island Heavy Artillery Regiment in the Rebellion, 1861–1865.* Providence: Published for the Third R. I. H. Art. Vet. Association by J. A. and R. A. Reid, 1879.

Dyer, Thomas G., ed. *To Raise Myself a Little: The Diaries and Letters of Jennie, a Georgia Teacher, 1851–1886.* Athens: University of Georgia Press, 1982.

Felton, Rebecca Latimer. *Country Life in Georgia in the Days of My Youth.* Atlanta: Index Printing Company, 1919.

Gorgas, Josiah. "Notes on the Ordnance Department of the Confederate Government." *Southern Historical Society Papers* 12 (January–February 1884): 66–94.

Hanckel, Thomas M., ed. *Sermons of the Right Reverend Stephen Elliott, D. D.* New York: Pott and Amery, 1867.

Harn, Julia E. "Old Canoochee-Ogeechee Chronicles." *Georgia Historical Quarterly* 16 (March 1932): 298–311.

Hayes, John D., ed. *Samuel Francis DuPont: A Selection from His Civil War Letters.* 3 vols. Ithaca, N.Y.: Cornell University Press, 1969.

Higginson, Thomas Wentworth. *Army Life in a Black Regiment.* (East Lansing, Mich.). Michigan State University Press, 1960.

King, Spencer B., Jr., ed. *Rebel Lawyer: Letters of Theodorick W. Montfort, 1861–1862.* Athens: University of Georgia Press, 1965.

Lane, Mills, ed. *Marching Through Georgia.* New York: Arno Press, 1978.

LeConte, Joseph. *'Ware Sherman: A Journal of Three Months' Personal Experience in the Last Days of the Confederacy.* Berkeley: University of California Press, 1937.

Long, John Dixon. *Pictures of Slavery in Church and State.* Philadelphia: Published by the author, 1857.

Bibliography

Lyell, Charles A. *A Second Visit to the United States of North America.* 2 vols. London: J. Murray, 1849.

Morgan, Julia. *How It Was: Four Years Among the Rebels.* Nashville: Publishing House, Methodist Episcopal Church, South, 1892.

Myers, Robert Manson, ed. *The Children of Pride: A True Story of Georgia and the Civil War.* New Haven: Yale University Press, 1972.

Phillips, Ulrich B., ed. *Plantation and Frontier Documents.* 2 vols. Cleveland: Arthur H. Clark Company, 1909.

Pollard, Edward A. *Black Diamonds, Gathered in the Darkey Homes of the South.* New York: Pudney & Russell, 1859.

Rawick, George P., et al., eds. *The American Slave: A Composite Autobiography.* 31 vols. in three series. Westport, Conn., and London: Greenwood Press, 1972–1977.

Sherman, William T. *Memoirs of General William T. Sherman.* 2d ed., revised and corrected. 2 vols. New York and London: D. Appleton and Company, 1931.

Sherwood, Julia L., and Samuel Boykin, eds. *Memoir of Adiel Sherwood.* Philadelphia: Grant and Faires, 1884.

Simms, James M. *The First Colored Baptist Church in North America.* Philadelphia: J. B. Lippincott, 1888.

Starobin, Robert S., ed. *Blacks in Bondage: Letters of American Slaves.* New York: New Viewpoints–Franklin Watt Inc., 1974.

Stephens, Alexander H. *A Constitutional View of the Late War Between the States.* 2 vols. Philadelphia, Cincinnati and Atlanta: National Publishing Company, 1868.

Taylor, Susie King. *Reminiscences of My Life in Camp.* Boston: Published by the Author, 1902.

Thompson, Robert Means, and Richard Wainwright, eds. *Confidential Correspondence of Gustavus Vasa Fox, Assistant Secretary of the Navy, 1861–1865.* 2 vols. New York: Printed for the Naval History Society by the De Vinne Press, 1918–1919.

Toombs, Samuel. *Reminiscences of the War, Comprising a Detailed Account of the Experiences of the Thirteenth Regiment New Jersey Volunteers in Camp, on the March, and in Battle.* Orange, N.J.: Journal Office, 1878.

Turner, J[oseph] A[ddison], "What Are We To Do?" *De Bow's Review* 29 [Vol. 4, New Series] (July 1860): 70–77.

Wiley, Bell I., ed. *Letters of Warren Akin, Confederate Congressman.* Athens: University of Georgia Press, 1959.

Bibliography

Williams, George Washington. *A History of the Negro Troops in the War of the Rebellion, 1861–1865.* New York: Harper and Brothers, 1888.

SECONDARY SOURCES

Books

Aptheker, Herbert. *American Negro Slave Revolts.* New York: International Publishers, 1969.

Avery, I. W. *The History of the State of Georgia from 1850 to 1881.* New York: Brown and Derby, 1881.

Batts, H[enry] Lewis. *History of the First Baptist Church of Christ at Macon, Georgia, 1826–1968.* Macon: Southern Press Inc., 1968–69.

Berlin, Ira. *Slaves Without Masters: The Free Negro in the Antebellum South.* New York: Pantheon Books, 1974.

Black, Robert C., III. *The Railroads of the Confederacy.* Chapel Hill: University of North Carolina Press, 1952.

Blassingame, John W. *Black New Orleans, 1860–1880.* Chicago: University of Chicago Press, 1973.

———. *The Slave Community: Plantation Life in the Antebellum South.* Rev. ed. New York: Oxford University Press, 1979.

Boles, John B. *The Great Revival: Origins of the Southern Evangelical Mind, 1787–1805.* Lexington: University Press of Kentucky, 1972.

Bolt, Christine, and Seymour Drescher, eds. *Antislavery, Religion and Reform: Essays in Memory of Roger Anstey.* Folkestone, England, and Hamden, Conn.: Archon Books, 1980.

Bracey, John H., August Meier, and Elliott Rudwick, eds. *Black Nationalism in America.* Indianapolis and New York: Bobbs-Merrill, 1970.

Bryan, T. Conn. *Confederate Georgia.* Athens: University of Georgia Press, 1953.

Carter, E. R. *The Black Side: A Partial History of the Business, Religious, and Educational Side of the Negro in Atlanta, Ga.* Atlanta: n.p., 1894.

Cate, Margaret Davis. *Early Days of Coastal Georgia.* St. Simons Island, Ga.: Fort Frederica Association, 1955.

Channing, Steven A. *Crisis of Fear: Secession in South Carolina.* New York: Simon and Schuster, 1970.

Coleman, Kenneth. *Confederate Athens.* Athens: University of Georgia Press, 1967.

Bibliography

Coleman, Kenneth, et al. *A History of Georgia.* Athens: University of Georgia Press, 1977.

Corley, Florence Fleming. *Confederate City: Augusta, Georgia, 1860–1865.* Columbia: University of South Carolina Press, 1960.

Cornish, Dudley Taylor. *The Sable Arm: Negro Troops in the Union Army, 1861–1865.* New York: W. W. Norton, 1966.

Coulter, E. Merton. *The Confederate States of America, 1861–1865.* Baton Rouge: Louisiana State University Press, 1950.

_____. *Old Petersburg and the Broad River Valley of Georgia.* Athens: University of Georgia Press, 1965.

Crenshaw, Ollinger. *The Slave States in the Presidential Election of 1860.* Johns Hopkins University Studies in Historical and Political Science, Series 63, No. 3. Baltimore: Johns Hopkins University Press, 1945.

Cunningham, Horace H. *Doctors in Gray.* Baton Rouge: Louisiana State University Press, 1962.

Cunyus, Lucy Josephine. *The History of Bartow County, Formerly Cass.* [Cartersville, Ga.]: Tribune Publishing Co., 1933.

Davis, David Brion. *The Problem of Slavery in the Age of Revolution, 1770–1823.* Ithaca: Cornell University Press, 1975.

Degler, Carl N. *The Other South: Southern Dissenters in the Nineteenth Century.* New York: Harper and Row, 1974.

Dew, Charles B. *Ironmaker to the Confederacy: Joseph R. Anderson and the Tredegar Iron Works.* New Haven: Yale University Press, 1966.

Drago, Edmund L. *Black Politicians and Reconstruction in Georgia: A Splendid Failure.* Baton Rouge: Louisiana State University Press, 1982.

DuBois, W. E. B. *Black Reconstruction in America.* New York: Meridian Books, 1963.

_____. *The Negro Artisan: A Social Study.* Atlanta: Atlanta University Press, 1902.

DuBois, W. E. B., and Augustus G. Dill. *The Negro American Artisan.* Atlanta: Atlanta University Press, 1912.

Durden, Robert F. *The Gray and the Black: The Confederate Debate on Emancipation.* Baton Rouge: Louisiana State University Press, 1972.

Eaton, Clement. *The Freedom of Thought Struggle in the Old South.* New York: Harper and Row, 1964.

_____. *A History of the Southern Confederacy.* New York: Free Press, 1954.

Escott, Paul D. *Slavery Remembered: A Record of Twentieth-Century Slave Narratives.* Chapel Hill: University of North Carolina Press, 1979.

Fladeland, Betty. *Men and Brothers: Anglo-American Antislavery Cooperation.* Urbana: University of Illinois Press, 1972.

Bibliography

Flanders, Ralph Betts. *Plantation Slavery in Georgia*. Chapel Hill: University of North Carolina Press, 1933.

Fogel, Robert William, and Stanley L. Engerman. *Time on the Cross: The Economics of American Negro Slavery*. 2 vols. Boston: Little, Brown, 1974.

Foner, Eric. *Free Soil, Free Labor, Free Men: The Ideology of the Republican Party Before the Civil War*. New York: Oxford University Press, 1970.

Fredrickson, George M. *The Black Image in the White Mind: The Debate on Afro-American Character and Destiny, 1817–1914*. New York: Harper and Row, 1971.

Genovese, Eugene D. *In Red and Black. Marxian Explorations in Southern and Afro-American History*. New York: Pantheon Books, 1971.

———. *The Political Economy of Slavery*. New York: Vintage Books, 1965.

———. *Roll, Jordan, Roll: The World the Slaves Made*. New York: Pantheon Books, 1974.

Goff, Richard B. *Confederate Supply*. Durham: Duke University Press, 1969.

Goldin, Claudia D. *Urban Slavery in the American South, 1820–1860: A Quantitative Study*. Chicago: University of Chicago Press, 1976.

Gutman, Herbert G. *The Black Family in Slavery and Freedom, 1750–1925*. New York: Pantheon Books, 1976.

Hahn, Steven. *The Roots of Southern Populism: Yeoman Farmers and the Transformation of the Georgia Upcountry, 1850–1890*. New York: Oxford University Press, 1983.

Harlan, Louis R. *Booker T. Washington: The Making of a Black Leader, 1856–1901*. New York: Oxford University Press, 1972.

Harrison, William P. *The Gospel Among the Slaves*. Nashville: Publishing House of the M.E. Church, South, 1893.

Hartz, Louis. *The Liberal Tradition in America*. New York: Harcourt, Brace, 1955.

Heath, Milton S. *Constructive Liberalism: The Role of the State in Economic Development in Georgia to 1860*. Cambridge: Harvard University Press, 1954.

Hill, Herbert. *Anger and Beyond: The Negro Writer in the United States*. New York: Harper and Row, 1966.

Hill, Louise B. *Joseph E. Brown and the Confederacy*. Chapel Hill: University of North Carolina Press, 1939.

Holifield, E. Brooks. *The Gentlemen Theologians: American Theology in Southern Culture, 1795–1860*. Durham: Duke University Press, 1978.

Hoole, William Stanley. *Vizetelly Covers the Confederacy*. Confederate Centennial Studies No. 4. Tuscaloosa: Lost Cause Press, 1957.

House, Albert Virgil., ed. *Planter Management and Capitalism in Ante-Bellum Georgia: The Journal of Hugh Fraser Grant, Ricegrower*. Columbia University Studies in the

History of American Agriculture, No. 13. New York: Columbia University Press, 1954.

Hynds, Ernest C. *Antebellum Athens and Clarke County.* Athens: University of Georgia Press, 1974.

Jenkins, William S. *Pro-Slavery Thought in the Old South.* Chapel Hill: University of North Carolina Press, 1935.

Johnson, Michael Paul. *Toward a Patriarchal Republic.* Baton Rouge: Louisiana State University Press, 1977.

Jones, Jacqueline. *Soldiers of Light and Love: Northern Teachers and Georgia Blacks, 1865– 1873.* Chapel Hill: University of North Carolina Press, 1980.

Jones, James P. *Yankee Blitzkrieg: Wilson's Raid Through Alabama and Georgia.* Athens: University of Georgia Press, 1976.

Jordan, Winthrop D. *White Over Black: American Attitudes Toward the Negro. 1550– 1812.* Chapel Hill: University of North Carolina Press, for the Institute of Early American History and Culture, 1968.

Kilpatrick, W. L. *The Hephzibah Baptist Association Centennial, 1794–1894.* Augusta, Ga.: Richards & Shaver, 1894.

Lawrence, Alexander A. *A Present for Mr. Lincoln: The Story of Savannah from Secession to Sherman.* Macon, Ga.: Ardivan Press, 1961.

Levine, Lawrence W. *Black Culture and Black Consciousness.* New York: Oxford University Press, 1977.

Lonn, Ella. *Salt as a Factor in the Confederacy.* University Ala.: University of Albama Press, 1965.

Loveland, Anne C. *Southern Evangelicals and the Social Order, 1800–1860.* Baton Rouge: Louisiana State University Press, 1980.

McDaniel, Susie Blaylock. *Official History of Catoosa County, Georgia, 1853–1953.* Dalton, Ga.: Gregory Printing and Office Supply, 1953.

Magdol, Edward. *A Right to the Land: Essays on the Freedmen's Community.* Westport, Conn., and London: Greenwood Press, 1977.

Malone, Henry Thompson. *The Episcopal Church in Georgia, 1733–1957.* Atlanta: Protestant Episcopal Church in the Diocese of Atlanta, 1960.

Massey, Mary Elizabeth. *Bonnet Brigades: American Women and the Civil War.* New York: Alfred A. Knopf, 1966.

———. *Refugee Life in the Confederacy.* Baton Rouge: Louisiana State University Press, 1964.

Mathews, Donald G. *Religion in the Old South.* Chicago: University of Chicago Press, 1977.

Meier, August. *Negro Thought in America, 1880–1915.* Ann Arbor: University of Michigan Press, 1963.

Miller, Floyd J. *The Search for a Black Nationality: Black Immigration and Colonization, 1787–1863.* Urbana: University of Illinois Press, 1975.

Montgomery, Horace. *Johnny Cobb: Confederate Aristocrat.* Athens: University of Georgia Press, 1964.

Moore, Albert B. *Conscription and Conflict in the Confederacy.* New York: Macmillan Company, 1924.

Nevins, Allan. *The Emergence of Lincoln: Prologue to Civil War, 1859–1861.* New York: Charles Scribner's Sons, 1950.

———. *The Statesmanship of the Civil War.* New York and London: Macmillan Company, 1962.

Nichols, James L. *Confederate Engineers.* Confederate Centennial Studies No. 5. Tuscaloosa: Lost Cause Press, 1957.

Oates, Stephen B. *To Purge This Land with Blood: A Biography of John Brown.* New York: Harper and Row, 1970.

Oubre, Claude F. *Forty Acres and a Mule: The Freedmen's Bureau and Black Land Ownership.* Baton Rouge: Louisiana State University Press, 1978.

Owens, Harry P., and James J. Cooke, eds. *The Old South in the Crucible of War.* Jackson: University Press of Mississippi, 1983.

Owsley, Frank L. *State Rights in the Confederacy.* Chicago: University of Chicago Press, 1931.

Parks, Joseph H. *Joseph E. Brown of Georgia.* Baton Rouge: Louisiana State University Press, 1977.

Parrish, Lydia. *Slave Songs of the Georgia Sea Islands.* Hatboro, Pa.: Folklore Associates, 1965.

Phillips, Ulrich B. *American Negro Slavery.* Baton Rouge: Louisiana State University Press, 1966.

———. *Georgia and State Rights.* Washington, D.C.: Government Printing Office, 1902.

———. *A History of Transportation in the Eastern Cotton Belt.* New York: Columbia University Press, 1908.

———. *Life and Labor in the Old South.* Boston: Little, Brown and Company, 1929.

———. *The Life of Robert Toombs.* New York: Macmillan Company, 1913.

Powell, Lawrence N. *New Masters: Northern Planters During the Civil War and Reconstruction.* New Haven: Yale University Press, 1979.

Quarles, Benjamin. *The Negro in the Civil War.* Boston: Little, Brown and Company, 1953.

Bibliography

Raboteau, Albert J. *Slave Religion: The "Invisible Institution" in the Ante-Bellum South.* New York: Oxford University Press, 1978.

Ransom, Roger L., and Richard Sutch. *One Kind of Freedom: The Economic Consequences of Emancipation.* Cambridge: Cambridge University Press, 1977.

Rawick, George. *From Sundown to Sunup: The Making of the Black Community.* Contributions in Afro-American and African Studies, No. 11. Westport, Conn. Greenwood Press, 1972.

Redkey, Edwin S. *Black Exodus: Black Nationalist and Back-to-Africa Movements, 1890–1910.* New Haven: Yale University Press, 1969.

Reynolds, Donald E. *Editors Make War: Southern Newspapers in the Secession Crisis.* Nashville: Vanderbilt University Press, 1970.

Ripley, C. Peter. *Slaves and Freedmen in Civil War Louisiana.* Baton Rouge: Louisiana State University Press, 1976.

Roark, James L. *Masters Without Slaves: Southern Planters in the Civil War and Reconstruction.* New York: W. W. Norton, 1977.

Rogers, William Warren. *Ante-Bellum Thomas County, 1825–1861.* Tallahassee: Florida State University Press, 1963.

————. *Thomas County During the Civil War.* Tallahassee: Florida State University Press, 1964.

Rose, Willie Lee. *Rehearsal for Reconstruction: The Port Royal Experiment.* New York: Vintage Books, 1964.

Savannah Unit, Federal Writers' Project, Works Progress Administration of Georgia. *Savannah River Plantations.* Edited by Mary Granger. Savannah: Georgia Historical Society, 1947.

Savannah Unit, Georgia Writers' Project, Works Projects Administration. *Drums and Shadows: Survival Studies Among the Georgia Coastal Negroes.* 1940. Reprint. Westport, Conn.: Greenwood Press, 1973.

Scarborough, Ruth. *The Opposition to Slavery in Georgia Prior to 1860.* Nashville: George Peabody College for Teachers, 1933.

Scarborough, William Kauffman. *The Overseer: Plantation Management in the Old South.* Baton Rouge: Louisiana State University Press, 1966.

Scott, Anne Firor. *The Southern Lady: From Pedestal to Politics, 1830–1930.* Chicago: University of Chicago Press, 1970.

Sellers, Charles Grier, ed. *The Southerner as American.* Chapel Hill: University of North Carolina Press, 1960.

Sellers, James B. *Slavery in Alabama.* University, Ala.: University of Alabama Press, 1950.

Bibliography

Smith, George G. *The Life and Times of George Foster Pierce, D. D., LL. D.* Sparta, Ga.: Hancock Publishing Co., 1888.

Sobel, Mechal. *Trabelin' On: The Slave Journey to an Afro-Baptist Faith.* Westport, Conn., and London: Greenwood Press, 1979.

Stampp, Kenneth M. *The Imperilled Union: Essays on the Background of the Civil War.* New York: Oxford University Press, 1980.

_____. *The Peculiar Institution: Slavery in the Ante-Bellum South.* New York: Vintage Books, 1956.

Standard, Diffie William. *Columbus, Georgia in the Confederacy.* New York: William-Frederick Press, 1954.

Starobin, Robert S. *Industrial Slavery in the Old South.* New York: Oxford University Press, 1970.

Steel, Edward M., Jr. *T. Butler King of Georgia.* Athens: University of Georgia Press, 1964.

Still, William N., Jr. *Iron Afloat: The Story of the Confederate Armorclads.* Nashville: Vanderbilt University Press, 1971.

Takaki, Ronald T. *A Pro-Slavery Crusade: The Agitation to Reopen the African Slave Trade.* New York: Free Press, 1971.

Thomas, Emory M. *The Confederacy as a Revolutionary Experience.* Englewood Cliffs, N.J.: Prentice-Hall, 1971.

_____. *The Confederate Nation.* New York: Harper and Row, 1979.

Thompson, Ernest Trice. *Presbyterians in the South.* 3 vols. Richmond: John Knox Press, 1963–1973.

Todd, Richard C. *Confederate Finance.* Athens: University of Georgia Press, 1954.

Trelease, Allen W. *White Terror: The Ku Klux Klan Conspiracy and Reconstruction.* New York: Harper and Row, 1971.

Tushnet, Mark. *The American Law of Slavery, 1810–1860.* Princeton: Princeton University Press, 1981.

Vandiver, Frank E. *Ploughshares into Swords: Josiah Gorgas and Confederate Ordnance.* Austin: University of Texas Press, 1952.

Wade, John Donald. *Augustus Baldwin Longstreet: A Study in the Development of Culture in the South.* Edited with an introduction by M. Thomas Inge. Athens: University of Georgia Press, 1969.

Wade, Richard C. *Slavery in the Cities: The South, 1820–1860.* New York: Oxford University Press, 1964.

Wikramanayake, Marina. *A World in Shadow: The Free Black in Antebellum South Carolina.* Columbia: University of South Carolina Press, 1973.

Wiley, Bell I. *Confederate Women.* Westport, Conn.: Greenwood Press, 1975.

Bibliography

_____. *Southern Negroes, 1861–1865.* New Haven: Yale University Press, 1938.

Williamson, Joel. *After Slavery: The Negro in South Carolina During Reconstruction, 1861–1877.* Chapel Hill: University of North Carolina Press, 1965.

Wood, Betty. *Slavery in Colonial Georgia, 1730–1775.* Athens: University of Georgia Press, 1984.

Wood, Peter H. *Black Majority: Negroes in Colonial South Carolina from 1670 through the Stono Rebellion.* New York: Alfred A. Knopf, 1974.

Wyatt-Brown, Bertram. *Southern Honor: Ethics and Behavior in the Old South.* New York: Oxford University Press, 1982.

Articles

Addington, Wendell G. "Slave Insurrections in Texas." *Journal of Negro History* 35 (October 1950): 408–34.

Almand, Bond. "The Preparation and Adoption of the Code of 1863." *Georgia Bar Journal* 14 (November 1951): 161–70.

Aptheker, Herbert. "The Negro in the Union Navy." *Journal of Negro History* 32 (April 1947): 169–200.

Bell, Howard H. "Negro Nationalism in the 1850s." *Journal of Negro Education* 35 (Winter 1966): 100–104.

Black, Robert C. "The Railroads of Georgia in the Confederate War Effort." *Journal of Southern History* 13 (November 1947): 510–34.

Blassingame, John W. "Before the Ghetto: The Making of the Black Community in Savannah, Georgia, 1865–1880." *Journal of Social History* 6 (Summer 1973): 463–88.

Bonner, James C. "Sherman at Milledgeville in 1864." *Journal of Southern History* 22 (August 1956): 273–91.

Breeden, James O. "A Medical History of the Later Stages of the Atlanta Campaign." *Journal of Southern History* 35 (February 1969): 31–59.

Bryan, T. Conn. "The Secession of Georgia." *Georgia Historical Quarterly* 31 (June 1947): 89–111.

Burnett, Edmund Cody, ed. "Some Confederate Letters: Alabama, Georgia, and Tennessee." *Georgia Historical Quarterly* 21 (March 1937): 188–203.

Carter, Dan T. "The Anatomy of Fear: The Christmas Day Insurrection Scare of 1865." *Journal of Southern History* 42 (August 1976): 345–64.

Charlton, Walter G. "A Judge and a Grand Jury." In *Report of the Thirty First Annual Session of the Georgia Bar Association.* Macon: J. W. Burke Co., 1914.

Cimbala, Paul A. "The 'Talisman Power': Davis Tillson, the Freedmen's Bureau, and Free Labor in Reconstruction Georgia, 1865–1866." *Civil War History* 28 (June 1982): 153–71.

Coulter, E. Merton. "Robert Gould Shaw and the Burning of Darien, Georgia." *Civil War History* 5 (December 1959): 363–73.

———. "Slavery and Freedom in Athens, Georgia, 1860–1866." *Georgia Historical Quarterly* 49 (September 1965): 264–93.

Covington, James W. "Cuban Bloodhounds and the Seminoles." *Florida Historical Quarterly* 33 (October 1954): 111–19.

Crenshaw, Ollinger. "The Psychological Background of the Election of 1860 in the South." *North Carolina Historical Review* 19 (July 1942): 260–79.

Daniel, W. Harrison. "Southern Protestantism and the Negro, 1860–1865." *North Carolina Historical Review* 41 (Summer 1964): 338–59.

Davis, John W. "George Liele and Andrew Bryan, Pioneer Negro Baptist Preachers." *Journal of Negro History* 3 (April 1918): 119–27.

Dew, Charles B: "Black Ironworkers and the Slave Insurrection Panic of 1856." *Journal of Southern History* 41 (August 1975): 321–38.

———. "David Ross and the Oxford Iron Works: A Study of Industrial Slavery in the Early Nineteenth Century South." *William and Mary Quarterly* 31 (April 1974): 189–224.

———. "Disciplining Slave Ironworkers in the Antebellum South: Coercion, Conciliation and Accommodation." *American Historical Review* 79 (April 1974): 393–418.

Donnelly, Ralph W. "The Bartow County Saltpetre Works." *Georgia Historical Quarterly* 54 (Fall 1970): 305–19.

Drago, Edmund L. "How Sherman's March Through Georgia Affected the Slaves." *Georgia Historical Quarterly* 57 (Fall 1973): 361–75.

Eisterhold, John A. "Savannah: Lumber Center of the South Atlantic." *Georgia Historical Quarterly* 57 (Winter 1973): 526–43.

Escott, Paul D. "The Context of Freedom: Georgia's Slaves During the Civil War." *Georgia Historical Quarterly* 58 (Spring 1974): 79–104.

Flanigan, Daniel J. "Criminal Procedure in Slave Trials in the Antebellum South." *Journal of Southern History* 40 (November 1974): 537–64.

Gifford, James M. "Anti-Black Bias in Antebellum Source Materials: Lucius J. Gartrell and the Gideon Will Case." *Louisiana Studies* 14 (Summer 1975): 189–97

———. "The Cuthbert Conspiracy: An Episode in African Colonization." *South Atlantic Quarterly* 79 (Summer 1980): 312–20.

Bibliography

_____. "Emily Tubman and the African Colonization Movement in Georgia." *Georgia Historical Quarterly* 59 (Spring 1975): 10–24.

Gottlieb, Manuel. "The Land Question in Georgia During Reconstruction." *Science and Society* 3 (Summer 1939): 356–88.

Griffin, Richard W. "The Origins of the Industrial Revolution in Georgia: Cotton Textiles, 1810–1865." *Georgia Historical Quarterly* 42 (December 1958): 355–75.

Haunton, Richard H. "Law and Order in Savannah, 1850–1860." *Georgia Historical Quarterly* 56 (Spring 1972): 1–24.

Heard, George Alexander. "St. Simons Island During the War Between the States." *Georgia Historical Quarterly* 22 (September 1938): 249–72.

Hoffman, Edwin D. "From Slavery to Self-Reliance: The Record of Achievement of the Freedmen of the Sea Island Region." *Journal of Negro History* 41 (January 1956): 8–42.

Huff, Lawrence. "Joseph Addison Turner's Role in Georgia Politics, 1851–1860." *Georgia Historical Quarterly* 50 (March 1966): 1–13.

_____. "The Literary Publications of Joseph Addison Turner." *Georgia Historical Quarterly* 46 (September 1962): 223–36.

Johnson, Whittington B. "Free Blacks in Antebellum Augusta, Georgia: A Demographic and Economic Profile." *Richmond County History* (Winter 1982): 10–21.

_____. "Free Blacks in Antebellum Savannah: An Economic Profile." *Georgia Historical Quarterly* 64 (Winter 1980): 418–31.

Jones, Jacqueline. " 'My Mother Was Much of a Woman': Black Women, Work, and the Family Under Slavery." *Feminist Studies* 8 (Summer 1982): 235–70.

Kilson, Marion D. deB. "Towards Freedom: An Analysis of Slave Revolts in the United States." *Phylon* 25 (Summer 1964): 175–87.

Kolchin, Peter. "Reevaluating the Antebellum Slave Community: A Comparative Perspective." *Journal of American History* 70 (December 1983): 579–601.

Mathews, Donald G. "Charles Colcock Jones and the Southern Evangelical Crusade to Form a Biracial Community." *Journal of Southern History* 41 (August 1975): 299–320.

Meier, August. "The Emergence of Negro Nationalism (A Study in Ideologies)." *Midwest Journal* 4 (Winter 1951–1952): 96–104.

Mitchell, Stevens. "Atlanta, the Industrial Heart of the Confederacy." *Atlanta Historical Bulletin* 7 (May 1930): 20–28.

Mohr, Clarence L. "Before Sherman: Georgia Blacks and the Union War Effort, 1861–1864." *Journal of Southern History* 45 (August 1979): 331–52.

383

Bibliography

———. "Harrison Berry: A Black Pamphleteer in Georgia During Slavery and Freedom." *Georgia Historical Quarterly* 67 (Summer 1983): 189–205.

———. "Slavery in Oglethorpe County, Georgia, 1773–1865." *Phylon* 23 (Spring 1972): 4–21.

Morgan, Philip D. "The Ownership of Property by Slaves in the Mid-Nineteenth Century Low Country." *Journal of Southern History* 49 (August 1983): 399–420.

———. "Work and Culture: The Task System and the World of Lowcountry Blacks, 1700 to 1880." *William and Mary Quarterly* 39 (October 1982): 563–99.

Mullin, Gerald W. "Rethinking American Negro Slavery from the Vantage Point of the Colonial Era." *Louisiana Studies* 12 (Summer 1973): 378–422.

Nelson, Bernard H. "Legislative Control of the Southern Free Negro, 1861–1865." *Catholic Historical Review* 32 (April 1946): 28–46.

Phillips, Ulrich B. "The Origin and Growth of the Southern Black Belts." *American Historical Review* 11 (July 1906): 798–816.

"The Presbyterian Church in Georgia on Secession and Slavery." *Georgia Historical Quarterly* 1 (September 1917): 263–65.

Proctor, William G., Jr. "Slavery in Southwest Georgia." *Georgia Historical Quarterly* 49 (September 1965): 1–22.

Robinson, Armstead L. "In the Shadow of Old John Brown: Insurrection Anxiety and Confederate Mobilization, 1861–1863." *Journal of Negro History* 65 (Fall 1980): 279–97.

Taylor, Rosser H. "Humanizing the Slave Code of North Carolina." *North Carolina Historical Review* 2 (July 1925): 323–31.

Thornberry, Jerry. "Northerners and the Atlanta Freedmen, 1865–1869." *Prologue* 6 (Winter 1974): 236–51.

Trexler, Harrison A. "The Opposition of Planters to the Employment of Slaves as Laborers by the Confederacy." *Mississippi Valley Historical Review* 27 (September 1940): 211–24.

Turner, Maxine. "Naval and River Operations on the Apalachicola and Chattahoochee Rivers, 1861–1865." *Alabama Historical Quarterly* 36 (Fall–Winter 1974): 187–266.

Wax, Darold D. "'New Negroes Are Always in Demand': The Slave Trade in Eighteenth Century Georgia." *Georgia Historical Quarterly* 68 (Summer 1984): 193–220.

White, William W. "The Texas Slave Insurrection of 1860." *Southwestern Historical Quarterly* 52 (January 1949): 259–85.

Wiley, Bell I. "The Movement to Humanize the Institution of Slavery During the Confederacy." *Emory University Quarterly* 5 (December 1949): 207–20.

Bibliography

Wish, Harvey. "The Slave Insurrection Panic of 1856." *Journal of Southern History* 5 (May 1939): 218–39.

Theses and Dissertations

Byrne, William A. "Slavery in Savannah, Georgia During the Civil War." M.A. thesis, Florida State University, 1971.

Cousins, Phyllis M. "A History of the 33rd United States Colored Troops." M.A. thesis, Howard University, 1961.

Debats, Donald Arthur. "Elites and Masses: Political Structure, Communication and Behavior in Ante-Bellum Georgia." Ph.D. dissertation, University of Wisconsin, 1973.

Gassman, Wade Banister. "A History of Rome and Floyd County, Georgia in the Civil War." M.A. thesis, Emory University, 1966.

Gifford, James M. "The African Colonization Movement in Georgia, 1817–1860." Ph.D. dissertation, University of Georgia, 1977.

Haunton, Richard Herbert. "Savannah in the 1850s." Ph.D. dissertation, Emory University, 1968.

Hendricks, George L. "Union Army Occupation of the Southern Seaboard, 1861–1865." Ph.D. dissertation, Columbia University, 1954.

Howard, Cary. "The Georgia Reaction to David Walker's Appeal." M.A. thesis, University of Georgia, 1967.

Jordan, Mildred. "Georgia's Confederate Hospitals." M.A. thesis: Emory University, 1942.

Lovett, Bobby Lee. "The Negro in Tennessee, 1861–1865: A Socio-Military History of the Civil War Era." Ph.D. dissertation, University of Arkansas, 1978.

Mohr, Clarence L. "Georgia Blacks During Secession and Civil War, 1859–1865." Ph.D. dissertation, University of Georgia, 1975.

Owens, James L. "The Negro in Georgia During Reconstruction, 1864–1872." Ph.D. dissertation, University of Georgia, 1975.

Singer, Ralph Benjamin, Jr. "Confederate Atlanta." Ph.D. dissertation, University of Georgia, 1973.

Sweat, Edward Forrest. "The Free Negro in Antebellum Georgia." Ph.D. dissertation, Indiana University, 1957.

Thomas, Eugene Marvin III. "The Columbus, Georgia *Enquirer*, 1855–1865." M.A. thesis, University of Georgia, 1971.

Valuska, David Lawrence. "The Negro in the Union Navy, 1861–1865." Ph.D. dissertation, Lehigh University, 1973.

INDEX

Abandonment of slaves, 204–206

Abolitionists, 3, 4, 5, 6, 7, 8, 24–41 passim, 58, 59, 60, 61, 217

African slave trade, xvi, 47, 239–40

Agriculture, 101, 142, 210, 212; on St. Simons Island, 80, 82; on sea islands, 82, 101; on land reserved for black settlement by Sherman, 96; effects of removal on, 112–16; wartime role of women in, 221–31. *See also* Task system

Akin, Mary F., 226–27

Akin, Warren, 226–27, 228

Alatoona Iron Works, 151

Alcohol: illegal sale of to slaves, 8, 44, 307 (n. 65)

Alexander, Adam L., 211

Alexander, Peter Wellington, 135

Allen, Henry W., 276

Amason, Mr., 38

Amelioration of slavery, 235–36; prewar sources of support for, 239–47; Toombs champions cause of, 241–42; motives of advocates of, 246; wartime reform movement, 247–61; importance of debate over, 261–62; arguments for, 262–67. *See also* Slavery reform movement

American Colonization Society, xix, 8, 11, 17, 18, 61, 62, 313 (n. 100)

Anderson, Edward C., 53

Andrews, Eliza Frances, 265

Arming of slaves: Confederate debate over, 270, 273–83; Cleburne proposal, 274–75; support for among Confederate soldiers, 278–79; authorized by Confederate Congress, 283; begins

with black enlistment, 283–85

Armstrong, Capt. Charles R., 127

Arson. *See* Incendiarism; "Texas Troubles"

Artisans and craftsmen, slave, 166–70, 187–88

Athens Iron Manufacturing Company, 152

Atlanta: statistics on hospital work force in, 131–35; wartime growth of, 193–94; Mayor's Court cases involving blacks in, 207–208

Augusta: ordnance installations in, 144, 146, 149, 194; wartime growth of, 194–95

Augusta Cotton Factory, 194

Baptists, 243, 244, 245; as leaders of wartime movement for slavery reform, 247–65 passim

Barrow, David Crenshaw, 157, 215, 285

Bartow County Saltpetre Works, 155

Bartow Iron Works, 152, 173

Bass, "Uncle" Dick, 227–28

Beasley, Mary (black teacher), 209

Beauregard, Gen. P. G. T., 121

Benger, Charles (black musician), 286–87, 288

Berry, Harrison (slave pamphleteer), 58–64, 209

Bigham, B. H., 169

Black military units (Union), 76, 85–86, 86–92, 95

Black resistance, 52, 54–56; to forced removal, 102–103, 110–11; to Confederate impressment, 171–72; as a bargaining tactic, 181

387

Index

Index